The Shifting Realities
of Philip K. Dick

BOOKS BY **Lawrence Sutin**

The Shifting Realities of Philip K. Dick:
    Selected Literary and Philosophical Writings

Divine Invasions:
    A Life of Philip K. Dick

The Shifting Realities of Philip K. Dick

Selected Literary and Philosophical Writings

Edited and with an Introduction by Lawrence Sutin

Vintage Books

A Division of Random House, Inc.

New York

FIRST VINTAGE BOOKS EDITION, FEBRUARY 1995

Some essays and stories have previously appeared in: *Imagination, Stories of Science Fiction and Fantasy, the PKDS Newsletter, Eternity Science Fiction, Old Series, The Real World, Scintillation, Interzone, Niekas, Oblique, Lighthouse, Foundation, New Worlds, Just SF, SelecTV Guide, Obtain Cite,* and *SF Commentary.*

Grateful acknowledgment is made to Frank C. Bertrand for permission to reprint "Philip K. Dick on Philosophy: A Brief Interview" (*Niekas*, No. 36, 1988). Originally published as "Philip K. Dick et la Philosophie: Une Courte Interview" translated by Sylvie Laine (*Yellow Submarine*, No. 41, September 1986). Reprinted by permission of Frank C. Bertrand.

The following essays and stories have been previously published: "Strange Memories of Death" and "How to Build a Universe That Doesn't Fall Apart Two Days Later" appeared in *I Hope I Shall Arrive Soon*, edited by Mark Hurst and Paul Williams. "The Double: Bill Symposium" appeared in *The Double: Bill Symposium*, published by DB Press, 1969, edited by Bill Mallardi and Bill Bowers. "Who Is an SF Writer?" appeared in *Science Fiction: The Academy Awakening* (1974), edited by Willis McNelly, published by the College English Association. "The Moon Plaque" appeared in *Men on the Moon*, an Ace Anthology, edited by Donald A. Wollheim. "Introduction to *Blood Money*" appeared in the 1985 Blue Jay Publications edition of that novel. "Introduction to *The Golden Man*" appeared in *The Golden Man*, edited by Mark Hurst. "Predictions" appeared in *The Book of Predictions*, edited by David Wallechinsky (Morrow, New York, 1981). "Headnote for 'Beyond Lies the Wub'" appeared in *First Voyages*, edited by Damon Knight, Martin H. Greenberg, and Joseph D. Olander (Avon, New York, 1981). "The Android and the Human" and "Man, Android, and Machine" appeared in *The Dark-Haired Girl*, published by Mark V. Ziesing (1988).

Book design by M. Kristen Bearse

To Mab, for her ceaseless fascination and patience with Philip K. Dick, and to Henry, always the most attentive reader of the *Exegesis*.

The editor would also like to thank Douglas A. Mackey for his kind assistance in tracing prior publication data for certain of the writings included herein.

Contents

Part Two
Writings on Science Fiction and Related Ideas

Part Three
Works Related to *The Man in the High Castle*
and Its Proposed Sequel

Part Four
Plot Proposals and Outlines

Part Five

Essays and Speeches

Part Six

Selections from the *Exegesis*

Introduction

BY LAWRENCE SUTIN

This is a first-time collection, in book form, of significant nonfiction writings—essays, journals, plot scenarios, speeches, and interviews—by Philip K. Dick from throughout his career. These writings establish, I believe, that Dick was not only a visionary creator of speculative fiction but also an illuminating and original thinker on issues ranging from the merging of quantum physics and metaphysics; to the potential scope of virtual reality and its unforeseen personal and political consequences; to the discomforting relation between schizophrenia (and other psychiatric diagnoses) and societal "joint hallucinations"; to, not least, the challenge to primary human values posed in an age of technological distance and spiritual despair.

The bulk of these writings have either never before been published, or have appeared only in obscure and out-of-print publications. Dick saw himself first and foremost as a fiction writer, and there can be no question that it is in his stories and his novels—both science fiction (SF) and mainstream—that Dick's most permanent legacy resides. As for his nonfiction writings, those few essays and speeches that he published in his lifetime attracted scant attention. In certain cases, this was justified—their style and quality were markedly uneven; indeed, the same may be said with respect to the contents of this volume, many of which—the *Exegesis* entries—Dick had no intention of publishing in his lifetime and hence no reason to revise and polish. (He may—there is no direct evidence in his private writings to support the supposition—have hoped that they be discovered and published after his death.)

But the lack of attention paid to Dick's nonfictional works is due to factors that go beyond unevenness of quality. To this day one finds, in SF critical circles, sharp resistance to the notion that Dick's ideas—divorced from the immediate entertainment context of his fiction—could possibly be worthy of serious consideration. It is as if, for these critics, to declare that certain of Dick's ideas make serious sense is to diminish his importance as the ultimate "mad" SF genius—a patronizing role assigned him by these selfsame critics. But it is nonsensical to maintain, in the face of the plain evidence of the fictional texts themselves, not to mention his own writings on SF in this volume, that Dick's ideas and his fictional realms are divisible dualities rather than the permeable whole of a life's work. Thankfully, this kind of critical parochialism is diminishing even within the SF world. And as for the world at large, Dick is, at long last, receiving his due as a writer of *both* imaginative depth and intellectual power. Indeed, the story of his emergence into sudden literary "respectability" is a revelatory parable as to the fierce cultural strictures that, in America, dominate the type and degree of attention paid to an author and his works.

Philip K. Dick (1928–82), author of more than fifty volumes of novels and stories, has become, since his death, the focus of one of the most remarkable literary reappraisals of modern times. From his longtime status as a patronized "pulp" writer of "trashy" science fiction, Dick has now emerged—in the minds of a broad range of critics and fellow artists—as one of the most unique and visionary talents in the history of American literature.

This astonishing turnabout in recognition of Dick is evidenced both by the intensity of the praise bestowed on him and the range of voices that concur in it. Art Spiegelman, author/illustrator of *Maus*, has written: "What Franz Kafka was to the first half of the twentieth century, Philip K. Dick is to the second half." Ursula Le Guin, who has acknowledged Dick's strong influence on her own acclaimed SF novels, points to him as "our own homegrown Borges." Timothy Leary hails Dick as "a major twenty-first-century writer, a 'fictional philosopher' of the quantum age." Jean Baudrillard, a leader of the postmodernist critical movement in France, cites Dick as one of the greatest experimental writers of our era. New Age thinker Terrence McKenna writes of Dick the philosopher as "this incredible genius, this gentle, long-suffering, beauty-worshiping man." Dick appears on the cover of *The New Republic* while the critical essay within declares that "Dick's novels demand attention. . . . He is both lucid and strange, practical and paranoid." An electronic-music opera with a libretto based on the Dick novel *Valis* premieres to great acclaim in the Pompidou Center in Paris. The renowned Mabou Mines theater group performs a dramatic adaptation of the Dick novel *Flow My Tears, the Policeman Said* in Boston and New York. Punk and industrial rock bands take their names from Dick titles and pay homage to his books in their lyrics. Hollywood adapts a Dick novel (*Do Androids Dream of Electric Sheep?*) and a story ("I Can Remember It for You Wholesale") into the movies *Blade Runner* and *Total Recall*, while an acclaimed French film adaptation of yet another novel (*Confessions of a Crap-Artist*) was released in America in the summer of 1993 under the title *Barjo*. In the past two years, Dick has been the subject of laudatory front-page features in *The New York Times Book Review* and the *L.A. Weekly*—the opposite poles, one might say, of an overall mainstream acceptance. The headline for the *L.A. Weekly* feature sums up the thrust of the critical turnaround: "The Novelist of the '90s Has Been Dead Eight Years."

What makes this posthumous triumph all the more wrenching is the knowledge that, during his lifetime, Dick could succeed in reaching a wide readership only within the "ghetto" of the (SF) genre—a critically derided "ghetto" that effectively prevented serious consideration of his works from without. Dick wrote a number of mainstream literary novels (including the above-mentioned *Confessions of a Crap-Artist*), most of which have been published posthumously. But the greatest of his fictional works fall within the SF genre, which allowed Dick a conceptual and imaginative freedom that was severely crimped by the strictures of consensual reality favored by the mainstream. Even within the SF genre, Dick was considered something of an odd figure, with his penchant for plots that emphasized metaphysical speculations as opposed to "hard" science predictions. Still, the sheer vividness, dark humor, and textured detail with which Dick rendered his spiraling alternate universes and the oh so human characters who inhabited them won over a sizable number of SF readers. In a writing career that spanned three decades, Dick produced a number of stories and novels that are widely regarded as SF classics; these include *Time out of Joint* (1959), *Martian Time-Slip* (1962), *The Three Stigmata of Palmer Eldritch* (1965), *Ubik* (1969), *A Scanner Darkly* (1977), and *Valis* (1981).

In 1963, Dick was awarded the highest honor that SF has to bestow: the Hugo Award for *The Man in the High Castle*, a novel that exemplifies Dick's trademark blending of SF plot structure (as to which the number one rule is constantly to *amaze* the reader) and philosophical mazemaking (with a no-holds-barred skepticism that allowed for *all* possibilities). Dick was fervent in his view that SF was the genre par excellence for the exploration of new and challenging concepts.

As Dick himself explained in an epistolary interview (with critic Frank Bertrand) included herein: "Central to SF is the idea as dynamism. Events evolve out of an idea impacting on living creatures and their society. The idea must *always* be a novelty. . . . There is SF because the human brain craves sensory and intellectual stimulation before everything else, and the eccentric view provides unlimited stimulation, the eccentric view and the invented world."

High Castle contains a horde of stimulating ideas, beginning with the basic plot: a post–World War II world in which the Axis powers apparently have prevailed and the United States is a conquered land divided between Japan (the West) and Germany (the East). While the Japanese are relatively compassionate conquerors, the Nazis have extended their brutal methods throughout their dominions. Evil has become, under their reign, a palpable daily horror. One of the characters, a Swiss diplomat who is secretly working against the Nazis, sees them as the products of a collective psychic upheaval (described in terms that evidence Dick's indebtedness to C. G. Jung) that has obliterated the distinction between the human and the divine by reversing the sacrificial pattern of the Christian eucharist:

> They [the Nazis] want to be the agents, not the victims, of history. They identify with God's power and believe they are godlike. That is their basic madness. They are overcome by some archetype; their egos have expanded psychotically so that they cannot tell where they begin and the godhead leaves off. It is not *hubris*, not pride; it is inflation of the ego to its ultimate—confusion between him who worships and that which is worshiped. Man has not eaten God; God has eaten man.

But beneath this apparent, horrific reality there exists—for those who can experience it—an alternate world in which the Allies are victorious and life has retained its capacity for goodness. To reach this alternate world is no easy matter; pain and shock may be necessary to open one's eyes, or the enlightening aid of *The Grasshopper Lies Heavy,* the novel-within-the-novel in *High Castle* that reveals the true state of affairs for those who read with intelligence, heart, and an open mind.

In 1974, perhaps the most tumultuous year—for reasons shortly to be discussed—in his signally tumultuous life, Dick contemplated writing a novelistic sequel to *High Castle,* but his inward repugnance at returning to an extended reimagining of the Nazi mentality prevented him from completing this project. The two chapters he did complete are published for the first time in this volume, as is the "Biographical Material on Hawthorne Abendsen" (1974).

Dick himself would come to hope, in the final decade of his writing life, that his own novels and stories could fulfill a role analogous to that of Abendsen for his readers: to alert them that the consensual reality that grimly governed their daily lives (the "Black Iron Prison," as Dick would come to call it in his philosophical journal, the *Exegesis*) might not be as impregnable as it seemed. This is not to say that Dick saw himself as a prophet or as one possessing an undeniable Truth of life (though Dick could sound—*temporarily*—convinced while exploring the possibilities of an idea that intrigued him.) On the contrary, Dick could be a relentless critic of his own theories and beliefs. He was also quite willing to satirize himself broadly (as the would-be mystic Horselover Fat) and his penchant for "wild" speculations in his autobiographical novel *Valis* (1981): "Fat must have come up with more theories than there are stars in the universe. Every day he developed a new one, more cunning, more exciting and more fucked." In his philosophical writings, Dick would don, dwell within, and then discard one theory after another—as so many imaginative masks or personae—in his quest to unravel the mysteries of his two great themes: What is human? What is real? What makes Dick such a unique voice, both in his fiction and—equally—in the nonfiction writings collected in this book, was not the answers he reached (for he held to none), but rather the imaginative range and depth of his questioning, and the joy and brilliance and wild nerve with which he pursued it.

Philosophical issues were always at the heart of Dick's subject matter as a writer. He sold his first SF story back in 1951, at age twenty-two. Even by then, his course was set: He would explore the basic mysteries of existence and of human character. In *Michael in the 'Fifties*, an unpublished novel by Kleo Mini (Dick's second wife, to whom he was married for most of the fifties decade), the psychological makeup of the title character is based loosely on Dick and displays the same intense scrutiny of existence that Mini remembers in her husband at the very start of his SF writing career. Here is a dialogue between Michael and wife Kate, based to some extent on Mini herself. Kate speaks first:

> "I think you [Michael]—sometimes—want to pull away from the world. Away from me, away from everything I think of as real. Away from your house and your car and your cat. Sometimes you're very far away from all of us. And sometimes I think I'm like a string that brings you back to earth, holds you down to the earth."
>
> She was right, he thought. She was real, as real as the crab grass and the kitchen table.
>
> "Where is it you go, Michael?"
>
> "I don't want to go anywhere, Kate. But I think there are different kinds of reality. And the car and the house and the cat are not all there is. Living like we do—on the edge, in a way—we're always so busy scraping along, trying to get by, that it keeps us, it keeps *me* from dealing with the other reality, the meaning of everything."[1]

In his interview with Bertrand, Dick offered a summary of his early philosophical influences:

> I first became interested in philosophy in high school when I realized one day that all space is the same size; it is only the material boundaries encompassing it that differ. After that there came to me the realization (which I found later in Hume) that causality is a perception in the observer and not a datum of external reality. In college I was given Plato to read and thereupon became aware of the possible existence of a metaphysical realm beyond or above the sensory world. I came to understand that the human mind could conceive of a realm of which the empirical world was epiphenomenal. Finally I came to believe that in a

certain sense the empirical world was not truly real, at least not as real as the archetypal realm beyond it. At this point I despaired of the veracity of sense-data. Hence in novel after novel that I write I question the reality of the world that the characters' percept-systems report.

This condensed history of philosophical influences tells only part of the story of Dick's development as a writer. There are, to be sure, a good number of philosophical and spiritual perspectives that mattered greatly to Dick but are not listed above. But a more basic factor was the difficult childhood Dick endured, which included the early divorce of his parents, frequent Depression era cross-country moves with his financially strapped and emotionally distant mother, and bouts of vertigo and agoraphobia that interfered with Dick's schooling and friendships and caused his mother to have him examined by at least two psychiatrists. One of these psychiatrists speculated that Dick might be suffering from schizophrenia—a diagnostic possibility that severely frightened the boy and would haunt the grown man all his life.

Throughout Dick's speculations, there is the underlying sense of a dark pain and of shattering experiences that had left him grappling for his place in the shared world (*koinos kosmos*, in the Greek of Heraclitus, a thinker whom Dick greatly admired) and struggling to evade the madness of solitary delusion (*idios kosmos*, private world; from *idios* comes the English "idiot"—one who is cut off from that which is happening around him). Though fear lurked strongly within him, Dick insisted on staring madness in the face and asking if it, too, could lay claim to a kind of knowledge. Thus, in "Drugs, Hallucinations, and the Quest for Reality," a 1964 essay included herein, Dick argued that what is called schizophrenic or psychotic "hallucination" may be, in many cases, the result of extremely broad and sensitive perceptions that most "sane" persons learn to screen out of their consciousness. The Kantian *a priori* categories of space and time are examples of such screens; Kant claimed that these were necessary for the mental ordering of phenomenal reality, which would otherwise remain a hopeless perceptual chaos to human minds. In his essay, Dick theorized that, to the extent that our mental and sensory awareness happens to extend beyond these socially ratified screens, any one of us may become subject to "hallucinations"—which are, in essence, *un-*

shared realities. While it is possible that "mystical" insights may ensue, there is a greater likelihood—and a fearfully tragic one it is—that we may find ourselves in a hell realm of utter mental isolation:

> In the light of this, the idea of hallucinating takes on a very different character; hallucinations, whether induced by psychosis, hypnosis, drugs, toxins, etc., may be merely quantitatively different from what we see, not qualitatively so. In other words, too much is emanating from the neurological apparatus of the organism, over and beyond the structural, organizing necessity. . . . No-name entities or aspects begin to appear, and since the person does not know what they are—that is, what they're called or what they mean—he cannot communicate with other persons about them. This breakdown of verbal communication is the fatal index that somewhere along the line the person is experiencing reality in a way too altered to fit into his own prior worldview and too radical to allow empathic linkage with other persons.

There is an interesting parallel between Dick's emphasis here on a societally based definition of hallucinations—as perceptions unshared by others—and the insight offered by the eminent anthropologist Edward T. Hall in his *Beyond Culture*: "Perceptual aberrations are not restricted to psychoses but can also be *situational* in character, particularly in instances of great stress, excitation, or drug influences."[2] Instances, that is, in which, in Dick's words, "too much is emanating from the neurological apparatus of the organism."

In his 1965 essay "Schizophrenia and the Book of Changes" (also included), Dick sought to give the fearful and isolated perceptions of the schizophrenic an analytical coherence that might extend beyond the purely personal to a new viewpoint on human experience:

> What distinguishes schizophrenic existence from that which the rest of us like to imagine we enjoy is the element of time. The schizophrenic is having it all *now*, whether he wants it or not; the whole can of film has descended on him, whereas we watch it progress frame by frame. So for him, causality does not exist. Instead, the a-causal connective principle which [quantum physicist] Wolfgang Pauli called Syncronicity is operating in all situations—not merely as one factor at work,

as with us. Like a person under LSD, the schizophrenic is engulfed in an endless now. It's not too much fun.

Dick described himself, in this essay, as "schizoid effective"—a "pre-schizophrenic personality." This fearful dancing on the high wire of self-diagnostics is a recurrent element in Dick's essays and journals. Two opposite possibilities set the boundaries: the fear that he might be insane ("psychotic" and "schizophrenic" were his most common terms), and the possibility that he might, through an encompassing intellectual under-standing (*anamnesis*, the recollection of the archetypal realm of Ideas of Plato), win spiritual redemption—freedom from his crippling fears, and a haven from the deluded and sorrowful world.

There was, for Dick, a certain sense in which his own writings might alleviate some of the sorrow—for his readers and for himself—by at least openly acknowledging the doubts and questions that existence posed for those who had eyes to see. As he wrote in one *Exegesis* entry:

I am a fictionalizing philosopher, not a novelist; my novel & story-writ-ing ability is employed as a means to formulate my perception. The core of my writing is not art but *truth*. Thus what I tell is the truth, yet I can do nothing to alleviate it, either by deed or explanation. Yet this seems somehow to help a certain kind of sensitive troubled person, for whom I speak. I think I understand the common ingredient in those whom my writing helps: they cannot or will not blunt their own intima-tions about the irrational, mysterious nature of reality, &, for them, my corpus of writing is one long ratiocination regarding this inexplicable reality, an integration & presentation, analysis & response & personal history.[3]

One aspect of that "personal history" that has continued to intrigue his readers is the bizarre and powerful series of dreams, visions, and voices that flooded Dick's consciousness in February and March 1974 (or "2-3-74," Dick's shorthand for that period) and stood for him as the cen-tral—and, ultimately, inexplicable—event of his life. These inspired what has become known as the *"Valis* Trilogy"—the final three novels of Dick's life that have earned both critical praise and a broad readership (through their recent simultaneous reissuance as Vintage trade editions):

Valis (1981), *The Divine Invasion* (1981), and *The Transmigration of Timothy Archer* (1982). In all three novels, Dick explores the anguish and entropic emptiness of an earthly realm in which God (or whatever alternative name we give to the divine) remains unknown and perhaps unknowable. But also, in all of these works, Dick offers the hope that divine knowledge and redemption may yet be granted—even to modern, scuffling souls who have trouble paying their rent and keeping their marriages together. There is a striking thematic resemblance between these novels and the speculations of the Gnostic thinkers of the early centuries of the Christian era. Indeed, in the definitive modern edition of Gnostic scriptures, *The Nag Hammadi Library* (1988), an "Afterword" singles out Dick (along with Jung, Hermann Hesse, and Harold Bloom) as a preeminent modern interpreter of Gnostic beliefs.

As we have seen, even prior to the *"Valis* Trilogy," philosophical and spiritual questions had formed the underpinnings of Dick's SF "alternate" worlds and "alien" intelligences. But Dick had harbored a carefully limited view of himself, through the first two decades of his writing career, as one who fervently posed ultimate questions but lacked—as a matter of personal experience—any real encounter with a higher source of being. After 2-3-74, this changed to an extent. By his very nature, Dick was not a man to arrive at—or even to *wish* to arrive at—a simple conclusion about any life event, much less as complex and unsettling a series of events as 2-3-74. But through all of his wrangling, one fundamental fact emerges plainly: 2-3-74 served as a soul-shaking inspiration for Dick as a writer and thinker. The pratfalls and paradoxes of his SF plots had begun to seem to him—after two decades of prolific exploration—mere entertainments. Not that Dick did not wish to entertain. On the contrary, it was one of his paramount concerns as a writer: He loved the *excitement* of a good SF plot, as is amply testified to in his essays on SF included in this volume. But one of the strongest facets of his character—and one that sets Dick aside from the abundance of writers who dabble in metaphysical puzzles out of sheer amusement—was his conviction that *answers* could be attained by those who persisted in asking questions. Imagination, intelligence, and yearning insistence could prevail. Now, in his final years, there was a new passion: the driving necessity of getting to the truth of what had happened to him in those months.

Was "2-3-74" a case of genuine mystical experiences, or a contact with "higher" (or simply "other") forms of intelligence, or a conscious manipulation of his mind by unknown persons, or a purely private outbreak of psychotic symptoms? Dick considered each of these possibilities, as well as others too numerous to summarize here, in his eight-thousand-page *Exegesis* (subtitled by Dick *Apologia pro Mea Vita*, to emphasize its central importance). The *Exegesis* was a journal—handwritten, for the most part—at which Dick labored night after night for eight years, until his death in 1982, in an attempt to explain 2-3-74 to his own satisfaction. He never succeeded. The *Exegesis* is, at times, a wild and wayward human record: Eight years' worth of impassioned journaling through the dead of the night (Dick's preferred time for creative effort), with no expressed intention of publication in his own lifetime, could not but result in highly uneven streaks of writing. But the *Exegesis* is also replete with passages that confirm Dick's standing as a subtle thinker and an astonishing guide to hidden possibilities of existence. A previous collection, *In Pursuit of Valis: Selections from the Exegesis* (Underwood/Miller, 1991), edited by the present writer, has won critical praise for Dick as a philosophical and spiritual thinker. Robert Anton Wilson (coauthor of the popular *Illuminatus* trilogy) wrote: "Dick explains 'mystic' states better than any visionary writer of the past." In *Gnosis*, reviewer John Shirley declared: "Deluded or spiritually liberated, Dick was a genius, and that genius shines through every page of this book." Further unpublished selections of the *Exegesis* appear in this volume—including a full-length essay, titled (in the parodic pulp style that Dick employed with masterly effect in his fictional works) "The Ultra Hidden (Cryptic) Doctrine: The Secret Meaning of the Great Systems of Theosophy of the World, Openly Revealed for the First Time."

As is exemplified by this flamboyant title, there is something in the nature of Dick's raptly pell-mell style that may well put off those readers who think they know what "serious" writing must look and sound like. Of course, it was just such fixed canons of "serious" discourse that Dick devoted himself to dismantling—or, in the more fashionable postmodern jargon that has come into prominence since his death, "deconstructing"—in many of the essays included in this book.

Dick is, as a matter both of style and of content, an uncategorizable thinker. One can dub him a "philosopher," and indeed he warrants the title in its original Greek meaning as one who loved wisdom and truly believed in the value of uninhibited questioning—a rarity in this day and age, in which the word "metaphysical" has become a synonym for "pointless." But Dick has none of the systematic rigor and impersonality of tone that mark modern-day philosophical analysis for most readers. He adheres to no single philosophical school, though he feels free enough to wander through the hallways, so to speak, of each and every school of West and East down through the ages. He defends no propositions; rather, he samples them, explores them to their heights and the depths, then moves on. He proposes ultimate answers—a goodly number of them, in fact—and then confesses that he himself cannot choose among them. Especially in the *Exegesis*, Dick is sometimes moved to exclamations of unphilosophical joy; at other times the despair expressed on the page is a fearful thing. Dick clearly does not fit the modern mold of the "philosopher"; his true affinity is with the pre-Socratic thinkers, whose gnomic and evocative writings—adamant, fragmented personal visions of the universe, its nature and purpose—have resisted definitive textual analysis for more than two millennia.

If one attempts to label Dick as a "mystic," similar difficulties arise. First, the term "mystic" seems to imply, by its standard usage in theological literature, that Dick definitely made contact with a divine reality or "saw God," as modern parlance goes. This conclusion is, of course, unwarranted. Dick himself never made up his mind as to whether it was God or "psychosis" or "something other" that he contacted in 2-3-74. Indeterminacy is the central characteristic of the *Exegesis*. The sheer strangeness of Dick's visions, coupled with his self-confessed "nervous breakdowns," have led some readers and critics to conclude that 2-3-74 can be seen only as the product of mental illness; the diagnoses offered are legion. To be sure, attempts at posthumous diagnosis of Dick are doomed to be highly speculative, particularly when psychiatrists and psychologists who treated him at various times of his life themselves disagreed widely over his mental state (most placed him as neurotic in some form, and at least one found him quite normal). Quite aside from the difficulties of such diagnosis, there is the further concern that diagnostics per se are useful when applied to a living patient under treatment but are singularly reductive when employed as a simplistic categorizing label for a substantial body of writings by a deceased author. There is, in truth, no psychiatric term yet devised that does justice to the vividness and complexity of his writings—and their impact on the psyches of his readers. To read Dick with attention is to participate—startlingly—in his unique vision, which frequently violates consensus assumptions about the nature of "reality," but retains nonetheless a brilliant coherence and emotional depth that signal anything but the workings of a madman, howsoever the facts of his life may be thrashed over and diagnosed by amateur analysts. Critic Alexander Star has aptly delineated the boundary between the man and the impact of his work: "Dick's sanity was open to question. But throughout his career he wrote with qualities that are rare in a science fiction writer, or in any writer at all. These included a sure feel for the detritus and debris, the obsolescent object-world, of postwar suburbia; a sharp historical wit; and a searching moral subtlety and concern."[4]

To focus on a rigid binary definition of sane or insane constitutes, in the case of Dick and his work, a puerile simplification. The further the combined bodies of knowledge of psychology, anthropology, and history of religions progress, the less clear it seems that bright-line divisions among "religious," "shamanic," and "psychotic" states is possible or even useful in the absence of a careful appreciation of the cultural and personal contexts of the experiencer. This is *not* to argue that Dick even remotely resembles an "enlightened" mystic; it is well to remember that Dick's forte was questions, not answers; those who would see his ideas as fodder for a "cult" merely reflect their own hunger for conditioned thought. Dick's experiences, as reflected in the writings in the present volume, reflect a root indeterminacy, a persistent puzzlement and skepticism that underlie even his wildest speculations. To follow Dick along his metaphysical quest will, however, provide its own unique rewards for the reader who is able to maintain an open mind.

For example, one of the elements of his 2-3-74 experience was a series of "phosphene graphics" visions, which included, in one instance, a sighting of the Golden Rectangle of Greek aesthetics, which represented, in that culture, perfect architectural proportion as reflected in structures such as the Parthenon. Dick also became fascinated, during this period, with the Fibonacci logarithmic series, named after the thirteenth-century mathematician Leonardo Fibonacci of Pisa, who utilized it to demonstrate a frequent structural analogy among spiral forms in nature, as in certain seashells, leaves, and rock formations. Subsequent research has extended the analogy to the spin of hurricane winds and the DNA double helix, as well as to the underlying theorems of fractal mathematics and computer imaging. Dick believed that the Golden Triangle and the Fibonacci series were keys to interpreting the archetypal truths being revealed in the "phosphene graphics"; these speculations appear frequently in the *Exegesis* and are featured in Dick's novel *Valis* and in the speech "If You Find This World Bad, You Should See Some of the Others," included in this volume. Nonetheless, the skeptical reader is likely to give them short shrift, consigning them as mere gibberish.

But now consider the pervasive influence of phosphene graphics in shamanic visions and world religions, as summarized by anthropologist Michael Ripinsky-Naxon:

> Somewhere in the neural network of the brain and the retina is spurred a phenomenon [phosphenes] that actuates inner sight, or luminous visions, and which may constitute the basis for an objective, physical framework for the visions encountered among religious adepts such as shamans and mystics. . . . Carl G. Jung, observing the transcultural character of the neurally stimulated phosphene shapes, pioneered the idea that certain archetypal symbols might originate in the personal experience of such luminous designs. . . . The almost visionary, later paintings, executed in an asylum, by Vincent van Gogh, exhibit phosphene patterns, as do many unskilled crayon drawings of youngsters between the ages of two and four years. As can be also expected, a large number of designs encountered in ancient and aboriginal cultures display phosphene-like characters.[5]

Ripinsky-Naxon goes on to consider the archetypal symbol of the spiral specifically:

> If we . . . recognize the spiral to be an archetypal pattern and its schematic representations as the labyrinth, then this conception may help elucidate our understanding of why this motif has been used to symbolize the unknown origin-point leading to the Hereafter, the cave, the tomb, and the womb of the Great Mother. The tomb, as has been noted, was constructed in resemblance of the body of the Great Mother, whose energy and procreative sexuality are conveyed through the element of the spiral.[6]

In this regard, note that Dick believed (see "If You Find This World Bad . . .") that he sighted, through the vision of the Golden Rectangle, the goddess Aphrodite, or the sexual aspect of the Great Mother. As for the importance of the Great Mother to Dick both philosophically and psychologically, the reader may consult his speech "The Android and the Human" in the present volume.

Again, the point here is not to seek to argue on behalf of Dick as an inspired seer, or even—necessarily—as a "sane" human being. (There is no "proof" possible as to the sanity or insanity of Philip K. Dick.)[7] Rather, it is to challenge the reader to resist labels and to plunge into the ideas expressed in the texts themselves, and to wrest from them what seems useful and vital without regard to predisposing diagnostic labels. One might further urge that readers suspend their tendency to read Dick's metaphysical writings with *belief* or *disbelief* foremost in mind. For Dick, as the writings themselves reveal, had no pointedly persuasive intentions with respect to the reader. In turn, those readers who refuse to worry over whether Dick persuades them on any particular points may find that he illumines any number of prospective paths for further exploration. There is a beauty and a visionary intensity to the possibilities Dick offers, as in "Cosmogony and Cosmology," a 1978 essay in which Dick sought to distill key concepts of the *Exegesis*. The divine form discussed is that of a righteous Godhead (akin to the redeeming Logos of the Gnostics) who has lost the memory of himself as the true creator and has ceded control of the earthly realm to a blind and ignorant demiurge or "artifact." This "artifact" (akin to the Gnostic Archon) holds all humans in its delusional thrall, and even the Godhead must struggle against it.[8]

Observe how Dick, in tracing out the possibilities of this spiritual viewpoint, employs the narrative gifts of a fiction master to create a haunting parable of a fallen and amnesiac god who must wander for centuries through his own creations to win his own redemption:

> He [the Creator] no longer knows why he has done all this to himself. He does not remember. He has allowed himself to become enslaved to his own artifact, deluded by it, coerced by it, finally killed by it. He, the living, is at the mercy of the mechanical. The servant has become the master, and the master the servant. And the master either renounced voluntarily his memory of how this happened and why, or

else his memory was eradicated by the servant. Either way, he is the artifact's victim.

But the artifact is teaching him, painfully, by degrees, over thousands of years, to remember—who he is and what he is. The servant-become-master is attempting to restore the master's lost memories and hence his true identity.

One might speculate that he constructed the artifact—not to delude him—but to restore his memory. However, perhaps the artifact then revolted and did *not* do its job. It keeps him in ignorance.

The artifact must be fought; i.e., disobeyed. And then memory will return. It is a piece of the Godhead *(Urgrund)* which has somehow been captured by the artifact (the servant); it now holds that piece—or pieces—hostage. How cruel it is to them, these fragments of its legitimate master! When will it change?

When the pieces remember and are restored. First they must wake up and then they must return.

If all of this seems impossibly speculative to the reader, it may be still more unsettling to realize that there is a direct parallel between the ideas expressed by Dick above and the cosmological theories posed by highly respected quantum physicists such as David Bohm. In *The Holographic Universe*, Michael Talbot offers a summary of Bohm's viewpoint on the "implicate" and "explicate" orders of the cosmos that is strikingly analogous to the Urgrund/artifact dichotomy posed by Dick:

As we have seen, according to Bohm the apparent separateness of consciousness and matter is an illusion, an artifact that occurs only after both have unfolded into the explicate world of objects and sequential time. If there is no division between mind and matter in the implicate, the ground from which all things spring, then it is not unusual to expect that reality might still be shot through with traces of this deep connectivity. [Fellow physicist F. David] Peat believes that synchronicities are therefore "flaws" in the fabric of reality, momentary fissures that allow us a brief glimpse of the immense and unitary order underlying all of nature. . . . According to Peat, when we experience a synchronicity, what we are really experiencing "is the human mind operating, for a moment, in its true order and extending throughout society and nature, moving through orders of increasing subtlety, reaching past the source of mind and matter into creativity itself."[9]

Dick was hardly an expert in quantum physics theories, though he did read in the field sporadically. As the essay "Drugs, Hallucinations, and the Quest for Reality" attests, he was especially interested in the concept of synchronicity posed by physicist Wolfgang Pauli (who worked in conjunction with C. G. Jung in formulating this theory). But the key parallels between Dick's writings—both fiction and nonfiction—and the current insights of quantum physics do not seem, based on the evidence of the *Exegesis* and other personal writings by Dick, to have been based on reading, but rather on an experiential grappling on Dick's part that proved synchronous, as it were, with the findings of the quantum physicists. For example, in his 1977 speech "If You Find This World Bad, You Should See Some of the Others," included herein—a speech that predates any widespread public discussion of the quantum physics notion that the known structure of the cosmos may aptly be described by the metaphor of a hologram—we find Dick asking, based on his experiences of 2-3-74, "Do we collectively dwell in a kind of laser hologram, real creatures in a manufactured quasi-world, a stage set within whose artifacts and creatures a mind moves that is determined to remain unknown?"

Nor is quantum physics the only field in which Dick's speculations find a revelatory context. Consider the concept of "fake fakes," which is put to use in so many of Dick's novels and stories and which is explored persistently in his nonfiction writings as well. Examples included in the present volume may be found in the outline for a proposed (but never completed) novel *Joe Protagoras Is Alive and Living on Earth,* as well as in the proposal for a script (never written) for the television series *Mission: Impossible* and in the 1978 speech (likely never delivered) "How to Build a Universe That Doesn't Fall Apart Two Days Later." In essence, a "fake fake" is—despite its seeming status as a mere contradiction that equates into "genuine"—a radically new ontological category that takes on significance precisely because it perplexingly mimics (and even threatens to supersede) our "ordinary" or consensual reality. Hence the "fake fake" is no mere SF plot prop—although Dick certainly employed it to dazzling effect as just such a prop—but is also a commentary on the inundation of our world by mechanical and computer-generated simulacra.

In the field of art, Marcel Duchamp explored a similar range of ideas with his concept of the "readymade," a found object that Duchamp would ironically designate as a work of art, at times adding his own visual or linguistic touches (in which case the object became a "readymade aided"). In his 1961 essay "Apropos of 'Readymades,'" Duchamp broached paradoxes that serve to elucidate certain aesthetic possibilities of a world in which Dickian "fake fakes" proliferate. Wrote Duchamp:

> At another time wanting to expose the basic antimony between art and readymades I imagined a "reciprocal readymade": use a Rembrandt as an ironing board! . . .
>
> Another aspect of the "readymade" is its lack of uniqueness . . . the replica of a "readymade" delivering the same message; in fact nearly every one of the "readymades" existing today is not an original in the conventional sense.
>
> A final remark to this egomaniac's discourse. Since the tubes of paint used by the artist are manufactured and readymade products we must conclude that all the paintings in the world are "readymades aided" and also works of assemblage.[10]

The "fake fake" of Dick and the "readymade" (and its permutations) of Duchamp are, at root, cognate ideas expressing the shimmering indeterminacy between originals and simulacra that is the hallmark of the virtual reality—both as metaphor and as technology—of postindustrial society. It was Walter Benjamin, in his seminal 1936 essay "The Work of Art in the Age of Mechanical Reproduction," who first clearly delineated this tension. But it was Philip K. Dick, in numerous works including the pointedly titled *The Simulacra* (1964), who first created a body of fiction that brought the tension to life. The concept of the "simulacrum" has since become a staple of postmodernist criticism—thus the praise offered by Baudrillard of Dick's works as "a total simulation without origin, past or future."

A brief note on the principles of selection of writings included in the present volume: The primary goal was to set forth the best of Dick's nonfictional efforts. But there was also the secondary aim of offering a representative sampling of his different nonfictional modes—autobiographical;

informal free flights of ideas (in the cozy obscurity of SF fanzines); critical examinations of the SF genre and of his own works in particular; and extended philosophical and theological analyses. In writing of his own life, Dick could range from brutal honesty to blatant fabulistic enhancements. No effort has been made in this volume to sort out "truth" from "fiction" in his autobiographical accounts. (Readers interested in one effort to do so may consult my *Divine Invasions: A Life of Philip K. Dick*.)

There are, in addition, selections herein from Dick's fiction: (1) two brief excerpts from an early unpublished Dick mainstream novel—*Gather Yourselves Together* (written in 1949)—featuring autobiographical elements bearing on Dick's *experience* of reality; and (2) the two completed chapters of the proposed sequel to *The Man in the High Castle*—tentatively titled, at one point, as *To Scare the Dead*—which have long deserved publication, and, in addition, benefit from being read in conjunction with "Naziism and the High Castle" and "Biographical Material on Hawthorne Abendsen."

For all selections, the year cited with the title is the year of first publication; or, if the piece is unpublished, the year in which it was written (in the case of the *Exegesis*, the year provided represents, in some cases, my best estimate based on internal textual clues); or if the piece was published significantly later than the writing thereof, the year it was written followed by the year of publication.

At his best, as evidenced both by his fiction and by his finest metaphysical speculations, Dick joins the great creators of parable and paradox of this century—a lineage that includes G. K. Chesterton, Franz Kafka, René Daumal, Jorge Luis Borges, Samuel Beckett, Flann O'Brien, and Italo Calvino.

Notes

1.   I would like to thank Kleo Mini for permission to quote from *Michael in the 'Fifties*, which offers a valuable portrait not only of Dick but also of the Berkeley milieu in which he came of age.

2.   Edward T. Hall, *Beyond Culture* (New York: Anchor Books, 1976, 1981), p. 229.

3.   Philip K. Dick, *In Pursuit of Valis: Selections from the Exegesis*, ed. Lawrence Sutin (Novato, Calif./Lancaster, Pa.: Underwood-Miller, 1991), p. 161.

4.   Alexander Star, "The God in the Trash," *The New Republic* (December 6, 1993), p. 34.

5.   Michael Ripinsky-Naxon, *The Nature of Shamanism* (Albany: State University of New York Press, 1993), pp. 148–50.

6.   Ibid., p. 150.

7.   There is a considerable range of quality in the attempts to apply diagnostic measures to Dick's life and writings. Jay Kinney, for example, offers a thoughtful and subtle comparison between schizophrenic and shamanic states in his "Wrestling with Angels: The Mystical Dilemma of Philip K. Dick" (published in *In Pursuit of Valis*). In the writings of Gregg Rickman, however, diagnoses of Dick abound and are relentlessly flogged despite the highly inconclusive evidence. Paul Williams, the onetime literary executor of the Dick estate, provides a sound assessment of Rickman's egregious mode of analysis in his *To The High Castle, Philip K. Dick: A Life (1928–1962)* (Long Beach, Calif.: Fragments West/ The Valentine Press, 1989), of Dick as a potential victim of child abuse. See "The Rickmanization of PKD" in the "Philip K. Dick Society Newsletter," No. 24 (May 1990).

8.   For those readers who would insist upon viewing Dick as a "mad" charlatan tossing about ideas he could not comprehend as truly as might a "sane" and reasonable scholar, the following case study—in miniature—may prove illuminating.

The late Ioan P. Couliano, an acclaimed historian of religious thought who taught at the University of Chicago Divinity School and worked as a scholarly collaborator with the eminent Mircea Eliade, had occasion to examine one novel of the *"Valis* Trilogy"—*The Divine Invasion*—in his landmark survey of Gnostic thought *The Tree of Gnosis* (New York: HarperCollins, 1992). Couliano's judgment of the thematic influences in that novel was intended to rebut those who, in Couliano's view, too carelessly cited Dick as an example of a "Gnostic" science fiction writer:

"A closer look at the novel shows that, indeed, Dick took inspiration from Jewish and Jewish-Christian apocalyptic literature (especially *The Vision of Isaiah*), yet his novel, which describes the descent of God to the earth through the first heaven controlled by the troops of Belial the Opponent, and God's encounter with his wisdom in a kindergarten, makes no use of gnostic material."

Now compare this with an analysis by Dick himself, written in 1979, in the concluding pages of an unpublished outline of the novel in progress (then titled *Valis Regained*) that would become *The Divine Invasion*. Note that Dick himself recognizes the absence of a fundamental Gnostic good-evil dualism in this novel. He also makes reference to Isaiah (though his source is the Bible, not the apocalyptic text cited by Couliano):

"In the first novel, *Valis*, the protagonist Horselover Fat was obsessed—and for good reason: His girlfriend had killed herself—by the problem of evil. He finally came to the conclusion that two gods exist, which is to say a bitheism, each contending against the other. Although *Valis Regained* draws heavily on the bitheism of the Qumran people, it basically presents another view, not syntonic to Horselover Fat: monotheism, with the notion that evil has no true existence of its own but borrows its existence, or is lent its existence, from the one God. *Valis Regained* bases its theology on the extraordinary passage in Isaiah 45:6–7 [the capitalization is Dick's own]:

". . . so that men from the rising and the setting sun

may know that there is none but I:

I am the LORD, there is no other;

I make the light, I create darkness,

author alike of prosperity and trouble.

I, the LORD, do all these things."

Had Couliano taken the time to study the first novel in the trilogy—*Valis*—it is possible that his judgment as to the presence of Gnostic ideas in Dick's work would have changed. Nonetheless, the comparison of these two quotations is useful not only as a validation of Dick's knowing use of religious source material but also as a fair warning to all those who would paste a doctrinal label of any sort on Dick's work. Dick's viewpoints were multifold, indeterminate, and changeable; he cannot rightly be described by any "ism."

9. Michael Talbot, *The Holographic Universe* (New York: Harper Perennial, 1992), pp. 79–80.

10. Marcel Duchamp, *Salt Seller: The Writings of Marcel Duchamp (Marchand du Sel)* (New York: Oxford University Press, 1973), p. 142.

Note to the Vintage edition: Two inadvertent errors in the dating of "The Two Completed Chapters of a Proposed Sequel to *The Man in the High Castle*" and the *Exegesis* entry on page 328 have been corrected in this paperback edition.

Part One

Autobiographical Writings

The writings in this section have been grouped together by the fact that their content focuses exclusively or primarily on Dick's life. It will be obvious to the reader, however, that many of the writings included in other sections of this volume contain autobiographical elements as well. In his writings, Dick frequently drew upon events in his life to elucidate his ideas, and, in like manner, drew upon the ideas that most fascinated him at any given time to elucidate past events.

The two selections from the mainstream novel *Gather Yourselves Together* (1949) vividly portray the psyche of the young and innocent protagonist Carl, who bears a close resemblance to the young Philip K. Dick. These are certainly not autobiographical passages, but they nonetheless offer insight into the modes of thought and feeling of the apprentice writer coming of age. This novel was published in a limited edition by WCS Books in 1994.

"Introducing the Author" was first published (with an accompanying photograph of Dick) on the inside front cover of *Imagination: Stories of Science and Fantasy* (February 1953).

"Biographical Material on Philip K. Dick" (1968) was apparently prepared for the use of one of Dick's publishers. It is published here for the first time.

"Self Portrait" was first published, according to Paul Williams, "in mid- or late 1968 for a Danish magazine or fanzine edited by Jannick Storm." It first appeared in English in the *Philip K. Dick Society (PKDS) Newsletter* (edited by Williams), No. 2, December 1983.

"Notes Made Late at Night by a Weary SF Writer," written in 1968, was first published in *Eternity Science Fiction*, Old Series, No. 1, July 1972. It was reprinted in the *PKDS Newsletter*, Nos. 22–23, December 1989.

The two autobiographical sketches—each titled "Biographical

Material on Philip K. Dick" and written in 1972 and 1973, respectively—are published here for the first time.

"Memories Found in a Bill from a Small Animal Vet" first appeared in *The Real World*, No. 5, February–March 1976.

"The Short, Happy Life of a Science Fiction Writer" first appeared in *Scintillation*, Vol. 3, No. 3, June 1976.

"Strange Memories of Death," written in 1979, first appeared in *Interzone*, Summer 1984, and was republished in the Dick essay-story collection *I Hope I Shall Arrive Soon*, edited by Mark Hurst and Paul Williams.

The 1980 epistolary exchange with critic Frank Bertrand—titled (in Dick's typed transcript) "Philip K. Dick on Philosophy: A Brief Interview"—was first published in *Niekas*, No. 36, in 1988. The version published here comes from the typed transcript in the possession of the Dick Estate.

Two Fragments from the Mainstream Novel
Gather Yourselves Together (1949)

This was what happened to all the things that came out of the wet earth, out of the filthy slime and mold. All things that lived, big and little. They appeared, struggling out of the sticky wetness. And then, after a time, they died.

Carl looked up at the day again, at the sunlight and the hills. It did not look the same, now, as it had looked a few moments before. Perhaps he saw it more clearly than he had a moment ago. The sky, blue and pure, stretched out as far as the eye could see. But blood and feathers came from the sky. The sky was beautiful when he stood a long way off from it. But when he saw too closely, it was not pretty. It was ugly and bitter.

The sky was held together with tacks and gum and sticky tape. It cracked and was mended, cracked and was mended again. It crumbled and sagged, rotted and swayed in the wind, and like the sky in the children's story, part of it fell to earth.

Carl walked on slowly. He stepped off the road and climbed a narrow dirt ridge. Soon he was going up the side of a grassy slope, breathing deeply and taking big steps. He stopped for a moment, turning to look back.

Already the Company and its property had become small, down below him. Shrunk, dwindling away. Carl sat down on a rock. The world was quiet and still around him. Nothing stirred. His world. His silent, personal world.

But he did not understand it. So how could it be his world? He had come out to smile at the flowers and grass. But he had found something more, something that he could not smile at. Something that was not pleasant at all. Something that he did not like nor understand nor want.

So it was not his world. If it were his world he would have made it differently. It had been put together wrong. Very much wrong. Put together in ways that he could not approve of.

The silent bird, lying in the road. It reminded him of something. His thoughts wandered. What did it remind him of? A strange feeling drifted through him. This had happened before. This very thing. He had gone out and found something terrible. Something that did not make sense. Something he could not explain or understand.

After a while he remembered. The cat. The dying old cat, with its broken ears, one eye gone, its body thin and dry with patches of loose hair. The cat and the bird. Other things. Flies buzzing around. Streams of ants. Things dying, disappearing silently, drifting away. With no one to watch or care.

He had never understood it, this thing that he found, in the great warm world. It had no meaning. No sense. Was there some purpose? Some reason?

When he understood the cat was dead he had gone back inside the house, walking slowly, deep in thought. Back inside, to his room, his things. His microscope. His stamps and maps and drawings and books. They had meaning. Purpose. Their existence had reason to it. He could look at them and understand them.

Carl sat on the hillside, thinking about his childhood. It was not so long ago. Not so very many years in the past. He could feel the memories rising up around him, seeping up on all sides of him. Sights, smells. Tastes. His past was very much with him. It was close, just below the surface. Waiting to come up. His room. His microscope. The drawings he had made.

He sat and remembered about them.

* * * *

Her breasts amazed him. They did not jut out and up. They did not swell, pressing forward as the drawings had shown them. They hung down, and when she bent over they fell away from her. They bounced and swung when she picked up her clothes, bending over and reaching down to dress. They were not hard cups at all, but flesh like the rest of her, soft pale flesh. Like wineskins hanging on tent walls in Middle East villages. Sacks, wobbling flesh sacks that much [sic; must] have got in her way every now and then.

She buttoned her short red pants and fastened her gray blouse around her. She sat down to tie her sandals. Now she looked the same as she always had, not white, bare, chunky. Her breasts were again curves under her blouse, not bulging wineskins hanging down. In the close-fitting pants and blouse she looked taller and slimmer.

She finished dressing and went off, across the lawn. He lost sight of her. She had disappeared. It was finished. He relaxed. His blood subsided. His heart began to return to normal, the color draining out of his cheeks and ears. He sighed, letting out his breath.

Had it really happened? He felt dazed. In a way he was disappointed. She had been white and short, bulging here and there. With legs for walking and feet for standing. Her body was like all bodies, a physical creation, an instrument, a machine. It had come into the world the same way as other things, from the dust and wet slime. After a while it would wither and sag and crack and bend, and the tape and glue and tacks would give way to let it sink back down into the ground again, from which it had come.

It would break and wear out. It would fade and pass away, like the grass and the flowers, the great fir trees above him, like the hills and the earth itself. It was a part of the ordinary world, a material thing like other material things. Subject to the same laws. Acting in the same way.

He thought suddenly of his drawings, the pinups he had copied, all the notions and images that had crowded into his mind as he sat in his stuffy room with the sunlight shining through the drapes. He smiled. Well, at least he had gained a new understanding. He had lost all the cherished images and illusions, but he understood something now that had eluded him before. Bodies, his body, her body, all were about the same. All were part of the same world. There was nothing outside the world, no great realm of the phantom soul, the region of the sublime. There was only this—what he saw with his eyes. The trees and sun and water. He, Barbara, everyone and everything, were parts of this. There was nothing else.

And it was not as if his secret inner world, the spirit world that he had nourished so long, had suddenly come crashing down around him. There were no ruins and sad remains to pick over. Rather, all the dreams and notions he had held so long had abruptly winked out of existence. Vanished silently, like a soap bubble. Gone forever. As if they had never existed.

"Introducing the Author" (1953)

Once, when I was very young, I came across a magazine directly below the comic books called *Stirring Science Stories*. I bought it, finally, and carried it home, reading it along the way. Here were ideas, vital and imaginative. Men moving across the universe, down into subatomic particles, into time; there was no limit. One society, one given environment was transcended. Stf [abbreviation for "scientifiction," an early alternate term for "science fiction"] was Faustian; it carried a person up and beyond.

I was twelve years old, then. But I saw in stf the same thing I see now: a medium in which the full play of human imagination can operate, ordered, of course, by reason and consistent development. Over the years stf has grown, matured toward greater social awareness and responsibility.

I became interested in writing stf when I saw it emerge from the ray gun stage into studies of man in various types and complexities of society.

I enjoy writing stf; it is essentially communication between myself and others as interested as I in knowing where present forces are taking us. My wife and my cat, Magnificat, are a little worried about my preoccupation with stf. Like most stf readers I have files and stacks of magazines, boxes of notes and data, parts of unfinished stories, a huge desk full of related material in various stages. The neighbors say I seem to "read and write a lot." But I think we will see our devotion pay off. We may yet live to be present when the public libraries begin to carry the stf magazines, and someday, perhaps even the school libraries.

—PHILIP K. DICK

9

"Biographical Material
on Philip K. Dick" (1968)

Philip K. Dick attended the University of California, operated a record store, was an advertising copywriter, had a classical music program on station KSMO, lives now in San Rafael, and is interested in hallucinogens and snuff. Born Chicago, December 16, 1928. Although bearded, aging and portly, is a fanatical girl-watcher; does everything but carry a measuring tape. Sold his first story November 1951 and has had no occupation except that of science fiction writer since. Has to his credit twenty-seven books, of which twenty-six are novels. First novel: 1954. In June 1953 had stories in seven magazines simultaneously. Won the Hugo for best novel 1962, *Man in the High Castle*. Married, has two daughters and young, pretty, nervous wife, Nancy, who is afraid of the telephone. In two years (1963, '64) wrote and sold twelve novels, plus many magazine-length stories. Loves ducks and sheep; lives on a slough where wild ducks pause in their migrations. Lost his seventeen sheep in his most recent divorce action. Has owned a strange variety of cats, including one—Horace—who all his life asked an invisible question which no one could answer. Spends most of his time listening to first Scarlatti and then the Jefferson Airplane, then *Götterdämmerung*, in an attempt to fit them all together. Has many phobias and seldom goes anywhere, but loves to have people come over to his small, nice place on the water. Owes creditors a fortune, which he does not have. Warning: don't lend him any money. In addition he will steal your pills. Considers his best work to be the novel *Do Androids Dream of Electric Sheep?* recently published by Doubleday, because it deals with the misfortunes of animals and imagines a society in which a person's dog or cat is worth more as a status symbol (and costs more) than his house or car.

"Self Portrait" (1968)

Chicago: I was born there, on December 16, 1928. It was a frigid city, and the home of gangsters; it was also a real city and I appreciated that. Fortunately, however, my mother and father moved us to the Bay Area in California, and I learned that weather could be good, could be friendly rather than harsh. So, like most people in California, I was not born here but drifted here (I was about a year old at the time).

What, in those days, could be collected as evidence that I would someday be a writer? My mother (who is still living) wrote with the hope of having a literary success. She failed. But she taught me to admire writing . . . whereas my father viewed football games as transcending everything else. The marriage between them did not last, and when I was five they separated, my father moving to Reno, Nevada, my mother and I—and my grandfather, grandmother, and aunt—remaining in Berkeley in a huge old blue house.

Cowboy songs were my main love then. Music, in fact, has played a major role throughout my life. But in those days—when I was six—I wore a cowboy suit and listened to cowboy music on the radio. That and the funny papers were my whole world.

It is odd to think that a child could grow up during the Depression and not know it. I never heard the word. Of course I knew that my mother was broke most of the time, but I never managed to extrapolate from this. It seemed to me that the dull quality of the society around me—the city streets and their houses—came from the fact that all motorcars were black. Traffic progressed like a great and never-ending funeral.

But we had our amusements. In the winter of 1934 my mother moved the two of us to Washington, D.C. This gave me the sudden opportunity to find out what really awful weather was like . . . and yet we enjoyed it.

11

We had our sleds in winter and our Flexies (sleds with wheels) in summer. In Washington, summer is a horror beyond the telling of it. I think it warped my mind—warped that in a fine conjunction of the fact that my mother and I had nowhere to live. We stayed with friends. Year in, year out. I did not do well (what seven-year-old child would?) and so I was sent to a school specializing in "disturbed" children. I was disturbed in regard to the fact that I was afraid of eating. The boarding school could not handle me because I weighed less each month, and was never seen to eat a string bean. My literary career, however, began to emerge, in the form of poetry. I wrote my first poem thus:

I saw a little birdy
Sitting in the tree
I saw a little birdy
looking out at me.
Then the kitty saw the birdy and there wasn't none to see,
For the cat ate him up in the morning.

This poem was enthusiastically received on Parents' Day, and my future was assured (although, of course, no one knew it; not then, anyhow). There then followed a long period in which I did nothing in particular except go to school—which I loathed—and fiddle with my stamp collection (which I still have), plus other boywise activities such as marbles, flipcards, bolobats, and the newly evented comic books, such as Tip Top Comics, King Comics, and Popular Comics. My ten-cent allowance each week went first to candy (Necco wafers, chocolate bar, and jujubes), and, after that, Tip Top Comics. Comic books were scorned by adults, who assumed and hoped they, as a literary medium, would soon disappear. They did not. And then there was the lurid section of the Hearst newspapers, which on Sunday told of mummies still alive in caves, and lost Atlantis, and the Sargasso Sea. The American Weekly, this quasi-magazine was called. Today we would dismiss it as "pseudo-science," but in those days, the midthirties, it was quite convincing. I dreamed of finding the Sargasso Sea and all the ships tangled up there, their corpses dangling over the rails and their coffers filled with pirate gold. I realize now that I was doomed to failure by the very fact that the Sargasso Sea did not exist—or anyhow it did not capture many Spanish gold-bearing ships-of-the-line. So much for childhood dreams.

About 1939 my mother took me back to Berkeley and we began to have cats. We lived in the Berkeley hills, which in those days were mostly vacant lots. Mice rustled about, and so did cats. I began to think of cats as a necessary part of the household—a view I hold even more strongly today (at present my wife and I have two, but the male, Willis, is worth at least five regular cats [I will return to this subject later]).

And, at about the same time, I discovered the Oz books. It seemed like a small matter, my utter avidity to read each and every Oz book. Librarians haughtily told me that they "did not stock such fantastic material," their reasoning being that books of fantasy led a child into a dreamworld and made it difficult for him to adjust properly to the "real" world. But my interest in the Oz books was, in point of fact, the beginning of my love for fantasy, and, by extension, science fiction.

I was twelve when I read my first SF magazine . . . it was called *Stirring Science Stories* and ran, I think, four issues. The editor was Don Wollheim, who later on (1954) bought my first novel . . . and many since. I came across the magazine quite by accident; I was actually looking for *Popular Science*. I was most amazed. Stories about science? At once I recognized the magic which I had found, in earlier times, in the Oz books—this magic now coupled not with magic wands but with science, and set in the future, where, as we all know, science will play more and more of a role in our lives. Such has come about, but I am not too happy about that. In any case my view became magic equals science . . . and science (of the future) equals magic. I have still not lost that view, and our idea then (I was twelve, remember) that science would prove to play a greater part in our lives—well, we were right, for better or worse. I, for one, bet on science as helping us. I have yet to see how it fundamentally endangers us, even with the H-bomb lurking about. Science has given more lives than it has taken; we must remember that.

In high school I held a little job in a record and radio store, sweeping and cleaning, but never, oh never, talking to the customers. Now here my longtime love of music rose to the surface, and I began to study and grasp huge areas of the map of music; by fourteen I could recognize virtually any symphony or opera, identify any classical tune hummed or whistled at me. And, through this, I was promoted to Record Clerk, First Class. Music—and phonograph records—became my life; I planned to make it my whole future. I would advance up the ladder, step by step, and eventually I would manage a record store and then at last I would own one. I forgot about SF; in fact, I no longer even read it. Like the radio serial *Jack Armstrong, the All-American Boy!* SF fell into place as an interest of childhood. But I still liked to write, so I wrote little literary bits which I hoped to sell to *The New Yorker* (I never did). Meanwhile I gorged myself on modern classics of literature: Proust and Pound, Kafka and Dos Passos, Pascal—but now we're getting into the older literature, and my list could go on forever. Let us say simply that I gained a working knowledge of literature from *The Anabasis* to *Ulysses*. I was not educated on SF but on well-recognized serious writing by authors all over the world.

I came back to SF—and ultimately SF writing—in an odd way. Anthony Boucher, the most dearly loved and equally important person in SF, had a program of vocal music on a local radio station, and due to my interest in classical music I listened to the program. I got to meet him— he came to the record store in which I worked—and we had a long talk. I discovered that a person could be not only mature, but mature and educated, and still enjoy SF. Tony Boucher had entered my life, and by doing so, had determined its whole basic direction.

Tony had a weekly class on writing, which he conducted in his home. I decided to go, and Tony dutifully read my painful first efforts. The literary ones he did not respond to, but to my surprise he seemed quite taken with a short fantasy, which I had done; he seemed to be weighing it in almost terms of economic worth. This caused me to begin writing more and more fantasy stories, and then SF. In October of 1951, when I was twenty-one years old [Dick is mistaken here; he was twenty-two], I sold my first story: a tiny fantasy to *F&SF*, the magazine that Tony Boucher edited. I began to mail off stories to other SF magazines, and lo and behold, *Planet Stories* bought a short story of mine. In a blaze of Faust-like fire I abruptly quit my job at the record shop, forgot my career in records, and began to write all the time (how I did it I don't yet know; I worked until four each morning). Within the month after quitting my job I made a sale to *Astounding* (now called *Analog*) and *Galaxy*. They paid very well, and I knew then that I would never give up trying to build my life around a science fiction career.

In 1953 I sold stories to fifteen different magazines; in one month, June, I had stories in seven magazines on the stands at once. I turned out story after story, and they were all bought. And yet—

With only a few exceptions, my magazine-length stories were second-rate. Standards were low in the early '50s. I did not know many technical skills in writing that are essential . . . the viewpoint problem, for example. Yet, I was selling; I was making a good living, and at the 1954 Science Fiction World Convention, I was very readily recognized and singled out . . . I recall someone taking a photograph of A. E. Van Vogt and me and someone saying, "The old and the new." But what a miserable excuse for "the new"! And how much the field was losing by Van Vogt's leaving it!

I knew that I was in serious trouble. For example, Van Vogt, in such works as *The World of Null A*, wrote novels; I did not. Maybe that was it; maybe I should try an SF novel.

For months I prepared carefully. I assembled characters and plots, several plots all woven together, and then wrote everything into the book that I could think up. It was bought by Don Wollheim at Ace Books and titled *Solar Lottery*. Tony Boucher reviewed it well in the *New York Herald Tribune*; the review in *Analog* was favorable, and in *Infinity*, Damon Knight devoted his entire column to it—and all in praise.

Standing there at that point I did some deep thinking. It seemed to me that magazine-length writing was going downhill—and not paying very much. You might get $20 for a story and $4,000 for a novel. So I decided to bet everything on the novel; I wrote *The World Jones Made*, and later on, *The Man Who Japed*. And then a novel that seemed to be a genuine breakthrough for me: *Eye in the Sky*. Tony gave it the Best Novel of the Year rating, and in another magazine, *Venture*, Ted Sturgeon called it "the kind of small trickle of good sf which justifies reading all the worthless stuff." Well, I had been right. I was a better novel writer than a short-story writer. Money had nothing to do with it; I liked writing novels and they went over well.

But then, at that point, my private life began to become violent and mixed up. My marriage of eight years broke up; I moved out into the country, met an artistically inclined woman who had just lost her husband. We met in October and the next April we had gotten married in Ensenada, Mexico. I had her and three girls to take care of, and for two years I was unable to produce anything except hack work. At last I gave up and went to work for my wife, in her jewelry business. I was miserable. As a child the misery had come from outside in the form of no money, no heat, no place to live; with Anne I could not fulfill myself because her own creative drive was so strong that she often declared that my creative work "got in her way." Even in the jewelry making I merely polished pieces that she designed. My sense of self-worth began to flag, so I hitched myself to the priest of our times, the psychologist-psychiatrist, and asked his advice. "Go home," he said, "and forget the jewelry business. Forget that you have a five-bedroom, three-bathroom house, with three girls to raise—and a fourth coming. Go home, sit down at your typewriter; forget income taxes, even How to Make Money. And simply write a good book, a book you really believe in. You can stop fixing breakfast for the kids and assisting your wife in her welding. *Write a book.*"

I did so, without preamble; I simply sat down and wrote. And what I wrote was *The Man in the High Castle.* It sold right away, received a number of reviews suggesting that it should win the Hugo, and then, one day, I got a letter from my agent congratulating me for winning the Hugo. Another point had been passed in my career—and, as before, I didn't realize it. All I knew was that I wanted to write more and more books; the books got better and the publishers were more interested in them.

Now, most readers do not know how little SF writers were paid. I had been earning about $6,000 a year. In the year following the Hugo award, I earned $12,000, and close to that in the subsequent years (1965–68). And I wrote at a fantastic speed; I produced twelve novels in two years . . . which must be a record of some sort. I could never do this again—the physical stress was enormous . . . but the Hugo was there to tell me that what I wanted to write was what a good number of readers wanted to read. Amazing as it seems!

Recently I have sat back, reflecting on my twenty-eight novels, which I have sold between 1954 and 1968, wondering which are good. What have I accomplished? Here I am, thirty-nine years old, rather moth-eaten and shaggy, taking snuff, listening to Schubert songs on the phonograph . . . "although bearded, elderly, and portly," someone said about me, "he is still a confirmed girl-watcher." This is true. And cat-watcher. They are the great joy for me, and I wish I could squeeze Willis, my huge orange and white tom, into a novel, or if they make a movie of *Do Androids Dream of Electric Sheep?* Willis could play a walk-on part (no lines), and we would both be happy. Four years ago I divorced my jewelry-welding wife and married a very sweet girl who paints. We now have a baby and we must find a larger house (we did find one, and, as I'm writing this, we are preparing to move into it: four bedrooms and two bathrooms and a level backyard, fenced, where Isa can play safely). So that is my nonliterary life: I have a very young wife whom I love, and a baby whom I almost love (she's a terrible pest), and a tomcat whom I cherish and adore. What about the books? How do I feel about them?

I enjoyed writing all of them. But I think that if I could only choose a few, which, for example, might escape World War Three, I would choose, first, *Eye in the Sky* [1956]. Then *The Man in the High Castle* [1962]. *Martian Time-Slip* [1964] (published by Ballantine). *Dr. Bloodmoney* [1965] (a recent Ace novel). Then *The Zap Gun* [1967] and *The Penultimate Truth* [1964], both of which I wrote at the same time. And finally another Ace book, *The Simulacra* [1964].

But this list leaves out the most vital of them all: *The Three Stigmata of Palmer Eldritch* [1965]. I am afraid of that book; it deals with absolute evil, and I wrote it during a great crisis in my religious beliefs. I decided to write a novel dealing with absolute evil as personified in the form of a "human." When the galleys came from Doubleday I couldn't correct them because I could not bear to read the text, and this is still true.

Two other books should perhaps be on this list, both very new Doubleday novels: *Do Androids Dream of Electric Sheep?* [1968] and another as yet untitled [*Ubik* (1969)]. *Do Androids* has sold very well and has been eyed intently by a film company who has in fact purchased an option on it. My wife thinks it's a good book. I like it for one thing: It deals with a society in which animals are adored and rare, and a man who owns a real sheep is Somebody . . . and feels for that sheep a vast bond of love and empathy. Willis, my tomcat, strides silently over the pages of that book, being important as he is, with his long golden twitching tail. Make them understand, he says to me, that animals are really that important right now. He says this, and then eats up all the food we had been warming for our baby. Some cats are far too pushy. The next thing he'll want to do is write SF novels. I hope he does. None of them will sell.

"Notes Made Late at Night by a Weary SF Writer" (1968, 1972)

Here I am, almost forty years old. Seventeen years ago I sold my first story, a great and wonderful moment in my life that will never come again. By 1954 I was known as a short story writer; in June 1953 I had seven stories on the stands, including one in *Analog*, *Galaxy*, and *F&SF*, and so on down. Ah, 1954. I wrote my first novel, *Solar Lottery*; it sold 150,000 copies of itself and then vanished, only to reappear again a few years ago. It was reviewed well, except in *Galaxy*. Tony Boucher liked it; so did Damon Knight. But I wonder why I wrote it—it and the twenty-four novels since. Out of love, I suppose; I love science fiction, both to read it and to write it. We who write it do not get paid very much. This is the harsh and overwhelming truth: Writing SF does not pay, and so writer after writer either dies trying to earn a living or leaves the field . . . to go into another, unrelated field, as for example Frank Herbert, who works for a newspaper and writes Hugo-winning SF in his spare time. I wish I could do that: hold an unrelated job and write SF after dinner each night, or early in the dawn. Then the pressure would be off. Let me tell you about that pressure. The average SF novel obtains between $1,500 and $2,000. Hence an SF writer who can write two novels a year—and sell them— gets back between $3,000 and $4,000 a year . . . which he can't live on. He can try, instead, to write three novels a year, plus a number of stories. With luck, and unending effort, he can raise his income to about $6,000 a year. At best, I have managed to earn $12,000 in one year; usually it runs less, and the effort of trying to bring in more money collapses me for as much as two years on end. During these two-year dry periods the only money coming in is for what are called "residuals." These include foreign sales, reprint in paperback, magazine serialization, TV and radio purchases, etc. It is awful, these dry periods, when you exist on the uncertain drip-drop of residuals. For example, an air mail letter arrives from one's agent. It contains royalty payments in the sum of $1.67. And the next week an air mail letter comes with a check for $4.50. And yet we who write SF go on, to some extent. As I say, it's love for the field.

What is there about SF that draws us? What is SF anyhow? It grips fans; it grips editors; it grips writers. And none make any money. When I ponder this I see always in my mind Henry Kuttner's *Fairy Chessmen* with its opening paragraph, the doorknob that winks at the protagonist. When I ponder this I also see—outside my mind, right beside my desk—a complete file of *Unknown* and *Unknown Worlds*, plus *Astounding* back to October 1933 . . . these being guarded by a nine-hundred-pound fireproof file cabinet, separated from the world, separated from life. Hence separated from decay and wear. Hence separate from time. I paid $390 for this fireproof file, which protects these magazines. After my wife and daughter these mean more to me than anything else I own—or hope to own.

The magic that grips us is in there, in the file. I have captured it, whatever it is.

As to my own writing. Reading it does not mean anything to me, all considerations as to how good it is or isn't, what I do well and what I do badly (such as putting in the kitchen sink, as Ted Sturgeon phrased it, in regard to *The Three Stigmata*). What matters to me is the *writing*, the act of manufacturing the novel, because while I am doing it, at that particular moment, I am in the world I'm writing about. It is real to me, completely and utterly. Then, when I'm finished, and have to stop, withdraw from that world *forever*—that destroys me. The men and women have ceased talking. They no longer move. I'm alone, without much money, and, as I said before, nearly forty. Where is Mr. Tagomi, the protagonist in *Man in the High Castle*? He has left me; we are cut off from each other. To read the novel does not restore Mr. Tagomi, place him once again where I can hear him talk. Once written, the novel speaks generally to everyone, not specifically to me. When a novel of mine comes out I have no more relationship to it than has anyone who reads it—far less, in fact, because I have the memory of Mr. Tagomi and all the others . . . Gino Molinari, for example, in *Now Wait for Last Year*, or Leo Bulero in *Three Stigmata*. My friends are dead, and as much as I love my wife, daughter, cat—none of these nor all of these is enough. The vacuum is terrible. Don't write for a living; sell shoelaces. Don't let it happen to you.

I promise myself: I will never write another novel. I will never again imagine people from whom I will eventually be cut off. I tell myself this . . . and, secretly and cautiously, I begin another book.

"Biographical Material
on Philip K. Dick" (1972)

In 1969 Paul Williams said of Philip K. Dick, "I must tell you this . . . Philip K. Dick will have more impact on the consciousness of this century than William Faulkner, Norman Mailer, or Kurt Vonnegut Jr." Author of thirty-one novels and almost two hundred stories published from 1951 on, he won the Hugo Award in 1963 for the Best Science Fiction Novel of the Year, *Man in the High Castle* [1962]. His reputation, especially in intellectual circles, is worldwide; in France, for example, he has more novels in print than has any other science fiction author. The first U.S. science fiction novel to appear in Poland will be his recent Doubleday novel, *Ubik* [1969], acclaimed by Patrice Duvic of Éditions OPTA, Paris (winner of the award for publisher of the year at the 1972 World Science Fiction Convention in L.A.) as "one of the most important books ever published." In February 1972 he spoke as Guest of Honor at the Second Vancouver Science Fiction Convention and lectured at the University of British Columbia. His most notable novels include *Do Androids Dream of Electric Sheep?* [1968], *Maze of Death* [1970], *We Can Build You* [1972], *Martian Time-Slip* [1964], *Dr. Bloodmoney* [1964], *The Three Stigmata of Palmer Eldritch* [1965], *Ubik* [1969], and *[The] Man in the High Castle* [1962]. Some of his best stories have been published in the paperback collection *The Preserving Machine* [1969]. Born in Chicago in 1928, Philip K. Dick has spent most of his life in the Bay Area, having attended the University of California at Berkeley. During the late fifties he lived in Point Reyes Station, Marin County, and in the early sixties in San Rafael. Now he resides in the Los Angeles area, where he lectures and writes. His early novels dealt with future societies of an antiutopian nature; in later novels he pioneered an "inner space" multiple-reality universe presented as hallucinations drug trauma [sic]. His story "Faith of Our Fathers" in Harlan Ellison's mind-shattering anthology *Dangerous Visions* [1967] received a Hugo nomination and is considered one of the most "dangerous visions" in that superb collection. Recently he completed a massive new novel for Doubleday titled *Flow My Tears, the Policeman Said* [later published in 1974] and is currently working on a science fiction novel of a different sort: a study of one girl's mind projected onto the universe, in which her qualities, lifestyle, and values form not merely a sociological enclave but the entire world of reality. Its working title is *Kathy-Jamis-Linda* and threatens to occupy him for what remains of his life. In it he contrasts the authentic human versus what he calls the "android," the reflex machine posing as a living being.

"Biographical Material on Philip K. Dick" (1973)

Professional science fiction writer since 1951, with almost two hundred stories and thirty-five novels sold. In 1963 *Man in the High Castle* [1962] won the Hugo Award for Best Science Fiction Novel of the year. Phil Dick was born on December 16, 1928 in Chicago but has lived most of his life in California. He attended the University of California at Berkeley but dropped out because of his antiwar convictions. His great passion is music: German Lieder, Wagner. He majored in German and greatly loves the works of Schiller, Heine, Goethe, Junger, Brecht. At one time he ran a classical music radio program and operated a record store. He is married, has three children, and a cat named Fred, and because of his experiences in Canada in the rehabilitation of drug addicts, is at work now on a major novel dealing with the tragedy of lives ruined by involvement with drugs. He identifies strongly with the protests and the angers of the younger generations versus the older establishment, and has lectured both in the U.S.A. and in Canada at universities and on the radio and in articles published throughout the world in favor of the rebellion of youth against age. His radicalism goes deeper than politics; it has become a worldview expressed growingly in his writing. Most of all he tries to express in his novels the fight against oppression of the free human spirit, of whatever kind: any tyranny, such as drug addiction or a police state or manipulative psychological techniques. The ordinary citizen, without political or economic power, is the hero of all his novels, and is his hero, too, his hope for the future.

"Memories Found in a Bill
from a Small Animal Vet" (1976)

> *Hark! Each tree its silence breaks.*
> —NICHOLAS BRADY (1692)

When I first met Theodore Sturgeon, who wrote *More Than Human*, this good man said to me right off, "What sort of universe is it that causes a man like Tony Boucher to die of cancer?" I had been wondering the same thing ever since Tony Boucher died [in 1968]. So had Ted Sturgeon, although he didn't expect me to give an answer. He just wanted to show me what he—Ted Sturgeon—was like. I've found I can do that, too: let people know about me by asking that. It shows that I cared a lot about one of the warmest men who ever lived. Tony was warm and at the same time when he stood in the midst of a group of people, sweat came out on his forehead from fear. Nobody ever wrote that about him but it's true. He was terrified all the time. He told me so once, in so many words. He loved people, but one time I encountered him on the electric train going to the opera and he was scared. He was a music critic and he did reviewing for *The New York Times* and edited a magazine and wrote novels and stories. But he was scared to take a drive across town.

Tony loved the universe and the universe frightened him, and I think I know where his head was at. A lot of people who are timid are that way because they love too much. They're afraid it'll all fall through. Naturally, it did with Tony. He died in middle age. Now, I ask you, what good did it do him to be scared? He used to carry his rare old 78 records to radio station KPFA every week for his program "Golden Voices," wrapping them in a towel so they wouldn't get broken. One time I decided to give Tony all my rare opera and vocal records, just plain give them to him as a

24

gift of my loving him. I phoned him up. "I got Tiana Lemnitz and Ger-
hard Husch," I told him. Tony replied shyly, "They are my idols." He was
a Roman Catholic, the only one we knew, so that was a strong statement.
Before I could get the records to him he was dead. "I feel tired half the
day," he had said. "I can't work as much as I used to. I think I'm ill." I
explained I had the same thing. That was eight or so years ago. The doctor
told him he had a bruised rib and taped it up. Someday I will meet that
doctor on the street. Tony got bad advice from everyone who could talk.

We used to play poker. Tony loved opera and poker and science fiction and mystery stories. He had a little writing class. This was after he was
famous and edited *Fantasy and Science Fiction Magazine* and he charged
one dollar a night when you showed up. He read your whole manuscript.
He told you how rotten it was, and you went away and wrote something
good. I never figured out how he accomplished that. Criticism like that is
supposed to crush you. "Maybe it's because when Tony reads your story
it's like he's reading it in Latin," Ron Goulart, a fellow student, said. Tony
taught me to write, and my first sale was to him. I still can remember that
nobody understood the story but he, even after it was printed. It's still in
print, twenty-two years later, in a college-level sf course manual put out by
Ginn and Company. There're only about fifteen hundred words to the
story, about as short as this. After the printing of the story, Ginn and Company prints an impromptu discussion I had with a high school class about
the story. All the kids understand the story. It's about a dog and how he
sees garbagemen coming to steal the precious food that the family stores
up every day until the heavily constructed metal urn is full and then these
Roogs come and steal the harvest just when it's ripe and perfect. The dog
tries to warn the family, but it's always early in the morning and his barking just annoys them. The story ends when the family decides they have
to get rid of the dog, due to his barking, at which point one of the Roogs or
garbagemen says to the dog, "We'll be back to get the people pretty soon."
I never could understand why no one but Tony Boucher could understand the story (I sent it to him in 1951). I guess in those days my view of
garbagemen was not shared universally, and now by 1971 when the high
school class discussed it with me, I guess it is. "But garbagemen don't eat
people," a lady anthologizer [SF editor Judith Merril] pointed out to me
in 1952. I had trouble answering that. *Something* comes and carries off
and devours people who are sleeping in tranquillity. Like Tony . . . some-

thing got to him. I think the dog who cried "ROOG! ROOG!" was trying to warn me and Tony. I got the warning and escaped—well, we'll see about that; time will tell—but Tony stayed at his post. You see, when you're so scared of the universe (or Roogs, if you will), to stay at your post takes courage of the kind they can't write about, because (1) they don't know how and (2) they don't notice in the first place, except maybe Ted Sturgeon, with all his own love, and his total lack of fear. He must have known how scared Tony was, and to be that scared and for the Roogs to get you . . . it's so goddam symmetrical, isn't it?

However, Tony is still alive, I discovered last year [1974]. My cat had begun to behave in an odd way, keeping watch over me in a quiet fashion, and I saw that he had changed. This was after he ran away and returned, wild and dirty, crapping on the rug in fear; we took him to the vet and the vet calmed him down and healed him. After that, Pinky had what I call a spiritual quality, except that he wouldn't eat meat. He would tremble whenever we tried to feed it to him. For five months he'd been lost, living in the gutter, seeing God knows what; I wish I knew. Anyhow, after he was changed—in the twinkling of an eye; that is, while at the vet's—he wouldn't ever do anything cruel. Yet I knew Pinky was afraid, because once I almost shut the refrigerator door on him and he did a three-cushion bank shot of himself off the walls to escape, and clocked a velocity unique for a pink sheeplike thing that usually just sat and gazed ahead. Pinky had trouble breathing because of his heavy fur and what they call hairballs. Tony had asthma terribly and needed it cold. Pinky would sit by the door to get the cold air from under the crack, and struggle to breathe. I will not write a teaser article here; Pinky died of cancer suddenly; he was three years old, very young for a cat. It was totally unexpected. The vet diagnosed it as something else, which could be cured.

I hadn't realized Pinky was Tony Boucher, out of love served up by the universe again, until I had this dream about Tony the Tiger, the cereal box character who offers you Sugar Frosted Flakes. In my dream I stood at one end of a light-struck glade, and at the other a great tiger came out slowly, with delight, and I knew we were together again. Tony the Tiger and me. My joy was unbounded. When I woke up I tried to think who I knew named Tony. I had other strange experiences after Pinky died. I dreamed about a "Mrs. Donlevy," who was incredibly tall—I could see only her feet and ankles—and she was serving me a plate of milk on the back porch and there was a vacant lot where I could roam at will, forever. It was the Elysian Vacant Lot, which the Greeks believed in, just my size. Also, the day Pinky died, at the vet's, that evening as I stood in the bathroom I felt my wife put her hand on my shoulder, firmly, to console me. Turning, I saw no one. I also dreamed this dream: I had the album notes for *Don Pasquale* and at the end the conductor had added a note: five strings of catgut like a cat's cradle, like a musical stave. It was a final hello from Pinky, who was Tony Boucher; in the dream the album was an old 78 one, a rare classic, a favorite of Tony's.

Tony or Pinky, I guess names don't count, was a lousy hunter all his life. One time he caught a gopher and ran up our apartment stairs with it. He placed it in his dish, where he was fed, because that was orderly, and of course the gopher got up at once and ran off. Tony felt that things belonged in their places, being an obsessively tidy person, his enormous collection of books and records was arranged the same way — each object in its proper place, and a proper place for each object. He should have tolerated more chaos in the universe. However, he recaught the gopher and ate it, all except the teeth.

Tony, or Pinky, was my guide; he taught me to write, and he stayed with me when I was sick back in 1972 and 1973, lying beside me day after day. That's why my wife, Tessa, brought him over, because I had pneumonia and needed help and we had no money for a doctor. (I think now in that regard I lucked out; he would have told me I had a bruised rib.) When the pain was really bad, Pinky used to lie on my body until I realized that he was trying to figure out which part of me was sick. He knew it was just one part, around the middle of my body. He did his best and I recovered but he did not. That was my friend.

Most cats fear the clattering arrival of the garbagemen each week, but Pinky detested them. Under our bed fixed, set eyes, but no Pinky was visible. Just the eyes, waiting for the bastards to go.

Four nights before Pinky unexpectedly died, before we knew he had cancer — I started to say, before he had been diagnosed as having a bruised rib — he and Tessa and I, as was our custom, were lying on the big bed, and I saw a uniform pale white light slowly fill the room. I thought the angel of death had come for me and I began praying in Latin: *"Tremens factus sum ego, et timeo,"* and so forth. Tessa gritted her teeth, but Pinky sat there, front feet tucked under him, impassive. I knew there was no place to hide, like under the bed. Every child knows that. And it looks bad.

It never occurred to me that death was arriving for anyone but me, which shows my attitude. I saw us all as painted ducks, on a painted sea, and thought of the thirteenth-century Arabic poem about "Once he will miss, twice he will miss. All the world's one level plain for him on which he hunts for flowers." We were as conspicuous as—well, anyhow, finally I gave up praying, but I remember in particular I kept crying out, "*Mors stupebit et natura*," which I thought meant that death stood stupefied, as if in surprise (as in, "I was stupefied to learn that my car had been towed away." It means just standing there impotently. That maybe is not what *Merriam-Webster* 3 says, but it is what I say).

Pinky never noticed the pale white light; as was his custom he seemed awake, but dozing. I think he was humming to himself. Later when I slept, toward morning, I dreamed a disturbing dream: The report of a gun fired close to my ear: a dreadful shotgun blast, and when I looked I saw a woman lying dying. I went for aid, but got on to one of those electric trolley buses by mistake, along with three Gestapo agents (I dream that a lot). We rode around forever while I tried vainly to short-circuit the power cables of the bus or trolley car, whatever it was—no luck. The Gestapo agents remained confident in that smug way they have and read newspapers and smoked. They knew they had me.

"The Short, Happy Life
of a Science Fiction Writer" (1976)

I would like to speak to my friends, here, to let them know that (1) all the dreadful things they have heard have befallen me have indeed befallen me, and (2) I am fine anyhow. In February I had a heart attack. The paramedics came—I was alone in the house at the time—and it was just like a scene in the TV program *Emergency*. They arrived two minutes after I phoned them, and pretty soon they were monitoring my vital life signs, and then it was to the county hospital to the Intensive Cardiac Care Unit. I hovered between life and death, telling jokes and falling in love with one nurse named Beth, who always wore pink.

But I write this to say that I recovered completely, until I saw the bill for $2,000 anyhow, which brings up the point that it was to the county hospital that I was taken; I didn't have any money, and none of the other Orange County hospitals would accept me. My view here is, Thank God for a hospital that will take you if you're broke, asking no questions, just saving your life and billing you later. But . . .

When I was sprung eleven days later I had forty cents, no more. Some food at home in the freezer. My total income for that month was nine dollars. March was no better, and by mid-April they were going to shut off the utilities. Every phone call was someone wanting money. My agent, God bless him, loaned me money, and here is where I want to say something that at the time didn't affect my head, but that when I told it later to a dude, he got really funny and said, "That sums up the situation of the artist better than I've ever heard it summed up before." There was a French royalty check on its way by mail from Paris to my agent, and I phoned, desperately, to see if it had arrived yet, since much of it was to go to me. The check arrived, the previous day. My agent could hear the fear in my voice, the shaking; I was three months overdue in my child support payments—and he said, in an oddly soft voice, "You know, Phil, you are one of the most respected writers in the world." I barely listened; all I knew was that I wouldn't be spending thirty days in Orange County jail for nonsupport, as Jim Croce says in one of his songs.

What I want to stress is not that I am either one of the most respected writers in the world or that my agent thinks so or said so but that here I am, after twenty-five years of professional SF writing, getting notices that they are going to turn off the water and gas and electricity if I don't pay in three days, and I say, What has it all been for? Well, recently I read an article by Barry Malzberg in F&SF [*Fantasy and Science Fiction*, a prominent SF magazine] in which he says he's leaving SF forever because— well, read it yourself; it is the greatest bunch of whining I ever heard in my life. I don't propose to whine, although probably what I've said so far seems to be whining. Really, though, I am more asking a question than making a statement, whining or otherwise. What have twenty-five years of work done to make me financially secure? I have a new novel coming out next January [1977] by Doubleday (*A Scanner Darkly*), which I honestly believe to be the best work I've ever done. I have the collaboration with Roger Zelazny coming out this year, the novel *Deus Irae* [1976]—there was that long article on me in *Rolling Stone* ["The Worlds of Philip K. Dick," November 6, 1975, by Paul Williams], which gave me a lot of publicity, and (and here it comes; get ready) I am *just about* to make it big. The key words: *just about to*. It is another case of waiting for Godot; the little boy says, "Mr. Godot isn't coming today, but surely he'll come tomorrow." But I say, If it does come for me, will it matter? Will it make up for twenty-five years of shivering with fear as to whether, when I get up in the morning, the electricity will still be turned on?

One time in early 1972 I came home and the utility company had shut off the electricity, and put a padlock on my circuit-breaker box. I got my tool kit, got out tools, and cut through the padlock and turned the power back on again. Technically, that's a crime, but the utility people were so surprised that they let me get away with it. I paid them the next day, but if you cut that padlock, you go into the slammer. I cite this to show that my fears are not merely neurotic. And the house that I was in then—it was repossessed by the finance company that held the mortgage. So these are real and valid fears. After I moved down here to Southern

California I had to start out from the bottom all over again; no car, no furniture, no house. And one day down here I got up and the electricity had been turned off. In early 1973 down here I was in bed with pneumonia, with no phone, no money to go to a doctor, to buy medication—I remember that very well, because while I was lying there propped up in bed (so I could breathe), Mr. Death walked into my bedroom. Really. I saw him as clear as I see you now, my friends. He wore a sharp, modern, polyester suit and carried a briefcase, which he opened to reveal some simple puzzles, the sort you give grammar school children. I failed to pass, and Mr. Death said, "Then you can come with me." And I saw (I'm not kidding you) a vision of a long winding road up a hillside, with many trees, to a sort of lovely large safe-looking old building, which was a sanitarium of some kind. "I'm taking you there," he said. "These tests prove that your brain is totally burned out, so now you can rest. You can rest up there at the top of the hill forever." And I was flooded with a sense of total joy and relief. However, at that moment my chick came into the bedroom, on impulse, to see how I was. And I realized who I'd been talking to. After that I began to mend.

You will say, now, that this piece I am writing rambles, and it is supposed to, having no topic but the head of the author writing it, which is well known to be a rambling head that produces rambling writing—with even a bit of chaos thrown in. What is my point? My point is that (1) twenty-five years of devoted writing haven't in any way given me financial security; (2) the fact that I am sure my new novel, *A Scanner Darkly*, is my best novel doesn't stop the fear; (3) I am not quitting. It's going to take more than all this to make me give up science fiction writing, for one simple reason. I love to write it. I am working on a thing now, called, *To Scare the Dead*, and already I've done two hundred thousand words of notes. It won't produce any financial security. The big break, just around the corner, will never come. One of these days I'll be back in the hospital, sick as hell, but I'll no doubt get out . . . and receive another $2,000 bill I have to pay off or go to jail. There are, in human beings, irrational drives. "Why don't you get a *real* job?" people say to me, mostly in fun, but not always in fun, and sometimes I say it to myself. They [sic; the big break] will always be on its way but not quite here yet; my agent will always help me (I should mention that he is Scott Meredith, and I've been with him about twenty-four years, and in 1973 when my son Christopher was born,

Scott sent him the most beautiful silver rattle you ever saw)—I guess there are eternal verities in the universe, all right, and the one that appeals to me is that man will keep on striving no matter how many times he is pushed down, which was what Faulkner said so thrillingly in his Nobel Prize speech. Man will be planning and scheming amid the ruins; the sound of his voice will still be heard.

So that is what's happened to me recently: three times in the hospital in a couple of years (plus the pneumonia), months of really being poor . . . one day I had to box up and mail off my collection of *Unknown* and *Unknown Worlds*, which was complete and which I had held on to through thick and thin, just to pay the landlord, BUT:

In this business of being an SF writer I have met either face-to-face, or talked with on the phone, or gotten letters from, some of the best goddamn human beings in the world. Schoolkids, for instance. Last week a black chick in Oakland. Today a guy from West Germany. Yesterday I wrote to a Swedish guy who came to this country mainly to meet me (sorry if that sounds egoish, but the point is, that was back in 1971, and we're still writing back and forth: Goran Bengtson; you may have seen letters of his printed in fanzines). I'm looking now in the stack, very huge and sloppy, beside my typewriter. A chick who did her master's thesis on me.

Oh yes. I find another letter, too. The return address:

OFFICE OF THE DISTRICT ATTORNEY.

So you can see what I mean, as my heart skips a beat and thuds to itself with the old, old fear.

Dear Carl [editor of *Scintillation*, in which this piece appeared],

You should have received by now the five-page piece I wrote for you, yesterday. Well, I decided to send the carbon off to Germany, to Uwe Anton, who has asked me for something and to whom I'd already sent some fragments of *Deus Irae*, the new novel coming out by me and Roger Zelazny (Anton is putting together a PKD issue, you see). Today I added three more pages to go with the five, to be printed in Germany only, and then I thought, Shit. Why not send *you* the carbons on these pages and see if you want to add them, perhaps explaining that Phil had originally intended them for the German printing only . . . although I sort of say that in the pages themselves. It's up to you. In any case, here are three additional pages to the untitled piece I mailed you on May first, and you are welcome to print them or not. Okay? But on second thought it seemed sort of chicken-shit for me to say stuff abroad and not here in the U.S. You'll see what I mean when you read the enclosed.

This ends the part written to be published in the United States, but for my German friends I would like to add a little more. [The subsequent language did appear in the U.S. publication.]

During 1974 we who opposed the Nixon tyranny here exhausted ourselves in forcing that tyranny out of office, only to discover, the next year, that underneath it lay an even greater abuse of power and threat to freedom: a secret police apparatus that had worked since the forties, completely invisible in terms of its lawless acts against Americans. In fact, something much like the police state that I depicted in *Flow My Tears, the Policeman Said* has come to light, and really to the astonishment of us all. I recall that back in the fifties, about 1953, two FBI agents came to visit me and asked me to spy on my wife, who at that time was attending the University of California at Berkeley and knew people—students— who were politically active. From then on, the secret political police apparatus grew.

And yet it was a thrilling year in 1974 when we began to dislodge what we thought was the tyranny . . . but then found the greater one, the intelligence community one, which really we cannot dislodge. The American people have lost the will to combat this tyranny; it has lasted too long, and we are tired. *I* am tired. As the disclosures came about the CIA and FBI, I could not believe them. What could I do? What could anyone do? It was not a question of one particular evil president, but all the presidents starting with Franklin Roosevelt: even our heroic ones, such as Kennedy. Freedom won only a limited victory in August 1974 when Nixon was forced out of office; the political police apparatus remains and will remain, and we cannot vote on this issue. I myself have given up, as our newspapers say most Americans have, with a sense that we are *helpless*. True, under the Freedom of Information Act, I was able to get the CIA to admit that they had indeed opened my mail to the Soviet Union and photographed it, and also I obtained my file from the FBI, or anyhow portions of it; I would have to go to court to get the rest. At that point, perhaps only a coincidence, I suffered my heart attack, as if my body had given up. As if my body was saying, "No more. It is futile." Now the thirty-day time limit is past; I can't go to court. And perhaps it's just as well. Perhaps my days of being a fighter for freedom are over, due to age, due to worry, but due mostly to the discovery—and existence—of the enormity of the secret political police apparatus that has so long existed in this country, and the dreadful things they have done (e.g., to Dr. King, for instance, who was a hero to me).

Personally, back in March 1974, I had the overwhelming conviction that God Himself had decided to depose Nixon. Few of my friends believe in God, much less that He would or was actually intervening. I mentioned it to Marcel Thaon of Robert Laffont publishers, France, and he wrote in an article accompanying their printing of my novel *Eye in the Sky*:

> *On sait combien l'affaire Watergate a frappé qui a été en butte par ailleurs à de nombreuses agressions voilées de l'administration Nixon. Comme le disait Klein a l'époque, Dick propose que le décrochage systématique de l'ordre etabli—par la désobéissance civique par exemple—peut seul faire échec au pouvoir. Il pense par ailleurs que c'est Dieu qui un jour en a eu assez de Nixon et s'en est débarrassé—mélangeant une fois de plus politique et religion.*

> [One knows how much the Watergate affair affected those who were exposed, in addition, to the other hidden aggressions of the Nixon administration. As Klein said at the time, Dick proposes that the blowing up of the established order—by civil disobedience, for example—could only check their power. He thinks, in addition, that God had had enough of Nixon and got rid of him—blending politics and religion one more time.]

I write this to my German friends and not to my American friends because my American friends, like myself, have become too weary to fight or care anymore. We fought a wonderful battle to dislodge Nixon, but our energy was gone, then. Perhaps, as I truly believe, that energy came directly from God, Who inspired and animated us, Who hurled us into battle. But what now? Months of depression have fallen over us here, we who were the activists. On TV, Senator Frank Church (God bless him) said that the U.S. intelligence organizations had become as bad as the KGB. *Ach Weh!*

So my novel in progress [ultimately crystallized as *Valis* (1981)] has nothing to do with politics; it has to do with the mystery religions of the first century B.C. and what they had discovered about restoring the faculties that man possessed before the Fall (Calvin spoke of man once having "supernatural faculties which were stripped away," and this fascinates me as the basis for a novel). But I am no longer politically active, and this will show up in my writing. This is sad, but I grow old; I grow old. I have not made my peace with the "straight" society, but at the same time I am too weak, too worn out by illness and fear, to do anything but try to make financial ends meet; I mean, to pay the water bill and gas bill and electricity bill. Perhaps it will not be the political secret police who will get me in the end but the district attorney for failure to pay back child support, an entirely unpolitical crime!

And yet . . . God may return, and inspire us again, to fight *when the time is right.* In my heart I wait for that day. Will it be long in coming? *"Wenn kommst du mein Heil . . . Ich komme dein Teil."* (When comes my salvation . . . I come as your portion.) And meanwhile I say to myself, *"Hab' Mut!"* (Have courage!)

[The following letter, to the editor of the fanzine *Scintillation*, in which this essay was first published, was attached as an epilogue.]

Just within the last two days I've read two separate articles, one in *Rolling Stone,* the other the editorial in the May 17, 1976, *New Yorker,* which so horribly bear out my fears expressed in the last three pages I sent you that I want to call them to your attention. Hopefully, you can call them to your readers' attention. The RS piece is titled: "The Hughes-Nixon-Lansky Connection: The Secret Alliances of the CIA from WWII to Watergate," by Howard Kohn. Look for it. Anyhow, the article suggests, incredibly, that Nixon may have been set up by the CIA, since "Deep Throat," who provided all the leaked secrets to Bob Woodward and Carl Bernstein at *The Washington Post,* turns out to be Robert Bennett, a CIA front man . . . which Woodward and Bernstein never realized. There seem to have been crucial segments of the puzzle that Woodward and Bernstein never got on to.

Carl, I think we were sold another crock; the exposure of the cover-up was itself a cover-up! What the RS piece points to is truly dreadful, far beyond what Woodward and Bernstein found. Would you believe that "Watergate," as they found it, was a CIA red herring? Incredible.

"Strange Memories of Death" (1979, 1984)

I woke up this morning and felt the chill of October [1979] in the apartment, as if the seasons understood the calendar. What had I dreamed? Vain thoughts of a woman I had loved. Something depressed me. I took a mental audit. Everything was in fact fine; this would be a good month. But I felt the chill.

Oh, Christ, I thought. Today is the day they evict the Lysol Lady.

Nobody likes the Lysol lady. She is insane. No one has ever heard her say a word and she won't look at you. Sometimes when you are descending the stairs she is coming up and she turns wordlessly around and retreats and uses the elevator instead. Everybody can smell the Lysol she uses. Magical horrors contaminate her apartment, apparently, so she uses Lysol. God damn! As I fix coffee I think, maybe the owners have already evicted her, at dawn, while I still slept. While I was having vain dreams about a woman I loved who dumped me. Of course, I was dreaming about the hateful Lysol Lady and the authorities coming to her door at 5:00 A.M. The new owners are a huge firm of real estate developers. They'd do it at dawn.

The Lysol Lady hides in her apartment and knows that October is here, October first is here, and they are going to bust in and throw her and her stuff out in the street. Now is she going to speak? I imagine her pressed against the wall in silence. However, it is not as simple as that. Al Newcum, the sales representative of South Orange Investments, has told me that the Lysol Lady wants Legal Aid. This is bad news because it screws up our doing anything for her. She is crazy but not crazy enough. If it could be proved that she did not understand the situation a team from Orange County Mental Health could come in as her advocates and explain to South Orange Investments that you cannot legally evict a person

37

with diminished capacity. Why the hell did she get it together to go to Legal Aid?

The time is 9:00 A.M. I can go downstairs to the sales office and ask Al Newcum if they've evicted the Lysol Lady yet, or if she is in her apartment, hiding in silence, waiting. They are evicting her because the building, made up of fifty-six units, has been converted to condominiums. Virtually everyone has moved, since we were all legally notified four months ago. You have one hundred and twenty days to leave or buy your apartment and South Orange Investments will pay $200 of your moving costs. This is the law. You also have first refusal on your rental unit. I am buying mine. I am staying. For $52,000 I get to be around when they evict the Lysol Lady who is crazy and doesn't have $52,000. Now I wish I had moved.

Going downstairs to the newspaper vending machine I buy today's *Los Angeles Times*. A girl who shot up a schoolyard of children "because she didn't like Mondays" is pleading guilty. She will soon get probation. She took a gun and shot schoolchildren because, in effect, she had nothing else to do. Well, today is Monday; she is in court on a Monday, the day she hates. Is there no limit to madness? I wonder about myself. First of all, I doubt if my apartment is worth $52,000. I am staying because I am both afraid to move—afraid of something new, of change—and because I am lazy. No, that isn't it. I like this building and I live near friends and near stores that mean something to me. I've been here three and a half years. It is a good, solid building with security gates and deadbolt locks. I have two cats and they like the closed patio; they can go outside and be safe from dogs. Probably I am thought of as the Cat Man. So everyone has moved out, but the Lysol Lady and the Cat Man stay on.

What bothers me is that I know that the only thing separating me from the Lysol Lady, who is crazy, is the money in my savings account. Money is the official seal of sanity. The Lysol Lady, perhaps, is afraid to move. She is like me. She just wants to stay where she has stayed for several years, doing what she's been doing. She uses the laundry machines a lot, washing and spin-drying her clothes again and again. This is where I encounter her: I am coming into the laundry room and she is there at the machines to be sure no one steals her laundry. Why won't she look at you? Keeping her face turned away . . . what purpose is served? I sense hate. She hates every other human being. But now consider her situation:

Those she hates are going to close in on her. What fear she must feel! She gazes about in her apartment waiting for the knock on the door; she watches the clock and understands!

To the north of us, in Los Angeles, the conversion of rental units to condominiums has been effectively blocked by the city council. Those who rent won out. This is a great victory but it does not help the Lysol Lady. This is Orange County. Money rules. The very poor live to the east of me: the Mexicans in their barrio. Sometimes when our security gates open to admit cars the Chicano women run in with baskets of dirty laundry; they want to use our machines, having none of their own. The people who lived here in the building resented this. When you have even a little money—money enough to live in a modern, full-security, all-electric building—you resent a great deal.

Well, I have to find out if the Lysol Lady has been evicted yet. There is no way to tell by looking at her window; the drapes are always shut. So I go downstairs to the sales office to see Al. However, Al is not there; the office is locked. Then I remember that Al flew to Sacramento on the weekend to get some crucial legal papers that the state lost. He hasn't returned. If the Lysol Lady wasn't crazy I could knock on her door and talk to her; I could find out that way. But this is precisely the focus of the tragedy; any knock will frighten her. This is her condition. This is the illness itself. So I stand by the fountain that the developers have constructed, and I admire the planter boxes of flowers that they have had brought in . . . they have really made the building look good. It formerly looked like a prison. Now it has become a garden. The developers put a great deal of money into painting and landscaping and in fact rebuilding the whole entrance. Water and flowers and French doors . . . and the Lysol Lady silent in her apartment waiting for the knock.

Perhaps I could tape a note to the Lysol Lady's door. It could read:

> MADAM, I AM SYMPATHETIC TO YOUR POSITION AND
> WOULD LIKE TO ASSIST YOU. IF YOU WISH ME TO
> ASSIST YOU, I LIVE UPSTAIRS IN APARTMENT C-1.

How would I sign it? Fellow loony, maybe. Fellow loony with $52,000 who is legally here whereas you are, in the eyes of the law, a squatter. As of midnight last night. Although the day before it was as much your apartment as mine is mine.

I go back upstairs to my apartment with the idea of writing a letter to the woman I once loved and last night dreamed about. All sorts of phrases pass through my mind. I will re-create the vanished relationship with one letter. Such is the power of my words.

What crap. She is gone forever. I don't even have her current address. Laboriously, I could track her down through mutual friends, and then say what?

> MY DARLING, I HAVE FINALLY COME TO MY SENSES.
> I REALIZE THE FULL EXTENT OF MY INDEBTEDNESS
> TO YOU. CONSIDERING THE SHORT TIME WE WERE
> TOGETHER YOU DID MORE FOR ME THAN ANYONE ELSE
> IN MY LIFE. IT IS EVIDENT TO ME THAT I HAVE
> MADE A DISASTROUS ERROR. COULD WE HAVE DINNER
> TOGETHER?

As I repeat this hyperbole in my mind the thought comes to me that it would be horrible but funny if I wrote that letter and then by mistake or design taped it to the Lysol Lady's door. How would she react? Jesus Christ! It would kill her or cure her! Meanwhile I could write my departed loved one, *die ferne Geliebte*, as follows:

> MADAM, YOU ARE TOTALLY NUTS. EVERYONE WITHIN
> MILES IS AWARE OF IT. YOUR PROBLEM IS OF YOUR
> OWN MAKING. SHIP UP, SHAPE UP, GET YOUR ACT
> TOGETHER, BORROW SOME MONEY, HIRE A BETTER
> LAWYER, BUY A GUN, SHOOT UP A SCHOOLYARD. IF
> I CAN ASSIST YOU, I LIVE IN APARTMENT C-1.

Maybe the plight of the Lysol Lady is funny and I am too depressed by the coming of autumn to realize it. Maybe there will be some good mail today; after all, yesterday was a mail holiday. I will get two days of mail today. That will cheer me up. What in fact is going on is that I am feeling sorry for myself; today is Monday and, like the girl in court pleading guilty, I hate Mondays.

Brenda Spenser pleaded guilty to the charge of shooting eleven people, two of whom died. She is seventeen years old, small and very pretty, like one of those she shot. The thought enters my mind that perhaps the Lysol Lady has a gun in her apartment, a thought that should have come to me a long time ago. Perhaps South Orange Investments thought of it. Perhaps this is why Al Newcum's office is locked up today; he is not in Sacramento but in hiding. Although, of course, he could be hiding in Sacramento, accomplishing two things at once.

An excellent therapist I once knew made the point that in almost all cases of criminal psychotic acting-out there was an easier alternative that the disturbed person overlooked. Brenda Spenser, for instance, could have walked to the local supermarket and bought a carton of chocolate milk instead of shooting eleven people, most of them children. The psychotic person actually chooses the more difficult path; he forces his way uphill. It is not true that he takes the line of least resistance, but he thinks that he does. There, precisely, lies his error. The basis of psychosis, in a nutshell, is the chronic inability to see the easy way out. All the behavior, all that constitutes psychotic activity and the psychotic lifestyle, stems from this perceptual flaw.

Sitting in isolation and silence in her antiseptic apartment, waiting for the inexorable knock on the door, the Lysol Lady had contrived to put herself in the most difficult circumstances possible. What was easy was made hard. What was hard was transmuted, finally, into the impossible, and there the psychotic lifestyle ends, when the impossible closes in and there are no options at all, even difficult ones. That is the rest of the definition of psychosis: At the end there lies a dead end. And, at that point, the psychotic person freezes. If you have ever seen it happen—well, it is an amazing sight. The person congeals like a motor that has seized. It occurs suddenly. One moment the person is in motion—the pistons are going up and down frantically—and then it's an inert block. That is because the path has run out for that person, the path he probably got on to years before. It is kinetic death. "Place there is none," St. Augustine wrote. "We go backward and forward, and there is no place." And then the cessation comes and there is only place.

The spot where the Lysol Lady had trapped herself was her own apartment, but it was no longer her own apartment. She had found a place at which to psychologically die and then South Orange Investments had taken it away from her. They had robbed her of her own grave.

What I can't get out of my mind is the notion that my fate is tied to that of the Lysol Lady. A fiscal entry in the computer at Mutual Savings divides us and it is a mythical division: It is real only so long as people such as South Orange Investments—specifically South Orange Investments—are willing to agree that it is real. It seems to me to be nothing more than a social convention, such as wearing matching socks. In another way, it's like the value of gold. The value of gold is what people agree on, which is like a game played by children. "Let's agree that that tree is third base." Suppose my television set worked because my friends and I agreed that it worked. We could sit before a blank screen forever that way. In that case it could be said that the Lysol Lady's failure lay in not having entered into a compact with the rest of us, a consensus. Underlying everything else there is this unwritten contract to which the Lysol Lady is not a party. But I am amazed to think that the failure to enter into an agreement palpably childish and irrational leads inevitably to kinetic death, to total stoppage of the organism.

Argued this way, one could say that the Lysol Lady had failed to be a child. The element that had taken over her life was the element of the grim. She never smiled. No one had ever seen her do anything but glower in a vague, undirected way.

Perhaps, then, she played a grimmer game rather than no game; perhaps her game was one of combat, in which case she now had what she wanted, even though she was losing. It was at least a situation she understood. South Orange Investments had entered the Lysol Lady's world. Perhaps being a squatter rather than a tenant was satisfying to her. Maybe we all secretly will everything that happens to us. In that case does the psychotic person will his own ultimate kinetic death, his own dead-end path? Does he play to lose?

I didn't see Al Newcum that day but I did see him the next day; he had returned from Sacramento and opened up his office.

"Is the woman in B-15 still there?" I asked him. "Or did you evict her?"

"Mrs. Archer?" Newcum said. "Oh, the other morning she moved out; she's gone. The Santa Ana Housing Authority found her a place over on Bristol." He leaned back in his swivel chair and crossed his legs; his slacks, as always, were sharply creased. "She went to them a couple of weeks ago."

"An apartment she can afford?" I asked.

"They picked up the bill. They're paying her rent; she talked them into it. She's a hardship case."

"Christ," I said. "I wish someone would pay my rent."

"You're not paying rent," Newcum said. "You're buying your apartment."

"Philip K. Dick on Philosophy: A Brief Interview," Conducted by Frank C. Bertrand (1980, 1988)

INTRODUCTION [BY BERTRAND]:   The following interview was conducted by mail in January 1980. Intended to be but the beginning of a long, in-depth discussion and exploration of P. K. Dick's interest in philosophy and the manifestation of that interest in his stories and novels, it was cut short by a disagreement over how best to continue, by letter or by phone. Nonetheless, what P. K. Dick has to say is a brief but informative overview of his interest in philosophy.

FB: I would like to start by asking a cliché question phrased a bit differ-ently. How do you define science fiction? In asking this, though, I do not seek a "dictionary"-type definition, but rather what is it about a work of fiction that when you read it causes you to say this is science fiction?

PKD: SF presents in fictional form an eccentric view of the normal or a normal view of the world that is not our world. Not all stories set in the future or on other planets are SF (some are space adventures), and some SF is set in the past or present (time travel or alternate world stories). It is not mimetic of the real world. Central to SF is the idea as dynamism. Events evolve out of an idea impacting on living creatures and their soci-ety. The idea must *always* be a novelty. This is the core issue of SF, even bad SF. That events accord with known scientific truths distinguishes SF from fantasy. Good SF tells a reader something he does not know about a possible world. Thus both the news (novel idea) and possible world (set-ting) are inventions by the author and not descriptions. Finally, SF makes what would otherwise be an intellectual abstraction concrete; it does this by locating the idea in a specific time and place, which requires the inventing of that time and place. Characters need not differ from characters in non-SF; it is what they encounter and must deal with that differ[s].

FB: *Why* is there science fiction? That is, why is it written, why is it read? Would literature be better or worse off if it had never come into existence? Just what function does SF fulfill in literature and for those who choose to read it, or write it?

PKD: There is SF because the human brain craves sensory and intellectual stimulation before anything else, and the eccentric view provides unlimited stimulation, the eccentric view, and the invented world. It is written because the human mind naturally creates, and in creating the world of an SF story the ultimate in human imagination is brought into use; thus SF is an ultimate product of and for the human mind. The function of SF psychologically is to cut the reader loose from the actual world that he inhabits; it deconstructs time, space, reality. Those who read it probably have difficulty adjusting to their world, for whatever reason; they may be ahead of it in terms of their perceptions and concepts or they may simply be neurotic, or·they may have an abundance of imagination. Basically, they enjoy abstract thought. Also, they have a sense of the magic of science: science viewed not as utilitarian but as explorative. The writer of SF has in his possession ideas not yet committed to print; his mind is an extension of the corpus of already written SF. He is SF's probe into the future, its vanguard. There is not a vast difference between reading SF and writing it. In both cases there is a joy in the novel—i.e. new—idea.

FB: Would you please recount just when it was that you first became interested in philosophy? Was it a particular course or book or idea that initially generated your interest? Or a particular teacher? In high school, before, after?

PKD: I first became interested in philosophy in high school when I realized one day that all space is the same size; it is only the material boundaries encompassing it that differ. After that there came to me the realization (which I found later in Hume) that causality is a perception in the observer and not a datum of external reality. In college I was given Plato to read and thereupon became aware of the possible existence of a metaphysical realm beyond or above the sensory world. I came to understand that the human mind could conceive of a realm of which the empirical world was epiphenomenal. Finally I came to believe that in a certain sense the empirical world was not truly real, at least not as real as the archetypal realm beyond it. At this point I despaired of the veracity of sense data. Hence in novel after novel that I write I question the reality of the world that the characters' percept-systems report. Ultimately I became an acosmic panentheist, led to this point by decades of skepticism.

FB: Once your interest in philosophy was sparked, how did you then pursue this interest? What books did you at *first* read? What courses if any did you take in philosophy?

PKD: I dropped out of college very early and began to write, pursuing my interest in philosophy on my own. My main sources were poets, not philosophers: Yeats and Wordsworth and the seventeenth-century English metaphysical poets, Goethe, and then overt philosophers such as Spinoza and Leibnitz and Plotinus—the last influencing me greatly. Early on I read Alfred North Whitehead and Bergson and became well grounded in process philosophy. I did take a basic survey course in philosophy at the University of California at Berkeley, but was asked to leave when I inquired as to the pragmatic value of Platonism. The Pre-Socratics always fascinated me, in particular Pythagoras, Parmenides, Heraclitus, and Empedocles. I still view God as Xenophanes viewed him. Gradually my interest in philosophy passed over into an interest in theology. Like the early Greeks I am a believer in parapsychism. Of all the metaphysical systems in philosophy I feel the greatest affinity for that of Spinoza, with his dictum *"Deus sive substantia sive natura"*; to me this sums up everything (viz., God i.e. reality i.e. nature). After flirting with bitheism for years I have settled down to monotheism; I regard even Christianity and later Judaism as basically dualistic and hence unacceptable. To me the truth was first uttered (insofar as we know) when Xenophanes of Colophon, an Ionian, stated, "One god there is . . . in no way like mortal creatures either in bodily form or in the thought of his mind. The whole of him sees, the whole of him thinks, the whole of him hears. He stays always motionless in the same place; it is not fitting that he should move about now this way, now that. But, effortlessly, he wields all things by the thought of his mind." My interest in Pythagoras came from reading Wordsworth's "Ode," and from there I passed on to Neo-Platonism and to the Pre-Socratics. The German *Aufklarung* influenced me, especially Schiller and his ideas of freedom; I read his "Wars of the Dutch Lowlands" and the "Wallenstein" trilogy. Spinoza's views regarding the worth of democracy also influenced me. Especially I studied the Thirty Years' War and the issues involved, and am sympathetic to the Protestant side, in particular the valorous Dutch. When I was twenty-one I wrote a piece on the superiority of the American governmental system of checks and balances, praising it above all other systems of government either in modern times or in antiquity; I got a copy to the then governor of California, Earl Warren, to which he replied, "It is a gratifying experience to receive such an expression of appreciation of the government for which all of us work and serve. And although it may be that others have the same depth of feeling you express, few are so articulate. Certainly your letter is unique in my experience, and I have received many through my years in public office." That was in the year 1952, when my first stories were published. It coincides, therefore, with my appearance as an author in the world of SF.

Part Two

Writings on Science Fiction
and Related Ideas

The essays in this section concern themselves primarily with the nature of the SF genre, the role of the SF writer, and speculation on future scientific possibilities.

"Pessimism in Science Fiction" (1955) was first published in *Oblique*, No. 6, December 1955, a fanzine edited by Clifford Gould.

"Will the Atomic Bomb Ever Be Perfected, and If So, What Becomes of Robert Heinlein?" was first published in the fanzine *Lighthouse*, No. 14, October 1966, edited by Terry Carr. The style represents Dick at his most informal, employing the open and uninhibited fanzine forum to orate, opine, and vent at will. It is not Dick's most impressive work, although it has its moments of humor and of dark insight, as in its brief remarks on the difficult relationship between Dick and his mother. There was a tempest in a teapot when, in the subsequent issue of *Lighthouse* (No. 15, August 1967), an SF fan wrote a letter attacking Dick for the callousness of his remarks both as to Heinlein and as to Dick's mother, and implying that Dick had suffered permanent brain damage from his use of LSD. In point of fact, Dick did not suffer from brain damage and was rather prone, during the sixties, to exaggerate his LSD usage greatly (he used the drug on only a handful of occasions, finding it far too frightening for his liking). Dick replied to this attack in the following issue with blustering outrage, implying that he might bring a suit for libel; the letter-writer apologized and the matter was dropped, to the evident relief of both parties. Dick never relented in his animus toward his mother; with regard to Heinlein, however, Dick's attitude changed considerably. See Dick's "Introduction" to *The Golden Man* story collection in this same section.

"The *Double: Bill* Symposium" replies by Dick were included in the pamphlet volume *The Double: Bill Symposium*, published by D:B Press (1969), which included the responses of ninety-four SF writers.

The two editors were Bill Mallardi and Bill Bowers. The questionnaire was prepared by Lloyd Biggle, Jr.

"That Moon Plaque" first appeared in *Men on the Moon* (1969), an Ace anthology edited by Donald A. Wollheim, an important figure in Dick's publishing career.

"Who Is an SF Writer?" was first published, in truncated form, in *Science Fiction: The Academic Awakening* (1974), a College English Association (Shreveport, Louisiana) chapbook. The editor was Willis E. McNelly, an English professor at the University of California at Fullerton with whom Dick enjoyed friendly relations. The essay appears here for the first time in its full typescript length, which is roughly one-third longer than the original published version.

"Michelson-Morley Experiment Reappraised" first appeared under the title (supplied by an editor) as "Scientists Claim: We Are Center of the Universe" in *New Worlds*, No. 216, September 1979.

"Introduction" to *Dr. Bloodmoney*, written in 1979, was first published in the 1985 Bluejay Books edition of that novel.

"Introduction" to *The Golden Man* first appeared under the title (supplied by an editor) "The Lucky Dog Pet Store" in *Foundation*, No. 17, September 1979. It was republished, with minor changes, as the "Introduction" to *The Golden Man* (1980) story collection edited by Mark Hurst. The story notes that concluded this essay were republished in the five-volume *Collected Stories of Philip K. Dick* (1987). The opening essay on his SF writing, not included in the *Collected Stories*, is presented here.

The "Book Review" (1980) of *The Cybernetic Imagination in Science Fiction*, by Patricia Warrick, has never before been published. It is unclear if Dick ever submitted it to any publication. It is important to note that this review may well have been written in a moment of temporary pique; Dick and Warrick carried on—both before and after this review was written—a voluminous correspondence on philosophical and spiritual matters, and Dick frequently praised and thanked Warrick, in this correspondence, for her insights and support. Nonetheless, the review is worth publishing because it does accurately reflect the high degree of suspicion, even animosity, that Dick felt toward "mainstream" academicians who sought to adopt SF, as it were, and make it respectable or "important." At the same time, as Dick confesses in his

"Introduction" to *The Golden Man*, the lack of mainstream attention for his work was a source of pain for him.

"My Definition of Science Fiction" was first published in *Just: SF*, Vol. 1, No. 1 (1981), edited by John Betancourt.

"Predictions" was first included in *The Book of Predictions* (New York: Morrow, 1981) by David Wallechinsky.

"Universe Makers . . . and Breakers" (1981) first appeared in *SelecTV Guide*, February 15–March 28, 1981. This guide was issued by Dick's cable company, and his payment for writing the piece was a free year of cable service. See my prefatory comments to "Notes on *Do Androids Dream of Electric Sheep?*" (1968), in a subsequent section, for further information on Dick's views on the film *Blade Runner* (1982). "Universe Makers . . ." was reprinted in *Radio Free PKD* (the successor to *PKDS Newsletter*, edited by Gregory Lee), No. 1, February 1993.

"Headnote" for "Beyond Lies the Wub," written in 1980, first appeared in accompaniment with the reprinted story in *First Voyages* (New York: Avon, 1981), an SF anthology edited by Damon Knight, Martin H. Greenberg, and Joseph D. Olander. It was reprinted in *PKDS Newsletter*, No. 24, May 1990, and in *Radio Free PKD*, No. 3, October 1993. This headnote was not reprinted in the available *Collected Stories* volumes; hence its inclusion here.

"Pessimism in Science Fiction" (1955)

Since science fiction concerns the future of human society, the worldwide loss of faith in science and in scientific progress is bound to cause convulsions in the SF field. This loss of faith in the idea of progress, in a "brighter tomorrow," extends over our whole cultural milieu; the dour tone of recent science fiction is an effect, not a cause. If a modern science fiction writer mirrors this sense of doom, he is only doing what any responsible writer does: If a writer feels that present-day saber-rattling and drum-beating are leading the world to war, he has no choice but to reproduce his feelings in his writings—unless he is writing purely for profit, in which case he *never* reproduces his feelings, only those sentiments that he feels will be commercially acceptable.

All responsible writers, to some degree, have become involuntary criers of doom, because doom is in the wind; but science fiction writers more so, since science fiction has always been a protest medium. In science fiction, a writer is not merely inclined to act out the Cassandra role; he is absolutely obliged to—unless, of course, he honestly thinks he will wake up some morning and find that the high-minded Martians have sneaked off with all our bombs and armaments, for our own good.

Of course, doom stories become monotonous, since there are infinite bright, successful, nondoom futures, but only one *doom*; that is war. Once *the* war-doom story has been written, there is not much to say; and Ray Bradbury has written that story at least once. So the responsible science fiction writer repeats himself, since although there are many things he might write about, there is only one horrible future he really *believes* in: The rest are exercises in logic, imagination, and writing skill. If the writer honestly believes we are moving toward racial suicide, then skillful, cheerful stories become—although interesting—mere fiddle-scraping.

54

But a natural hope, taking the place of legitimate optimism, crowds us into preferring these pleasant substitutes. Well, they are a lot of fun, just as detective novels were a lot of fun in the thirties. And the question is *not*: Which makes more enjoyable reading? Because nobody would seriously debate that one. After all, pleasant exercises in imagination and logic are supposed to be pleasant; and the doom stories are merely intended to call attention to reality. The latter activity has never been popular.

In a sense, the job of the science fiction writer in continuing to write pessimistically if he feels pessimistic, is a worsening of the spot every one of us is in; the SF writer will be cooked no deader than anybody else. But the SF writer has all day to brood; brooding, ar at least thinking, is his job. If the SF writer is requested not to think about doom, if it's immoral to write about an approaching war, then it certainly is an evil thing to worry about it.

The only really legitimate complaint that can be raised against doom stories (outside of the complaint that they are all the same and hence only one really adequate doom story is required) is that there have always been war and danger, and that the sense of doom may be misplaced. This is a good argument, and I am beginning to believe it. A doom story never offers a solution to the problem: It merely utters the problem over and over again. Well, assuming we accept the existence of the problem (the approaching war), perhaps a more realistic or at least more valuable function would be to seek, in our science fiction stories, partial solutions to the menace. *How* are we going to survive? *What* will our world be like after a few (or a lot) of us have survived?

Rather than writing stories about doom, perhaps we should take the doom for granted and go on from there. Make the ruined world of ash a premise: State it in paragraph one, and get it over with, rather than winding up with it at the very end. And make the central theme or idea of the story an attempt by the characters to solve the problem of postwar survival.

At worst, we can suppose that nobody will survive. But this is like taking pictures of coal bins at midnight: It can be done, but if there is nothing there, then what the hell. It is quite possible that a few dozen and even a very large number of people may survive the war, in which case a story dealing with various attempts at setting up societies can be developed. Of course, we want to avoid the English doom novel: the struggling primitive colony of the postmachine type, the "back to nature" thing. Let's bypass that, and presume basic technology; maybe not atomic-powered rocket ships, but at least gasoline combustion engines and telephones.

However, I can't seriously believe that much of our cultural pattern or physical assets will survive the next fifty years. Our present social continuum is disintegrating rapidly; if war doesn't burst it apart, it obviously will corrode away. At the very best, at the most optimistic, there won't be any death and destruction. I'll assume the brighter side, the possibility of a limited war and only partial retrogression—Bradbury is perhaps too pessimistic—but to avoid the topic of war and cultural retrogression, as some schools of science fiction writers and editors have done, is unrealistic and downright irresponsible.

Such pollyanna noises are designed to increase circulation. They shouldn't fool anybody who reads newspapers.

"Will the Atomic Bomb Ever Be Perfected, and If So, What Becomes of Robert Heinlein?" (1966)

Recently I took yet another dose of LSD-25, and as a result certain dull but persistent thoughts have come creeping into my head. I will herein retail [sic; retell] a few of them, in chaotic form. If you find them all false, good for you. If you find them all true, good for you likewise.

The real origin of science fiction lay in the seventeenth-century novels of exploration in fabulous lands. Therefore Jules Verne's story of travel to the moon is not SF because they go by rocket but because of *where* they go. It would be as much SF if they went by rubber band.

Very few SF stories come true. Fortunately. Those such as *Waldo* are freaks and prove nothing.

Because of a present-day rocket travel to Mars et al., the general public is at last willing to accept SF as reasonable. They have stopped laughing, but they have not started reading. They probably never will, because reading is too hard for them. But now we know that we were right. (Of course, we knew that all along. But it's nice to see it proved.)

No one makes any real money off good—I repeat, *good*—SF. This probably indicates that it has artistic worth. If Lorenzo de Medici were alive he would pick up the tab for A. E. van Vogt, not for John Updike.

The best SF novel I have read is Vonnegut's *Player Piano*, because it actually deals with men-women relationships (Paul Proteus and his bitch of a wife). In this matter the book is unique in the field. *Brave New World* only seems to do this; *1984* in this regard is awful.

If I were to dredge up one SF novel that, more than any others, would cause me to abandon SF entirely, it is Robert Heinlein's *Gulf.* It strikes me as fascism pure and simple, and—what is worse—put forth unattractively. Bleh.

Heinlein has done more to harm SF than has any other writer, I think— with the possible exception of George O. Smith. The dialogue in *Stranger in a Strange Land* has to be read to be believed. "Give the little lady a box of cigars!" a character cries, meaning that the girl has said something that is correct. One wonders what the rejoinder would be if a truly inspired remark had to be answered, rather than a routine statement; it would probably burst the book's gizzard.

Once I read a terrific short story in *If* by an unknown writer named Robert Gilbert. It was poetry, beauty, love, perfection, and I wrote him and told him so. He wrote back and said he'd written the story while listening to Harry James records.

I started reading SF in 1941. I'm old.

There is one accurate way—and only one—by which you can tell you are growing old. It is when the SF magazines that you bought new on the stand at the time they came out have begun to turn the same yellow color as the ones you picked up as collectors' items from specialty dealers . . . i.e., already ancient.

Is it possible that Lovecraft saw the truth? That realms and wickedness such as he describes, for example in *The Strange Case of Charles Dexter Ward,* actually exist? Imagine taking a dose of LSD and finding yourself in Salem. You would go mad.

Religion ought never to show up in SF except from a sociological standpoint, as in *Gather, Darkness* [a novel by Fritz Leiber]. God per se, as a character, ruins a good SF story; and this is as true of my own stuff as anyone else's. Therefore I deplore my *Palmer Eldritch* book in that regard. But people who are a bit mystically inclined like it. I don't. I wish I had never written it; there are too many horrid forces loose in it. When I wrote it I had been taking certain chemicals and I could see the awful landscape that I depicted. But not now. Thank God. *Agnus Dei qui tollis peccata mundi* [Lamb of God who lifts the sins of the world].

Avram Davidson [an SF writer] fascinates me—as a person, I mean. He is a mixture of a little boy and a very wise old man, and his eyes always twinkle as if he were a defrocked Santa Claus. With beard dyed black.

I'll give anyone fifteen cents who can imagine [SF editor] Tony Boucher as a small boy. Obviously, Tony was always as he is now. But even more difficult to imagine is the strange truth that once there was no Tony Boucher at all. This is clearly impossible. I think there must always have been a Tony Boucher; if not the one we know, then some other, very much like him.

I have written and sold twenty-three novels, and all are terrible except one. But I am not sure which one.

If Beethoven had lived just one additional year he would have entered a fourth period of his evolving talent. We can imagine this by listening to his last composition, the alternate ending for the thirteenth quartet. What we cannot imagine is—what about later, in his old age? Suppose he, like Verdi, like Haydn, had lived to compose in his eighties. Under LSD I have a vision of a seventh or eighth period of Beethoven: string quartets with chorus and four soloists.

Out of all the SF that I have read, one story still means more to me than any others: It is Harry Bates's *Alas, All Thinking*. It is the beginning and the end of literate science fiction. Alas.

For fifteen years, the entire period in which I have written SF, I have never seen my agent or even talked to him on the phone. I wonder what sort of person he is, assuming he exists at all. When I call his number his receptionist says, "Mr. Meredith isn't here right now. Will you talk to Mr. Rib Frimble?" Or some such unlikely name. On the basis of that, in my next call I ask not for Mr. Meredith but for Mr. Frimble. Then the receptionist says, "Mr. Frimble is out, sir; will you talk to Mr. Dead?" And so it goes.

If I knew what a hallucination was I would know what reality was. I have examined the topic thoroughly, and I assert that it is impossible to have a hallucination; it goes against reason and common sense. Those who claim to have had them are probably lying. (I have had a few myself.)

Once in a while somebody in the neighborhood who is rich enough to own a hedge, and is always busily clipping it, asks me why I write SF. I never have an answer. There are several other questions that get asked but that obtain no response at all from me. They are:

1. Where do you get your plots?
2. Do you put people you know into your stories?
3. Why aren't you selling to *Playboy*? Everyone else is. I hear it pays a hell of a lot.
4. Isn't science fiction mainly for kids?

Let me illustrate what I mean when I say I have no answer to these; I will do herein what I generally do.

> Answer to 1: Oh, well, plots; well, you can find them almost anywhere. I mean, there're a lot of plots. Say, talking to you gives me an idea for a plot. There's this humanoid superior mutant, see, who has to hide himself because the mass man has no understanding of him or his superior, evolved aims—etc.
> Answer to 2: No.
> Answer to 3: I don't know. I guess I'm a failure. What other possibility can there be? And it was lousy of you to ask.
> Answer to 4: No, SF is not for kids. Or maybe it is; I don't know who reads it. There're roughly 150,000 people who comprise the readership, and that's not a great number. And even if it does appeal to kids—so what?

You can see how weak these answers are. And I've had fifteen years in which to think up better answers. Obviously I never will.

The TV news announcer says tonight that a ninety-one-year-old man has married a ninety-two-year-old woman. It is enough to bring tears to your eyes. What do they have in store for them? What chance is there, every time they close their eyes, that they will ever open them again? The small and unimportant silent creatures are far finer and worth a great deal more than Robert Heinlein will ever know.

Loneliness is the great curse that hangs over a writer. A while ago I wrote twelve novels in a row, plus fourteen magazine pieces. I did it out of loneliness. It constituted communication for me. At last the loneliness grew too great and I stopped writing; I left my then-wife and then-children and took a great journey. The great journey ended up in Bay Area fandom, and for a short while I ceased to be lonely. Then it came back, late one night. Now I know it will never go away. This is my payment for twenty-three novels and one hundred magazine pieces. It's no one's fault. That's just the way it is.

My mother shows her love for me by clipping out certain magazine and newspaper articles, which she gives me. These articles prove that the tranquilizers that I take do permanent brain damage. It's nice, a mother's love.

Under LSD I saw radiant colors, especially the pinks and reds; they shone like God Himself. Is that what God is? Color? But at least this time I didn't have to die, go to hell, be tormented, and then raised up by means of Christ's death on the cross into eternal salvation. As I said to J. G. Newkom [a friend of Dick at this time] when I was free of the drug, "I don't mind going through the Day of Judgment again, after I die, but I just hope it won't last so long." Under LSD you can spend 1.96 eternities, if not 2.08.

In fifteen years of professional writing I haven't gotten a jot or a tittle better. My first story, Roog, is as good as—if not better than—the five I did last month. This seems very strange to me, because certainly through all those years I've learned a good deal about writing . . . and in addition my general store of worldly wisdom has increased. Maybe there are only a given number of original ideas in each person; he uses them up and that is that. Like an old baseball player, he no longer has anything to offer. I will say one thing in favor of my writing, however, which I hope is true: I am original (except where I copy my own previous work). I no longer write "like Cyril Kornbluth" or "like A. E. van Vogt." But in that case I can no longer blame them for my faults.

A publisher in England asked me to write a blurb for a collection of my short stories. In this country someone else writes them, usually someone who has not read the book. I would like to have started the blurb by saying, "These dull and uninteresting stories . . ." etc. But I suppose I had better not.

Thus endeth my thoughts.

"The *Double: Bill* Symposium":
Replies to "A Questionnaire for
Professional SF Writers and Editors"
(1969)

Question 1: *For what reason or reasons do you write science fiction in preference to other classes of literature?*

Its audience is not hamstrung by middle-class prejudices and will listen to genuinely new ideas. There is less of an emphasis on mere style and more on content—as should be. It is a man's field, and hence a happy ending is not required—as in all the fiction fields dominated by women. It is one of the few branches of serious fiction in which humor plays a major role (thereby making SF more complete, as was Shakespeare's work). Being one of the oldest modes of fiction known to the Western world, it embodies some of the most subtle, ancient, and far-reaching dreams, ideas, and aspirations of which thinking man is capable. In essence, it's the broadest field of fiction, permitting the most far-ranging and advanced concepts of every possible type; no variety of idea can be excluded from SF; everything is its property.

Question 2: What do you consider the raison d'être, *the chief value of science fiction?*

To present in fiction form new ideas too difficult or too vague as yet to be presented as scientific fact (e.g., Psionics). And ideas that are not scientific fact, never will be, but that are fascinating conjectures—in other words, *possible* or alternate science systems. World views that we can't "believe" in but that interest us (as, for example, we find interesting the medieval worldview but simply cannot any longer accept it as "true"). So

SF presents to us, in addition to the worldview, which we actually adopt, a great range of "as if" views: The possession of these have the effect of making our minds flexible: We are capable of seeing alternate viewpoints as coequal with our own.

Question 3: What is your appraisal of the relationship of science fiction to the "mainstream" of literature?

SF fails to explore the depths of interpersonal human relationships, and this is its lack; however, on a purely intellectual level it possesses more conceptual ideas as such, and hence in this respect is superior to mainstream or quality fiction. And (supra) it does not need to dwell on mere style as such but can range farther in terms of its content. But SF (excepting Bradbury) is for younger, more optimistic people, who haven't yet truly suffered at the hands of life; quality fiction tends—and rightly so—to deal with the defeated, those who have lost the first bloom . . . hence quality fiction is more mature than SF—alas.

Question 4: Do you believe that participating in fandom, fanzines, and conventions would be a benefit or a hindrance to would-be writers?

A benefit, but not a very great one. It would be a benefit if the fans allowed the writer to do the talking, instead of trying to instruct him. It is the job of the writer to do the telling; he should not be turned into a listener. But the concepts in SF writing are not derived from fandom, from within the field, anyhow; they are—or at least should be—derived from the wide world itself, its far shores in particular. From everywhere but SF fandom.

Question 5: What source or sources would you recommend to beginning writers as having been, in your experience, the most productive of ideas for science fiction stories?

Journals that deal in the most advanced research of clinical psychology, especially the work of the European existential analysis school. C. G. Jung. Oriental writings such as those on Zen Buddhism, Taoism, etc. Really authoritative—as compared with popularizations—historical works (e.g., *The Brutal Friendship*). Medieval works, especially those dealing with crafts, such as glass blowing—and science, alchemy, religion, etc.

Greek philosophy, Roman literature of every sort. Persian religious texts. Renaissance studies on the theory of art. German dramatic writings of the Romantic period.

Question 6: Do you feel that a beginning science fiction writer should concentrate on short stories as opposed to novels—or vice versa? Why?

Short stories first, to master this easier form. Then, very slowly, work toward longer pieces, say up to twenty-five thousand words. Then at last try a full-size (i.e., sixty-thousand-word) novel, based on the structure of some writer who is admired. I, for instance, based my first novels on the structure used by A. E. van Vogt. Later, when I was more sure of myself, I departed from this. Be sure, however, that you select a writer who is skilled in the novel form (for instance, don't select Ray Bradbury).

Question 7: What suggestions can you offer to the beginning writer concerning the development of "realistic" characters and writing effective dialogue?

Read modern "quality" writing, especially the short pieces of Algren, Styron, Herb Gold, the so-called New School writers. And the fine left-wing writers of the thirties, such as Dos Passos, Richard Wright, and go back as far as Dreiser and Hawthorne—try to stick to American writers (including, of course, Hemingway and Gertrude Stein) because it is among the American writers that realistic dialogue has developed. Try the French realistics, such as Flaubert, for plot and characterization. Avoid Proust and other subjective-type writers. And by all means intently study James Joyce; everything from his early short stories to *The Wake*.

Question 8: Do you believe that an effective novel requires a message or moral? Please comment.

Absolutely not! The notion that a novel needs a moral or message is a bourgeois concept. In the days of the aristocracy it was recognized that art did not need to instruct or elevate; it could be a success by merely entertaining. One should never look down on entertainment; Mozart string quartets do not instruct—show me a moral or message in, say, the late Beethoven. Music is pure; literature can be, too; it becomes more pure as it drops its intention of improving and instructing the audience. The writer is not a bit superior in morals than his audience anyway—and frequently he's inferior to them. What moral can he really teach them? What he has to offer is his ideas.

Question 9: To what extent do you think it possible to detect a writer's viewpoints as to politics, religion, or moral problems through examination of his stories?

If the writer is a good one, it's impossible. Only a bad writer details his personal viewpoints in his fiction. However, it is always possible that some good writing may be found in an "instructive" work. But at the moment I can't think of any (e.g., Ray Bradbury. There is no way, in reading his work, to tell really what his personal views are; the writer in this case disappears entirely, and his story reveals itself on its own. This is the way it ought to be.). It is one of the cardinal errors of literary criticism to believe that the author's own views can be inferred from his writing; Freud, for instance, makes this really ugly error again and again. A successful writer can adopt any viewpoint that his characters must needs possess in order to function; this is the measure of his craft, this ability to free his work of his own prejudices.

Question 10: During your formative writings, what one author influenced you the most? What other factors such as background, education, etc., were important influences?

Van Vogt influenced me the most. Also Tony Boucher (i.e., his critical views, not his fiction). Also my interest in the Japanese novelists in the French Department of Tokyo University, who wrote after World War Two. And my interest in Depth Psychology and drugs. And in "stream of consciousness" writing, as with James Joyce. And—but I wouldn't recommend this for the would-be writer—my own "nervous breakdown," which I experienced at nineteen and then again at twenty-four and at thirty-three. Suffering of this sort educates your viewpoint, but at the expense of your creature-comfort principle; it may make you a better writer but the cost is far too great.

Question 11: What do you consider the greatest weakness of science fiction today?

Its inability to explore the subtle, intricate relationships that exist between the sexes. Men, in their relationship with women, get themselves into the most goddamn difficult circumstances, and SF ignores—or is unable to deal with—this fundamental aspect of adult life. Therefore SF remains preadult, and therefore appeals—more or less—to preadults. If SF explored the man-woman aspect of life it would not lose its readers as those readers reach maturity. SF simply must learn to do this or it will always be retarded—as it is now. The novel *Player Piano* is an exception to this, and I suggest that every SF fan and especially every would-be writer study again and again the details of this superb novel, which deal specifically with the relationship of the protagonist and his wife.

"That Moon Plaque" (1969)

In no way should problems here on Earth detract from the glory of the *Apollo 11* moon flight. Similar problems led to the colonization of the New World back in the seventeenth and eighteenth centuries: poverty, lack of opportunity, even starvation. Sometimes the presence of grave social problems is a stimulus to exploration; man searches relentlessly for a way out of his problems, and in doing so he presses at every door, hoping to find one that will lead him somewhere that is new and different. And it must be recognized that the moon flight has acted and will continue to act as a flare lighting up the powerful abilities of man, his capacity to do what has never been done before. It is an indication of what can be done, and should make, by its existence, a new awareness grow in us as to what we can do. We should, because of it, be more optimistic as to what we can do here on Earth; it is proof of our strength and tenacity, not an indication that we are forgetting domestic goals. And, in addition, it was essential that we send a man to the moon; exploration is natural to man; it is virtually an instinct. It is, at least, a force in man so powerful that it cannot be denied. The moon flight was inevitable and is a new measure of ourselves.

"Who Is an SF Writer?" (1974)

The delight which SF writers show when encountering one another personally, at conventions or on panels or during lectures, indicates some common element shared by them, novices and old pros alike. There always emerges a psychological rapport, even if the ideas and politics in their respective works clash head-on; it is as if absolutely opposite themes in their published work—which might be expected to create a personal barrier when the writers meet face to face—this barrier is never there, and a feeling when a group of SF writers gathers is always one of a family rejoined, lost friends refound or new friends made—friends among whom there is a fundamental basis of outlook or at least of personality structure. Nearly always it is characterized by a mutual respect, and this respect on the part of each writer is for the others as persons, not merely a respect for their work. We are linked as if scattered members of a once tightly knit ethnic group which has been scattered, but then momentarily reunited. I have felt this with no other group of people: Something special is there in us, that not only is common but which binds us rather than separates us as one finds, say, in the social gatherings of the so-called "New York literary writers," in which chronic jealousy and envy and sour carping impede personal contact. To my knowledge, this camraderie and rapport is at least currently unique in the arts; and it means something; it tells something about us.

On meeting a new SF writer who has just gotten into print, we never feel crowded or insecure; we feel strangely happy, and tell him so and encourage him: We *welcome* him. And I think this is because we know that the very fact that he has chosen to write SF rather than other types of fiction—or other careers in general—tells us something about him already. I know one element that allows us to prejudge favorably any new pro SF writer to our midst: There just cannot be a profit motive as this person's working dynamism because there is no profit financially in writing SF; the average high school teacher, to name another underpaid group, makes almost twice what I make, and all my income comes from writing SF. So we know this to start with: Facing a new young pro SF writer I know first of all what he is *not* driven by; he is out of the hands of one of the great corrupting drives, that for great wealth—and I might add great fame and prestige as well, because we don't get those either. I know, when I meet a new pro writer, that he must in some sense truly love to write SF, at all costs, or he would be in other, greener pastures.

But what is the positive motivation and personality that I feel, say, that Geo. Effinger, a new SF writer whom I met in August of last year, can be assumed to have? "I know where your head is," is what I think when I meet a man or woman who has just published his first SF piece. I know you don't want fame, power, the big best seller, fortune—and therefore I know that you must want to or even need to write SF. One SF writer said to me one day, "I'd write it even if they paid nothing." Vanity to see your name in print? No, just an awareness that this is a *chosen* field, and chosen by him; he is not being forced to live out the ambitions of his thwarted parents and their aspirations that their son "amount to something," as, for example, by becoming a doctor or a lawyer—all those good, classy, well-paying professions. His drive must be intrinsic; it is impossible to imagine one's mother saying, "I hope my son will grow up to be an SF writer." What is there in the SF writer, old pro like myself (twenty-two years of selling) or a new one after his initial sale, is a belief in the *value* of science fiction. Not necessarily a belief in his own ability to write the Great American SF Novel and be remembered forever—novice pros are very shy and unpushy and humble—but his belief in the significant meaning of his field. And he would not see this specific field as a high-value field unless he had read SF by other authors, previous authors, and had some sense of the nature of what SF is, can do, will be.

If anything, assuming he is going to write and sell, he will be looked down on; people will say, "But are you doing any *serious* writing?," meaning, of course, that they do not share this mystique, this understanding and conviction of what SF is. He actually risks losing status rather than gaining it. Not, of course, by his colleagues, but by those people who think SF consists of George Pal budget films about the Anchovie That Ate New

York, such as one sees on TV late at night; he knows that this is not what SF is, really. Even if he can't come through with massive talent, the attitude is still there: SF is an accretional field, built up layer by layer, year by year with constant reference to all that has come before. Unlike the Western story writer, you do not sell the same story twice, with new character names and a new title; each time you must produce something genuinely new. The SF reader—all exceptions granted—insists on one thing before all else: The new stories and novels must not duplicate those that came before, and woe unto the novice writer who does not know all the SF classics back to 1930; he must—and almost certainly did—absorb them before he began writing himself. What he did, what I did back in 1951 when I sold my first story, was to go on to the next step in structure of fictionalized thought that is the growing public property of all SF readers and writers. In this sense SF must be avant-garde. And so it is. And the motivation I think that underlies many of us—certainly it did me—was to add one more bit of stone to a mosaic whose pattern, whose final gestalt, has not been explicated or frozen yet on the printed page. It is as if an SF writer is created when he reads a story by a previous writer and then says, "Next it could be that . . ." meaning this book, this story, this underlying theme should be carried on. Heinlein has written what he calls "future history," and much of SF is. And much of the motivation that drives the SF writer is the motivation to "make" history—contribute what he sees, his perception of ". . . and then what happened?" to what all the rest of us have already done. It is a great colloquy among all of us, writers and fans and editors alike. Somewhere back in the past (I would say about 1900) this colloquy began, and voice after voice has joined in, little frogs and big in little puddles and big, but all croaking their sublime song . . . because they sense a *continuity* and the possibility, the opportunity, the ethical need, if you will, for them to add onto this growing "future history."

I've watched high school kids grow from an avid reading appreciation of SF to their first hesitant submission, their first sale—they may disappear soon, or become only one of many, or become like Ted Sturgeon a unique and powerfully lovely contributor . . . in any case there is a tremendous motivation to make the statement, the written submission. "Nobody has thought yet of *this*," the SF writer says when an idea comes to him, but it is not merely an *outre* idea that he senses germinating in his head; it is an addition and a contribution to a vast, extant body. In the sciences proper, when experimental work reveals some law or principle previously unknown, the researcher knows he must publish his results; why determine that such-and-such is a universal scientific principle and then say nothing about it? This shows the affinity between the SF writer and the true scientist; having discovered something new, it is incumbent on him—morally incumbent—to publish a little piece in print about it, whether that publishing will make him immortal or rich—the ethic is the same. In fact it would be purposeless, for example, to determine in scrupulous laboratory conditions that mice fed on nothing but canned mackerel live twice as long as the control group and then, the experiment having been conducted and the results obtained, never mention it to anybody. So, I think, we in our field have that grand great drive of the true research scientist, to acquaint people with something heretofore overlooked. All other factors—the need to earn a living, to impress people, to be "immortal"—those are secondary; spin-offs, so to speak, if they do occur.

Probably what we see in an SF writer (I will use myself as an example) is a boy growing up and originally wanting to be a scientist (I wanted to be a paleontologist, for example). But science does not leave room for a factor vital to us: speculation. For example, an anthropologist finds a humanoid skull in Africa almost 3 million years old. He looks at it, subjects it to tests, and then in his article in *Nature* or *Scientific American* tells us what he actually found. But I can see myself there with Leakey finding those incredibly ancient humanoid skulls with an 800 cc brain skull, back at the 2.8-million-year striation, and as I see it, wild speculations *that I cannot prove* would come to my mind. If X, then Y. If true, humans lived that long ago—and I would imagine a whole culture, and speculate as in a voluntary dream, what that person's world might have been like. I do not mean his diet or how fast he could run or if he walked upright; this is legitimate for the hard sciences to deal with. What I see is what I suppose I would have to call a "fictional" environment that that skull tells me of. A story that that skull might wish to say. "Might" is the crucial word, because we don't know, we don't have the artifacts, and yet I see more than I hold in my hand. Each object is a clue, a key, to an entire world unlike our own—past, present, or future, it is not *this* immediate world, and this skull tells me of this other world, and this I must dream up myself. I have passed out of the domain of true science. If I wish to write about that

("What if these ancient humanoids had developed a method of controlling their environment by"—etc.) then I must write what we call science fiction. It is first of all the true scientific curiosity, in fact, true wondering, dreaming curiosity in general, that motivates us, plus a desire to fill in the missing pieces in the most startling or unusual way. To add to what is actually there, the concrete reality that can only say so much and no more, my own "glimpse" of another world. A world I will never see fully or even to a great extent, but toward which this one object has pointed.

It is not, however, that the SF writer is a thwarted scientist who couldn't make it legitimately and so turned to fantasy fiction, to dreams; it is more that this person is impatient to see all the rest not visible in the actual skull, and inventive enough to spin such a myth, a tale about "that other world" that touches ours only here and there. We as SF writers see many objects again and again as clues to other universes, other societies. We sense the rest, and this sensing can't be separated from literary, artistic imagination. "This rock," the phrase goes, "could tell many stories, of battles fought here, of deeds done and now forgotten; *if only it could talk.*" The SF writer senses that story, or many stories from the clues of tangible reality around him, and does the rest; he talks for the objects, the clues. He is driven to. He knows there is more, and he knows that he will not live long enough to see all the scientific data actually brought forth . . . they may never be. The writer, then, begins to sing about those battles and those deeds. He places them in the future only for convenience; it is the placing of the story mostly in an imaginary world, but bound by small actual clues to this world, that drives him into expression. It might be said that where Homer sang about Troy after those events, the SF writer wishes to sing about events ahead because he feels that this is really the only reasonable place where those events could occur. It is as if Homer wrote the *Iliad* before those events, and had he done so it would be authentic speculative or science fiction.

This shows, I think, the affinity between the SF writer and the scientist as such: But his impatience, his inventiveness, his discovery that the pieces and bits around him (and they can be in our present actual world or in other SF) tell stories not yet told and that without him might never get told—this is one facet characteristic of the SF writer's mind and shows why the term "science fiction" still lingers to describe what we do, even if we write about a purely religious society set not even in the future but in a parallel Earth. It is not that the stories are about science; it is that the writer is motivated along parallel lines motivating research scientists. But he is not content. He is stuck with a discontent; he must improve or change what he sees, not by going out and politically agitating but by looking deep into other possibilities and alternatives manufactured within his own head. He does not say, "We should pass laws regarding air pollution" and hence join ecology groups; his wish is the same—he detests righteously what he sees of decay and corruption in our society as much as anyone—but his manner of approaching the problem is acutely different.

He will create, on the basis of the known data or plausible data, how it could all be better, or how it could all be worse. His story or novel is in a sense a protest, but not a political one; it is a protest against concrete reality in an unusual way. He wishes to sing, rather than chant and carry signs. He will sing to us of hells far worse than what we actually endure, or better worlds, or just worlds in which these elements are simply not present: worlds based on other premises. I would say, he is an introverted activist, not an extroverted one. It does not occur to him, if he sees the freeways becoming death traps, to petition the city council for changes in speed laws and so on—he sees the dangers but, being an introvert, the idea of social action, of acting out publicly and politically, is not his natural response. He would look funny out there marching and chanting. He is self-conscious and shy. He will instead write down rather than act out.

So I would say, the SF writer shares a little of the political mentality just as he does the scientific. Scientists improve things by staying in their labs; activists go out and petition. The SF writer glimpses totalities, some good, some bad, some merely bizarre, and he wants to bring these glimpses to our attention. Hence he is also a literary figure as well as a little of the politician and the scientist; he is all three and probably something more. But to speak of his work as escapist—no view of SF, at least nowdays, could be less true. He is writing about reality with as much fervor and conviction as anyone could muster to get a bad zoning ordinance changed. This is his way, because he is none of the three types listed above but a fusion of all. Somewhere along the line he got the idea that words are things; they can exert force and accomplish desired ends. This he shares, with all writers, I suppose; but if you join this latter to his quasi-scientific basis and his quasi-political basis of personality structure, you can readily see that what he wishes to capture on paper, and his motivation, *in toto* are different from writers in other fields. They may wish to capture the lovely, the quaint—freeze one block of a Bronx slum circa 1930 and the life of it for all future generations to read—but the SF writer is not oriented toward freezing any one milieu except a vision—one vision after another—that he prepared in his own head. There is no actual boyhood world, once extant but now only a memory, gnawing at him; he is free and glad to write about an infinity of worlds, with no proclivity for the freezing of any one alone; for example, his own boyhood in a small town where there were nickel Cokes and so forth . . . he wishes to get down on paper all possibilities that seem important enough to him to be recorded and then at once communicate to others.

"Flexibility" is the key word here; it is the creating of multiverses, rather than a universe, that fascinates and drives him. "What if . . ." is always his starting premise. Part scientist, part political activist, but with the conviction of the magic power of the written word, and his restlessness, his impatience—he will spin one new world for you after the other, given a set of facts or even one sole datum to take off from. He wants to see possibilities, not actualities. But as I say, his possibilities are not escapist (although, again, much hack SF is escapist, particularly when tending toward power fantasies) because the source of them lies firmly rooted in reality. He is a dreamer with one eye open, always coldly appraising what is actually going on. And yet he thinks, "It doesn't have to be this way. Because what if we woke up one day and found that all the men were sterile except for . . ." and the scientist in him will bond him to possibilities that have validity for us, in contrast to stories about Hobbits and looking glasses. He is, as Santayana once said, "dreaming under the control of the object," which was Santayana's definition of our waking life: "dreaming under the control of the object," yes, but for the science fiction writer there is a capacity—and this is to me the thrilling part—however powerful that immediate object is, he is able to speculate us out of its total grip; it still holds us, but not absolutely. The SF writer is able to dissolve the normal absolute quality that the objects (our actual environment, our daily routine) have; he has cut us loose enough to put us in a third space, neither the concrete nor the abstract, but something unique, something connected to both and hence relevent. So we do cut loose, but with enough ties still remaining never to forget that we do live in one specific society at one specific time, and no legitimate SF writer would want us to forget that, want us to drift away inside our heads and ignore the actual problems around us. It is just that he is saying, "Hey, you know it occurs to me that if by chance such-and-such were to happen, *then* . . ." and it is the *then* that is fictional because this particular event (Washington, D.C., washed away by a mysterious tidal wave, etc., or whatever premise you wish), this event has not happened, probably will not, and we are not being asked to believe either that it has or that it will. It is just that the daily tyranny of our immediate world, which we generally succumb to, becoming passive in the hands of and accepting as immutable, this is broken, this tyranny of concrete reality.

Often SF readers and writers are accused of a sort of clinical syndrome, a reality-evading one such as is found in schizophrenics. One pictures the disturbed adolescent boy in his room avidly reading "Spicy Science Fiction Horror Tales" and escaping into lurid fantasy as a way out of solving his and society's problems. But a primary tendency in the schizophrenic is that he is unable to think abstractly to such an extent that his mentational processes become involuntarily tied to immediate stimuli, to what is called concrete thinking. The production of great tales of other societies in the future on other planets does not pander to the incipient schizophrenic, and anyhow if I am wrong about this I'm sure TV is doing a better job in this area anyhow, this pandering.

The authentic body of science fiction, by its truly reputable writers (and I believe most of us are), does not provide an alternative to facing reality because it deals, as I've said, with reality fundamentally and primarily, as opposed to the genre of fantasy, and the writers are not clinically disturbed either; I have met many, many of my colleagues over the years, and I find them genial, warm, friendly people who hate the isolation imposed on them by the tragically solitary act of having to go off and lock oneself into one's study for a year to do a novel, not allowing any interruptions . . . writing is a lonely profession, at least I have found it so, and this is what I hold against my work: not that it allows me to escape into the "fantasies" of my novels but that it cuts me off from wife, children, and friends. I resent that. We all do. I find that there is enough extroversion in SF writers to cause them to yearn, to strive—and very successfully—to relate to other people; they are not motivated by the wish to withdraw, but by the *necessity* of solitude involved in the mechanics of the work itself. They have, let me say, enough extroversion to seek out whenever possible their colleagues and fans, to lecture, to speak on the radio and TV, to be interviewed . . . but then they *must* go back into that lonely little office for a period of time that, not counting food breaks and sleep breaks, may run, for a good novel, two years.

They resent this; they would love to sit and chat forever, and must force themselves back into their office or studio. They do not flee; they are *forced* that way, whereas, I think, the true scientist may be more introverted and might greet with real relief his withdrawal from human contact to do his work. This brings up one more point, crucial, I think, in determining what sort of person becomes an SF writer: He has a warmer heart than the scientist, and would like to play and chat and be close to others, and he resents this aspect of his work; he is torn within, and when he can, emerges from his studio to fraternize with whomever he can buttonhole. Probably, as I do, most SF writers, like most fiction writers in general, solve this by creating characters in their stories to keep them company during the long, lonely, isolated chore of work. I have a strong feeling, having met so many of my colleagues over the years, that there is almost universally among them a love of human beings and a concern for them, a desire for closeness that, in itself, might explain why the SF writer chose that field rather than one of the pure sciences. SF writers are not loners. Caught halfway between going out to petition versus retiring into solitude—caught between the political activist and the pure scientist— they have or at least I have found SF a workable compromise: I can be with my characters when I write, I can love them and support their anguished hopes as I would my "actual" friends—we do, in the final analysis, write about people, however idea-oriented our stories—and yet I don't have to be manning the barricades, be out on the street waving a banner, where I really don't belong.

I have seen real love shown among SF writers who came together at one of the many conventions—a great authentic fondness for their colleagues, not as writers, but as close friends. I'm sure this isn't unique to SF, and yet even other kinds of writers do not seem to exhibit this extended family quality that we have—they seem more competitive, more pitted against one another, hoping the new novel by their colleague will fail, will not turn out good. SF writers have none of that. We are a body, a corporate group working, as in the Byzantine days, on some great mosaic, upon which finally no individual name will be stamped; we are friends and we admire one another in a warm and personal way. We ratify one another and sense our identity as humans as being intimately connected with this fraternal spirit. There are few if any cold schizoid SF writers; when you meet a Ray Bradbury or a Ted Sturgeon or a Norman Spinrad or an A. E. van Vogt you find a warm person longing to know you, too; you are part of a family that goes back decades and into which we perpetually welcome others: There are no sterile, aseptic white smocks, no cruel or detached interactions among us. Writing SF requires a humanization of the person, or, put another way, I doubt if that person would want to write SF unless he had in him these empathic needs and qualities. Too timid to demonstrate, too warm to retreat to a sterile lab and experiment on objects or animals, too excited and impatient to allow all knowledge to be confined to the limits of absolute certitude — we live in a world of what a radio SF show once called "possible maybes," and this world attracts persons who are not loners but are lonely; and between those two distinctions there is a crucial difference.

"Michelson-Morley Experiment Reappraised" (1979)

The failure of the famous Michelson-Morley experiment in 1881, in which the absolute velocity of the Earth moving through luminiferous ether proved to be zero, gave rise to Einstein's Relativity Theory, which holds that the concept "absolute velocity" is meaningless. However, scientists at UCLA, using more sophisticated laser techniques, have suggested a more probable significance of the null result: that in fact the Earth does not move and that Copernicus was a crypto-Pythagorean determined to vindicate an ancient and discredited heliocentric solar system model. In a meeting of Southern California astronomers and astrophysicists it was proposed that (1) the geocentric solar system be restored as the proper model, and (2) that Copernicus be dug up and admonished. As a side issue, Einstein will be regarded with mild disfavor and some amusement, but scientists attending the meeting could not agree on the amount of amusement to be formally proposed.

"Introduction" to *Dr. Bloodmoney* (1979, 1985)

Well, I predicted wrong when I wrote *Dr. Bloodmoney* back in 1964. Events that I foresaw never came about, and as you read this novel you will see what I mean. But it is not the job, really, of science fiction to predict. Science fiction only *seems* to predict. It's like the aliens on *Star Trek*, all of whom speak English. A literary convention is involved, here. Nothing more.

I am amused, however, to see what specifically I got wrong. Worst of all, I totally misread the future of the manned space program. But this only shows how rapidly history unfolds. In *Dr. Bloodmoney* I have one American circling the world forever. This is obvious nonsense; either there would be many Americans—and many Russians, for that matter— or none at all.

Of course, the major item that I got wrong is the End of the World. Back in 1964 I was expecting it anytime; I kept checking my watch. Horace Gold, who edited *Galaxy* magazine, once chided me for anticipating global wipe-out within the next week. That was back around 1954; I anticipated it by 1964. Well, such were the fears of the times. Right now we have other worries. Our problem seems to be paying our debts with incredibly inflated dollars, finding gas for our cars—much more mundane worries. Less cosmic.

Oddly, these are the sort of worries that assail the characters in *Dr. Bloodmoney* in their post-World War Three world. There are horses pulling cars. Eyeglasses are rare and treasured. A man who manufactures cigarettes is honored wherever he goes. Of supreme value is someone who can fix things. Society has reverted, but not to the brutal level that we might expect. Rather, it has become rural in nature. The vast cities are

gone, and, in their place, a sort of countryside exists that is not awful at all.
I must add, however, that in no sense does it resemble any world that we
actually have.

But then, of course, we haven't had World War Three.

In my opinion, this is an extremely hopeful novel. It does not posit the
end of human civilization as a result of the next war. People are still
around and they are still coping. Those who survive, anyhow, are fairly
lucky in their new lives. What is interesting is the subtle change in the
relative power status of the survivors. Take Hoppy Harrington, who has no
arms or legs. Before the bomb hits, Hoppy is marginal in terms of power.
He is fortunate if he can get any kind of job at all. But in the postwar world
this is not the case. Hoppy is elevated by stealthy increments until, at last,
he is a menace to a man not even on the planet's surface; Hoppy has
become a demigod, and a complex one at that. He is not really evil, in the
ᴣual sense . . . but here is an instance of the abuse of power: evil emanating from power per se. It is not so much that Hoppy is evil but that his
power is evil.

In the satellite, Walt Dangerfield is transformed from a man assisting
the fragmented postwar society, giving it unity and strength, raising its
morale, to a man desperate for help from it, a man who is becoming
weaker day by day. He signifies isolation, which is the horror of the many
down below: isolation and a loss of the objects and values that comprised
their original world. As time passes, Walt Dangerfield must gain strength
from those on the planet's surface, rather than giving strength to them.
And into the vacuum created comes Hoppy Harrington, who epitomizes
the monster in us: the person who is hungry. Not hungry for food but
hungry for coercive control over others. This drive in Hoppy stems from a
physical deprivation. It is compensation for what he lacked from birth.
Hoppy is incomplete, and he will complete himself at the expense of the
entire world; he will psychologically devour it.

You will note in *Dr. Bloodmoney* an account of a test conducted in 1972
that turned out to be a catastrophe, and, of course, there was in fact no
such test and no such catastrophe. But then, there was no such person as
Dr. Bluthgeld. This is a work of fiction. And yet at a certain level it is not.
The West Marin County area where much of the novel is set is an area

that I knew well. When I wrote the novel I lived in that area. Many of the features that I describe are real. So a great deal of the veridical is blended in with the fiction. As do some of the characters, I searched for wild mushrooms in West Marin, and I found the varieties they find (and avoided the varieties they avoid). It is one of the most beautiful areas in the United States, and is called by the Sierra Club "The Island in Time." When I lived there in the late fifties and early sixties it was set apart from the rest of California and therefore seemed to me a natural locus for a postwar microcosm of society. Already, in fact, West Marin was a little world. When I read over *Dr. Bloodmoney* I discover, to my pleasure, that I have captured in words much of that little world that I so loved—a little world from which I am now separated by time and distance.

My favorite character in the novel is the TV salesman Stuart McConchie, who happens to be black. In 1964, when I wrote *Dr. Bloodmoney*, it was daring to have a major character be a black man. My God, how much change has taken place in these recent years! But what an excellent change, one we can be proud of. In my first novel, *Solar Lottery*, I had a black man as captain of a spaceship—daring, indeed, for a novel published in 1955. Stuart is in my opinion the focus of the novel, and he appears first. It is through his eyes that we initially see Dr. Bluthgeld, which is to say, Dr. Bloodmoney. Stuart's reaction is simple; he is seeing a lunatic, and that is that. Bonny Keller, however, knowing Dr. Bluthgeld more intimately, holds a more complex view of the man. Frankly, I tend to see Bluthgeld as Stuart McConchie sees him. I am, so to speak, Stuart McConchie, and at one time *I* was a TV salesman at a store on Shattuck Avenue in Berkeley. Like Stuart, I used to sweep the sidewalk in front of the store in the early morning, noticing the cute girls on their way to work. So I do have to confess to an overly simple view of Doctor Bluthgeld: I hate him and I hate everything he stands for. He is the alien and the enemy. I cannot fathom his mind; I cannot understand his hates. It is not the Russians I fear; it is the Dr. Bluthgelds, the Dr. Bloodmoneys, in our own society that terrify me. I am sure that to the extent that they know me, or would know me, they hate me back and would do exactly to me what I would do to them.

"And, sure enough as Stuart watched, leaning on his broom, the furtive first nut of the day sidled guiltily toward the psychiatrist's office."

This is our initial glimpse of Dr. Bloodmoney: through the eyes of a man pushing a broom. I am with the man pushing the broom, here at the beginning of the novel and all the way to the end. Stuart McConchie is an astute man, and in seeing Dr. Bloodmoney he has experienced a moment of instant insight that Bonny Keller in her years of personal, intimate knowledge lacks. I admit to prejudice, here. I think the first response by the man pushing the broom can be trusted. Doctor Bloodmoney is sick, and sick in a way that is dangerous to the rest of us. And much of the evil in our world now emanates from such men, because such men do exist.

So in writing *Dr. Bloodmoney* in 1964 I may have erred in many of my predictions, but upon rereading the novel recently I sensed a basic accuracy in it—an accuracy about human beings and their power to survive. Not survive as beasts, either, but as genuine humans doing genuinely human things. There are no supermen in this novel. There are no heroic deeds. There are some very poor predictions on my part, I must admit; but about the people themselves and their strength and tenacity and vitality . . . there I think I foresaw accurately. Because, of course, I was not predicting; I was only describing what I saw around me, the men and women and children and animals, the life of this planet that has been, is, and will be, no matter what happens.

I am proud of the people in this novel. And, as I say, I would like to number myself as one of them. I once pushed a broom on the sidewalk of Shattuck Avenue in Berkeley and I felt the joy and sense of busy activity and industry that Stuart feels, the excitement, the sense of the future.

And, as the novel depicts, despite the war—the war that did not in fact happen—it is a good future. I would have enjoyed being there with them in their microcosm, their postwar West Marin world.

"Introduction" to *The Golden Man* (1980)

When I see these stories of mine, written over three decades, I think of the Lucky Dog Pet Store. There's a good reason for that. It has to do with an aspect of not just my life but with the lives of most freelance writers. It's called poverty.

I laugh about it now, and even feel a little nostalgia, because in many ways those were the happiest goddamn days of my life, especially back in the early fifties, when my writing career began. But we were poor; in fact, we—my wife, Kleo, and I—were *poor* poor. We didn't enjoy it a bit. Poverty does not build character. That is a myth. But it does make you into a good bookkeeper; you count accurately and you count money, little money, again and again. Before you leave the house to grocery shop you know exactly what you can spend, and you know exactly what you are going to buy, because if you screw up you will not eat the next day and maybe not the day after that.

So anyhow there I am at the Lucky Dog Pet Store on San Pablo Avenue, in Berkeley, California, in the fifties, buying a pound of ground horsemeat. The reasons why I'm a freelance writer and living in poverty is (and I'm admitting this for the first time) that I am terrified of Authority Figures like bosses and cops and teachers; I want to be a freelance writer so I can be my own boss. It makes sense. I had quit my job managing a record department at a music store; all night every night I was writing short stories, both SF and mainstream . . . and selling the SF. I don't really enjoy the taste or texture of horsemeat; it's too sweet . . . but I also do enjoy not having to be behind a counter at exactly 9:00 A.M., wearing a suit and tie and saying, "Yes, ma'am, can I help you?" and so forth. . . . I enjoyed being thrown out of the University of California at Berkeley because I wouldn't take ROTC . . . boy, an Authority Figure in a uniform is *the*

Authority Figure!—and all of a sudden, as I hand over the thirty-five cents to the Lucky Dog Pet Store man, I find myself once more facing my personal nemesis. Out of the blue, I am once again confronted by an Authority Figure. There is no escape from your nemesis; I had forgotten that.

The man says, "You're buying this horsemeat and you are eating it yourselves."

He now stands nine feet tall and weighs three hundred pounds. He is glaring down at me. I am, in my mind, five years old again, and I have spilled glue on the floor in kindergarten.

"Yes, sir," I admit. I want to tell him, Look: I stay up all night writing SF stories and I'm real poor but I know things will get better, and I have a wife I love, and a cat named Magnificat, and a little old house I'm buying at the rate of $25-a-month payments, which is all I can afford. But this man is interested in only one aspect of my desperate (but hopeful) life. I know what he is going to tell me. I have always known. The horsemeat they sell at the Lucky Dog Pet Store is only for animal consumption. But Kleo and I are eating it ourselves, and now we are before the judge; the Great Assize has come; I am caught in another Wrong Act.

I half expect the man to say, "You have a bad attitude."

That was my problem then and it's my problem now; I have a bad attitude. In a nutshell, I fear authority but at the same time I resent it—the authority *and* my own fear—so I rebel. And writing SF is a way to rebel. I rebelled against ROTC at U.C. Berkeley and got expelled; in fact, told never to come back. I walked off my job at the record store one day and never came back. Later on I was to oppose the Vietnam War and get my files blown open and my papers gone through and stolen, as was written about in *Rolling Stone*. Everything I do is generated by my bad attitude, from riding the bus to fighting for my country. I even have a bad attitude toward publishers; I am always behind in meeting deadlines (I'm behind in this one, for instance).

Yet—SF is a rebellious art form and it needs writers and readers and bad attitudes—an attitude of "Why?" or "How come?" or "Who says?" This gets sublimated into such themes as appear in my writing as "Is the universe real?" "Are we all really human, or are some of us just reflex machines?" I have a lot of anger in me. I always have had. Last week my doctor told me that my blood pressure is elevated again and there now seems to be a cardiac complication. I got mad. Death makes me mad.

Human and animal suffering make me mad; whenever one of my cats dies I curse God and I mean it; I feel fury at him. I'd like to get him here where I could interrogate him, tell him that I think the world is screwed up, that man didn't sin and fall but was pushed—which is bad enough—but was then sold the lie that he is basically sinful, which I know he is not.

I have known all kinds of people (I turned fifty a while ago and I'm angry about that; I've lived a long time), and those were by and large good people. I model the characters in my novels and stories on them. Now and again one of these people dies, and that makes me mad—*really* mad, as mad as I can get. "You took my cat," I want to say to God, "and then you took my girlfriend. What are you doing? Listen to me; listen! It's wrong what you're doing."

Basically, I am not serene. I grew up in Berkeley and inherited from it the social consciousness that spread out over this country in the sixties and got rid of Nixon and ended the Vietnam War, plus a lot of other good things, the whole civil rights movement. Everyone in Berkeley gets mad at the drop of a hat. I used to get mad at the FBI agents who dropped by to visit with me week after week (Mr. George Smith and Mr. George Scruggs of the Red Squad), and I got mad at friends of mine who were members of the Communist Party; I got thrown out of the only meeting of the CP-USA I ever attended because I leaped to my feet and vigorously (i.e., angrily) argued against what they were saying.

That was in the early fifties, and now here we are in the very late seventies and I am still mad. Right now I am furious because of my best friend, a girl named Doris, twenty-four years old. She has cancer. I am in love with someone who could die anytime, and it makes fury against God and the world race through me, elevating my blood pressure and stepping up my heartbeat. And so I write. I want to write about people I love, and put them into a fictional world spun out of my own mind, not the world we actually have because the world we actually have does not meet my standards. Okay, so I should revise my standards; I'm out of step. I should yield to reality. I have never yielded to reality. That's what SF is all about. If you wish to yield to reality, go read Philip Roth; read the New York literary establishment mainstream best-selling writers. But you are reading SF and I am writing it for you. I want to show you, in my writing, what I love (my friends) and what I savagely hate (what happens to them).

I have watched Doris suffer unspeakably, undergo torment in her fight against cancer to a degree that I cannot believe. One time I ran out of the apartment and up to a friend's place, literally ran. My doctor had told me that Doris wouldn't live much longer and I should say good-bye to her and tell her it was because she was dying. I tried to and couldn't and then I panicked and ran. At my friend's house we sat around and listened to weird records (I'm into weird music in general, both in classical and in rock; it's a comfort). He is a writer, too, a young SF writer named K. W. Jeter—a good one. We just sat there and then I said aloud, really just pondering aloud, "The worst part of it is I'm beginning to lose my sense of humor about cancer." Then I realized what I'd said, and he realized, and we both collapsed into laughter.

So I do get to laugh. Our situation, the human situation, is, in the final analysis, neither grim nor meaningful but funny. What else can you call it? The wisest people are the clowns, like Harpo Marx, who would not speak. If I could have anything I want I would like God to listen to what Harpo was not saying, and understand why Harpo would not talk. Remember, Harpo *could* talk. He just wouldn't. Maybe there was nothing to say; everything has been said. Or maybe, had he spoken, he would have pointed out something too terrible, something we should not be aware of. I don't know. Maybe you can tell me.

Writing is a lonely way of life. You shut yourself up in your study and work and work. For instance, I have had the same agent for twenty-seven years and I've never met him because he is in New York and I'm in California. (I saw him once on TV, on the Tom Snyder *Tomorrow Show,* and my agent is one mean dude. He really plays hardball, which is what an agent is supposed to do.) I've met many other SF writers and become close friends with a number of them. For instance, I've known Harlan Ellison since 1954. Harlan hates my guts. When we were at the Metz Second Annual SF Festival last year, in France, see, Harlan tore into me; we were in the bar at the hotel, and all kinds of people, mostly French, were standing around. Harlan shredded me. It was fine; I loved it. It was sort of like a bad acid trip; you just have to kick back and enjoy; there is no alternative.

But I love that little bastard. He is a person who really exists. Likewise Van Vogt and Ted Sturgeon and Roger Zelazny and, most of all, Norman Spinrad and Tom Disch, my two main men in all the world. The loneliness of the writing *per se* is offset by the fraternity of writers. Last year a dream of mine of almost forty years was realized: I met Robert Heinlein. It was his writing, and A. E. Van Vogt's, that got me interested in SF, and I consider Heinlein my spiritual father, even though our political ideologies are totally at variance. Several years ago, when I was ill, Heinlein offered his help, anything he could do, and we had never met; he would phone me to cheer me up and see how I was doing. He wanted to buy me an electric typewriter, God bless him—one of the few true gentlemen in this world. I don't agree with any ideas he puts forth in his writing, but that is neither here nor there. One time when I owed the IRS a lot of money and couldn't raise it, Heinlein loaned the money to me. I think a great deal of him and his wife; I dedicated a book to them in appreciation. Robert Heinlein is a fine-looking man, very impressive and very military in stance; you can tell he has a military background, even to the haircut. He knows I'm a flipped-out freak and still he helped me and my wife when we were in trouble. That is the best in humanity, there; that is who and what I love.

My friend Doris who has cancer used to be Norman Spinrad's girl-friend. Norman and I have been close for years; we've done a lot of insane things together. Norman and I both get hysterical and start raving. Norman has the worst temper of any living mortal. He knows it. Beethoven was the same way. I now have no temper at all, which is probably why my blood pressure is so high; I can't get any of my anger out of my system. I don't really know—in the final analysis—who I'm mad at. I really envy Norman his ability to get it out of his system. He is an excellent writer and an excellent friend. This is what I get from being an SF writer: not fame and fortune, but good friends. That's what makes it worth it to me. Wives come and go; girlfriends come and go; we SF writers stay together until we literally die . . . which I may do at any time (probably to my own secret relief). Meanwhile I am writing this "Introduction" to The Golden Man, rereading stories that span a thirty-year period of writing, thinking back, remembering the Lucky Dog Pet Store, my days in Berkeley, my political involvement and how The Man got on my ass because of it. . . . I still have a residual fear in me, but I do believe that the reign of police intrigue and terror is over in this country (for a time, anyhow). I now sleep okay. But there was a time when I sat up all night in fear, waiting for the knock on the door. I was finally asked to "come downtown," as they call it, and for hours the police interrogated me. I was even called in by OSI (Air Force

Intelligence) and questioned by them; it had to do with terrorist activities in Marin County—not terrorist activities by the authorities this time, but by black ex-cons from San Quentin. It turned out that the house behind mine was owned by a group of them. The police thought we were in league; they kept showing me photos of black guys and asking did I know them. At that point I wouldn't have been able to answer. That was a really scary day for little Phil.

So if you thought writers live a bookish, cloistered life you are wrong, at least in my case. I was even in the street for a couple of years; the dope scene. Parts of that scene were funny and wonderful and other parts were hideous. I wrote about it in *A Scanner Darkly*, so I won't write about it here. The one good thing about my being in the street was that the people didn't know I was a well-known SF writer, or if they did, they didn't care. They just wanted to know what I had that they could rip off and sell. At the end of the two years everything I owned was gone—literally, including my house. I flew to Canada as guest of honor at the Vancouver SF Convention, lectured at the University of B.C., and decided to stay there. The hell with the dope scene. I had temporarily stopped writing; it was a bad time for me. I had fallen in love with several unscrupulous street girls. . . . I drove an old Pontiac convertible modified with a four-barrel carb and wide tires, and no brakes, and we were always in trouble, always facing problems we couldn't handle. It wasn't until I left Canada and flew down here to Orange County that I got my head together and back to writing. I met a very straight girl and married her, and we had a little baby we call Christopher. He is now five. They left me a couple of years ago. Well, as Vonnegut says, so it goes. What else can you say? It's like the whole of reality: You either laugh or—I guess fold and die.

One thing I've found that I can do that I really enjoy is rereading my own writing, earlier stories and novels especially. It induces mental time travel, the same way certain songs you hear on the radio do (for instance, when I hear Don McLean sing "Vincent" I at once see a girl named Linda wearing a miniskirt and driving her yellow Camaro; we're on our way to an expensive restaurant and I am worrying if I'll be able to pay the bill and Linda is talking about how she is in love with an older SF writer and I imagine—oh, vain folly!—that she means me, but it turns out she means Norman Spinrad, whom I introduced her to); the whole thing returns, an eerie feeling that I'm sure you've experienced. People have told me that everything about me, every facet of my life, psyche, experiences, dreams, and fears, are laid out explicitly in my writing, that from the corpus of my work I can be absolutely and precisely inferred. This is true. So when I read my writing, like these stories in this collection, I take a trip through my own head and life, only it is my earlier head and my earlier life. I abreact, as the psychiatrists say. There's the dope theme. There's the philosophical theme, especially the vast epistemological doubts that began when I was briefly attending U.C. Berkeley. Friends who are dead are in my stories and novels. Names of streets! I even put my agent's address in one, as a character's address. (Harlan once put his own phone number in a story, which he was to regret later.) And of course, in my writing, there is the constant theme of music, love of, preoccupation with, music. Music is the single thread making my life into a coherency.

You see, had I not become a writer I'd be somewhere in the music industry now, almost certainly the record industry. I remember back in the midsixties when I first heard Linda Ronstadt; she was a guest on Glen Campbell's TV show, and no one had ever heard of her. I went nuts listening to her and looking at her. I had been a buyer in retail records and it had been my job to spot new talent that was hot property, and, seeing and hearing Ronstadt, I knew I was hearing one of the great people in the business; I could see down the pipe of time into the future. Later, when she'd recorded a few records, none of them hits, all of which I faithfully bought, I calculated to the exact *month* when she'd make it big. I even wrote Capitol Records and told them; I said, the next record Ronstadt cuts will be the beginning of a career unparalleled in the record industry. Her next record was "Heart Like a Wheel." Capitol didn't answer my letter, but what the hell; I was right, and happy to be right. But, see, that's what I'd be into now, had I not gone into writing SF. My fantasy number that I run in my head is, I discover Linda Ronstadt, and am remembered as the scout for Capitol who signed her. I would have wanted that on my gravestone:

HE DISCOVERED LINDA RONSTADT
AND SIGNED HER UP!

My friends are caustically and disdainfully amused by my fantasy life about discovering Ronstadt and Grace Slick and Streisand and so forth. I have a good stereo system (at least my cartridge and speakers are good) and I own a huge record collection, and every night from 11:00 P.M. to 5:00 A.M. I write while wearing my Stax electrostatic top-of-line headphones. It's my job and my vice mixed together. You can't hope for better than that: having your job and your sin commingled. There I am, writing away, and into my ears is pouring Bonnie Koloc and no one can hear it but me. The joker is, though, that there's no one but me here anyhow, all the wives and girlfriends having long since left. That's another of the ills of writing; because it is such a solitary occupation, and requires such long-term concentrated attention, it tends to drive your wife or girlfriend away, anyhow, whoever you're living with. It's probably the most painful price the writer pays. All I have to keep me company are two cats. Like my doper friends (ex-doper friends, since most of them are dead now) my cats don't know I'm a well-known writer, and, as with my doper friends, I prefer it that way.

When I was in France, I had the interesting experience of being famous. I am the best-liked SF writer there, best of all in the entire whole complete world (I tell you that for what it's worth). I was Guest of Honor at the Metz Festival, which I mentioned, and I delivered a speech that, typically, made no sense whatever. Even the French couldn't understand it, despite a translation. Something goes haywire in my brain when I write speeches; I think I imagine I'm a reincarnation of Zoroaster bringing news of God. So I try to make as few speeches as possible. Call me up, offer me a lot of money to deliver a speech, and I'll give a tacky pretext to get out of doing it; I'll say anything, palpably a lie. But it was fantastic (in the sense of not real) to be in France and see all my books in expensive beautiful editions instead of little paperbacks with what Spinrad calls "peeled eyeball" covers. Owners of bookstores came to shake my hand. The Metz City Council had a dinner and a reception for us writers. Harlan was there, as I mentioned; so was Roger Zelazny and John Brunner and Harry Harrison and Robert Sheckley. I had never met Sheckley before; he is a gentle man. Brunner, like me, has gotten stout. We all had endless meals together; Brunner made sure everyone knew he spoke French. Harry Harrison sang the Fascist national anthem in Italian in a loud voice, which showed what he thought of prestige (Harry is the iconoclast of the known universe). Editors and publishers skulked everywhere, as well as the media. I got interviewed from eight in the morning until three-thirty the next morning, and, as always, I said things that will come back to haunt me. It was the best week of my life. I think that there at Metz I was really happy for the first time—not because I was famous but because there was so much excitement in those people. The French get wildly excited about ordering from a menu; it's like the old political discussions we used to have back in Berkeley, only it's simply food involved. Which street to walk up involves ten French people gesticulating and yelling, and then running off in different directions. The French, like me and Spinrad, see the most improbable possibility in every situation, which is certainly why I am popular there. Take a number of possibilities, and the French and I will select the wildest. So I had come home at last. I could get hysterical among people acculturated to hysteria, people never able to make decisions or execute actions because of the drama in the very process of choosing. That's me: paralyzed by imagination. For me a flat tire on my car is (a) The End of the World; and (b) An Indication of Monsters (although I forget why).

This is why I love SF. I love to read it; I love to write it. The SF writer sees not just possibilities but *wild* possibilities. It's not just "What if . . ." It's "*My God; what if . . .*" In frenzy and hysteria. The Martians are always coming. Mr. Spock is the only one calm. This is why Spock has become a cult god to us; he calms our normal hysteria. He balances the proclivity of SF people to imagine the impossible.

KIRK (frantically):   Spock, the *Enterprise* is about to blow up!

SPOCK (calmly):   Negative, Captain; it's merely a faulty fuse.

Spock is always right, even when he's wrong. It's the tone of voice, the supernatural reasonability; this is not a man like us; this is a god. God talks this way; every one of us senses it instinctively. That's why they have Leonard Nimoy narrating pseudo-science TV programs. Nimoy can make anything sound plausible. They can be in search of a lost button or the elephants' graveyard, and Nimoy will calm our doubts and fears. I would like him as a psychotherapist; I would rush in frantically, filled with my usual hysterical fears, and he would banish them.

PHIL (hysterically):   Leonard, the sky is falling!

NIMOY (calmly):   Negative, Phil; it's merely a faulty fuse.

And I'd feel okay and my blood pressure would drop and I could resume work on the novel I'm three years behind on vis-à-vis my deadline.

In reading the stories included in this volume, you should bear in mind that most were written when SF was so looked down upon that it virtually was not there, in the eyes of all America. This was not funny, the derision felt toward SF writers. It made our lives wretched. Even in Berkeley—or especially in Berkeley—people would say, "But are you writing anything serious?" We made no money; few publishers published SF (Ace Books was the only regular book publisher of SF); and really cruel abuse was inflicted on us. To select SF writing as a career was an act of self-destruction; in fact, most *writers*, let alone other people, could not even conceive of someone considering it. The only non-SF writer who ever treated me with courtesy was Herbert Gold, whom I met at a literary party in San Francisco. He autographed a file card to me this way: "To a colleague, Philip K. Dick." I kept the card until the ink faded and was gone, and I still feel grateful to him for this charity. (Yes, that was what it was, then, to treat an SF writer with courtesy.) To get hold of a copy of my first published novel, *Solar Lottery*, I had to special-order it from the City Lights Bookshop in San Francisco, which specialized in the *outre*. So in my head I have to collate the experience in 1977 of the mayor of Metz shaking hands with me at an official city function, and the ordeal of the fifties when Kleo and I lived on $90 a month, when we could not even pay the fine on an overdue library book, and when I wanted to read a magazine I had to go to the library because I could not afford to buy it, when we were literally living on dog food. But I think you should know this—specifically, in case you are, say, in your twenties and rather poor and perhaps becoming filled with despair, whether you are an SF writer or not, whatever you want to make of your life. There can be a lot of fear, and often it is a justified fear. People do starve in America. My financial ordeal did not end in the fifties; as late as the midseventies I still could not pay my rent, nor afford to take Christopher to the doctor, nor own a car, nor have a phone. In the month that Christopher and his mother left me I earned $9, and that was just three years ago. Only the kindness of my agent, Scott Meredith, in loaning me money when I was broke got me through. In 1971, I actually had to beg friends for food. Now, look; I don't want sympathy; what I am trying to do is tell you that your crisis, your ordeal, assuming you have one, is not something that is going to be endless, and I want you to know that you will probably survive it through your courage and wits and sheer drive to live. I have seen uneducated street girls survive horrors that beggar description. I have seen the faces of men whose brains had been burned out by drugs, men who still could think enough to be able to realize what had happened to them; I watched their clumsy attempts to weather that which cannot be weathered. As in Heine's poem "Atlas," this line: "I carry that which can't be carried." And the next line is, "And in my body my heart would like to break!" But this is not the sole constituent of life, and it is not the sole theme in fiction, mine or anyone else's, except perhaps for the nihilist French existentialists. Kabir, the fifteenth-century Sufi poet, wrote, "If you have not lived through something, it is not true." So live through it; I mean, go all the way to the end. Only then can it be understood, not along the way.

If I had to come forth with an analysis of the anger that lies inside me, which expresses itself in so many subliminations, I would guess that probably what arouses my indignation is seeing the meaningless. That which is disorder, the force of entropy—there is no redemptive value of something that can't be understood, as far as I am concerned. My writing, in toto, is an attempt on my part to take my life and everything I've seen and done, and fashion it into a work that makes sense. I'm not sure I've been successful. First, I cannot falsify what I have seen. I see disorder and sorrow, and so I have to write about it; but I've seen bravery and humor, and so I put that in, too. But what does it all add up to? What is the vast overview that is going to impart sense into the entirety?

What helps for me—if help comes at all—is to find the mustard seed of the funny at the core of the horrible and futile. I've been researching ponderous and solemn theological matters for five years now, for my novel-in-progress, and much of the Wisdom of the World has passed from the printed page and into my brain, there to be processed and secreted in the form of more words: words in, words out, and a brain in the middle wearily trying to determine the meaning of it all. Anyhow, the other night I started on the article on Indian philosophy in the *Encyclopedia of Philos-*

ophy, an eight-volume learned reference set that I esteem. The time was 4:00 A.M.; I was exhausted—I have been working endlessly like this on this novel, doing this kind of research. And there, at the heart of this solemn article, was this:

"The Buddhist idealists used various arguments to show that perception does not yield knowledge of external objects distinct from the percipient. . . . The external world supposedly consists of a number of different objects, but they can be known as different only because there are different sorts of experiences 'of' them. Yet if the experiences are thus distinguishable, there is no need to hold the superfluous hypothesis of external objects. . . ."

In other words, by applying Ockham's razor to the basic Epistemological question of "What is reality?" the Buddhist idealists reach the conclusion that belief in an external world is a "superfluous hypothesis"; that is, it violates the Principle of Parsimony—which is the principle underlying all Western science. Thus the external world is abolished, and we can go about more important business—whatever that might be.

That night I went to bed laughing. I laughed for an hour. I am still laughing. Push philosophy and theology to their ultimate (and Buddhist idealism probably is the ultimate of both) and what do you wind up with? Nothing. Nothing exists (they also proved that the self doesn't exist, either). As I said earlier, there is only one way out: seeing it all as ultimately funny. Kabir, whom I quoted, saw dancing and joy and love as ways out, too; and he wrote about the sound of "the anklets on the feet of an insect as it walks." I would like to hear that sound; perhaps if I could my anger and fear, and my high blood pressure, would go away.

"Book Review" of *The Cybernetic Imagination in Science Fiction* (1980)

This is MIT Press's first effort to cope with the reality of science fiction. Although less than 300 pages, it weighs almost a pound and a half, compared to Ballantine Books' edition of Ted Sturgeon's classic *More Than Human*, which weighs exactly a quarter pound. Therefore Warrick's book must be six times as important as Sturgeon's. Her study, Warrick tells us, "is based on 225 stories and novels written between 1930 and 1977." She states her conclusions up front in her introduction: "This study demonstrates that much of the (science) fiction written since World War II is reactionary in its attitude toward computers and artificial intelligence. It is often ill informed about information theory and computer technology and lags behind present developments instead of anticipating the future." She then goes on to present a fully developed aesthetic approach by which to judge SF (here she does quite well). The three SF writers whom she deals with most fully are Asimov, Lem, and myself. I get the impression she considers the three of us important, and here lies my quarrel with her. As far as I am concerned the concept "important" is of no use in judging SF. I could quarrel with the vague style of the book (for instance, I cite ". . . a prison of false illusions" as being not only a double negative but also verbose, and "A shower of bizarre metaphors trails from Dick's imagination as it journeys through the patterns of possibilities in the evolving reciprocal relationship between man and his artificial constructs" and "He throws torches of possibility into his dark future, and their flashes of light reveal a survival," etc., as boring and sophomoric and a waste of the reader's time). But I would prefer to quarrel with the purpose of the book instead, and start out by saying that it has no purpose. It is a parasitic thing, and its very existence suggests that SF as a field is beginning to die, because only an entity waning and failing attracts such suckers as the academic sports of this sort. As Jesus says in Matthew 24:28: "Wherever the corpse is, there will the vultures gather."

The main complaint expressed repeatedly by Warrick in this book is SF's tendency to emit warnings about the dangers of technology—dangers to individual humans and human society generally. Well, it is just too bad, but it is a fact: Science fiction writers worry about trends, worry about possible dystopias growing out of the present, and this is a cardinal value of the field. Admittedly, there was a time when science and progress were assumed to be identical. If we worry now we have cause to. This is not due to ignorance of the state of the world and the breakthroughs in science. Warrick devotes an entire chapter to my stories and novels that deal with robots, and she quotes me—fairly—as saying: "The greatest change growing across our world these days is probably the momentum of the living towards reification, and at the same time a reciprocal entry into animation by the mechanical." Am I not to be allowed to view this with alarm? Who will legislate what SF writers will be allowed to write and to worry about? This book praises me by terming my writing important but it arrogates to itself the role of arbiter of viewpoint and proper concern. Viewpoint and concern in SF are a transaction among author, editor, and reader, to which the critic is a spectator. If the reader enjoys what I write, there you have it. If he does *not* enjoy it, there you have nothing. "Important" is a rule from another game that I am not playing. I did not begin to read or write SF for reasons dealing with importance. When I sat in high school geometry class secretly reading a copy of *Astounding* hidden within a textbook I was not seeking importance. I was seeking, probably, intellectual excitement. Mental stimulation.

If SF becomes annexed to the academic world it will buy into its own death, despite what Delany, Russ, Lem, and Le Guin may think; as with a single mind they woo academic approval as if it were some ultimate court. However, I look to my left and see a coverless, tattered copy of the July 1952 *Planet Stories*—my first published story appeared in it, and I received a lot of kidding from serious-minded people for selling to such a market and for reading such a "trashy" magazine, to use Lem's favorite term of derision. Frankly I would prefer the derision to the new praise; SF is now palatable to the educated, the lofty, and I say, Let me out. Professor Warrick's pound-and-a-half book with its expensive binding, paper, and dust jacket staggers you with its physical impression, but it has no soul and it will take *our* soul in what really seems to me to be brutal greed. Let us alone, Dr. Warrick; let us read our paperback novels with their peeled eyeball covers. Don't dignify us. Our power to stimulate human imagination and to delight is intrinsic to us already. Quite frankly, we were doing fine before you came along.

"My Definition of Science Fiction" (1981)

I will define science fiction, first, by saying what SF is *not*. It cannot be defined as "a story (or novel or play) set in the future," since there exists such a thing as space adventure, which is set in the future but is not SF. It is just that: adventure, fights, and wars in the future in space involving superadvanced technology. Why, then, is it not science fiction? It would seem to be, and Doris Lessing (e.g.) supposes that it is. However, space adventure *lacks the distinct new idea* that is the essential ingredient. Also, there can be science fiction set in the present: the alternate-world story or novel. So if we separate SF from the future and also from ultra-advanced technology, what then do we have that *can* be called SF? We have a fictitious world; that is the first step: It is a society that does not in fact exist, but is predicated on our known society—that is, our known society acts as a jumping-off point for it; the society advances out of our own in some way, perhaps orthogonally, as with the alternate-world story or novel. It is our world dislocated by some kind of mental effort on the part of the author, our world transformed into that which it is not or not yet. This world must differ from the given in at least one way, and this one way must be sufficient to give rise to events that could not occur in our society—or in any known society present or past. There must be a coherent idea involved in this dislocation; that is, the dislocation must be a conceptual one, not merely a trivial or a bizarre one—*this* is the essence of science fiction, the conceptual dislocation within the society so that as a result a new society is generated in the author's mind, transferred to paper, and from paper it occurs as a convulsive shock in the reader's mind, *the shock of dysrecognition*. He knows that it is not his actual world that he is reading about.

Now, to separate science fiction from fantasy. This is impossible to do, and a moment's thought will show why. Take Psionics; take mutants such as we find in Ted Sturgeon's wonderful *More Than Human.* If the reader believes that such mutants could exist, then he will view Sturgeon's novel as science fiction. If, however, he believes that such mutants are, like wizards and dragons, not possible, nor will ever be possible, then he is reading a fantasy novel. Fantasy involves that which general opinion regards as impossible; science fiction involves that which general opinion regards as possible under the right circumstances. This is in essence a judgment call, since what is possible and what is not [cannot be] objectively known but is, rather, a subjective belief on the part of the reader.

Now to define *good* science fiction. The conceptual dislocation—the new idea, in other words—must be truly new (or a new variation on an old one) and it must be intellectually stimulating to the reader; it must invade his mind and wake it up to the possibility of something he had not up to then thought of. Thus "good science fiction" is a value term, not an objective thing, and yet, I think, there really is such a thing, objectively, as good science fiction.

I think Dr. Willis McNelly at the California State University at Fullerton put it best when he said that the true protagonist of an SF story or novel is an idea and not a person. If it is good SF the idea is new, it is stimulating, and, probably most important of all, it sets off a chain reaction of ramification ideas in the mind of the reader; it so to speak unlocks the reader's mind so that that mind, like the author's, begins to create. Thus SF is creative and it inspires creativity, which mainstream fiction by and large does not do. We who read SF (I am speaking as a reader now, not a writer) read it because we love to experience this chain reaction of ideas being set off in our mind by something we read, something with a new idea in it; hence the very best science fiction ultimately winds up being a collaboration between author and reader, in which both create— and *enjoy* doing it: Joy is the essential and final ingredient of science fiction, the joy of discovery of newness.

"Predictions" by Philip K. Dick
Included in *The Book of Predictions* (1981)

1983
*The Soviet Union will develop an operational particle-beam accelerator, making missile attack against that country impossible. At the same time the USSR will deploy this weapon as a satellite killer. The United States will turn, then, to nerve gas.

1984
*The United States will perfect a system by which hydrogen, stored in metal hydrides, will serve as a fuel source, eliminating the need for oil.

1985
*By or before this date there will be a titanic nuclear accident either in the USSR or in the United States, resulting in a shutting down of all nuclear power plants.

1986
*Such satellites as *HEA0-2* will uncover vast, unsuspected high-energy phenomena in the universe, indicating that there is sufficient mass to collapse the universe back when it has reached its expansion limit.

1989
*The United States and the Soviet Union will agree to set up one vast metacomputer as a central source for information available to the entire world; this will be essential due to the huge amount of information coming into existence.

1993
*An artificial life form will be created in a lab, probably in the USSR, thus reducing our interest in locating life forms on other planets.

1995

*Computer use by ordinary citizens (already available in 1980) will transform the public from passive viewers of TV into mentally alert, highly trained, information-processing experts.

1997

*The first closed-dome colonies will be successfully established on Luna and on Mars. Through DNA modification, quasi-mutant humans will be created who can survive under non-Terran conditions, i.e., alien environments.

1998

*The Soviet Union will test a propulsion drive that moves a starship at the velocity of light; a pilot ship will set out for Proxima Centaurus, soon to be followed by an American ship.

2000

*An alien virus, brought back by an interplanetary ship, will decimate the population of Earth but leave the colonies on Luna and Mars intact.

2010

*Using tachyons (particles that move backward in time) as a carrier, the Soviet Union will attempt to alter the past with scientific information.

"Universe Makers . . . and Breakers" (1981)

[The opening biographical note
was written by Dick himself.]

Philip K. Dick is the author of 48 books and 150 stories, with four movies currently in the works. He has won the Hugo Award, the John W. Campbell Memorial Award, the Graouilly d'Or Award of France, the British Science Fiction Award, and the *Playboy* Award for Best New Contributor of Fiction for 1980 [for the story "Frozen Journey," later retitled "I Hope I Shall Arrive Soon"]. This February, Bantam Books releases his new novel *Valis*, and in April Simon & Schuster its sequel *The Divine Invasion*. The London Times wrote of him, "One of the most original practitioners now writing any kind of fiction, Philip K. Dick makes most of the European avant-garde seem navel-gazers in a cul-de-sac." He lives in Santa Ana, Orange County, California, and has been a *SelecTV* subscriber for over two years.

Science fiction films have put one over on us. Like the veil of *maya*, your special effects department down there in Hollywood can now simulate anything the mind can imagine . . . and you thought it was all real. No, they really don't blow up planets. It's true; they make it up. And a great deal of skillful imagining is going on these days. Not content with destroying whole planets, inventive scriptwriters and directors will soon be bringing you peculiar new universes with inhabitants to match. Watch for it. What you thought an alien looked like . . . well, it is going to look a lot worse. What burst through Kane's shirt in *Alien* is not the end of the line of monsters but more the beginning.

It takes megabucks to match the imaginations behind sci-fi films, and that money exists because the profits are there. Not for the story line of the film; that isn't what Hollywood goes for, now that Hitchcock has left us. Why do you need a story line if your special effects department can simulate anything? Graphic, visual impact has replaced story. Authors of science-fiction novels know this and grumble; what they wrote is not what you get when the film is finished. But this is as it should be. We are seeing a story, not being told it.

Ridley Scott, who directed *Alien* and who now intends to bring into existence a $15 million film based on my novel *Do Androids Dream of Electric Sheep?*, confessed to an interviewer from *Omni* magazine that he "found the novel too difficult to read," despite the fact that the novel appeared as a mass-circulation paperback. On the other hand I was able rather easily to read the screenplay (it will be called *Blade Runner*). It was terrific. It bore no relation to the book. Oddly, in some ways it was better. (I had a hell of a time getting my hands on the screenplay. No one involved in the *Blade Runner* project has ever spoken to me. But that's okay; I haven't spoken to them.) What my story will become is one titanic lurid collision of androids being blown up, androids killing humans, general confusion and murder, all very exciting to watch. Makes my book seem dull by comparison.

Still, you wouldn't want to see my novel on the screen because it is full of people conversing, plus the personal problems of the protagonist. These matters don't translate to the screen. And why translate them, since a novel is a story in words, whereas a movie is an event that moves? They're not called movies for nothing. I have no complaints.

Sometimes we sci-fi writers tell ourselves that the recent mass excitement over our wares is due to the successes in the actual space program, all those manned and unmanned probes, all those pictures sent back of moons no one knew existed, not to mention rings that are braided together in an affront to known laws of physics. But this isn't the case. The real reason for the wild financial successes of recent sci-fi films is: Human imagination takes a quantum-leap breakthrough by the special effects people; films such as *Close Encounters* and *Alien* and *2001* would be just terrific, just as awe-inspiring and wonderful if we were still driving Model A Fords—perhaps even more so.

The fact is, spaceships no longer dangle on strings, no longer fizz, hesitate, or wobble past you, as in the old Flash Gordon serials. The monsters are no longer inflated rubber toys haltingly mimicking what the average ten-year-old could dream up. There is great sophistication at the dream factory these days. If I as an author can think it up, they can build it in such a way as to scare or amaze you, and in all cases convince you. And this is why, really, sci-fi films work now, in contrast to the old days, when kids at Saturday afternoon matinees hooted and giggled at Lon Chaney, Jr., emerging from a fake swamp to inflict the mummy's curse on yet another idiotic lady.

As a writer, though, I'd sort of like to see some of my ideas, not just special effects of my ideas, used. For all its dazzling graphic impact, *Alien* (to take one example) had nothing new to bring us in the way of concepts that awaken the mind rather than the senses. A monster is a monster, and a spaceship is a spaceship. *Star Trek*, years ago, delved more into provocative ideas than most big-budget sci-fi films today, and some of the finest authors in the science-fiction field wrote those hour TV episodes. I'm getting a little tired of people turning out to be robots, harmless-looking life forms evolving into stupendous but predictable space squids, and, most of all, World War Two's Battle of Midway refought in outer space. But I must admit that the eerie, mystical, almost religious subtheme in *Star Wars* and *The Empire Strikes Back* enchanted me. Now and then the sense of wonder *is* there. Okay, if they would just stop blowing up the orbiting space station at the end—but it looks so nice, that acid-trip color-burst display. This is the great written rule: Sci-fi films end not with a whimper but a bang. And maybe that's as it should be, in the best of all visual galaxies.

"Headnote" for "Beyond Lies the Wub" (1981)

The idea I wanted to get down on paper had to do with the definition of "human." The dramatic way I trapped the idea was to present ourselves, the literal humans, and then an alien life form that exhibits the deeper traits that I associate with humanity: not a biped with an enlarged cortex—a forked radish that thinks, to paraphrase the old saying—but an organism that is human in terms of its soul.

I'm sorry if the word "soul" offends you, but I can think of no other term. Certainly, when I wrote the story "Beyond Lies the Wub" back in my youth in politically active Berkeley, I myself would never have thought of the crucial ingredient in the wub being a soul; I was a fireball radical and atheist, and religion was totally foreign to me. However, even in those days (I was about twenty-two years old) I was casting about in an effort to contrast the truly human from what I was later to call the "android or reflex machine" that looks human but is not—the subject of the speech I gave in Vancouver in 1972 ["The Android and the Human," included herein]—twenty years after "Beyond Lies the Wub" was published. The germ of the idea behind the speech lies in this, my first published story. It has to do with empathy, or, as it was called in earlier times, *caritas* or *agape*.

In this story, empathy (on the part of the wub, who looks like a big pig and has the feelings of a man) becomes an actual weapon for survival. Empathy is defined as the ability to put yourself in someone else's place. The wub does this even better than we ordinarily suppose could be done: Its spiritual capacity is its literal salvation. The wub was my idea of a higher life form; it was then and it is now. On the other hand, Captain Franco (the name is deliberately based on General Franco of Spain, which is my concession in the story to political considerations) looks on other creatures in terms of sheer utility; they are objects to him, and he pays the ultimate price for this total failure of empathy. So I show empathy possessing a survival value; in terms of interspecies competition, empathy gives you the edge. Not a bad idea for a very early story by a very young person!

I liked the blurbs that *Planet Stories* printed for "Beyond Lies the Wub." On the title page of the magazine they wrote:

Many men talk like philosophers and live like fools, proclaimed the slovenly wub, after death.

And ahead of the story proper they wrote:

The slovenly wub might well have said: Many men talk like philosophers and live like fools.

Reader reaction to the story was excellent, and Jack O'Sullivan, editor of *Planet,* wrote to tell me that in his opinion it was a very fine little story— whereupon he paid me something like $15. It was my introduction to pulp payment rates.

Just a week ago while going through my closet I came across an ancient pulp magazine with ragged edges, its cover missing, its pages yellow. . . . Wondering what it was, I picked it up—and found that this ancient remnant, this artifact from another epoch, was indeed the July 1952 issue of *Planet Stories* with my first published story in it. Profound emotions touched me as I gazed down at the illustration for "Wub"; it is a superb little illo [illustration], done by Vestal, and under it is written, " 'The Wub, sir,' Peterson said. 'It spoke!' " Well, here we are in the eighties, twenty-eight years later, and the gentle wub still speaks. May he always speak . . . and may other humans always listen.

Part Three

Works Related to
The Man in the High Castle
and Its Proposed Sequel

Readers should consult the "Introduction" to this volume for a discussion of the Dick novel *The Man in the High Castle* (1962), which won the Hugo Award for Best Science-Fiction Novel the following year.

"Naziism and the High Castle" was first published in the science-fiction fanzine *Niekas* in September 1964. It was written in response to a politically charged review of *High Castle* in an earlier issue of *Niekas* by fellow SF writer (and friend) Poul Anderson. It was reprinted in the *Philip K. Dick Society Newsletter*, No. 14 (June 1987). As the essay raises a number of unusually important factual issues, it is essential to note that the assertion by Dick that "many" Jewish refugees who lived, during World War Two, under Japanese rule in the Far East "set up Hitler organizations" and performed the Nazi salute is utterly unsubstantiated by the numerous scholarly studies that I have consulted. Dick's own source for this assertion is unknown.

Both the "Biographical Material on Hawthorne Abendsen" (1974) and the two chapters (1964) of the proposed sequel to *High Castle* are published here for the first time. The quality of the two chapters is remarkable; see the "Introduction" for a discussion of the factors that led Dick to abandon this project. One historical clarification is in order: In the first chapter, reference is made to the suicide of Field Marshal Rommel by shooting. In fact, he poisoned himself. It should also be noted that an audiotape cassette released as *PKDS Newsletter*, Nos. 9–10 (January 1986) includes, as one of its sides, notes dictated by Dick (whose arm was in a splint due to a shoulder injury, which precluded him from his usual typing) on this proposed novel. The tape describes one scene in which Hawthorne Abendsen is brutally interrogated by the Nazis as to the truth of the *Nebenwelt* (or alternate universe) in which the Allies, not the Nazis, were triumphant. But Abendsen cannot provide them with the truth—*he does not know*. The secret is ever elusive.

"Naziism and *The High Castle*" (1964)

Many moon have passed since white man (i.e., Poul Anderson) review my book *Man in the High Castle*, and fen [sic; perhaps "fan" intended] (e.g., too many to note, with, however, one exception, a certain John Boardman) have commented, not on the book nor review per se, but on Naziism—which is right and proper, because *that* is the true topic, far more so than any novel or any review, and only proves that I am right: We are still very much afraid, still rightly so very much disturbed, and, as Harry Warner so correctly said, ". . . we might identify with the war guilt of the Germans because they're so similar to us. . . ."

However, although these comments, etc., took place back in March, I have just now seen them, and would also like to comment.

John Boardman calls Dr. Friedrich Foerster "the greatest modern critic of Germany." There is no *one* "greatest modern critic," etc., of anything; this is just a way of saying that you believe your source, and it is right that you should believe your source; however, I will dispute his uniqueness, or any claim to his Platonic Ideal-type perfection as a sole and utter source. Even though, as a matter of fact, I agree with the quoted passage from him (v. John Boardman's comments March '64 *Niekas*). In fact it is just this sort of thinking that worries me (however, it is early in the morning, I have not had breakfast yet, so everything worries me; let it go). Anyhow, we just cannot say for sure if there are "two Germanies" in the sense of two traditions of thought, or that Naziism is the absolute culmination, the logical fulfillment, of all that is German; we don't know; please, let's admit our ignorance. We know *what* they did, we know what their *stated* ideologies were . . . but we do not actually know *why*, in the deepest sense, they—i.e., the Nazis—did it. Truly. I have talked to some of them. All they knew was that they were afraid—afraid as we are, but not afraid of the same things: They were afraid of us, of the U.K., of Russia (which we are, too, now), and—most of all, of the Jews, which we are not, and which we cannot comprehend; i.e., this fear. To us, a Jew is, for example, a nice tall guy with a glass in his hand next to us at a party. To them—well, there the curtain falls. But a Nazi friend of mine, living in the United States after the war, started to enter an apartment with me, and I said, "By the way, this fellow who lives here is named Bob Goldstein," and my Nazi friend actually paled and blanched (i.e., drew back); he was literally afraid to go into the apartment—and, in addition, he felt somatic, horrible aversion. Why? Ask Hannah Arendt, whom I regard as the "greatest modern critic of Germany," a Jew herself. I feel even *she,* raised among them, does not know. It is subrational; it is psychological, not logical. Why do some people fear cats or streetcars or redheaded goats? They themselves do not know. Phobia is phobia; it springs, as Freud and Jung and H. S. Sullivan showed, from depths of the self unknown to the self. *Ipse dixit.*

Please forgive me if I ramble, but you see: I feel that simple, clear "answers" to this question ("Why the Nazis did what they did, and will we do it, and are we also guilty?") defy us; they cannot be had. Are we guilty of what the mad, subrational "planners" in Washington, D.C., are doing right now? I don't know. Was some old village German lady in 1939 "guilty" of a decision at Eichmann's bureau in Berlin? There are a few established facts, however, that we should remember. (1) When Himmler asked for and got the chance to witness an execution of innocent, harmless Jewish people (by firing squad), he had a convulsion of horror; he fainted, fell to the floor, rolled in a spasm of anguish; his aides had to drag him to his feet; and, there and then, Himmler decreed that no more Jews "were to be shot, but that some merciful method, painless and instant" had to be found. Remember, mark, this. So even this unman, this thing, reified into the top ranks of Nazi officialdom, had "feelings." (Hitler would neither have cared to watch, and if he had, he would not have had any emotional, ethical reaction; mark that, too.) Also, the *Wermark Soldaten* (the average German soldier) hated the *Schwarzers,* the SS . . . knew them as murderers. Mark that. German citizens poked bread into the sealed cattle cars carrying Jews to their death through the Reich; read that and ponder. Remarque records a German playing the theme from Beethoven's *Fidelio* that depicts the prisoners—unjustly held by a tyranny—as they are at last, for a moment, let up to see the light—playing this as a team of Jewish concentration camp victims are led down the street past his house. Even German whores came to the walls of the death camps, hoping "to do something for" those within. In other words, good (and I will not put quotes around that word) impulses broke out constantly among average Germans as and when they became aware of what was being done to the Jews; many, admittedly, spat on, kicked, jeered at, Jews being hauled off . . . but not all. *"Die Stille im Lande"* [the quiet in the land] the Nazis called these Germans who did not approve of the racial policies; these Germans knew that if they showed themselves they, too, would be killed. Mark this: The first inhabitants of the concentration camps were non-Jewish Germans. And it did mean death, during the war, for a German citizen to show any dissent from official policy; a German woman, for example, was imprisoned because the newspaper with which she lined her garbage pail had on it a photo of Hitler; this was decreed by the court (the so-called *Reichs Gericht*) a "crime against the state." They made it stick!

Yet, the German people, or a good part of them, better than half, voted, legally voted, Hitler into power, and knowing his racial views. Read Goebbels' early diaries; the *Partei* had the support of the working class—not the bourgeoisie. Mark that, too: The working class swung from supporting the Communists and the moderate socialists to the Nazis. Why? Well, I can hazard a guess. The Nazis, like the big city political bosses who used to run Chicago and New York and Boston, were always "open," always there and ready to listen, to help, to dole out food and support . . . and the Germans were starving, dying, being evicted, being deprived; it was the Depression, remember, and the people, as our people, were desperate. One of our favorite folk singers of today in those days (late '30s) not only sang against our support of the U.K. and defense plant activity but drawlingly spoke of being listed as a "Japanese spy"; in other words, this "now liberal, one of us" great folk singer—his initials are P.S.—was *for* Nazi Germany—because of the German-Russian Pact. World Communism and Naziism were cooperating, for a time; the Nazis were *not* "rightists"; they were coleftists—at least until the Nazi tanks entered the Russian-controlled half of ex-Poland.

In his comments in *Niekas* George H. Wells speaks of "Jewish nationalists," and that they "were overlooked." This is a point, too; at the time of the rise of anti-Jewish ideology among non-Jewish-Germans, the *Jewish*-Germans were beginning, in great part, to think—as not Germans or even Europeans, but as nationalists of the soon-to-be-reborn national state of Israel. (Moses Mendelssohn pleaded with the people not to accept this, but to "come out and be part of the European community"; generally, he failed.) So: We saw Jews, in Germany, arrive at the same idea as the pre-Nazi "racists," such as Wagner, and it always seems that Richard Wagner is the goat in this; he *invented* the idea that Jews were aliens, hostile to Germany. Catcrap. A thorough study of Wagner's ideas shows that he broke with Nietzsche in the end, saw a redemption of Germany (i.e., of man per se) in Christian love, not in military bombast (vide *Parsifal*). So even among the famous pre-Nazi theoreticians we don't find the uniformity of outlook; what we do find, however, is the Englishmen Stuart House Chamberlain, and Carl Rhodes . . . and of course Nietzsche; but we find *English madmen-thinkers* right at the "heart of darkness," so to speak. Teaching the idea, as Hannah Arendt says, of a small, worldwide elite of Nordics who will run things: a top caste who will tell the "darkies," i.e., the rest of us, where to go . . . and "where to go" may be into the false shower baths that are really cyanide gas chambers. Yes, Harry Warner, writing in *Niekas*, is right: We squirm and we remember because it is not "them" but "us" who thought those awful thoughts, and hence instigated those awful deeds; and the "us" includes the Jewish nationalist fanatics, some of whom live today in Israel, who invade schools, break up grammar school class meetings with their quasi-military (I think the form is paramilitary) thugs . . . because the teacher of the class is not racially "correct." In this case, however, not sufficiently Jewish, rather than sufficiently German.

The Zionists drove *one million* Arabs out of Israel, and those Arabs, supported—i.e., kept from starving—by the Quakers, are the greatest single lot of displaced persons on earth today. And don't let anyone tell you that those Arabs (i.e., non-Jews and hence aliens, although their people had lived there for two thousand years) *wanted* to leave. They were terrorized into leaving, and they cannot return. So the victims of World War Two have become the arrogant nationalists, ready to go to war (vide the Suez crisis) with their neighbors as soon as assured of adequate military support (and again it is Britain who gives it, Britain and France).

This is all dreadful. In the Jewish refugee settlements in the Far East under the Japanese during World War Two, many Jews set up Hitler organizations, including the Nazi (or Roman, if you prefer) salute.

We like to think of the victims of tyranny and cruelty as innocent (e.g., Chessman). But often the victim is blood-stained, too; i.e., he has participated actively in the situation that has at last claimed his life. Many Jews today won't ride in a VW, and some won't even listen to the music of Beethoven; is this not as neurotic and "sick" as was the nineteenth-century ideologies of blood, race, and land being taught by both Germans and Jewish-Germans? Personally, I enjoy telling fanatical nationalistic, blood-oriented Jewish friends a fact they generally don't know: Many of the medieval German knight-poets, the minnesingers, were—Jewish.

So, Dr. Friedrich Foerster, "the greatest modern critic of Germany" to the contrary, there are now, have always been, at least two, and probably three, seven, nine Germanies; i.e., worldviews held by Germans. J. S. Bach considered himself a Pole (his monarch was under fief to a Polish king.) But we call Bach a German because he spoke German. Tony Boucher speaks German, and perfectly; is he, therefore, a German, hence a Nazi? The German Jews spoke German . . . and remember, a Jewish violinist's hand was broken by a Zionist fanatic swinging a lead pipe because that violinist dared to play a Richard Strauss piece in concert in Israel. . . . Is this not the Brown Shirts of the thirties once more, or is it not?

When a Jewish fanatic friend of mine calls me a "gentile" I simply say, "Call me a *goy* and let it go at that." Because, if I am a "gentile," then two thousand years of evolution in human thought has been abandoned.

And if he won't ride in my VW—which was probably made in New York, not Germany, and was certainly, for sure, sold me by a Jewish person, Leon Felton of San Rafael—then I will not allow him to eat a bagel in my presence. (I am, of course, joking; I am trying to show this: That we can no more hold a people responsible than we can hold any other mythical, semantic, nonactual entity responsible; German$_1$ is not German$_2$ and German$_2$ is not German$_3$ and so forth. Just as, in this country, you and I did not bomb those little Negro schoolchildren in that church Sunday school . . . you know goddamn well we did not, and if we, you and I, could catch the white bastards—or rather just plain bastards—who did it, we would work just as much and quick vengeance on them as any Negro mob would or could.)

I am not a "white man." My German friends are not "Germans," nor my Jewish friends "Jews." I am a nominalist. To me, there are only individual entities, not group entities such as race, blood, people, etc. For example, I am an Anglo-Catholic; yet my views differ from those of my vicar, and his do—enormously—from the bishop of the diocese—whose views *I* happen to agree with, Bishop Pike. And so forth.

I will not walk out of a room when a German enters any more than I would have walked out of a room when a Jew entered. Nor will I allow myself to be a "gentile"—i.e., a member of a *race*—to my Jewish friends. If they don't like me, let them hit *me*, as an individual, one right in the eye; let's see them hit a race—as the Nazis tried to do—one right in the eye. It won't work; the Nazis failed: Israel exists, and Jews exist. And—let us face it: Germany exists. Let's live in the present and for the future, not dwelling neurotically on the outrages of the past. Ludwig von Beethoven did not light the fires at Dachau. Leonard Bernstein did not hit that Jewish violinist on the hand with a piece of lead pipe. Okay? And *salve*, as the Romans used to say. Or, as we Anglo-Catholics say, may the peace and love of God be with you. Germans included. And, please, Jews, too.

"Biographical Material
on Hawthorne Abendsen" (1974)

I am, of course, one of Mr. Abendsen's admirers; my own works, such as they are, have been influenced strongly by his, in particular my novel *Man in the High Castle* (Berkley Books, U.S.A., 1974 [a reprint paperback edition]).

It goes without saying that *The Grasshopper Lies Heavy* (its German title, *Schwer Liegt die Heuschrecke* [München: Konig Verlag, 1974] is perhaps more familiar to us) has become Hawthorne Abendsen's most renowned book, although "underground" both in printing and distribution, due to its political and religious nature. Although *Grasshopper* offended the Authorities, they themselves studied it with keen professional intent, for it outlines major historic "possibilities" of an "alternate world," of a sort familiar to SF readers, in which the Axis is not favorably described, thus causing Mr. Abendsen and his family to seek an uneasy and certainly temporary sanctuary in the Rocky Mountain states between the two more militant zones of the United States, partitioned off by treaty after the defeat of the Communist-Plutocrat Alliance.

Further writing by Mr. Abendsen, who lives as modest and conventional a family life as possible, in view of his vulnerability to police reprisal for his famous underground novel in which the Axis *lost* the war, is meager; most appear in the form of hasty letters printed in nonprofit "fanzines," as they are called, outside the United States—for obvious reasons.

The Two Completed Chapters
of a Proposed Sequel to
The Man in the High Castle (1964)

ONE

On the morning of August fifth, 1956, Reichsmarshal Hermann Göring flew north from the big Luftwaffe base located at Miami, Florida. He had not wakened in a good mood; on his mind, like an iron press, rested the recent memory of the Little *Doktor*'s appointment as chancellor of Germany and all German-occupied territory. And when one ponders, Göring thought, it was after all my bombers that defeated England and won for us the war; the Ministry of Propaganda did nothing more than whip up and excoriate the people to a useless but fashionable enthusiasm.

Below him the *Gau* of Virginia passed; his R-15 Messerschmitt rocket flew low enough for him to glimpse black specks: slaves working the fields in the God-ordained manner, both timeless and circular. It appealed to reason and to good sense. But nothing could please him today.

He had not properly anticipated the death of the old chancellor, Bormann. Others had, as, for example, Goebbels himself—not to mention the eager eggheads in the higher SS. Keeping politically alert, however, had not benefited the Reichsführer SS, Reinhardt Heydrich, who chafed, fumed, and wrote many memos at his permanent headquarters on Prinz-Albrechtstrasse, home in Berlin. I wonder what he intends? the Reichsmarshal mused. Supposedly a concentration of Waffen-SS troops and armor, specifically the Leibstandarte Division, commanded by old, dependable Sepp Dietrich, had gathered in order to protect Heydrich from removal—Dr. Goebbels had certainly by now considered that—and in addition to threaten the party, should it fish for a loyalty oath to the new chancellor by the generals, something Bormann had been unable to do. And then, meditating, he wondered once again if he had been wise to leave the Miami Luftwaffe base, his center of protection throughout the current crisis. After all, Baldur von Scherach, the head of the Hitler Youth, had been arrested on Goebbels' order. But Goebbels had been jealous of von Scherach since the success of Project Farmland: the draining of the Mediterranean. The project—Scherach's one achievement—had been popular with the masses whom Goebbels appealed to, so there lay a conflict of interests . . . resolved a few days ago by von Sherach's arrest.

Of course, in a showdown the Wehrmacht had an advantage: possession, solely and exclusively, of the hydrogen bomb. For years the SS had sent its agents skulking about army installations, trying to learn enough to build a nuclear reactor of their own. Evidently they had failed. But any government, representing either the party or the SS—or a third force, perhaps a coalition—would need the generals, in particular the support of the supreme wartime field marshal, General Rommel, living now in retirement, but still vigorous. And still hating the party and the SS for his removal as Military Governor of German-occupied America a few years after Capitulation Day—a day that he believed in his arrogant ignorance he had personally brought about at Cairo. Whereas the knocking out of the English radar network by the Luftwaffe had achieved the victory, as every German schoolboy knew.

The autopilot of the R-15 bleeped, indicating that he had reached his destination, Albany, New York.

I hope, he thought, that Fritz Sacher has come up with proof of his contention. If so, I will reward him. The reward, carefully wrapped in cloth, lay in the rear compartment of the ship: a great bottle containing a uniquely deformed fetus, the product of medical experiments carried out by Dr. Seyss-Inquart. The father had been a Slav, the mother a Negress. The fetus, worked on by Seyss-Inquart's staff during its development in the womb, had a foot where its head should have been and eyes at the end of its feet. Only this one existed, and it had been part of the Reichsmarshal's collection of more than a hundred genetic sports. It was in fact the best. But pleasing Fritz Sacher came before the pride of collecting, at least if the research scientist's claims could be believed.

An armed patrol with dogs kept watch along the perimeter of Sacher's

New York estate, but it was through secrecy that the operation protected itself. Luftwaffe funds supported it; hence his knowledge. The Abwehr, Naval Counterintelligence, supplied men and so Admiral Canaris knew, too. He was not therefore surprised when, upon climbing from the R-15, he found both Sacher and Canaris waiting for him.

Puffing with the exertion of descending the rungs of his ship, Göring said, "I brought you a *Wunderkind*, Herr Sacher." He eyed Admiral Canaris, whom he did not like. "Nothing for you."

"*Der Dicke* [the Fat One] emulates the Japanese," Canaris said to no one in particular. "The giving of gifts. Ceremony." He examined his watch. "I'd like to get started." He started from the field, into the building that had once been a governor's mansion in the prewar days when America had governed itself.

"Try and guess the deformity of this," Göring said, reaching up to grasp the bulky, cloth-wrapped bottle.

"Who knows you're here, Reichsmarshal?" Sacher asked. "Anyone in the SS? We're especially concerned about the SS."

"Only my own people," Göring answered as he lifted down the bottle and held it out to the young scientist Sacher. "This one is novel; it will give you quite a lift."

Accepting the bottle, Sacher said, "Many thanks, Reichsmarshal. Your collection of enormities is well known. I remember as a schoolchild touring your villa near Brenner and seeing . . ." He had by now unwrapped the bottle. "A cephalopedalis. Well. How nice." He stared fixedly at the fetus floating gradually to the bottom of the bottle. "Must be worth at least a thousand *Reichsmarks* at home; even more here. I have as yet created no real collection myself; only a few—"

"Can we get started?" Admiral Canaris called sharply.

They entered the building. Göring and Canaris followed the white-robed research scientist down a hallway and into a large room that, the Reichsmarshal guessed, had once been a dining room. The two men sat at a table with papers and objects before them, neither of them particularly distinguished-looking; they both seemed ill-at-ease, and when they made out the Reichsmarshal they rose awkwardly in respect.

"These are the surviving members of the twelve-man *Kommando* group originally sent through our nexus," Sacher said. "That is now eighteen months ago that we first became aware of the parallel universe, which we then called *die Nebenwelt*, because it borders this, and is beside it constantly, plus being available by means of a weak spot, such as exists here. Such we have known the entire eighteen months. Now we can present accurate specifics relating to this *Nebenwelt*, and it is for this presentation, Herr Reichsmarshal, that Admiral Canaris and yourself have been asked to meet with me here. I introduce Herr Kohler and Herr Seligsohn to you; they will speak briefly on their encounter."

"I am Kohler," the shorter of the two men explained. Beside him his companion self-consciously reseated himself. In a squeaky, untrained voice Kohler continued, "We with others of our *Kommando* unit who survived the crossing from here to that world but who did not also survive the crossing back, as we did, lived ordinary lives in the *Nebenwelt* for virtually a year and a half, speaking the English language with facility, it being the language of this geographical area in that universe. We found it to be a reasonably satisfactory milieu, but overrun with Jews. We inquired, via the public library and through accidental contacts, as to why that would be, and also why English and not German dominates as the spoken and written language. As we had anticipated before our crossing—as Herr Sacher originally theorized—the *Nebenwelt* constitutes an alternate Earth to ours in which the Rome-Berlin-Tokyo Axis mishandled the war and allowed the Allied Nations of Communism and Plutocracy a victory by default. Because of this, America remains a number one Jew State, and the Bolsheviks control half the world, the other half; they have divided the world between them, as Dr. Goebbels predicted in event of an Axis defeat."

There was silence, then. No one spoke as the Reichsmarshal and Admiral Canaris pondered.

"Did you manage," Canaris asked presently, "to make out specifically why their war miscarried?"

Irritably, Göring said, "What does that matter? Technical details; for academic scholars." To Sacher he said, "Your *Nebenwelt* is a hallucination, a phantasm. It isn't real, not like this." He rapped his knuckles noisily against a nearby case filled with scientific texts.

Kohler said, "We brought back artifactual documentation."

"Faked," Göring said bitingly.

"It is up to me to determine that," Admiral Canaris pointed out. He walked to the table, bent to scrutinize the assembled papers and objects. "Why do you reject this idea ad hoc, Reichsmarshal?" He glanced inquiringly at Göring. "Is it that you can't conceive of this? As Herr Kohler says, we've known of it—at least theoretically—for a year and a half. You've had a long time to digest the idea, and now we have material brought back by men who've been living there. *I* find it intriguing." He picked up a massive book from the desk, thumbed through it intently. "But, of course, disturbing." He eyed Kohler, who remained doggedly on his feet, unwilling to back down. "We have here something called *The Rise and Fall of the Third Reich*, by William Shirer." Glancing at Kohler, he said, "I gather this will answer as to the 'technical details.' " His voice was withering.

"The period up to 1945," Kohler agreed, nodding. "I have read it several times; it is complete, absolutely the best I could find there. At several bookstores in New York I asked and was told this volume is totally comprehensive; it is certainly not one I selected at random." His voice rang with conviction. "And it certainly is not faked."

Sacher said, "While waiting for you, Admiral, and you, Reichsmarshal, to arrive here"—he took the book from Canaris, opened to a marked place—"I personally examined this. Let me read you."

"Just tell us," Canaris said.

"Their history," Sacher said, "apparently diverged from ours in the early thirties. President Roosevelt was *not* successfully assassinated and was in office in 1941 when America entered the war against the Axis."

"Bricker never became president?" Canaris said alertly.

"No, Herr Admiral." Sacher shook his head.

"In prosecuting the war," Kohler said, "Field Marshal Rommel failed to take Cairo and therefore never managed to link up with the German army coming down from Russia. Nor did the German army break the Russian lines; at a town called Stalingrad on the Volga the Communist hordes counterattacked and destroyed our entire Sixth Army corps."

Beside him Herr Seligsohn murmured, "And"—he did not look directly at Göring—"the Luftwaffe concentrated on bombing civilian population centers in Britain and did not put out of action their radar network. So, consequently, no invasion of the British Isles took place."

"Toward the end of the war," Kohler said, "the Anglo-Saxon powers developed the atomic bomb. The Jew Einstein suggested it in a letter to Roosevelt, although himself born in Germany; he betrayed his homeland."

Göring said, "Germany is not a homeland for any Jew."

Drily, Canaris said, "Herr Einstein seems to have agreed."

"They brought back material," Sacher said, "on the condition of Germany as it is now. It has been divided between the Anglo-Saxon powers and Communist Russia. Split in half, no longer a nation." He added, "Japan is as of this date a satellite of the United States. And communism has spread throughout the Orient; specifically into China." His voice was stony, impersonal, a mere recitation of facts without emotion. "It becomes evident how vital the assassination of Roosevelt was in shaping our world. If any one single event could be said to have—"

"I would be interested in knowing," Göring broke in, "how our great wartime Field Marshal Erwin Rommel, who lead us to victory in '47, fared in this so-called *Nebenwelt*. I cannot imagine him in defeat."

"After the loss of North Africa," Kohler said, "the field marshal was transferred to France to take command of the forces awaiting invasion from England. While en route by car he was spotted by a British Spitfire and machine-gunned, hence hospitalized. He did not command during the invasion of Festung Europa at its West Wall." He paused. And then in a low voice said, "There is more."

"Well?" Göring demanded.

"Field Marshal Rommel joined a group of traitors conspiring against the life of Adolf Hitler."

"That could never be," Göring said.

"Wait," Canaris said, gesturing tensely. "Let him finish."

"The plot failed," Kohler said. "The conspirators were strangled and hung from meathooks, which is appropriate. Erwin Rommel, being a soldier and former patriot, was allowed to shoot himself. He so did."

Again there was silence, long and strained.

"I think," Göring said at last, "that these so-called 'artifactual documentations' are forgeries put together by the Abwehr." He studied Admiral Canaris, trying to penetrate the slightly ironic mask that had, at his words, slid in place. "The motivation, however, is unclear to me. Obviously in part it is to slander the field marshal. The rest I do not understand." He made his voice harsh and affirmative, but inwardly he felt doubt, confusion. He needed time to digest all of this. Certainly this trumped-up "disclosure" related to the current political crisis in the Reich's politics; that much was clear. Intuitively he sensed that Admiral Canaris and his counterintelligence organization had engineered the venture; after all, Kohler and Seligsohn were Abwehr agents, as had been the entire *Kommando* squad.

And yet—it appeared true that an alternate universe did exist, as Sacher had, for a year and a half, declared. That much we did not dispute. If only he could send some of his own Luftwaffe people, loyal to him . . .

"I hasten to add, Herr Reichsmarshal," Kohler said, "that the decision to bomb English cities and not the radar network was not yours but the Führer's." He peered hopefully at Göring.

Pacing about, his arms folded, Admiral Canaris said, half to himself, "For several minutes now I have been thinking of something odd. In Japanese-controlled regions, specifically the Rocky Mountain states and the PSA, a book has been circulating; it is banned here, but my office has routinely examined it. They say it's very popular among the Japanese, for reasons I do not understand. It is a work of fiction, pure fiction, or at least so we have up to now supposed."

"The Grasshopper Lies Heavy," Göring said. He had read it; the ban on reading Hawthorne Abendsen's book did, of course, not apply to him. "A narrative of the world as it would be today if the Allied powers had won the war."

Canaris said, "And also an analysis of how the Allied Powers could have won. They could have won, this Abendsen alleges, if the Soviet Union had stopped General von Paulus at Stalingrad. Abendsen bases his fictional world specifically on that." Turning to Sacher he said, "This is a historical condition reported by these two *Kommandos*; this occurred in *Nebenwelt*, so it would appear to me that Abendsen's book is an account of *Nebenwelt*."

"Not quite," Kohler said. "Both Seligsohn and myself are familiar with Abendsen's book; there is a vague resemblance between the world he describes and the environment studied by us over the past eighteen months. But many details vary. The relationship fails to be precise. By example, in the book Rexford Tugwell is president at the time America enters the war; in *Nebenwelt*, Roosevelt still—"

"But Abendsen," Canaris persisted, "seems to have had at least a diffuse awareness of the *Nebenwelt*. Even if details differ, the resemblance is basic; to ignore it would be politically unwise."

"Why unwise?" Göring said.

Canaris gestured. "It means that Sacher has no monopoly as to access to *Nebenwelt*. If one man, Hawthorne Abendsen, is aware of it, then others can be—have already been, perhaps. We don't have the undivided control over egress that we need."

"Need for what?" Göring said. He had never been able to fathom the admiral's convoluted thinking, typical as it was of intelligence reasoning.

A veiled expression appeared on the admiral's face. Obviously choosing his words with care, he said, "Any military operation planned by the army would now of necessity be shelved—in view of this."

"Why?" Göring said, still not following. "What military undertaking is planned?" He thought at once of the space program, the colonization of Venus and Mars. So far, the Wehrmacht had stayed aloof; emigration had been handled solely by the SS. He wondered if at last the army intended to participate. Certainly it would help; so far the SS had signally failed to round up sufficient numbers of genetically adequate human specimens.

Canaris, however, switched to another area of the topic; slippery and deft, he eluded even a direct question. "A point-by-point comparison between Abendsen's imaginary alternate world and the *Nebenwelt* should be developed. I would like to know exactly how they compare and differ." He gestured. "It may be what the Japanese call synchronicity, a meaningless coincidence. Or rather what our own physicist Wolfgang Pauli calls synchronicity; I forget that the acausal connective concept is of German origin." He scowled. "It is their use of that damn oracle that confuses me, that *I Ching* they employ in the making of every decision. Fortunately the party has rejected it as degenerate oriental mysticism."

"The oracle," Kohler said, "exists in the *Nebenwelt*; we encountered it several times, although there is—we found—no widespread use. It does not appear at all in Abendsen's book, in the world he depicts."

"Another difference," Canaris said thoughtfully. He seemed for a time to chew on this point. "If we were to believe in the oracle," he said at last, "then we would suppose it to know of the existence of the *Nebenwelt*, inasmuch [as] it can be found there. Abendsen, I have read, makes use of the oracle; I understand, in fact, he plotted his book by means of the hexagrams. That might account for the resemblance of his fictional world to the *Nebenwelt.* But consider the hazard involved—the hazard to Germany. The oracle is attempting to inform those who rely on it that . . ." He broke off, again scowling. "I'm talking about it as if it were alive."

Göring said, "We did well to ban it in German-occupied territory. I remember how emphatic Dr. Goebbels was on that issue; he foamed at the mouth when that modern composer—what was his name?—declared in print that he used it to develop chord progressions."

"The Little *Doktor* foams at the mouth about everything he fails to understand," Canaris said.

"Who understands the oracle?" Göring asked. "Not even those who rely on it. Except for Pauli's theory of synchronicity there is no hypothesis for its operation at all. Except the ancient Chinese idea that invisible spirits determine which hexagram turns up." The subject bored him and he returned to the matter that had brought him here to Albany. "Sacher," he said briskly, "it is vital to Germany's internal and external security that the availability of the *Nebenwelt* be kept confidential. We can't throttle speculation because Abendsen's book has already raised the issue publicly; even in Germany most intellectuals are aware of its general outline, without, of course, having read it. Unfortunately it is not necessary to have read it; to know of its existence is enough. You understand what I mean." For the masses to speculate on another way of life, an existence minus German hegemony—that breached the unconditional identification with the *Gemeinschaft,* the folk community created back in '32 by the party and now half a world wide. The writer Hawthorne Abendsen had, by his book, done great harm, and all the machinery of the secret police, the Sicherheitsdienst, had not managed to keep bootlegged copies of *The Grasshopper* from showing up in such central *Gaus* as Berlin itself. In Hamburg especially, knowledge of—and possession of—the book defied the state security apparatus, vigilant as it continued to be.

We should have Abendsen picked up, Göring pondered. Seized by an SD Einsatz Gruppe and brought in for expert interrogation. I will call Heydrich about that, he decided, as soon as I'm out of here. Surprising that the Reichsführer SS has done nothing in that direction already.

Kohler said, "Shall I continue my description of the *Nebenwelt,* as well as explaining these artifactual documents?" He indicated the heap of items on his and Seligsohn's table.

"Do so," Göring said, and bent an ear to listen to the elaborate circumstantial report of another world, a mystifying universe in which the Axis had lost—unbelievably—the Second World War.

TWO

In the mirror-polished Daimler phaeton sedan the SS men who had met Captain Rudolf Wegener at Tempelhof Airfield chatted amiably as the car neared SS GHQ on Prinz-Albrechstrasse, where the crack Black Shirt division, Sepp Dietrich's Leibstandarte, had bivouacked itself with the expectation of successfully waiting out the great current crisis in domestic German affairs. Now Wegener could perceive the huge Tiger tanks of the division deployed strategically here and there, their 88mm cannons covering each intersection and building.

The show of military strength did not impress him. One tactical hydrogen bomb, lobbed by a Wehrmacht mortar, would erase the division of SS men and Heydrich himself. The Hangman, however, probably felt psychologically secure: The SS mentality thrived on the ostentatious display of finely executed, parade-style maneuvers such as these cordons of gleaming tanks.

When he had been escorted into Heydrich's big office he found the Reichsführer SS on the telephone.

"We already sent someone to do that," Heydrich was saying in his harsh, monotonous voice as he stared blankly through Wegener. "He wound up killed in a hotel room in Denver. His throat. Yes, someone slashed it. Yes, he was very close to reaching the Jew Abendsen." A pause. "No, he wasn't going to bring him here; why do that? What's he got to say besides what he said in his book?" Another pause, longer this time. "If you want him brought here," Heydrich said finally, "you'll have to tell me why. We're not an adjunct to the Luftwaffe. Okay, send someone yourself. Bomb him. Good-bye." Heydrich hung up, jotted a note on a pad of paper, then inclined his head to indicate a leather-covered chair placed before his desk. "The Reichsmarshal," he explained to Wegener, "all four hundred kilos of him. Sit down. You're the Abwehr man who's been in the Pacific States of America." He spread out fanwise a collection of folios, rummaged, and at last selected one, which he opened. "I've been reading about you. Did you enjoy the way the Japs run things? Slipshod, wouldn't you say? Of course, things aren't much better here, what with that nasty little crippled gutter rat Goebbels sneaking in as chancellor— temporarily. He'd kill us all in our beds while we slept. That's why I had you met at the airport."

"I appreciated it," Wegener said woodenly.

"In our opinion," Heydrich rattled away, "Bormann was murdered. So in no regard is Goebbels legal chancellor. Several SS lawyers have drawn up briefs for me to that effect. An election will have to be held, with all party members voting. The new leader of Germany must come from the party ranks, as Hitler originally intended. Goebbels, even if legally appointed, is too old—as are all the *Altparteigenosse*. I, of course, do not fit in that category."

"Not in the slightest," Wegener agreed.

"Did you make much headway as to informing the Japs about Operation Dandelion? Was General Tedeki interested?"

"I—know nothing about it," Wegener said.

"But you went there to inform the Japanese that we are on the verge of attacking them." Irritably, Heydrich said in a sharp voice, as if speaking to a foreigner, "Operation Dandelion—the attack on Japan. Your mission; you posed as a Swedish businessman." He leafed through the dossier. "You left Tempelhofer Field in one of those new Lufthanse 9-E rockets, under the name of Baynes. An SD agent talked with you en route; he gave the name Alex Lotze and pretended to be a painter; you pretended to be in plastics and polyesters. At the San Francisco airport you were met by a delegate from the ranking Jap Trade Mission, a Mr. Nobusuke Tagomi. A day later at his office in the *Nippon Times* Building the retired Chief of Staff of the Japanese Imperial Army, General Tedeki, met with the two of you and you informed him of the imminent attack on the home islands by the Wehrmacht—a surprise attack that the Japanese secret police, the Tokkoka, had no knowledge of."

Wegener said, "This is all new to me, this information."

"Balls," Heydrich said impatiently. "In fact, during your conference with General Tedeki and Mr. Tagomi, a squad of SD men attempted to force their way in and kill the three of you." He added, "They failed."

After a pause Wegener said huskily, "Mr. Tagomi is a good shot. He collects pistols of the U.S. Civil War and practices firing them."

"We wondered what happened. Bruno Kreuz von Meere, who is the

San Francisco head of the SD, theorized that it had been Kempeitai marksmen—the Japanese civil police—who had waited either outside or within Tagomi's office. Hmm; so Tagomi took care of Kreuz von Meere's men himself." He nodded, apparently glad to see the mystery cleared up. "So you betrayed your country. Is the entire Abwehr involved, or was it only you? What about Admiral Canaris himself?"

"He knows nothing about my trip," Wegener said, wondering if Heydrich had in his possession information to the contrary. The Reichsführer SS seemed to know everything else; why not this?

Heydrich, however, dropped the point; he turned to another topic. "In the Pacific States, did you encounter that Jew book in which our war effort fails? That *Grasshopper* book?"

"It's available there," Wegener said abstractly.

"You heard me talking to the Reichsmarshal; they want me to snatch Abendsen and bring him here, for reasons they won't divulge." Heydrich eyed Wegener intently. "We understand that a joint project exists in Albany, New York, in which your organization and the Luftwaffe are involved. Do you personally know anything about that?"

"No," he said, truthfully.

"As far as we can determine," Heydrich said, "this project is operating under the assumption that paralled worlds exist, of which we are one and Abendsen's world, written about as if imaginary fiction, is another. What success Sacher—he heads the project—has obtained we don't know. Perhaps none. The premise may be false. Or"—Heydrich gestured— "enough success to prove the premise, but not enough to open actually a doorway to another parallel world." He ticked the possibilities off methodically, using his fingers. "Or they have found a passageway through, but the other world—the *Nebenwelt*, I understand they call it—is not that which the Jew Abendsen depicts in his pseudo-fictional book. There are other possibilities." He reflected. "At most they have been able to reach several other worlds, of which Abendsen's is one."

"Hmm," Wegener said.

"What interests is that all at once the Reichsmarshal is interested in having Abendsen—not killed—but abducted and brought here; brought, specifically, to the Reichsmarshal's pro tem headquarters at the Luftwaffe base in Miami." Heydrich studied his extended fingers, then selected one. "This suggests that they wish to interrogate Abendsen regarding his

Grasshopper world . . . which further suggests to me that they have had some luck." He raised his eyes, regarded Wegener acutely. "Are you sure you know nothing about this? You're an Abwehr agent, and the Abwehr, we hear, is supplying the agents that Sacher means to—or has already, perhaps—"

"All my recent time," Wegener broke in, "has been spent in preparation for my visit to the PSA, now completed. There's no use talking to me; I can't help you. Up to now I haven't even heard of this project, presuming, as you say, it exists." It sounded doubtful to him: more like an imaginative fabrication by the brilliant, deranged minds of the higher SS, Heydrich included.

"Consider this, then," Heydrich said, folding his hands and tilting his chair back until he rested against the wall behind his desk. "You are legally a traitor to Germany; you deliberately and systematically carried top-secret military information to our enemy, directly to the Japanese general staff. Without a convocation of the Reichsgericht I could have you garroted and hung from a meathook. I could have your testicles crushed first, by means of pliers. I could have a solution of lye forced up your—"

"Your agency," Wegener said, managing to keep his voice reasonably steady, "can do nothing to an agent of Naval Counterintelligence. If I have to stand trial it will be a military court-martial, presided over by my superiors in the Abwehr."

"You want to bet?"

Wegener said, "I know for a certainty that your agency, in fact the entire SS, opposes Operation Dandelion. By your own statement you had me followed; you knew what I came for before I managed to meet with General Tedeki; you could have stopped me."

"We attempted to," Heydrich said smoothly. "At the *Nippon Times* Building."

"What's your point?"

Heydrich said, "You are, at this moment, at the dead center of the Waffen-SS division Leibstandarte. There is no way anyone, from the Abwehr or the Wehrmacht or the party or all three, could get you out of here. So if you transact any business it must be with me, and I am hard to do business with, which you may have heard. In this dossier on you"—he indicated the papers spread out on his desk—"details and documentation of your treason are laid out. Right now it is a very much open file, but I have the authority, despite all it contains, to make it perpetually inactive. No SD men will show up at 5:00 A.M. and cart you off to a final solution camp; no *Nacht und Nebel* [Night and Fog] action will ever take place in your direction—I guarantee it. In fact, I will make you an honorary colonel in the Waffen-SS; General Dietrich himself will bestow the citation on you." Heydrich picked up a phone receiver from his desk and said, "Get me Sepp Dietrich."

"I'm familiar with the mechanism," Wegener said. "I'm not interested." As soon as he became an honorary colonel in the SS he would be automatically under SS jurisdiction, taking his orders from Heydrich or even someone lower down in Heydrich's apparatus. Over the years innumerable Wehrmacht officers had received such commissions, without being aware of the consequences. Instant SS men, he thought grimly. Created by a stroke of Heydrich's pen.

Shrugging, Heydrich said, hanging up the phone, "It's up to you if you want to remain a captain in an organization that probably won't exist one year from now. Admiral Canaris has been skating over thin ice for years; it's only a question of time before he falls through . . . dragging the rest of you down with him."

"What is it you want me to do?" Wegener asked. "In exchange for letting me out of here?"

"Not merely 'letting you out.' In addition, as I explained, we'll guarantee your continual safety—from reprisals, for example, by your organization. To be protected by the SD is to be virtually beyond reach; you'll find yourself sleeping at night again, peacefully, and in these times of unpredictable political conflict that will be anomalous. I want you to do this: You will report back to your superiors in the Abwehr and give a report of your mission to San Francisco without mentioning your side trip here. You landed at Tempelhofer; you took a cab to Abwehr GHQ. All uneventful."

"And from then on," Wegener said, "I'm to report regularly to you or one of your subordinates about Sacher's project."

Heydrich eyed him.

"I may never get near Sacher's project," Wegener said.

"You'll hear talk. *We* have heard talk, and we have yet to penetrate Canaris' organization . . . until perhaps now. I'm not in a hurry; I agree that it will take time. Just so long as the information comes to us eventually. *Verstehst du?*"

"I understand you," Wegener said. He pondered, then decided to take a calculated risk. "You won't kill me," he said, "because it's to your advantage that I informed General Tedeki about Operation Dandelion. You'll make use of this as ammunition to persuade the party not to back the Wehrmacht; a surprise attack is now out of the question, and we all know that even though the Japanese lack the hydrogen bomb, they do have enormous intercept hardware. Even if the home islands are destroyed, their Chinese regions, their Manchukuo colony, the Philippines, the Pacific States of America, their holdings in Latin America—"

"I am familiar with the geography of the East Asia Co-Prosperity Sphere," Heydrich said drily.

"Plus the fact," Wegener said, "that the guidance systems of our missiles are imperfect—notoriously so. For example, we are familiar with our missile performance in Africa. Several years—"

"The guidance systems have been improved since then."

Wegener said, "You'll require my continued existence because I'm the only German national who knows from direct contact that the Japanese general staff is aware of Operation Dandelion. Without me, all that exists is your dossier on me, which could be faked. Or so the Wehrmacht generals will argue. In particular, Rommel."

"The field marshal is in retirement." Heydrich added, "And old."

"It is planned to restore him into service." The Abwehr had learned this several months ago. "He will, in fact, be made the highest military commander in the operation; as is well known, his unique strategic sense has not since been equaled. And his presence will make the campaign considerably more popular with the people, who regard him an *Übermensch*. The only hero of modern times; one would have to go back to Hindenburg."

"Or Adolf Hitler."

"Hitler's legendary reputation as a strategist has dimmed. The Wehrmacht knew his failings at the time; most of the German people know them now. As I'm sure you realize. You do keep tabs on such matters."

"It was the peresis of the brain," Heydrich said hotly. "If the Ur-Führer had not contracted that disease during his youthful days in Vienna, that Jew town—"

Rising to his feet, Wegener said, "This discussion, as far as I am concerned, is over. I am required to report back to my superiors as to my accomplishments. *Guten Tag.*"

Also standing, the Reichsführer SS started to speak. But then the intercom system on his desk buzzed. "Yes?" he said, depressing a key.

"General Skorzany to see you, sir," the intercom said.

"All right. Send him in." Heydrich folded his arms, rocked back and forth on his heels, reflecting.

A burly, gray-haired man, reasonably good-looking, with wary, intelligent eyes, wearing the uniform of a Waffen-SS general, entered Heydrich's office. He glanced at Wegener, sizing him up, then turned inquiringly to the Reichsführer SS.

To Wegener, Heydrich said, "Turn my suggestions over in your mind. For a time I will suspend any action vis-à-vis your activities recently in the Pacific States. I'll be in touch with you before the end of the week and I hope a favorable decision will occur to you. Keep it in mind that your position is not good."

Part Four

Plot Proposals and Outlines

This section contains examples of Dick at work sketching out his ideas—lucidly, and with a penchant both for dramatic possibilities and cognitive paradoxes—for the consideration of agents, editors, and potential television and film producers. All four of the selections date from the late 1960s, the only period in his life in which Dick seriously attempted to break into writing for television. (One of his finest early short stories, "Colony," had been adapted, in 1956, for the X *Minus One* radio program, devoted to SF dramatizations.) There is no evidence that he gained even the interested attention of anyone in that industry. The lure to attempt to do so may have stemmed from the success of certain of his SF peers, such as Harlan Ellison and Theodore Sturgeon, in placing scripts with the original *Star Trek* series.

The novel outline "Joe Protagoras Is Alive and Living on Earth" (1967) was first published posthumously in *New Worlds* #2, edited by David Garnett (Gollancz, London, 1992).

"Plot Idea for *Mission: Impossible*" (1967) and "TV Series Idea" (1967) have never before been published.

"Notes on *Do Androids Dream of Electric Sheep?*" (1968) was first published posthumously in *PKDS Newsletter*, No. 18 (August 1988). The notes were written for the benefit of Bertram Berman, a filmmaker who had, in that year, obtained a first option on the just released Dick novel *Do Androids Dream of Electric Sheep?* (1968). This novel was ultimately adapted (with no involvement by Berman) into the acclaimed film *Blade Runner* (1982). Dick was able to see some of the early rushes of that film before his death in 1982, and was decidedly enthusiastic. In an earlier stage of the production of *Blade Runner*, however, Dick was displeased with the then quality of the script (subsequently rewritten, to Dick's liking, by David Peoples) and vented his displeasure in "Universe Makers . . . and Breakers" (1981), included earlier in this volume. It is interesting to compare Dick's notes here with the film version of the novel—*Blade Runner*—that ultimately emerged.

"Joe Protagoras Is Alive
and Living on Earth" (1967)

Theme: A revolution which has brought forth conditions less favorable than the dictator planned. He is asked to resign in favor of an aspirant who says he can do better. But a group opposed to the aspirant takes the dictator into an alternate Earth where the aspirant, not the dictator, has ruled. Conditions are much worse. In fact, all the alternate worlds are worse. The aspirant ponders; he knows about this group and what they are doing. Solution: Aspirant has a team cross into alternate world and create fake fakes here and there, very subtle in character, which, when dictator finds them, will convince him that this *whole* alternate world is faked. So far, so good. But aspirant now goes too far: He plans out *entire* faked world (alternate Earth), where he rules superlatively. Aspirant knows that the dictator will be suspicious, will look for flaws, but aspirant is sure he can bring it off. Next step: What would group loyal to the dictator (the group who took him to real alternate worlds) do? They don't need to plant fake fakes in the "good alternative" because it's already wholly faked!

Plot: Joe Protagoras has a puny job—but in the overpopulated and economically malfunctioning socialist world of 2007 he is lucky to have any job at all. However, he has been saving up a sum of money by which to consult Mr. Job. This peculiar entity, with tens of thousands of outlets throughout Earth and its planetary colonies, is virtually alive, although artificial, and is important in the lives of Earth's hordes of jobless and near-jobless citizens. Mr. Job can tell Protagoras, after an analysis of his aptitudes and experience, where he can find a genuinely adequate career appointment; Mr. Job, through its network of multiple extensors, keeps computer-style tabs on all job openings everywhere. But consulting Mr. Job is expensive. Protagoras hasn't much "real" money saved up (i.e., metal coins, in contrast with the nearly worthless inflationary scrip floated by the government), but he can't wait any longer (among other things, his girlfriend is putting pressure on him). He accordingly enters one of Mr. Job's many booths (like a telephone booth), dials his facts in, drops his precious coins into the slot. He gets back a cryptic sentence-and-a-half: "Your twenty words are up," Mr. Job tells him, and then clicks off. Joe Protagoras leaves the booth, trying to decipher the oraclelike message, and at this point the novel shifts to its other main character.

Simon Herrlich, the ancient, tottering despot, has kept himself alive by means of artificial organs for far too many years—and has kept himself in Earth's top office at the same time. He is ill-liked by his heir, an ambitious aspirant named Arthur Self. For years, Self has been trying to persuade the Old Man to bow out voluntarily and hence turn everything over to him, i.e., to the younger, more virile Art Self. It is Self's contention that if he had been ruling all this time, Earth would be in better shape economically, politically, and socially—if not spiritually (i.e., ideologically, this being a totalitarian state).

From Self's viewpoint we learn about Project Almost, the breaking through to and investigation of alternate Earths. We learn about the scientist in charge of operating the inter-Earth project: Nick Edel, a close associate and good friend of Simon Herrlich—a man whom Self hates because it is Nick Edel who is, by means of his project, keeping Herrlich in office . . . inasmuch as all alternate Earths visited are worse than their own.

This section of the novel ends with Self conceiving the idea of sending his own teams across into one of the worst alternate worlds and planting "simulated forgeries"—in other words, fake fakes—with the idea of discrediting Edel's whole project by giving the alternate Earths the appearance of being phony. We see him visiting the REM Corporation, a huge industrial concern owned by the government (which, of course, owns every economic enterprise on Earth, this being a Communist-type society). We now meet Cynthia Stonemerchant, the director of REM Corporation, the elderly widow who manages this vast industrial cartel. She is quite hostile toward the old dictator; she is, in fact, in favor of a non-Communist government, with industries privately owned, as in a capitalist society. Therefore she is glad to have her factories produce the fake fakes that Self wants. Then, together, they hatch out the extraordinary idea of creating an entire fake alternate world, a world that Mrs. Stonemerchant and her technical staff will plan.

Unknown to Self, Mrs. Stonemerchant plans to construct a *capitalist* fake alternate world that is better than their own. She is not merely hostile toward Simon Herrlich; she is hostile toward Art Self as well. She is in fact hostile to their whole totalitarian society, and is doing this job for her own purposes.

We return to Joe Protagoras, who has managed—with the help of his girlfriend—to decipher the sentence-and-a-half that Mr. Job gave him. It is telling him to go to REM Corporation's Los Angeles branch and apply for the job technically listed as 20583-AR . . . a designation that means absolutely nothing to him; he has no idea what the job for which he will be applying consists of. But Mr. Job is never wrong, so Joe Protagoras quits the meager job he has, gathers his few possessions together (he has only a rented room, adequate housing being years away, due to the faulty economics of the government). Going by second-class surface bus, he sets off for Los Angeles.

When he reaches REM Corporation's Los Angeles branch and applies for job 20583-AR he discovers what it is. Designing rides for what is called an "amusement park," something that he has never even heard of. The personnel manager of REM, however, assures him that he is the man for the job (Joe Protagoras has given the personnel manager the same résumé he gave Mr. Job). "You'll do just fine," Mr. Bean assures him, and leads him to his bright, modern, high-class office. He is to begin work right away. Historical texts and technical manuals dealing with amusement parks are already in the office; Joe Protagoras begins to read, and we leave him. But before we return to the schemes of Art Self, we see Protagoras making an interesting inquiry. What is REM Corporation's product? What is his job *for*? He gets no answer from his new superiors; they know but won't tell him. "Just design good, scary, fun rides," he is told. "Pay special attention to Mr. Toad's Wild Ride from the twentieth-century amusement park called Disneyland; that is your prototype. Update it and you'll be on your way."

We of course know what REM Corporation is producing: the fake alternate world supposedly for Self's benefit, but actually for Mrs. Stonemerchant's personal purposes. In any case, Protagoras, the "little" protagonist, is now linked to Art Self, the "big" protagonist, as well as Mrs.

Stonemerchant, the third force at work on the world stage, or rather inter-worlds stage.

At this point all the characters will have been introduced. These are:

Elderly despot: Simon Herrlich

Aspirant: Arthur Self

Director of REM Corporation: Mrs. Cynthia Stonemerchant

Craftsman little protagonist: Joe Protagoras

Girlfriend of Protagoras: Abby Vercelli

Girl, party zealot for Simon Herrlich: Marleen Poole

Hatchetman thug for Herrlich: Patrick O'Connell

Tough goon for REM Corp: Mike Fox

Group of top officials loyal to Herrlich: Calvin Gold, Dan Hastings, Ian Kain

Spy and informer for Art Self: Demeter Troll

Wife (young) of Herrlich: Aulikki Mildmay

The plot continues as follows. Briefly, it's this: While REM Corporation is building the fake capitalist alternate world, Nick Edel's research work-ers *stumble onto a genuine capitalist alternate world.* This pleases no one; that is, neither Art Self nor the old despot (it would please Mrs. Stonemer-chant, of course, but both Herrlich and Self keep this startling informa-tion top-secret). It is a better world than any other alternative—including their own. This is one possibility that neither Self nor Herrlich antici-pated; wrapped up in their Communist ideology, they were absolutely certain that if a capitalist alternate world showed up (which in itself is considered by both of them unlikely), it would, of course, be awful.

Art Self crosses over to it, spends time there skulking about incognito, then returns to his own world. And, back in it, encounters almost at once a fake fake object!

What does this discovery mean? Two hypotheses are possible. (1) It—his own world—is real and someone has planted fake fakes there, as he himself has done in the alternate worlds; for instance, Mrs. Stonemer-chant, who may have learned about the real alternate capitalistic world. Or (2) his own world is entirely fake, and he has a false memory grafted into his brain by someone unknown to him but who is obviously out to destroy him. This someone could be either Herrlich's supporters in the party apparatus or Mrs. Stonemerchant's technicians. Hard to tell.

The maximum host of perplexities is now at its peak; from hereon the plot will unravel.

A. Protagoras is doing a strange sort of task for a purpose he does not know and for a corporation whose product is kept secret from him.

B. Mrs. Stonemerchant may or may not know about the discovery of an authentic capitalistic Earth. If she does find out, what will she do?

C. Art Self has found what appear to be fake fakes in his own world. What does this mean? Who put them there and why? Or is *everything* fake?

D. The old man, Simon Herrlich, has seen his hopes and dreams shattered, here at the end of his life, by the discovery that a capitalistic world would have been—is, in fact—far better than anything he and his world-revolution takeover can come up with. What should he do now? Renounce his own totalitarian society and attempt to bring capitalism back—with Mrs. Stonemerchant's help and that of other industrial directors who share her attitude?

The novel is resolved in this way. A team working for REM Corporation is discovered, by Self's personal police, planting fake fakes in his own world. That answers that. His world is real, and Mrs. Stonemerchant has tried to do to him what he did to Herrlich. Self therefore has his thugs kill Mrs. Stonemerchant (after a heavy pitched battle with her company goons), since he knows for a certainty that she is, in totalitarian jargon, plotting against him, obviously with the idea of undermining their socialist state. However, Mrs. Stonemerchant has made certain arrangements; the instant she dies, an automatic instrument goes into action; it drops into a mail slot many, many copies of a full statement of REM Corporation's activities, its creating of fake fakes at Self's command. This letter is addressed to every powerful official loyal to old Simon Herrlich, and within twenty-four hours the elderly despot learns what Self has been up to.

Self becomes, at once, a hunted criminal in a society where escape from the government police is impossible. He knows he can't escape Herrlich's agent, but at least he can take revenge vis-à-vis REM Corporation—which, he reasons, has brought about his downfall and certain death. He therefore, with all the resources he can muster, attacks REM Corporation's various branches, and, in a matter of hours, reduces most of them to rubble . . . killing the majority of the corporation's employees. Or so he thinks. Actually, Mrs. Stonemerchant had anticipated exactly this; upon her death, REM Corporation's employees began passing across to the alternate capitalist world via a pirated duplicate of Nick Edel's mechanism.

Again the novel focuses on Protagoras, who believes himself safe in this capitalist alternate world. However, he very soon makes a hideous discovery. This is not the authentic alternate capitalist world at all. Something—at least in his case—went wrong. This is the mere partly completed fake that REM Corporation was building for Self up to the time that Mrs. Stonemerchant learned of the existence of the real one. Here he finds, for example, the not yet functioning "rides" that he himself designed: a ghostly, lonely, echoing "amusement park," of which he is the sole patron; he is alone in this ersatz world, with no way to get back out.

The ending is not downbeat, however. REM Corporation has not removed its machinery, the autonomic building rigs by means of which they were constructing this "world." At the end of the book we find Joe Protagoras starting the great elaborate autonomic machines once more into action; if he can't leave this ersatz world, at least he can complete it—make it pleasant and habitable, including the building of ersatz "people" to keep him company. He is emperor of an entire landscape, and he is happy. Of all the major characters, Joe Protagoras came out the best—which the reader will agree is as it should be.

In this ending, the questions What is real? What is illusion? are answered (or anyhow the attempt will be made within the context of the novel). Joe Protagoras has gone from a "real" but unsatisfying world into an "unreal" but satisfying alternate. The test will be purely pragmatic. If this half-completed ersatz world is capable of answering Joe Protagoras' needs, *then it is real*—in the sense that it provides the material out of which he can fashion a reasonably tolerable life. In fact, the issue of "real" versus "unreal" is itself false; the authentic issue is: What will sustain life? What will permit a living organism to function? In answer to this, the ersatz, half-completed world is advantageous, because, among other things, it gives Joe Protagoras a field in which to work creatively (i.e., as he personally completes it). Instead of a bureaucrat he is now an artist, and this ersatz world is the lump of clay out of which he will fashion his own, idiosyncratic reality. Which, we realize, is the finest reality of all.

"Plot Idea for *Mission: Impossible*" (1967)

The mission is to take place in a Latin American country that is an ana-log for present-day Cuba. Formerly a hedonistic, self-serving dictator ruled, but a year or so ago he was overthrown *and killed* by a young, ideal-istic revolutionary. However, this left-wing revolutionary has allied him-self with "the other side"—i.e., the Communist states of Eastern Europe and Asia. The United States would, of course, like to see him deposed, but assassination is out of the question; the revolutionary's followers would know that the CIA had done it, and would become even more fa-natical and anti-West. So the mission is this: to find a way by which the revolutionary leader can be induced to come *voluntarily* to the United States—which will not only remove him from power in his own country but also will undermine the Marxist-oriented followers and demileaders backing him. But how can this be done?

The scheme worked out by the *Mission: Impossible* team is as follows. The revolutionary leader (from hereon referred to as R) is at present at a swank resort within the borders of his country—a pleasure palace left over from the previous dictator's reign. At this fashionable spot the R is confer-ring with heads of clandestine fighters operating in the mountains of other Latin American countries. R is therefore out of public circulation for a time. Using cinnamon as bait, the team captures and drugs the R and makes off with him—meanwhile making use of word cuts from audiotapes that the R made in the past: These individual word cuts are assembled so as to form an oral statement to the others gathered at the mansion to explain why the R has "temporarily departed." (I don't believe *Mission: Impossible* has used word cuts from audiotapes before, as was done in the movie *The Great Man.*) The team takes the R off to a building that they have taken over. They have made the interior of the building appear to be that of a mental sanitarium. When the R comes to, he is told by the chief "psychiatrist" (probably, of the team, Jim Phelps) that he has been in a complete catatonic schizophrenic state for well over a year. The time is the present, but the R has not ruled; he went mad in the hills, believing himself ruler of the entire country. It was a delusion that the previous dictator (from hereon referred to as D) was kicked out of office and then executed; the D is very much alive *and still in power*.

Here the magic fakery of the fertile minds of the team begins to operate. The D appears on TV, and this is not an old film or videotape; it is live, and in various ways alludes to the time—to the now. The D might even scathingly refer to the R as being hopelessly mad and in a sanitarium. Then there are faked newspapers. The R makes phone calls to his demileaders, and Barney cuts into the circuit, at which point Rollin tells the R that first one demileader and then another is either in the D's prisons or dead. The movement failed; it collapsed after the R became psychotic and could no longer keep things running. (The appearance of the D on the TV screen is done by Rollin, using his handy rubber-face apparatus.) But the most overwhelming fakery is yet to come.

When he took office, after deposing and killing the D, the R made an important speech; he remembers it well. It stated to the nation the aims and intentions that he intended to carry out; in this speech the R unmasked himself and informed his conquered country that he intended to lead it into "progressive anticapitalism," etc. The team therefore produces the following. They take the audio portion of the tape (or movie film) of that speech. Rollin, this time wearing a rubber face, etc., which makes him look like the R (repeat: like the *R*), only it is not the R speaking from the balcony of his new capitol building to huge masses of people: The video portion of the tape or film shows the R in a mental hospital—the very same one he is in now—wearing the standard clothes of a patient and delivering his speech to other patients and members of the hospital staff (the team accomplishes this via lip-sync plus Rollin's impersonation).

However, there has been a minor, technical error in the film. A pile of magazines is shown, and the R has noticed this same pile in the now—and the film is supposed to be at least a year old. The R now employs a bit of electronic gadget knowledge on his own; he manages to get a single frame of the film enlarged enough so that he can read the date on the top magazine. The magazine is current, not a year old. So the R realizes that this is all an illusion (the *Mission: Impossible* team does not know, however, that he has discovered this). But even though he knows this, he is still physically in their hands. How can he make contact with the outside world—i.e. his followers? After all, Barney has all the phones tied up, and Willy is skulking about outdoors with a Skoda rapid-fire hand weapon.

But the R is inventive and imaginative; after all, he did come down out of the hills and take over his country. The *Mission: Impossible* team, this time, is up against a person who is not only as resourceful as they are, but is so along some of the same lines—for example, electronic gadgetry, Barney's specialty. (I don't recall a *Mission: Impossible* episode in which the team faced someone expert in their own sort of electronic delusion sleight-of-hand before.)

There are two possible things that the R can do. (1) He can try to get hold of one of the team's walkie-talkies and rewire it so that it broadcasts over a much greater area, thus—hopefully—reaching a nearby outpost of the R's militia. Or (2) he might be able to splice into an underground phone cable that runs nearby (he now knows where he is geographically). But he can't be precisely sure where the phone cable is, and anyhow it's down deep, and he has no shovel or other tool by which to dig. Hence he decides to steal a walkie-talkie and rewire it.

Cinnamon is currently posing as a fellow patient. The R manages to steal the miniaturized walkie-talkie from her purse; he sneaks off to an unnoticed spot where he can work on it. Where else than the basement? He is able to pick the lock on the basement door, and starts down into the darkness of his hiding place—and then, when he turns the lights on, finds himself facing Barney's electronics center. Everything he needs is here. What a windfall!

First, to take care of Barney should he come back, the R rapidly lays a hot cable across the wooden basement steps—then he begins to work feverishly to alter the walkie-talkie, using Barney's tools and other equipment. Barney does come back, yanks out a pistol with a silencer on it, rushes down the stairs . . . and steps on the hot cable. He at once topples over, letting the gun bounce down the stairs to the floor, where the R waits. Alertly, the R snatches up the gun; now he doesn't need to rewire anything: He can fight his way out.

Leaving the building, he scampers across the lawn of the building, whereupon he encounters Willy. He shoots Willy, and Willy falls down, obviously dead. The R continues to scuttle away from the "mental hospital," entering a wooded area; he is soon successfully gone from the team's custody.

Segue to the R tramping wearily through the woods. Then, to his immense relief, he stumbles onto a paved road. Traffic will surely be coming soon; meanwhile he trudges along the road, still putting as much distance between himself and the MI team as possible.

(The viewer, at this point, thinks that not only has the R gotten away and the mission has failed, but also that Barney and Willy are dead.)

The R reaches a military picket shack, where several of his khaki-clad militiamen are lounging about. The R stumbles toward them. At the sight of him, the militiamen raise their rifles alarmingly. "It's me," the R pants. "Ernesto. Your leader, Ernest Guardia. Don't you recognize me?" Their faces remain hostile and cold, and then one of them fires. The R drops into safety behind a rock, and, with his silencer-equipped pistol, kills the several militiamen. All at once there is silence. The R alone remains alive.

Getting to his feet, he gaspingly staggers toward the picket shack, numbed by the impossible: his own militiamen firing at him. Inside the shack he discovers current newspapers and a radio receiver (but not a transmitter). After examining the newspapers and listening to the radio, he discovers that, during his absence, two of his demileaders have tried to seize power; the country is now split into two warring camps, and what is worse, the two adversaries have released hitherto secret papers that incriminate the R—this along the lines of the de-Stalinization in the USSR after Stalin's death.

What can he do? Even though the MI team failed, he has been deposed anyhow, during his absence. The incriminating papers that were released tell how, while in the hills, the R worked with CIA agents, inasmuch as that at that time the R had not come out for a "people's democracy" along Marxist, pro-China lines.

Obligingly, a small but high-speed plane lands in the rustic field behind the picket shack; the pilot gets out of his craft and saunters toward the shack, carrying various objects of a military nature. The R shoots him; the pilot obligingly falls to the ground, whereupon the R scuttles across the field and into the plane. In a moment he is airborne—and heading for the United States. Then the camera returns to the field, where the "dead" pilot lies; he is now getting leisurely to his feet to watch the plane depart, as are the "dead" militiamen. They grin. What does all this mean?

All this means that the R fell for a fraud within a fraud. The newspapers that he found in the picket shack were fakes. So was the radio broadcast that he heard: Barney did that, and Barney is very much alive. The team *intended* that the R "escape," that he "shoot" Willy and "electrocute" Barney, then flee the scene and make his way to the fake picket shack. The R did not in actuality leave the fake world and reenter the real world; no one seized power during his absence; there is no civil war; no incriminating documents were released; the "militiamen" and the pilot were spurious, and they did not die any more than Willy died; the gun, with its effective silencer, fired no bullets—no wonder the silencer was so effective! And now he is on his way to the United States; the MI team did its job: It only *appeared* to have lost control of the situation for a time . . . when in actuality everything went exactly as planned. The whole unmasking of the "mental hospital" and the fake newsreel of the R delivering his important speech—from the very beginning the team intended the R to discover the truth . . . right down to Rollin's rubber face and the lip-sync. *The R was too smart to be fooled by the fakery,* and the team knew this from the start. For the mission to work they had to include the R's discovering "everything" and go on from there.

Of course, when he reaches Florida, the R will fairly soon discover the truth—discover that there has been no seizure of power back home. But by this time the American authorities will have audio- and videotaped the R's formal statement that he is applying for formal sanctuary in the United States, and this will be sufficient to keep him from returning to his own country, for obvious reasons.

"TV Series Idea" (1967)

Location: The gray, foggy landscape of Heaven. "We Are Watching You, Inc.," a small guardian angel organization consisting of Anastasia Kelp, the owner, a Paul Douglas type; Miss Theola Feather, the phone operator, receptionist, and secretary; Morris Nimbleman, the research director; the protagonist, Herb DeWinter, in charge of field operations; Ludlow Orlawsky, sales manager; Fred Engstrom, repairman for the field equipment that Herb uses on his trips back and forth between Earth and Heaven. "We Are Watching You, Inc.," is a small outfit among several giants, but its record of bailing Earthlings out of jams is virtually 100 percent; it's a small but proud, fine old "handcrafted" firm, beset with worries—namely, that the Government will cancel its franchise due to its smallness (the other guardian angel firms have thousands of field operators, whereas WAWY, Inc., has only DeWinter, who is a slender, good-looking, young, slightly baffled type who seems to fumble things up until the last moment, whereat he miraculously comes through). Additional character: Mr. Vane, the expert from the Government who is ghostly—his voice booming through an echo chamber—and somehow always on hand, checking up on them. He has the power to close them for good, and his "audit" is much feared, although admittedly it would be just. Anastasia Kelp is realistic, aware that his small outfit is an anachronism and probably ought to give up, but he can't quite bring himself to resign and fold up tents. Everything at WAWY, Inc., is old-fashioned, even the telephones and wooden counters; it reeks of the early twentieth century, without chrome or gadgets—except the "magical" advanced electronic superscience gimmicks that the repairman Fred Engstrom provides Herb with at the start of each trip to Earth. Each time the gimmicks differ, according to the assignment. The gimmicks are really spectacular, so that Herb becomes a parody on James Bond with his magic attaché case, and when he is operating in the field and the locale is Earth, this is the dominant mood of the drama: a sort of supernatural James Bond type, except well-intentioned and unsophisticated and a bit bungling. When in Heaven, however, at WAWY, Inc., the locale is like an old-fashioned small store, with much personal relatedness between the employees so that they form a bickering, loving small family, with Anastasia Kelp, of course, as the father.

Each episode consists of a different field trip by Herb DeWinter. In each episode a client has come to WAWY, Inc., for help. A relative or loved one still on Earth is in trouble, and the client wants to hire the services of a professional Guardian Angel to bail that person out. Inasmuch as WAWY, Inc., is a small, marginal—but reputable—firm, it is bound to get a good many oddballs as clients . . . and this it does. The loved one or relative on Earth, too, is often wild or kookie, with a wild, kookie mess ensnaring him.

When he has left Heaven and the offices of WAWY, Inc., and has journeyed down to Earth, Herb routinely approaches the beleaguered loved one in this manner: He shows him or her his business card—he is, of course, wearing a natty New York-style suit of the latest cut—and says something like, "Mr. Peterson. My name is Herb DeWinter, from We Are Watching You, Incorporated. Your grandmother Hatte has hired me to look into your situation with an eye toward effectively bringing about a positive solution," etc. In other words, he lays it on the line; the beleaguered loved one knows who is assisting him and why. Double takes are as brief as possible; then the two of them get down to brass tacks, and the beleaguered loved one accepts Herb from then as he would accept any expert help proffered him in his dilemma. The shortness of the double takes can be explained by the urgent peril surrounding the beleaguered loved one; he can't *afford* to be skeptical, not at a time like this.

The drama of each episode consists of Herb DeWinter's efforts to collaborate with the beleaguered loved one in getting him out of his jam. He always does, but generally he makes it a lot worse before he extricates the victim, and often the victim is faster and brighter than he. Extra humor is supplied by the occasional tough Chicago syndicate-type enemies of the victim who also unhesitatingly accept Herb for what he is; for instance, he is sapped, knocked out, and his wallet examined by gunsels of the mobster. Mr. Big, the head of the mob, as did the victim, does very little double taking; he, too, accepts Herb at face value, but of course doubts cynically if Herb will be of much use. In addition, Mr. Big compares his electronic gimmicks with the supernatural magic ones that Herb is equipped with, and often Mr. Big's are more advanced (recall that WAWY, Inc., is quite obsolete: and not merely behind the times in Heaven but occasionally—although not inevitably—on Earth). Countering this is the occasional appearance of some gimmick rigged up at WAWY by Fred Engstrom, which is so potent as to be miraculous. So it can go either way, depending on the episode. The pendulum swings from miracle to complete bust of Herb's arsenal of wild supernatural gimmicks—the fact that any gimmick may work spectacularly or be a total dud—would help keep audience interest, in that the effect of these broad pendulum swings of electronic effectiveness on his part make him almost a superman in some episodes, an idiot in others. In fact, within the same episode there is no telling what the results will be the next time Herb dips into his ever-present attaché case; a good deal of suspense can be built up here.

The drama of struggle between the victim and those opposing him is always fought out beyond the pale of the law. If it were a situation in which actual, recognized legal bodies could cope with, Mr. DeWinter wouldn't be needed. In every case, the beleaguered loved one is isolated in his struggle, and this is what has caused the client up in Heaven to come to WAWY, Inc., for help.

Sometimes, in extremely sticky situations, the owner of the firm, Anastasia Kelp, appears to confer with Herb—appears without being called, in that Herb is always humiliated, not relieved, to see his shrewd, heavy-set, rough-talking employer. Kelp never really helps Herb solve the problem; he generally merely bickers with him in an effort to goad him into better work. The relationship between the two of them is highly turbulent, they being so different from each other.

In addition, Herb occasionally—but not usually more than once in an episode—"phones" Heaven to confer either with the repairmen Engstrom or the delightfully sexy receptionist or, less frequently, Kelp himself. Engstrom, a nervous, twitchy electronics genius type, is a good friend of Herb, and can often give him suggestions as to how to put the gear in the attaché case to work (almost always the gimmicks that Fred Engstrom has come up with are new to Herb). And, of course, everyone at WAWY, Inc., is watching Herb's progress on their Terrascreen. As is the apprehensive client—who occasionally manages to get hold of Herb when he calls up to Heaven and berates him old-ladywise. (This is a video intercom system, by the way; a mixture of science fiction and the supernatural: science fiction in the idea of a visual phone, but supernatural in that almost any object can be used as a Terrascreen, such as the mirror of the medicine cabinet in the bathroom; Herb is shaving, suddenly sees his lathered features dim, and in their place appears Anastasia Kelp's grumpy, irritated visage.)

And also Mr. Vane, the Government man—it is never made clear what this "government" is like, but obviously, by process of logical reasoning, he must either be God or represent God—tends to hang around the locale of the action on Earth, studying Herb's activities, pursuant to his—Vale's—job of auditing the firm to see if it "fills a genuine need." He never participates in the victim rescue, except insofar as he's inadvertently brought in by such extravagant moments as the total collapse of the building, etc.

Hence, in his job, Herb is under great pressure every episode; pressure from his boss Mr. Kelp, pressure from Mr. Vane, pressure from the victim's foes, and, of course, from the victim himself, who always expects absolutely spectacular, unlimited help from a representative from Heaven who has been hired as his professional guardian angel. He is, of course, disappointed each time, as is Kelp—and Vane appears always on the verge of writing *finis* to the firm—but then, as the final moments run out, Herb, with the help of Fred Engstrom and Miss Feather, manages to snatch final victory, and everyone can relax until next time. Reluctantly, with grudging admiration, Mr. Vane grants a temporary reprieve to the firm. The episode ends with Herb back in Heaven in the front office of the firm, and an identifying coda note closes each half hour: the entrance to the firm's office, with the shadow of a new client falling across it as the client prepares to enter.

Hence each episode begins and ends with a shadow—a different shadow—darkening the threshold of the firm's office, and all employees, plus Mr. Kelp, glancing up in unison with a mixture of apprehension and anticipation.

Sex enters mildly in Heaven à la Miss Feather, and more carnally in the form of certain female victims whom Herb has shown up to save. In this vein the drama a bit resembles the *Topper* novels. Herb, who is rather a small-town hick, although good-looking and certainly not regional, seems quite frequently to draw swanky, wealthy penthouse-type mistresses and wives as his victim-to-be-saved; he is naive, and so the sequel theme doesn't ever get very far—keeping the series fit for children. And, of course, being from Heaven, he can't very well have a deep interest in such goings-on. But now and then he is tempted.

Since Herb can appear anywhere on Earth, in any country, the locale of the Earth scenes is enormous. One episode can be with the Volpo in East Berlin, the next in Cambodia or Pocatello, Idaho. This permits the same international flavor as in *U.N.C.L.E.*-type series.

In periods of extreme danger for Herb, when he is unable to get some gimmick to work, Fred Engstrom occasionally actually comes to Earth in person; together, they tinker with the gadget, trying to figure out why it doesn't work. Engstrom, an electronic—but erratic—genius, often gets it to work—and sometimes work too well. Both men have the advantage, however, of being immortal; the building can disappear in a cloud of atomic particles, but, of course, neither is harmed. Here again is the superman theme, with humorous, even satiric overtones.

Much greater depth can be given the series if there is a particular evil "human" who shows up in various guises from time to time, while Herb is at work on Earth. This sinister man's name changes, and so does the modus operandi of his activities, but he is always pitted against Herb . . . this gives Herb's rescue activities the faint hint of being a perpetual crusade in the name of God and Good against Evil, as personified by the recurring evil figure who seems to haunt Earth. Of course, since this is basically an action-comedy series, philosophical undertones such as this will be played down, yet will be there for anyone who wants to pick them up.

The currency that WAWY, Inc., receives for its successful rescue efforts on Earth is the reprieve from extinction that Mr. Vane extends at the end of each episode. So over and above the fight in each episode to save the beleaguered victim on Earth, there is a perpetual fight on the part of Herb DeWinter, Anastasia Kelp, and others in the organization, which transcends the episodes: the fight to keep their identity; i.e. the fight to survive.

"Notes on *Do Androids Dream of Electric Sheep?*" (1968)

The initial question: Who is the viewpoint character? It must be either the bounty hunter Rick Deckard or Jack Isidore. Since Isidore is younger, were he to be the viewpoint character we would perhaps have something on the order of *The Graduate,* in which everyone over thirty is corrupt and an instrument of the Establishment, and young, free, innocent love wins out—an oddly corny theme for such a supposedly adult movie. In the novel, Isidore has a naive love directed toward the androids; Rick Deckard's view is that the androids are vicious machines that must be destroyed. These two different (and mutually exclusive) views, running parallel to each other in a twin-plot scheme, merge toward the end of the work, when Isidore is confronted by the cruelty of the androids as they cut the legs off the spider. Rick Deckard's view has won out, and the proof of this is that Isidore tells the bounty hunter where the androids are within the decayed apartment building. Since Deckard's view proves to be correct, perhaps he should be the viewpoint protagonist. We cannot come up with "love and innocence and faith conquer all," as was done—and I think wrongly—in the movie *The Graduate.*

But if Rick Deckard is the protagonist, then we are faced with a difficult problem (or perhaps I should say a problem that must be solved): the love that the bounty hunter feels toward animals, in contrast to his heartless murders of the androids. To love an animal more than a person is a deranged or cynical view—or so it might seem. We must learn very soon *why* Rick holds this view, which means an early proof for his view contrasted with Isidore's. Or is not this the major theme, this struggle between the two views—with proof *only at the end* that Rick Deckard's view was correct. In the novel we are *told* that androids lack human feeling, warmth, and empathic sensitivity, but we are not shown this in action until the meeting of Isidore and Deckard. But perhaps this is a good way to handle it; the contrast between Isidore and his views, in contrast to Deckard and his views, in some ways is the primary story. Notice I say "story" and not theme. The theme of the book tends to cluster around the religion of Mercerism and its emphasis on shared pain and mutual compassion, a rebirth of the primordial Christian view. Or is the basic theme the broad background, the total world in which they live, with their collective and general worship of animals, the decaying huge apartment buildings, and the "specials," like Jack Isidore—plus the running thread of their mutual empathy?

Casting is a vital question. Rick Deckard could, for example, be played by Gregory Peck (which makes him powerful and sensitive and wise), in contrast to Richard Widmark (which makes him a psychotic killer), with several lesser possibilities, such as Martin Balsam (which makes him virtually into an archetypal father figure), or someone like Ben Gazzara (which makes him bold, and a man of action). As to Isidore. He could be played, for example, by Dean Stockwell (which makes him sensitive and an introvert, living in a lonely world of his own making), or possibly Wally Cox, which makes him into Wally Cox. My theory (supra) calls for Deckard to be the protagonist, with views that the audience may not quite at first share but that at the end win out morally, psychologically, dramatically, and in all other ways. Hence I would favor someone like Gregory Peck to play Rick Deckard, and then Dean Stockwell to play Isidore. It seems to me that with each casting change—or decision—you have a whole new ball of wax. Think, for example, of the strong factor introduced if Rachael were played by a vibrant, hard girl such as Grace Slick (a bit of casting I would really plug for).

Of course, there is also the question of the *tone* of the picture; is this a touching story (Isidore protecting the androids and then, at the end, seeing what they are really like—his soap bubble world suddenly collapsing), or Isidore as funny (via Wally Cox, etc.), or gunplay action, as Deckard shoots one android after another, or as a broad general picture of a whole and entire world that is *ethnic* fundamentally, with many quaint and odd customs practiced with great solemnity by the natives, customs that include murder on a legal basis: "people" (i.e. the androids) without any legal rights of any sort. Also, the film could be procop or anticop, which reverts as a question to the deeper, earlier question of what age group is the protagonist going to be?

I personally feel that the bizarre, the odd, the eerie should be played up, the pataphysical quiddities of this world in which they live. One finds this, for example, of the whole element about fake live animals, and the new animal dealers who have replaced the new car dealers of our own time. The *strange*, the dreamlike (as in the time-lapse and space-lapse camerawork in *The Graduate*). It is a sort of pretend world . . . up to a point. And then the murders of the androids begin, and suddenly it is all real, all for keeps, and very much grim and unfunny.

One additional oddity: the fact that there are two Rachaels, the one whom Rick meets, and then the one Isidore meets. These are the same android, and some kind of imaginative camerawork—superimpositions or few-frame blinks back and forth between the two androids—is much needed, and could be a major attraction of the film. What must be made clear to the audience, however, [is] that these two Rachaels, each with its human colleague, are functioning at the same time; these are not a flashback but a simultaneous double life. For example, the android talking to Rick Deckard could say a phrase, and then when we pick the other Rachael up with Isidore, she could repeat the exact words—an audiotrack superimposition, with the voice echoing itself as in a sort of electronic echo chamber, much improved on our own. I think that (1) it is going to be hard to get across the desired effect, but (2) it will be worth the effort. The small plot-element of the Other Police Station could be eliminated entirely.

I am not sure that the Mood Organ material should, as in the novel, begin the piece. Perhaps instead we could have Jack Isidore driving his electric-animal-repair truck setting out at dawn. Technically, I think there should be a weapon, used in particular by the bounty hunters, that isn't merely another laser tube, such as one sees in *Star Trek* and *The Invaders*. Here again, something of imagination rather than cliché is needed. This includes the *sound* made by the weapon; it must be new and unusual, too. A sound, for example, that a champagne bottle makes when it pops its cork.

It seems to me that one strong point of the novel is the fact that it provides space for many moods and tones: There is the dramatic search and destruction of the androids, the tenderness felt toward live animals, the weird, deserted apartment building in which Jack Isidore lives—opportunities for humor, the peculiar, the very frightening, and, of course, the awe felt when Mercer is encountered. We can have a many-sided film . . . or, I would think, some of the moods (and plot, etc.) can be eliminated entirely, however important they are to the novel . . . and then remaining elements, such as Isidore and the Mercer theme, can be retained and built up more. But I do think that both the search and destroy androids theme must be retained (because of its connection—contrast—to Isidore's view), and because it all throughout the novel adds the quality of violence, of the chase . . . although, in regarding this, I wonder if the empathy test that Deckard gives prospective androids is adequate in the visual medium. Perhaps an entirely new type of test should be made up for this, or perhaps no test that is a question-and-answer test, but perhaps a measuring of brain-wave rhythms. This, too, is a vital area to be there with imagination, as with the kind of weapons used.

There could be room for more sex. E.g. Rick Deckard making love to Rachael and then dissolve to Isidore, trying same on his Rachael android, and fouling it all up, à la Peter Sellers. The possibilities here are enormous . . . to cite one reason, there is the exact duplication of sentences uttered by the two identical androids. Sentences to which Rick Deckard gives one kind of reply. Jack Isidore another. The Isidore romance could be a chilling travesty of the successful Rick Deckard makeout with the girl.

And this brings up the whole underlying subject: sexual relations between humans and androids. What is it like? What does it mean? Is it, for instance, like going to bed with a real woman? Or is it an awful, nighmarish, bad trip, where what is dead and inert seems alive and warm and capable of the most acute intimacy known to living creatures? Isn't this, this sexual union between Rick Deckard and Rachael Rosen—isn't it the *summa* of falsity and mechanical motions carried out minus any real feeling, as we understand the word? Feeling on each of their parts. Does in fact her mental—and physical—coldness numb the male, the human man, into an echo of it?

In the novel it is treated on page 165 [of the 1968 Doubleday first edition] in its most acute form, when, as Rachael and Rick prepare to go to bed, Rachael says to him, "Androids can't bear children . . . is that a loss? I really don't know; I have no way to tell. How does it feel to have a child? How does it feel to be born, for that matter? We're not born; we don't grow up; instead of dying from illness or old age, we wear out like ants. Ants again; that's what we are . . . chitinous reflex machines who aren't really alive. I'm not really alive! You're not going to bed with a woman."

And then a bit later Rachael says,

"I understand—they tell me—it's convincing if you don't think too much about it. But if you think too much, if you reflect on what you're doing—then you can't go on. For, ahem, physiological reasons."

Rick then bends and kisses her bare shoulder.

Now, this is about the extent of this subject as handled in the novel, but there are more possibilities, which might come out vividly in a film version. For example (to name the first that comes to my mind): Is this a way he can cheat vis-à-vis his wife Iran—in other words, is it all right to sleep with an android? It doesn't count, etc. In any case, the key question comes up on page 168, where Rachael asks, "Would you ever go to bed with an android again?" His answer to this is gracious, very politic, and yet somehow evasive. "If it was a girl," Rick says. "If she resembled you." But Rachael has already made the point that she is not a person; she is a type, a subform of androids in general. His relationship, by having intercourse with her, has melded him to—not an individual, human or android—but to a whole type or model, of which, theoretically, there could be tens of thousands. To whom, then, has he *really* given his erotic libido to? An army of rachael rosens, a horde of them, all identical? This undermines the meaning of love—at least sexual, erotic love—because the basic parity is undermined, one man for one woman (or at least one at a time). But he has, in effect, made love to them all!

Here, I think, the crucial questions of What is reality? and What is illusion? come up strongly. The whole sexual scene with Rachael (and, if used, the one between Isidore and Pris) could be dreamlike, but not in the usual sense, not the wishful, daydreaming contemplations of infinite women, infinite prowess, and so forth. This could be—not a vague dream—but a horrifyingly *mechanical* episode of half dream, half reality, with Rachael melting superficially—but by doing so, exposing a steel-and-solid-state electronic gear beneath. The more Rick strives to force her to become a woman—or, more accurately, to play the role of a woman—the more he encounters the core of unlife within her. In subtle ways (certainly not in gross ways) it should be shown that his attempt to make love to her as a woman for him is defeated by the tireless core of her electronic being. I don't mean that he opens a door in her chest, thus swinging her right breast away and exposing a maze of sensationally advanced selenoids and servo-assists and transistors. *This* is not the discovery he—and the audience—is making; this is already known. What is shown is just how far both the android woman and the human male can manage to force back the artificial and mechanical and smother it in their mutual yearnings. They are both pretending . . . but a good deal of ordinary, today and now sex is handled this way; during sex the faculty of judgment in many ways is suspended, by both partners. The question *here* is: How far can this go? Will that which both of them desire be successfully maintained, or will it, because of her makeup, recede farther and farther the deeper he goes—much to the bitter disappointment of both of them?

It seems to me that after the soothing, endearing words, a very hateful conclusion—or aftermath—could spring up between them; their mutually arranged act has made each worse off than before, and this could be well expressed by the mutual hatred and disappointment each now feels for the other.

With this miserable outcome, perhaps the segue to Isidore and Pris, from time to time, could reveal a more optimistic scene than would be expected. Ironically, it might be Isidore who succeeds—due to his worldly ignorance. And this would provide an augmented basis for his grief when the three andys die.

The failure of the sexual act between Rick and Rachael could, in the end, amount to a complete collapse of understanding between them, a theme on the order of A *Passage to India* [the E. M. Forster novel]. And if this deep and final estrangement aids Rick in his search-and-destroy mission against Pris Stratton—makes it possible, in fact, for him to kill her—then the sex theme will have served a vital purpose in terms of the book's plot (which up to now it really hasn't done; it was, in the printed form, sort of an interlude only). Yes, it could well be that Rick's recoiling from being close to Rachael—or trying his damn best to be close—may be vital in his determination—and success—in destroying the last three andys.

I will stop speculating at this point, and hopefully wait for a response, however slight it may well be, to what I've added here in the way of further analysis of the novel.

Part Five

Essays and Speeches

This section contains the principal published essays by Dick on matters other than science fiction.

"Drugs, Hallucinations, and the Quest for Reality" was first published in *Lighthouse* (edited by Terry Carr), No. 11, November 1964.

"Schizophrenia & *The Book of Changes*" was first published in *Niekas*, No. 11, March 1965. It was reprinted in the *PKDS Newsletter*, No. 14, June 1987.

"The Android and the Human," delivered as a speech by Dick at the University of British Columbia, Vancouver, in February 1972, was first published in *SF Commentary*, No. 31, December 1972. It was most recently reprinted in the eclectic Dick anthology *The Dark-Haired Girl* (1988), published by Mark V. Ziesing. This essay is Dick's most extended nonfictional foray into social ethics. The rape-related humor has aged very badly, and the celebration of random ripoffs as the means of warding off centralized oppression may not convince readers who live in crime-ridden neighborhoods. But the central distinction between the android and the human remains a suggestive one.

"Man, Android, and Machine" first appeared in the British anthology *Science Fiction at Large* (Gollancz, 1976), edited by Peter Nicholls, and was reprinted in *The Dark-Haired Girl*.

"If You Find This World Bad, You Should See Some of the Others" was delivered as a speech by Dick at the second Festival International de la Science-Fiction de Metz, France, in September 1977. It was first published in French translation in *L'Année 1977–78 de la S.-F. et du Fantastique* (Juilliard, 1978), edited by Jacques Goimard. Its first English publication came in the *PKDS Newsletter*, No. 27, August 1991.

"How to Build a Universe That Doesn't Fall Apart Two Days Later" was written as a speech but was likely never delivered. It was first published in *I Hope I Shall Arrive Soon* (1985).

"Cosmogony and Cosmology," dated January 23, 1978, was expressly intended by Dick as a summary of the key insights expressed in the *Exegesis* as of that time. It is included here as an essay because it was sent out in typed form by Dick to his agent, Russell Galen, although with no overt publishing intentions in mind. In this sense, it differs from the remainder of the *Exegesis*, which Dick kept to himself, but for occasional limited disclosures to friends. It was first published in a limited edition by Kerosina Books in 1987.

"The Tagore Letter" was first published in *Niekas*, No. 28, November 1981.

"Drugs, Hallucinations, and the Quest for Reality" (1964)

One long-past innocent day, in my prefolly youth, I came upon a statement in an undistinguished textbook on psychiatry that, as when Kant read Hume, woke me forever from my garden-of-eden slumber. "The psychotic does not merely think he sees four blue bivalves with floppy wings wandering up the wall; he *does* see them. An hallucination is not, strictly speaking, manufactured in the brain; it is received by the brain, like any 'real' sense datum, and the patient acts in response to this to-him-very-real perception of reality in as logical a way as we do to our sense data. In any way to suppose he only 'thinks he sees it' is to misunderstand totally the experience of psychosis."

Well, I have pondered this over the dreary years, while meantime the drug industry, psychiatrists, and certain naughty persons of dubious repute have done much to validate—and further explore—this topic, so that now we are faced with a psychiatric establishment little related to the simple good old days (circa 1900) when mental patients fell into one of two rigid classes: the insane, which meant simply that they were too ill to function in society, to wash and wax their car, pay their utility bills, drink one martini and still utter pleasant conversation, and hence had to be institutionalized . . . and the neurotic, which included all those wise enough to seek out psychiatric help, and for merely "hysterical" complaints, such as feeling a compulsion to untie everybody's shoes or count the number of small boys on tricycles passing their houses or offices, or for "neurotic" disorders that boiled down to anxiety felt out of proportion to the "reality situation," in particular specialized phobias such as a morbid, senseless dread that an unmanned space missile supposed to land in the Atlantic would instead strike dead-center in the patio on Sunday afternoon while the person in question was fixing charcoal-broiled hamburgers. No real relationship was seen between the "insane" who were—or should have been—in institutions and "neurotics" or "hysterical" individuals showing up for one hour of free-association a week; in fact, the belief that the insane (or as we would say now, the psychotic) had an ailment of a physical, rather than psychogenic, origin and the neurotic felt unnatural fears because of a traumatic event in his early childhood was so established that Freud's initial discovery had to do with creating a diagnostic basis upon which the doctor could decide into which group the ill person fell. If he proved psychotic, then depth psychology, psychoanalysis, was not for him—if neurotic, all that was needed was to bring the long-forgotten repressed traumatic sexual material out of the subconscious and into the light of day . . . whereupon the phobias and compulsions would vanish.

This looked to be a good thing, until Jung showed up and proved:

1. That hospitalized, full psychotics responded to psychotherapy as rapidly as neurotics, once the psychotic's private language had been comprehended, communication thereby being established. And

2. Many "neurotics," who were ambulatory, who held jobs, raised families, brushed their teeth regularly, were not what he had designated as "introverted neurotics" but in fact psychotics—specifically schizophrenics—in an early stage of a lifelong illness career. And *they* responded less well to psychoanalysis than anyone else.

This meant something. (A) Perhaps all mental illness, no matter how severe, might be psychogenic in origin. (B) A neurosis might not be an illness at all or even an illness symptom, but a construct of the brain to achieve stasis and avoid a far more serious breakdown; hence it might well be risky to tinker with someone's neurosis because under it might lie a full-blown psychosis—which would emerge at the point where the happy psychiatrist sits back and says, "See? You're no longer afraid of buses." Whereupon the patient then discovers that he is now afraid of everything, including life itself. And can no longer function at all.

So out went the whole great scheme of things, the subconscious, the repressed childhood sexual trauma—like a medieval flat-world map it referred to nothing, and was, possibly, even harmful to what are now designated as "borderline psychotics," which is a way of saying, "Those who can't function in society but do. I guess." How cloudy can an issue become? All theories, one by one, broke down; there were "rational" psychotics, whom we in our amusing way call paranoids, and there were—but enough. Because now we are at what I regard the crucial issue: that of the presence in the psychotic of not only delusions ("They're conspiring against me," etc.) but of hallucinations, which neurotics do not have. So perhaps in this regard we have a diagnostic basis, if not of the nature of the illness then at least of its severity. But one item crops up, here, that is rather unnerving. There is such a thing as negative hallucination—that is, instead of seeing what is not there, the patient cannot see what is. (Jung gives, I think, the most extraordinary example of this: a patient who saw people minus their heads—he saw them up to the neck only, and then nothing.) But what is even more scary is that this patient was not psychotic; he was absolutely for sure merely hysterical—as any stage hypnotist can testify, since such malperception can be induced in distinctly nonill people . . . as well as a good deal more, including that which when it occurs without the influence of the hypnotist is considered the *sine qua non* of psychosis, the positive hallucination.

We are now getting somewhere, and it is a frightening where. Because we have entered the landscape depicted by Richard Condon in his terrific novel *The Manchurian Candidate:* Not only can delusions and hallucinations be induced in virtually any person, but the added horror of "posthypnotic suggestion" gets thrown in for good measure . . . and, by the Pavlov Institute, all this for clearly worked-out political purposes. I don't think I'm wandering into fantasy here, because recall: Freud originally became involved in a form of psychotherapy that utilized hypnosis as its cardinal tool. In other words, all modern depth psychology—that which postulates some region of the mind unavailable to the person's conscious self, and which, on many an occasion, can preempt the self—grows from the observation of individuals acting out of complete convictions and perceptions and motivations implanted by "suggestion" during the hypnotic state. Suggestion? How weak a word; how little it conveys, compared to the experience itself. (I've undergone it and it is, beyond doubt, the most extraordinary thing that ever happened to me.) What the body of "suggestions" add up to for the hypnotized subject is nothing less than a new worldview superimposed on the subject's customary one; there is no limit to the extent of this induced new view or gestalt of data perceptions and organizing ideas within the mentational processes of the brain—no limit to its extent, its duration, or its departure not only from what we quaintly call "reality." And—this simply can't be, logically, but it is so—the subject can be altered physically, in terms of what he is able to do; he can lie rigid between two chairs and be stood on, so even the somatic portion of him is new . . . sometimes even to the point of contradicting what we know to be anatomically possible, as relating to the circulatory system, etc. (e.g., holding his arm extended for a considerable time); the time limit is imposed by purely physiological factors, and there simply can be no psychogenic explanation as to such a phenomenon, unless we wish to posit yoga or Psionic or—let's face it—magical powers. But powers of this sort by whom? The patient? The hypnotist? It makes no sense either way, unless we restore the seventeenth-century notion of wizards and those who are victims of wizardly spells . . . and where does *this* take us? I doubt if even John W. Campbell, Jr. [influential SF editor of *Astounding* magazine, whose rigid approach to SF plotting was disapproved of by Dick] would want to venture along this path.

However, perhaps we can construct something comprehensible out of this by recalling that there now appears some validation of extrasensory perceptions—and abilities. There is a relationship; as far back as 1900 Freud himself noted palpable evidence, during free association by his patients, of telepathic ability. (I really hate to have learned this, having jeered at ESP for years; but Freud's documentation alone—and he was an incredibly scrupulous observer—tends to strengthen the case for ESP.) And, recently, in absolutely reputable psychiatric journals, trained M.D. psychiatrists have given us the news that telepathic perceptions by their patients occur so frequently as to be beyond dispute. Ehrenwald, published by W. W. Norton, which is reputable, with a foreword by Gardner Murphy, goes so far as to construct an entire theory of mental illness based on firsthand observation of his severely disturbed patients that they are experiencing involuntary telepathic linkage; the paranoids, for example, receive as sense data the marginal, repressed, unspoken hostile thoughts and feelings of those around them; he declares that again and again, while passing through hospital wards, paranoid patients quoted to him word for word hostile thoughts that he was entertaining toward them—and, of course, concealing such thoughts, as we all do, in order to keep our interpersonal relationships functioning. So now, in my prolix, rambling way, I have gotten to my Big Scoop. Taking Ehrenwald's utterances at face value (that is, accepting them as true and using them as a postulate), we are faced with the clear and evident possibility that at least in the case of paranoids—or, anyhow, some paranoids—the "delusions" are not delusions at all, but are, on the contrary, accurate perceptions of an area of reality that the rest of us cannot (thank the Lord) reach. All right; now let's return to and reexamine the entire topic of mental illness, hallucinations both negative and positive, the hypnotic experience, pseudoschizophrenic sensory distortions brought about by chemicals such as LSD and organic toxins such as are found in some mushrooms, etc., and, to be absolutely certain that I make a fool of myself, I'll add mysticism, the mystical event called "conversion," such as happened to St. Paul. Ready? Okay.

Can a person be psychotic without hallucinating? Yes. The paranoids merely have "delusional ideas"; they see the same reality that we do, but interpret it differently, work it into their system.

Can a person hallucinate without being psychotic? Yes, as for example during the hypnotic state, under drugs, when ill with a high fever, poisoned—for many reasons.

What is the relationship between hallucination and worldview? The German psychological notion (more accurately Swiss) is that each individual has a structured, idiosyncratic, and in some regards unique way of picturing or experiencing—or whatever it is one does with—reality. It now is universally accepted that reality "in itself," as Kant put it, is really unknown to any sentient organism; the categories of organization, time, and space are mechanisms by which the living percept-systems, including the portions of the brain that receive the "raw" sense data, require the imposition of a subjective framework in order to turn what would otherwise be chaotic into an environment that is relatively constant, with enough abiding aspects so that the organism can imagine, on the basis of memory (the past) and observing (the present), what the future *probably* will be. Continuity is essential; one must be able to recognize a good deal of the external world in order to function (this, of course, is why the name problem is real and not a figment of medieval imagination; the logos, the word, turns chaos into separate and different objects).

A good deal of this organization is done within the percept system itself; that is, by less-than-conscious portions of the neurological apparatus, so by the time the "self" receives the sense data it has so to speak been automatically structured into the idiosyncratic worldview. The self (or ego or some damn fool thing) is therefore presented with material a good deal of which originated within its own being, at one level or another. In the light of this, the idea of hallucinating takes on a very different character; hallucinations, whether induced by psychosis, hypnosis, drugs, toxins, etc., may be merely quantitatively different from what we see, not qualitatively so. In other words, too much is emanating from the neurological apparatus of the organism, over and beyond the structural, organizing necessity. The percept system in a sense is overperceiving, is presenting the self portion of the brain too much. The cognitive processes, then, in particular the judging, reflecting frontal lobe, cannot encompass what it has been given, and for it—for the person—the world begins to become mysterious. No-name entities or aspects begin to appear, and, since the person does not know what they are—that is, what they're called or what they mean—he cannot communicate with other persons about them. This breakdown of verbal communication is the fatal index that somewhere along the line the person is experiencing reality in a way too altered to fit into his or her own prior worldview and too radical to allow empathic linkage with other persons.

But the crucial question as to where, at what stage, these perplexing aspects, augmentations, or warpages away from the commonly shared view begin, is not answered by any of this. We are aware today that a good deal of what we call "external reality" consists of a subjective framework by the percept system itself, and that there are probably as many different worldviews as individuals . . . but how do unwanted, even frightening, and certainly not commonly shared "hallucinations" creep in? Up until the last three or four years it would have been generally agreed that these invasions of the orderly continuity of world experience beyond doubt originate in the person, at some level of the neurological structure, but now, for the first time, really, the body of evidence has begun to swing the other way. Entirely new terms such as "expanded consciousness" are heard, terms indicating that research, especially with hallucinatory drugs, points to the probability, whether we like it or not, that, as in the case of Jan Ehrenwald's paranoids, the percept system of the organism is overperceiving, all right, and undoubtedly presenting the judging centers of the frontal lobe with data they can't handle, and this is bad because there can be no judgment under such circumstances, and no interpersonal life, due to the breakdown of the shared language—but the overperception emanates from outside the organism; the percept system of the organism is perceiving what is actually there, and it should not be doing so, because to do so is to make the cognitive process impossible, *however real the entities perceived are.* The problem actually seems to be that rather than "seeing what isn't there" the organism is seeing what *is* there—but no one else does, hence no semantic sign exists to depict the entity and therefore the organism cannot continue an empathic relationship with the members of his society. And this breakdown of empathy is double; they can't empathize his "world," and he can't theirs.

Hallucination, mental illness, drug experiences of "expanded consciousness" are menacing to the organism because of the social results. It is obvious, then, what role language plays in human life: It is the cardinal instrument by which the individual worldviews are linked so that a shared, for all intents and purposes common reality is constructed. What is actually subjective becomes objective—agreed on. So, viewed this way, sociologically and anthropologically, it does not matter where the hallucinations originate or even whether they are accurate—but unique and hence unshared—perceptions of "higher levels of reality unglimpsed ordinarily," even by the person himself.

Real or unreal, originating within the percept system or received validly by the percept system because, say, of some chemical agent not normally present and active in the brain's metabolism, the unshared world that we call "hallucinatory" is destructive: Alienation, isolation, a sense of everything being strange, of things altering and bending—all this is the logical result, until the individual, formerly a part of human culture, becomes an organic "windowless monad" [a description utilized by Leibnitz]. It does not matter that his reasoning faculties are unimpaired; it does not matter whether or not he feels "adequate emotion," those being the two classic criteria by which schizophrenia was diagnosed. Actually it seems to be that neither is impaired; faced with the sense data presented him, the individual does as well with it as we do with ours, and the same goes for his emotional life—he may display moods and feelings that to us can't be accounted for. But we are not perceiving what he is; the emotions are almost certainly appropriate in relation to what he perceives, i.e. experiences.

My own feeling, especially in view of the very recent laboratory find-

ings that some connection exists between schizophrenia and subsecre-
tions of the adrenal gland, is this: "The sane man does not know that everything is possible." In other words, the mentally ill person at one time or
another *knew too much*. And, as a result, so to speak, his head shut down.
A little knowledge may be a dangerous thing, but gadzooks—what about
too much knowledge? Death, as a factor of reality, perhaps should not be
known about at all, or, if that's impossible, then as little as one can manage. James Stephens, in his poem "The Whisperer" (from *Insurrections*,
Dublin, 1912), informs us of something I distinctly am not glad to know,
but now I know it, and I guess one finds it out sooner or later. Ironically, it
is that God Himself feels this:

> *I fashion you,*
> *and then for weal or woe,*
> *By business through,*
> *I care not how ye go,*
> *Or struggle, win or lose, nor do*
> *I want to know.*

One doesn't have to depend on hallucinations; one can unhinge oneself
by many other roads.

"Schizophrenia & *The Book of Changes*" (1965)

In many species of life forms, such as the grazing animals, a newborn individual is more or less thrust out into the *koinos kosmos* (the shared world) immediately. For a lamb or a pony, the *idios kosmos* (the personal world) ceases when the first light hits his eyes—but a human child, at birth, still has years of a kind of semireal existence ahead of him: semireal in the sense that until he is fifteen or sixteen years old he is able to some degree to remain not thoroughly born, not entirely on his own; fragments of the *idios kosmos* remain, and not all or even very much of the *koinos kosmos* has been forced onto him as yet. The full burden of the *koinos kosmos* does not weigh until what is delightfully referred to as "psychosexual maturity" strikes, which means those lovely days during high school epitomized by asking that cute girl in the row ahead of you if she'd like to go get a soda after school, and she saying "NO." That's it. The *koinos kosmos* has set in. Prepare, young man, for a long winter. Much more—and worse—lie ahead.

The preschizophrenic personality is generally called "schizoid effective" [sic; likely "affective" intended], which means that as an adolescent he still hopes that he won't have to ask the cute chick (or boy) in the next row for a date. Speaking in terms of my own schizoid-effective experience, one gazes at her for a year or so, mentally detailing all possible outcomes; the good ones go under the rubric "daydreams," the bad ones under "phobia." This bipolar internal war goes on endlessly; meanwhile the actual girl has no idea you're alive (and guess why: You're not). If the phobias win out (suppose I ask her and she says, "With *you?*" etc.), then the schizoid-effective kid physically bolts from the classroom with agoraphobia, which gradually widens into true schizophrenic avoidance of all human contact, or withdraws into phantasy, becomes, so to speak, his own Abe Merritt [a popular SF writer of the 1920s and 1930s]—or, if things go further wrong, his own H. P. Lovecraft. In any case, the girl is forgotten and the leap to psychosexual maturity never takes place, which wouldn't be bad in itself because really there are other things in life besides pretty girls (or so I'm told, anyhow). But it's the implication that's so ominous. What has happened will repeat itself again and again, wherever the kid runs head on into the *koinos kosmos*. And these are the years (fifteen years old to twenty-two) when he can no longer keep from running into it on almost every occasion. (Phone the dentist, Charley, and make an appointment to get that cavity patched," etc.) The *idios kosmos* is leaking away; he is gradually being thrust out of the postwomb womb. Biological aging is taking place, and he can't hold it back. His efforts to do so, if they continue, will later be called "an attempt to retreat from adult responsibility and reality," and if he is later diagnosed as schizophrenic, it will be said that he has "escaped from the real world into a phantasy one." This, while almost true, is just not quite correct. Because reality has an attribute that, if you'll ponder on't, you'll realize is the attribute that causes us to so designate it as reality: It *can't* be escaped. As a matter of fact, during his preschizophrenic life, during the schizoid-effective period, he has been somewhat doing this; he is now no longer able to. The deadly appearance, around nineteen, of schizophrenia, is not a retreat from reality, but on the contrary: the breaking out of reality all around him; its presence, not its absence from his vicinity. The lifelong fight to avoid it has ended in failure; he is engulfed in it. Gak!

What distinguishes schizophrenic existence from that which the rest of us like to imagine we enjoy is the element of time. The schizophrenic is having it all *now*, whether he wants it or not; the whole can of film has descended on him, whereas we watch it progress frame by frame. So for him, causality does not exist. Instead, the acausal connective principle that Wolfgang Pauli called synchronicity is operating in all situations—not merely as only one factor at work, as with us. Like a person under LSD, the schizophrenic is engulfed in an endless now. It's not too much fun.

At this point the *I Ching (The Book of Changes)* enters, since it works on the basis of synchronicity—and is a device by which synchronicity can be handled. Maybe you prefer the word "coincidence" to Pauli's word.

Anyhow, both terms refer to acausal connectives, or rather events linked in that manner, events occurring outside of time. Not a chain passing from yesterday to today to tomorrow but all taking place now. All chiming away now, like Leibnitz's preset clocks. And yet none having any causal connection with any of the others.

That events can take place outside of time is a discovery that strikes me as dismal. My first reaction was, "Good God, I was right; when you're at the dentist it *does* last forever." I'll let the mystics dilate on more favorable possibilities, such as eternal bliss. Anyhow, LSD has made this discovery available to everyone, and hence subject to consensual validation, hence within the realm of knowledge, hence a scientific fact (or just plain fact, if you prefer). Anybody can get into this state now, not just the schizophrenic. Yes, friends, you, too, can suffer forever; simply take 150 mg of LSD—and enjoy! If not satisfied, simply mail in—but enough. Because after two thousand years under LSD, participating in the Day of Judgment, one probably will be rather apathetic to asking for one's five dollars back.

But at least one has now learned what life is like during the catatonic schizophrenic state, and one does return from LSD within a short time period as computed within the *koinos kosmos* (roughly ten hours), however much longer it is in the *idios kosmos* (to rather understate the matter). For the catatonic schizophrenic the duration of this state is not only forever *idios kosmos*wise but also, unless lucky, *koinos kosmos*wise. To put it in zen terms, under LSD you experience eternity for only a short period (or, as *Planet Stories* used to phrase it, "Such-and-such," he screamed under his breath). So, within a nontime interval, all manner of elaborate and peculiar events can take place; whole epics can unfold in the fashion of the recent movie *Ben Hur*. (If you'd prefer to undergo the experience of LSD without taking it, imagine sitting through *Ben Hur* twenty times without the midpoint intermission. Got it? Keep it.)

This unfolding is not in any sense a causal progression; it is the vertical opening forth of synchronicity rather than the horizontal cause-and-effect sequence that we experience by clock time, and since it is timeless, it is unlimited in extent; it has no built-in end. So the universe of the schizophrenic is, again to understate it, somewhat large. Much too large. Ours, like the twice-daily measured squirt of toothpaste, is controlled and finite; we rub up against only as much reality as we can handle—or think we can handle, to be more accurate. Anyhow, we seem to manage to control its rate, just as, for example, we decide not to go on the freeway during rush-hour traffic but take that good old back road that nobody (sic) knows about except us. Well, it goes without saying that we eventually err; we take a wrong turn, generally when we're about sixty-five years of age; we drop dead from cardiac arrest, and despite years of experience in managing the flow of reality, we're just as dead as the psychotic stuck in the eternal now.

But, to repeat, this merely lies ahead of us, in the future; we haven't failed to get that annual medical checkup yet, or if we have, it wouldn't have revealed anything this time, except the usual ulcer. Our partial knowledge of reality is sufficient to get us by—for a while longer. Cause and effect bumble on, and we go with them; like good middle-class Americans we keep paying on our insurance policies, hoping to outbet the actuary tables. What will destroy us in the end is synchronicity; eventually we will arrive in a blind intersection at 4:00 A.M. the same time another idiot does, also tanked up with beer; both of us will then depart for the next life, with probably the same outcome there, too. Synchronicity, you see, can't be anticipated; that's one of its aspects.

Or can it? If it could . . . imagine being able to plot in advance, in systematic fashion, the approach of all meaningful coincidences. Is that *a priori*, by the very meaning of the word, not a contradiction? After all, a coincidence, or as Pauli called it, a manifestation of synchronicity, is by its very nature not dependent on the past; hence nothing exists as a harbinger of it (cf. David Hume on the topic; in particular the train whistle versus the train). This state, not knowing what is going to happen next and therefore having no way of controlling it, is the *sine qua non* of the unhappy world of the schizophrenic; he is helpless, passive, and instead of doing things, he is done to. Reality happens to him—a sort of perpetual auto accident, going on and on without relief.

Schizophrenics don't write and mail letters, don't go anywhere, don't make phone calls: They are written to by angry creditors and authority figures such as the San Francisco Police Department; they are phoned up by hostile relatives; every so often they are forcibly hauled off to the barber shop or dentist or funny farm. If, by some miracle, they hoist themselves into an active state, call HI 4-1234 and ask for a cab so they can visit their good friend the pope, a garbage truck will run into the taxi, and if, after getting out of the hospital (vide Horace Gold's experience a few years ago), another taxi is called and they try one more time, another garbage truck will appear and ram them again. They know this. They've had it happen. Synchronicity has been going on all the time; it's only news to *us* that such coincidences can happen.

Okay; so what can be done? For a schizophrenic, any method by which synchronicity can be coped with means possible survival; for us, it would be a great assist in the job of temporarily surviving . . . we both could use such a beat-the-house system.

This is what the *I Ching*, for three thousand years, has been and still is. It works (roughly 80 percent of the time, according to those such as Pauli who have analyzed it on a statistical basis). John Cage, the composer, uses it to derive chord progressions. Several physicists use it to plot the behavior of subatomic particles—thus getting around Heisenberg's unfortunate principle. I've used it to develop the direction of a novel (please reserve your comments for *Yandro*, if you will). Jung used it with patients to get around their psychological blind spots. Leibnitz based his binary system on it, the open-and-shut-gate idea, if not his entire philosophy of monadology . . . for what that's worth.

You, too, can use it: for betting on heavyweight bouts or getting your girl to acquiesce, for anything, in fact, that you want—except for foretelling the future. That, it can't do; it is not a fortunetelling device, despite what's been believed about it for centuries both in China and by Richard Wilhelm, who did the German translation now available in the Pantheon Press edition in an English version. (Helmut, Richard's son, who is also a Sinologist, has demonstrated this in articles in the *Eranos Jahrbucher* and in lectures; also available in English from Pantheon. And Legge, in the first English version circa 1900, demonstrated that, then.) True, the book *seems* to deal with the future; it lays before your eyes, for your scrutiny, a gestalt of the forces in operation that will *determine* the future. But these forces are at work now; they exist, so to speak, outside of time, as does the ablative absolute case in Latin. The book is analytical and diagnostic, not predictive. But so is a multiphasic physical exam; it tells you what is going on *now* in your body—and out of a knowledge of that, a competent doctor may possibly be able, to some extent, to predict what may happen in the future. ("Get that artery replaced, Mr. McNit, or next week or maybe even on the way home this afternoon you'll probably drop dead.")

By means of the *I Ching* the total configuration of the *koinos kosmos* can be scrutinized—which is why King Wen, in prison in 1100 B.C., composed it; he wasn't interested in the future: He wanted to know what was happening outside his cell that moment, what was becoming of his kingdom at the instant he cast the yarrow stalks and derived a hexagram. Knowledge of this sort is obviously of vast value to anyone, since, by means of it, a fairly good guess (repeat: *guess*) can be made about the future, and so one can decide what one ought to do (stay home all day, go outside briefly, go visit the pope, etc.).

However, if one is schizophrenic to any extent, and it is now resignedly realized by the psychiatric profession that a hell of a lot of us are, many more than was once realized, knowledge of this type, this absolute, total presentation of a pattern representing the entire *koinos kosmos* at this *Augenblick* [moment], consists of total knowledge period, in view of the fact that for the schizophrenic there is no future anyhow. So in proportion to the degree of schizophrenic involvement in time that we're stuck with—or in—we can gain yield from the *I Ching*. For a person who is completely schizophrenic (which is impossible, but let's imagine it, for purposes here), the derived hexagram is everything; when he has studied it plus all texts appended to it, he knows—literally—all there is to know. He can relax if the hexagram is favorable; if not, then he can feel worse: His fears were justified. Things *are* unendurable, as well as hopeless, as well as beyond his control. He may, for example, with complete justification ask the book, "Am I dead?" and the book will answer. We would ask, "Am I going to get killed in the near future?," and in reading our hexagram get some kind of insight—if we read the judgment, "Misfortune. Nothing that would further," we might decide not to shoot out into commuter traffic that evening on the way to North Beach—and we might thereby keep alive a few years longer, which certainly has utility value to anyone, schizophrenic or not.

But we can't live by the damn book, because to try to would be to surrender ourselves to static time—as King Wen was forced to do by losing his throne and being imprisoned for the rest of his life, and as present-day schizophrenics must, along with those of us nutty enough to belt down a draft of LSD. But we can make partial use of it; partial, as its ability to "forecast coming events" is highly partial—if not in the strict sense, as I just now said, nonexistent. Sure, we can tinker around and fix matters up so that it *does* depict the future precisely. But that would be to become schizophrenic, or anyhow more schizophrenic. It would be a greater loss than gain; we would have induced our future into being consumed by the present: To understand the future totally would be to have it now. Try that, and see how it feels. Because once the future is gone, the possibility of free, effective action of any kind is abolished. This, of course, is a theme that appears in SF constantly; if no other instance crosses your mind, recall my own novel *The World Jones Made*. By being a precog, Jones ultimately lost the power to act entirely; instead of being freed by his talent, he was paralyzed by it. You catchum?

It occurs to me to sum up this observation by saying this. If you're totally schizophrenic now, by all means use the *I Ching* for everything, including telling you when to take a bath and when to open a can of cat tuna for your cat Rover. If you're partially schizophrenic (no names, please), then use it for some situations—but sparingly; don't rely on it inordinately: save it for Big Questions, such as, "Should I marry her or merely keep on living with her in sin?" etc. If you're not schizophrenic at all (those in this class step to the foot of the room, or however the expression, made up by you nonschizophrenics, goes), kindly use the book a very, measured little—in controlled doses, along the lines of your wise, middle-class use of Gleam, or whatever that damn toothpaste calls itself. Use the book as a sort of (ugh) fun thing. Ask it the opposite sort of questions from what we partial schizophrenics do; don't ask it, "How can I extricate myself from the dreadful circumstances of complete decay into which I've for the fiftieth time fallen, due to my own stupidity?," etc., but on this line instead, "What happened to lost Atlantis?" or, "Where did I mislay the sporting green *this* morning?" Ask it questions the outcome of which can have no genuine bearing on your life, or even on your immediate conduct; in other words, don't "act out" on the basis of what the book hands you—comport yourself strictly as you should under LSD: Observe and enjoy what you see (or, if it's the hell world, observe and suffer through in silence and immobility), but let that be all, white man; you begin to act out in real life on basis of what you see and we put you in Shanghai People's Democratic Funny Farm doing stoop labor at harvest time.

I speak from experience. The Oracle—the *I Ching*—told me to write this piece. (True, this is a zen way out, being told by the *I Ching* to write a piece explaining why not to do what the *I Ching* advises. But for me it's too late; the book hooked me years ago. Got any suggestions as to how I can extricate myself from my morbid dependence on the book? Maybe I ought to ask it that. Hmmm. Excuse me; I'll be back at the typewriter sometime next year. If not later.) (I never could make out the future too well.)

"The Android and the Human" (1972)

It is the tendency of the so-called primitive mind to animate its environment. Modern depth psychology has requested us for years to withdraw these anthropomorphic projections from what is actually inanimate reality, to introject—that is, bring back into our own heads—the living quality that we, in ignorance, cast out onto the inert things surrounding us. Such introjection is said to be the mark of true maturity in the individual, and the authentic mark of civilization in contrast to mere social culture, such as one finds in a tribe. A native of Africa is said to view his surroundings as pulsing with a purpose, a life, that is actually within himself; once these childish projections are withdrawn, he sees that the world is dead and that life resides solely within himself. When he reaches this sophisticated point he is said to be either mature or sane. Or scientific. But one wonders: Has he not also, in this process, reified—that is, made into a thing—other people? Stones and rocks and trees may now be inanimate for him, but what about his friends? Has he now made them into stones, too?

This is, really, a psychological problem. And its solution, I think, is of less importance in any case than one might think, because, within the past decade, we have seen a trend not anticipated by our earnest psychologists—or by anyone else—that dwarfs that issue; our environment, and I mean our man-made world of machines, artificial constructs, computers, electronic systems, interlinking homeostatic components—all of this is in fact beginning more and more to possess what the earnest psychologists fear the primitive sees in his environment: animation. In a very real sense our environment is becoming alive, or at least quasi-alive, and in ways specifically and fundamentally analogous to ourselves. Cybernetics, a valuable recent scientific discipline, articulated by the late Norbert Wiener, saw valid comparisons between the behavior of machines and humans—with the view that a study of machines would yield valuable insights into the nature of our own behavior. By studying what goes wrong with a machine—for example, when two mutually exclusive tropisms function simultaneously in one of Grey Walter's synthetic turtles, producing fascinatingly intricate behavior in the befuddled turtles—one learns, perhaps, a new, more fruitful insight into what [in] humans was previously called "neurotic" behavior. But suppose the use of this analogy is turned the other way. Suppose—and I don't believe Wiener anticipated this—suppose a study of ourselves, our own nature, enables us to gain insight into the now extraordinary complex functioning and malfunctioning of mechanical and electronic constructs? In other words—and this is what I wish to stress in what I am saying here—it is now possible that we can learn about the artificial external environment around us, how it behaves, why, what it is up to, by analogizing from what we know about ourselves.

Machines are becoming more human, so to speak—at least in the sense that, as Wiener indicated, some meaningful comparison exists between human and mechanical behavior. But is it ourselves that we know first and foremost? Rather than learning about ourselves by studying our constructs, perhaps we should make the attempt to comprehend what our constructs are up to by looking into what we ourselves are up to.

Perhaps, really, what we are seeing is a gradual merging of the general nature of human activity and function into the activity and function of what we humans have built and surround[ed] ourselves with. A hundred years ago such a thought would have been absurd, rather than merely anthropomorphic. What could a man living in 1750 have learned about himself by observing the behavior of a donkey steam engine? Could he have watched it huffing and puffing and then extrapolated from its labor an insight into why he himself continually fell in love with one certain type of pretty young girl? This would not have been primitive thinking on his part; it would have been pathological. But now we find ourselves immersed in a world of our own making so intricate, so mysterious, that as Stanislaw Lem the eminent Polish science fiction writer theorizes, the time may come when, for example, a man may have to be restrained from attempting to rape a sewing machine. Let us hope, if that time comes, that it is a female sewing machine he fastens his intentions on. And one over the age of seventeen—hopefully, a very old treddle-operated Singer, although possibly, regrettably, past menopause.

I have, in some of my stories and novels, written about androids or robots or simulacra—the name doesn't matter; what is meant is artificial constructs masquerading as humans. Usually with a sinister purpose in mind. I suppose I took it for granted that if such a construct, a robot, for example, had a benign or anyhow decent purpose in mind, it would not need to so disguise itself. Now, to me, that then seems obsolete. The constructs do not mimic humans; they are, in many deep ways, *actually* human already. They are not trying to fool us, for a purpose of any sort; they merely follow lines we follow, in order that they, too, may overcome such common problems as the breakdown of vital parts, loss of power source, attack by such foes as storms, short-circuits—and I'm sure any one of us here can testify that a short-circuit, especially in our power supply, can ruin our entire day and make us utterly unable to get to our daily job, or, once at the office, useless as far as doing the work set forth on our desk.

What would occur to me now as a recasting of the robot-appearing-as-human theme would be a gleaming robot with a telescan lens and a helium-battery power pack, who, when jostled, bleeds. Underneath the metal hull is a heart such as we ourselves have. Perhaps I will write that. Or, as in stories already in print, a computer, when asked some ultimate question such as "Why is there water?" prints out 1 Corinthians. One story I wrote, which I'm afraid I failed to take seriously enough, dealt with a computer that, when able to answer a question put to it, ate the questioner. Presumably—I failed to go into this—had the computer been unable to answer a question, the human questioner would have eaten *it*. Anyhow, inadvertently I blended the human and the construct and didn't notice that such a blend might, in time, actually begin to become part of our reality. Like Lem, I think this will be so, more and more. But to project past Lem's idea: A time may come when, if a man tries to rape a sewing machine, the sewing machine will have him arrested and testify, perhaps even a little hysterically, against him in court. This leads to all sorts of spin-off ideas: false testimony by suborned sewing machines who accuse innocent men unfairly; paternity tests; and, of course, abortions for sewing machines that have become pregnant against their will. And would there be birth control pills for sewing machines? Probably, like one of my previous wives, certain sewing machines would complain that the pills made them overweight—or rather, in their case, that it made them sew irregular stitches. And there would be unreliable sewing machines that would forget to take their birth control pills. And, last but not least, there would have to be Planned Parenthood clinics at which sewing machines just off the assembly lines would be counseled as to the dangers of promiscuity, with severe warnings of venereal diseases visited on such immoral machines by an outraged God—Himself, no doubt, able to sew buttonholes and fancy needlework at a rate that would dazzle the credulous merely metal and plastic sewing machines, always ready, like ourselves, to kowtow before divine miracles.

I am being facetious about this, I suppose, but—the point is not merely a humorous one. Our electronic constructs are becoming so complex that to comprehend them we must now reverse the analogizing of cybernetics and try to reason from our own mentation and behavior to theirs—although I suppose to assign motive or purpose to them would be to enter the realm of paranoia; what machines *do* may resemble what we do, but certainly they do not have intent in the sense that we have; they have tropisms, they have purpose in the sense that we build them to accomplish certain ends and to react to certain stimuli. A pistol, for example, is built with the purpose of firing a metal slug that will damage, incapacitate, or kill someone, but this does not mean that the pistol *wants* to do this. And yet there we are entering the philosophical realm of Spinoza when he saw, and I think with great profundity, that if a falling stone could reason, it would think, "I *want* to fall at the rate of thirty-two feet per second per second." Free will for us—that is, when we feel desire, when we are conscious of wanting to do what we do—may be even for us an illusion; and depth psychology seems to substantiate this: Many of our drives in life originate from an unconscious that is beyond our control. We are as driven as are insects, although the term "instinct" is perhaps not applicable for us. Whatever the term, much of our behavior that we feel is the result of our will, may control us to the extent that for all practical purposes we are falling stones, doomed to drop at a rate prescribed by nature, as rigid and predictable as the force that creates a crystal. Each of us may feel himself unique, with an intrinsic destiny never before seen in the universe . . . and yet to God we may be millions of crystals, identical in the eyes of the Cosmic Scientist.

And—here is a thought not too pleasing—as the external world becomes more animate, we may find that we—the so-called humans—are becoming, and may to a great extent always have been, inanimate in the sense that we are led, directed by built-in tropisms, rather than leading. So we and our elaborately evolving computers may meet each other halfway. Someday a human being, named perhaps Fred White, may shoot a robot named Pete Something-or-Other, which has come out of a General Electric factory, and to his surprise see it weep and bleed. And the dying robot may shoot back and, to its surprise, see a wisp of gray smoke arise from the electric pump that it supposed was Mr. White's beating heart. It would be rather a great moment of truth for both of them.

I would like, then, to ask this: What is it, in our behavior, that we can call specifically human? That is special to us as a living species? And what is it that, at least up to now, we can consign as merely machine behavior, or, by extension, insect behavior, or reflex behavior? And I would include in this the kind of pseudohuman behavior exhibited by what were once living men—creatures who have, in ways I wish to discuss next, become instruments, means, rather than ends, and hence to me analogues of machines in the *bad* sense, in the sense that although biological life continues, metabolism goes on, the soul—for lack of a better term—is no longer there or is at least no longer active. And such does exist in our world—it always did, but the production of such inauthentic human activity has become a science of government and suchlike agencies now. The reduction of humans to mere use—men made into machines, serving a purpose that although "good" in the abstract sense has, for its accomplishment, employed what I regard as the greatest evil imaginable: the placing on what was a free man who laughed and cried and made mistakes and wandered off into foolishness and play a restriction that limits him, despite what he may imagine or think, to the fulfilling of an aim outside of his own personal—however puny—destiny. As if, so to speak, history has made him into its instrument. History, and men skilled in—and trained in—the use of manipulative techniques, equipped with devices, ideologically oriented themselves, in such a way that the use of these devices strikes them as a necessary, or at least desirable, method of bringing about some ultimately desired goal.

I think, at this point, of Tom Paine's comment about one or another party of the Europe of his time, "They admired the feathers and forgot the dying bird." And it is the "dying bird" that I am concerned with. The dying—and yet, I think, beginning once again to revive in the hearts of the new generation of kids coming into maturity—the dying bird of authentic humanness.

That is what I wish to say to you here, today. I wish to disclose my hope, my faith, in the kids who are emerging now. Their world, their values. And, simultaneously, their imperviousness to the false values, the false idols, the false hates of the previous generations. The fact that they, these fine, good kids, cannot be reached or moved or even touched by the "gravity"—to refer back to my previous metaphor—that has made us older persons fall, against our knowledge or will, at thirty-two feet per second throughout our lives . . . while believing that we *desired* it.

It is as if these kids, or at least many of them, some of them, are falling at a different rate, or, really, not falling at all. Walt Whitman's "Marching to the sound of other drummers" [this phrase, inexactly quoted, in fact belongs to Henry David Thoreau] might be rephrased this way: falling, not in response to unexamined, unchallenged, alleged "verities," but in response to a new and inner—and genuinely authentic—human desire.

Youth, of course, has always tended toward this; in fact, this is really a definition of youth. But right now it is so urgent, if, as I think, we are merging by degrees into homogeneity with our mechanical constructs, step by step, month by month, until a time will perhaps come when a writer, for example, will not stop writing because someone unplugged his electric typewriter but because someone unplugged *him*. But there are kids *now* who cannot be unplugged because no electric cord links them to any external power sources. Their hearts beat with an interior, private meaning. Their energy doesn't come from a pacemaker; it comes from a stubborn, almost absurdly perverse refusal to be "shucked"; that is, to be taken in by the slogans, the ideology—in fact, by any and all ideology itself, of whatever sort—that would reduce them to instruments of abstract causes, however "good." Back in California, where I came from, I have been living with such kids, participating, to the extent I can, in their emerging world. I would like to tell you about their world because—if we are lucky—something of that world, those values, that way of life, will shape the future of our total society, our utopia or anti-utopia of the future. As a science fiction writer, I must, of course, look continually ahead, always at the future. It is my hope—and I'd like to communicate it to you in the tremendous spirit of optimism that I feel so urgently and strongly—that our collective tomorrow exists in embryonic form in the heads, or rather in the hearts, of these kids who right now, at their young ages, are politically and sociologically powerless, unable even, by our California laws, to buy a bottle of beer or cigarette, to vote, to in any way shape, be consulted about, or bring into existence the official laws that govern them and our society. I think, really, I am saying this: If you are interested in the world of tomorrow you may learn something about it, or at least read about possibilities that may emerge to fashion it, in the pages of *Analog* and *F&SF* and *Amazing,* but actually, to find it in its authentic form, you will discover it as you observe a sixteen- or seventeen-year-old kid as he goes about his natural peregrinations, his normal day. Or, as we say in the San Francisco Bay Area, as you observe him "cruising around town to check out the action." This is what I have found. These kids that I have known, lived with, still know, in California, are my science fiction stories of tomorrow, my summation, at this point of my life as a person and a writer; they are what I look ahead to—and so keenly desire to see prevail. What, more than anything else I have ever encountered, I believe in. And would give my life for. My full measure of devotion, in this war we are fighting, to maintain, and augment, what is human about us, what is the core of ourselves and the source of our destiny. Our flight must be not only to the stars but into the nature of our own beings. Because it is not merely *where* we go, to Alpha Centauri or Betelgeuse, but what we are as we make our pilgrimages there. Our natures will be going there, too. *Ad astra*—but *per hominum.* [To the stars—but as men.] And we must never lose sight of that.

It would, after all, be rather dismaying, if the first two-legged entity to emerge on the surface of Mars from a Terran spacecraft were to declare, "Thanks be to God for letting me, letting me, click, letting, click, click . . . this is a recording." And then catch fire and explode as a couple of wires got crossed somewhere within its plastic chest. And probably even more dismaying to this construct would be the discovery when it returned to Earth that its "children" had been recycled along with the aluminum beer cans and Coca-Cola bottles as fragments of the urban pollution problem. And, finally, when this astronaut made of plastic and wiring and relays went down to the City Hall officials to complain, it would discover that its three-year guarantee had run out, and, since parts were no longer available to keep it functioning, its birth certificate had been canceled.

Of course, literally, we should not take this seriously. But as a metaphor—in some broad sense maybe we should scrutinize more closely the two-legged entities we plan to send up, for example, to man the orbiting space station. We do not want to learn three years from now that the alleged human crew had all married portions of the space station and had settled down to whirr happily forever after in connubial bliss. As in Ray Bradbury's superb story in which a fear-haunted citizen of Los Angeles discovers that the police car trailing him has no driver, that it is tailing him on its own, we should be sure that one of us sits in the driver's seat: In Mr. Bradbury's story the real horror, at least to me, is not that the police car has its own tropism as it hounds the protagonist but that, within the car, there is a vacuum. A place unfilled. The *absence* of something vital— that is the horrific part, the apocalyptic vision of a nightmare future. But I, myself, foresee something more optimistic: Had I written that story I would have had a teenager behind the wheel of the police car—he has stolen it while the policeman is in a coffee shop on his lunch break, and the kid is going to resell it by tearing it down into parts. This may sound a little cynical on my part, but wouldn't this be preferable? As we say in California, where I live, when the police come to investigate a burglary of your house, they find, when they are leaving, that someone has stripped the tires and motor and transmission from their car, and the officers must hitchhike back to headquarters. This thought may strike fear in the hearts of the establishment people, but frankly it makes me feel cheerful. Even the most base schemes of human beings are preferable to the most exalted tropisms of machines. I think this, right here, is one of the valid insights possessed by some of the new youth: Cars, even police cars, are expendable; can be replaced. They are really all alike. It is the person inside who, when gone, cannot be duplicated at any price. Even if we do not like him we cannot do without him. And once gone, he will never come back.

And then, too, if he is made into an android, he will never come back, never be again human. Or anyhow most likely will not.

As the children of our world fight to develop their new individuality, their almost surly disrespect for the verities we worship, they become for us—and by "us" I mean the establishment—a source of trouble. I do not necessarily mean politically active youth, those who organize into distinct societies with banners and slogans—to me that is a reduction into the past, however revolutionary these slogans may be. I refer to the intrinsic entities, the kids each of whom is on his own, doing what we call "his thing." He may, for example, not break the law by seating himself on the tracks before troop trains; his flouting of the law may consist of taking his car to a drive-in movie with four kids in the trunk to avoid having to pay. Still, a law is being broken. The first transgression has political, theoretical overtones; the second, a mere lack of agreement that one must always do what one is ordered to do—especially when the order comes from a posted, printed sign. In both cases there is disobedience. We might applaud the first as meaningful. The second, merely irresponsible. And yet it is in the second that I see a happier future. After all, there has always been in history movements of people organized in opposition to the governing powers. This is merely one group using force against another, the outs versus the ins. It has failed to produce a utopia so far. And I think always will.

Becoming what I call, for lack of a better term, an android, means, as I said, to allow oneself to become a means, or to be pounded down, manipulated, made into a means without one's knowledge or consent—the results are the same. But you cannot turn a human into an android if that human is going to break laws every chance he gets. Androidization requires obedience. And, most of all, *predictability*. It is precisely when a given person's response to any given situation can be predicted with scientific accuracy that the gates are open for the wholesale production of the android life form. What good is a flashlight if the bulb lights up only now and then when you press the button? Any machine must always work to be reliable. The android, like any other machine, must perform on cue. But our youth cannot be counted on to do this; it is unreliable. Either through laziness, short attention span, perversity, criminal tendencies—whatever label you wish to pin on the kid to explain his unreliability is fine. Each merely means: We can tell him and tell him what to do, but when the time comes for him to perform, all the subliminal instruction, all the ideological briefing, all the tranquilizing drugs, all the psychotherapy are a waste. He just plain will not jump when the whip is cracked.

And so he is of no use to us, the calcified, entrenched powers. He will not see to it that he acts as an instrument by which we both keep and augment those powers and the rewards—for ourselves—that go with them.

What has happened is that there has been too much persuasion. The television set, the newspapers—all the so-called mass media—have overdone it. Words have ceased to mean much to these kids; they have had to listen to too many. They cannot be taught because there has been too great an eagerness, too conspicuous a motive, to make them learn. The anti-utopia science fiction writers of fifteen years ago, and I was one of them, foresaw the mass communications propaganda machinery grinding everyone down into mediocrity and uniformity. But it is not coming out this way. While the car radio dins out the official view on the war in Vietnam, the young boy is disconnecting the speaker so that he can replace it with a tweeter and a woofer; in the middle of the government's harangue the speaker is unattached. And, as he expertly hooks up better audio components in his car, the boy fails even to notice that the voice on the radio is trying to tell him something. This skilled craftsman of a kid listens only to see whether there is any distortion, interference, or a frequency curve that isn't fully compensated. His head is turned toward immediate realities—the speaker itself—not the *flatuus voci* dinning from it.

The totalitarian society envisioned by George Orwell in 1984 should have arrived by now. The electronic gadgets are here. The government is here, ready to do what Orwell anticipated. So the power exists, the motive, and the electronic hardware. But these mean nothing, because, progressively more and more so, no one is listening. The new youth that I see is too stupid to read, too restless and bored to watch, too preoccupied to remember. The collective voice of the authorities is wasted on him; he rebels. But rebels not out of theoretical, ideological considerations, but only out of what might be called pure selfishness. Plus a careless lack of regard for the dread consequences that the authorities promise him if he fails to obey. He cannot be bribed because what he wants he can build, steal, or in some curious, intricate way acquire himself. He cannot be intimidated because on the streets and in his home he has seen and participated in so much violence that it fails to cow him. He merely gets out of its way when it threatens, or, if he can't escape, he fights back. When the locked police van comes to carry him off to the concentration camp, the guards will discover that while loading the van they have failed to note that another equally hopeless juvenile has slashed the tires. The van is out of commission. And while the tires are being replaced, some other youth siphons out all the gas from the gas tank for his souped-up Chevrolet and has sped off long ago.

The absolutely horrible technological society—that was our dream, our vision of the future. We could foresee nothing equipped with enough power, guile, or whatever to impede the coming of that dreadful, nightmare society. It never occurred to us that the delinquent kids might abort it out of the sheer perverse malice of their little individual souls, God bless them. Here, as in [sic] case in point, are two excerpts from the media; the first, quoted in that epitome of the nauseating, *Time*, is—so help me—what *Time* calls the "ultimate dream in telephone service once described by Harold S. Osborne, former chief engineer at AT&T: Whenever a baby is born anywhere in the world, he is given at birth a telephone number for life. As soon as he can talk, he is given a watchlike device with ten little buttons on one side and screen on the other. When he wishes to talk with anyone in the world, he will pull out the device and punch on the keys the number. Then, turning the device over, he will hear the voice of his friend and see his face on the screen, in color and in three dimensions. If he does not see him and hear him, he will know that his friend is dead."

I don't know; I really don't find this funny. It is really sad. It is heartbreaking. Anyhow, it is not going to happen. The kids have already seen to that. "Phone freaks," they are called, these particular kids. This is what the *L.A. Times* says, in an article dated earlier this year:

They (the phone freaks) all arrived carrying customized MFers—multifrequency tone signals—the phone-freak term for a blue box. The homemade MFers varied in size and design. One was a sophisticated pocket transistor built by a Ph.D. in engineering, another was the size of a cigar box with an acoustical coupler attaching to the phone receiver. So far, these phone freaks had devised twenty-two ways to make a free call without using credit cards. In case of a slip-up, the phone freaks also know how to detect "supervision," phone-company jargon for a nearly inaudible tone that comes on the line before anyone answers to register calling charges. As soon as phone freaks detect the dreaded "supervision," they hang up fast.

Captain Crunch was still in the phone booth pulling the red switches on his fancy computerized box. He got his name from the whistle found in the Cap'n Crunch breakfast cereal box. Crunch discovered that the whistle has a frequency of 2,600 cycles per second, the exact frequency the telephone company uses to indicate that a line is idle, and, of course, the first frequency phone freaks learn how to whistle to get "disconnect," which allows them to pass from one circuit to another. Crunch, intent, hunched over his box to read a list of country code numbers. He impersonated a phone man, gave precise technical information to the overseas operator and called Italy. In less than a minute he reached a professor of classical Greek writings at the University of Florence.

This is how the future has actually come out. None of us science fiction writers foresaw phone freaks. Fortunately, neither did the phone company, which otherwise would have taken over by now. But this is the difference between dire myth and war, merry reality. And it is the kids, unique, wonderful, unhampered by scruples in any traditional sense, that have made the difference.

Speaking in science fiction terms, I now foresee an anarchistic, totalitarian state ahead. Ten years from now a TV street reporter will ask some kid who is president of the United States, and the kid will admit that he doesn't know. "But the president can have you executed," the reporter will protest. "Or beaten or thrown into prison or all your rights taken away, all your property—everything." And the boy will reply, "Yeah, so could my father up to last month when he had his fatal coronary. He used to say the same thing." End of interview. And when the reporter goes to gather up his equipment he will find that one of his color 3-D stereo microphone-vidlens systems is missing; the kid has swiped it from him while the reporter was babbling on.

If, as it seems we are, [sic] in the process of becoming a totalitarian society in which the state apparatus is all-powerful, the ethics most important for the survival of the true, human individual would be: Cheat, lie, evade, fake it, be elsewhere, forge documents, build improved electronic gadgets in your garage that'll outwit the gadgets used by the authorities. If the television screen is going to watch you, rewire it late at night when you're permitted to turn it off—rewire it in such a way that the police flunky monitoring the transmission from your living room mirrors back *his* house. When you sign a confession under duress, forge the name of one of the political spies who's infiltrated your model-airplane club. Pay your fines in counterfeit money or rubber cheks or stolen credit cards. Give a false address. Arrive at the courthouse in a stolen car. Tell the judge that if he sentences you, you will substitute aspirin tablets for his daughter's birth control pills. Or put His Honor on a mailing list for pornographic magazines. Or, if all else fails, threaten him with your using his telephone-credit-card number to make unnecessary long-distance calls to cities on another planet. It will not be necessary to blow up the courthouse anymore. Simply find some way to defame the judge—you saw him driving home one night on the wrong side of the road with his headlights off and a fifth of Seagram's VO propped up against his steering wheel. And his bumper sticker that night read: *Grant Full Rights to Us Homosexuals.* He has, of course, torn off the sticker by now, but both you and ten of your friends witnessed it. And they are all at pay phones right now, ready to phone the news to the local papers. And, if he is so foolish as to sentence you, at least ask him to give back the little tape recorder you inadvertently left in his bedroom. Since the off-switch on it is broken, it has probably recorded its entire ten-day reel of tape by now. Results should be interesting. And if he tries to destroy the tape, you will have him arrested for vandalism, which in the totalitarian state of tomorrow will be the supreme crime. What is your life worth in his eyes compared with a $3 reel of Mylar tape? The tape is probably government property, like everything else, so to destroy it would be a crime against the state. The first step in a calculated, sinister insurrection.

I wonder if you recall the "brain mapping" developed by Penfield recently; he was able to locate the exact centers of the brain from which each sensation, emotion, and response came. By stimulating one minute area with an electrode, a laboratory rat was transfigured into a state of perpetual bliss. "They'll be doing that to all of us, too, soon," a pessimistic friend said to me regarding that. "Once the electrodes have been implanted, they can get us to feel, think, do anything they want." Well, to do this, the government would have to let out a contract for the manufacture of a billion sets of electrodes, and in their customary way, they would award the contract to the lowest bidder, who would build substandard electrodes out of secondhand parts.

The technicians implanting the electrodes in the brains of millions upon millions of people would become bored and careless, and, when the switch would be pressed for the total population to feel profound grief at the death of some government official—probably the minister of the interior, in charge of the slave-labor rehabilitation camps—it would all get folded up, and the population, like that laboratory rat, would go into collective seizures of merriment. Or the substandard wiring connecting the brains of the population with the Washington, D.C., thought control center would overload, and a surge of electricity would roll backward over the lines and set fire to the White House.

Or is this just wishful thinking on my part? A little fantasy about a future society we should really feel apprehensive about?

The continued elaboration of state tyranny such as we in science fiction circles anticipate in the world of tomorrow—our whole preoccupation with what we call the "anti-utopian" society—this growth of state invasion into the privacy of the individual, its knowing too much about him, and then, when it knows, or thinks it knows, something it frowns on, its power and capacity to squash the individual—as we thoroughly comprehend, this evil process utilizes technology as its instrument. The inventions of applied science, such as the almost miraculously sophisticated sensor devices right now traveling back from war use in Vietnam for adaptation to civilian use here—these passive infrared scanners, sniperscopes, these chrome boxes with dials and gauges that can penetrate brick and stone, can tell the user what is being said and done a mile away within a tightly sealed building, be it concrete bunker or apartment building, can, like the weapons before them, fall into what the authorities would call "the wrong hands"—that is, into the hands of the very people being monitored. Like all machines, these universal transmitters, recording devices, heat-pattern discriminators, don't in themselves care who they're used by or against. The predatory law-and-order vehicle speeding to the scene of a street fracas where, for example, some juvenile has dropped a water-filled balloon into the sports car of a wealthy taxpayer—this vehicle, however fast, however well-armed and animated by the spirit of righteous vengeance, can be spotted by the same lens by which its superiors became aware of the disturbance in the first place . . . and notification of its impending arrival on the scene can be flashed by the same walkie-talkie Army surplus gadget by which crowd control is maintained when blacks gather to protest for their just rights. Before the absolute power of the absolute state of tomorrow can achieve its victory it may find such things as this: When the police show up at your door to arrest you for thinking unapproved thoughts, a scanning sensor that you've bought and built into your door discriminates the intruders from customary friends and alerts you to your peril.

Let me give you an example. At the enormous civic center building in my county, a fantastic Buck Rogers type of plastic and chrome backdrop to a bad science fiction film, each visitor must pass through an electronic field that sets off an alarm if he has on him too much metal, be it keys, a watch, a pair of scissors, bomb, or .308 Winchester rifle. When the hoop pings—and it always pings for me—a uniformed policeman immediately fully searches the visitor. A sign warns that if any weapon is discovered on a visitor, it's all over for him—and the sign also warns that if any illegal drugs are found on a visitor during this weapons search, he's done for, too. Now, I think even you people up here in Canada are aware of the reason for this methodical weapons search of each visitor to the Marin County Civic Center—it has to do with the tragic shootout a year or so ago. But, and they officially posted notice of this, the visitor will be inspected for narcotics possession, too, and this has nothing to do with either the shootout or with any danger to the building itself or the persons within it. An electronic checkpoint legitimately set up to abort a situation in which explosives or weapons are brought into the Civic Center, has been assigned an added police function connected with the authentic issue only by the common thread of Penal Code violation. To visit the county library, which is in that building, you are subject to search—must, in fact, yield absolutely and unconditionally—for possession without the juridical protection, built into the very basis of our American civil rights system, that some clear and evident indication exist that you may be carrying narcotics before a search can be carried out against you. During the search I've even had the uniformed officer at the entrance examine the books and papers I was carrying, to see if they were acceptable. The next step, in the months to come, would be to have such mandatory checkpoints at busy intersections and at all public buildings—including banks and so forth. Once it has been established that the authorities can search you for illegal drugs because you're returning a book to the library, I think you can see just how far the tyranny of the state can go. Once it has provided itself with an electronic hoop that registers the presence of something we all carry on us: keys, a pair of fingernail clippers, coins. The *blip*, rather a quaint little sound, which you set off, opens a door not leading to the county library but to possible imprisonment. It is that blip that ushers in all the rest. And how many other blips are we setting off, or our children will be setting off, in contexts that we know nothing about yet? But my optimistic point: The kids of today, having been born into this all-pervasive society, are fully aware of and take for granted the activity of such devices. One afternoon when I was parking my car on the lot before a grocery store, I started, as usual, to lock all the car doors to keep the parcels in the backseat from being stolen. "Oh, you don't have to lock up ‡he car," the girl with me said. "This parking lot is under constant closed-circuit TV scan. Every car here and everyone is being watched all the time; nothing can happen." So we went inside the store, leaving the car unlocked. And, of course, she was right; born into this society, she has learned to know such things. And—I now have a passive infrared scanning system in my own home in Santa Venetia, connected with what is called a "digital transmitting box," which, when triggered off by the scanner, transmits a coded signal by direct line to the nearest law-enforcement agency, notifying them that intruders have entered my house. This totally self-operated electronic detection system functions whether I am home or not. It is able to discriminate between the presence of a human being and an animal. It has its own power supply. If the line leading from it is cut, grounded, or even tampered with, the signal is immediately released, or if any other part of the system is worked on. And Westinghouse will reinstall it wherever I live: I own the components for life. Eventually, Westinghouse Security hopes, all homes and businesses will be protected this way. The company has built and maintains a communications center near each community in this country. If there is no police agency willing or able to accept the signal, then their own communications center responds and guarantees to dispatch law enforcement personnel within four minutes—that is, the good guys with the good guns will be at your door within that time. It does not matter if the intruder enters with a passkey or blows in the whole side of the house, or as they tell me it's being done now, bores down through the roof—however he gets in, for whatever reason, the mechanism responds and transmits its signal. Only I can turn the system off. And if I forget to, then—I suppose, anyhow—it's all over for me.

Someone suggested, by the way, that perhaps this passive infrared scanner sweeping out the interior of my house constantly "might be watching me and reporting back to the authorities whatever I do right there in my living room." Well, what I am doing is sitting at my desk with pen and paper trying to figure out how to pay Westinghouse the $840 I owe them for the system. As I've got it worked out now, I think that if I sell everything I own, including my house, I can—oh, well. One other thing. If I enter the house—my house—and the system finds I'm carrying illegal narcotics on my person, it doesn't blip; it causes both me and the house and everything in it to self-destruct.

Street drugs, by the way, are a major problem in the area where I live—that is, the illegal drugs you buy on the street are often adulterated, cut, or just plain not what you're told they are. You wind up poisoned, dead, or just plain "burned," which means, "You don't get off," which means you paid $10 for a gram of milk sugar. So a number of free labs have been set up for the specific purpose of analyzing street drugs; you mail them a portion of the drug you've brought and they tell you what's in it, the idea being, of course, that if it has strychnine or flash powder in it, you should know before you take it. Well, the police saw through into the "real" purpose of these labs at one glance. They act as quality-control stations for the drug manufacturers. Let's say you're making Methedrine in your bathtub at home—a complicated process, but feasible—and so every time a new batch comes out, you mail a sample to one of these labs for analysis . . . and they write back, "No, you haven't got it quite right yet, but if you cook it for perhaps just five minutes longer . . ." This is what the police fear. This is how the police mentality works. And, interestingly, so does the drug-pusher mentality; the pushers are already doing precisely that. I don't know—to me it seems a sort of nice idea, the drug pushers interested in what they're selling. Back in the old days they cared only that you lived long enough to pay for what you purchased. After that, you were on your own.

Yes, as every responsible parent knows, street drugs are a problem, a menace to their kids. I completely, emphatically agree. At one time—you may have read this in biographical material accompanying my stories and novels—I was interested in experimenting with psychedelic drugs. That is over for me. Too many suicides, psychoses, organic—irreversible—damage to both heart and brain. But there are other drugs, not illegal, not street drugs, not cut with flash powder or milk sugar, and not mislabeled, that worry me even more. These are reputable, establishment drugs prescribed by reputable doctors or given in reputable hospitals, especially psychiatric hospitals. These are pacification drugs. I mention this in order to return to my main preoccupation, here: the human versus the android, and how the former can become—can, in fact, be made to become—the latter. The calculated, widespread, and thoroughly sanctioned use of specific tranquilizing drugs such as the phenothiazines may not, like certain illegal street drugs, produce permanent brain damage, but they can—and, God forbid, they do—produce what I am afraid I must call "soul" damage. Let me amplify.

It has been discovered recently that what we call mental illness or mental disturbance—such syndromes as the schizophrenias and the cyclothemic phenomena of manic-depression—may have to do with faulty brain metabolism, the failure of certain brain catalysts such as serotonin and noradrenaline to act properly. One theory holds that, under stress, too much amine oxidase production causes hallucinations, disorientation, and general mentational breakdown. Sudden shock, especially at random, and grief-producing, such as loss of someone or something dear, or the loss of something vital and taken for granted—this starts an overproduction of noradrenaline flowing down generally unused neural pathways, overloading brain circuits and producing behavior that we call psychotic. Mental illness, then, is a biochemical phenomenon. If certain drugs, such as the phenothiazines, are introduced, brain metabolism regains normal balance; the catalyst serotonin is utilized properly, and the patient recovers. Or if the MAOI drug is introduced—a mono amine oxidase inhibitor—response to stress becomes viable and the person is able to function normally. Or—and this right now is the Prince Charming hope of the medical profession—lithium carbonate, if taken by the disturbed patient, will limit an otherwise overabundant production or release of the hormone noradrenaline, which, most of all, acts to cause irrational thoughts and behavior of a socially unacceptable sort. The entire amplitude of feelings, wild grief, anger, fear, and all intense feelings will be reduced to proper measure by the presence of the lithium carbonate in the brain tissue. The person will become stable, predictable, not a menace to others. He will feel the same and think the same pretty much all day long, day after day. The authorities will not be greeted by any more sudden surprises emanating from him.

In the field of abnormal psychology, the schizoid personality structure is well defined; in it there is a continual paucity of feeling. The person thinks rather than feels his way through life. And as the great Swiss psychiatrist Carl Jung showed, this cannot be successfully maintained; one must meet most of crucial reality with a feeling response. Anyhow, there is a certain parallel between what I call the "android" personality and the schizoid. Both have a mechanical, reflex quality.

Once I heard a schizoid person express himself—in all seriousness— this way: "I receive signals from others. But I can't generate any of my own until I get recharged. By an injection." I am, I swear, quoting exactly. Imagine viewing oneself and others this way. Signals. As if from another star. The person has reified himself entirely, along with everyone around him. How awful. Here, clearly, the soul is dead or never lived.

Another quality of the android mind is an inability to make exceptions. Perhaps this is the essence of it: the failure to drop a response when it fails to accomplish results, but rather to repeat it, over and over again. Lower life forms are skillful in offering the same response continually, as are flashlights. An attempt was made once to use a pigeon as a quality-control technician on an assembly line. Part after part, endless thousands of them, passed by the pigeon hour after hour, and the keen eye of the pigeon viewed them for deviations from the acceptable tolerance. The pigeon could discern a deviation smaller than that which a human, doing the same quality control, could. When the pigeon saw a part that was mismade, it pecked a button, which rejected the part, and at the same time dropped a grain of corn to the pigeon as a reward. The pigeon could go eighteen hours without fatigue and loved its work. Even when the grain of corn failed—due to the supply running out, I guess—the pigeon continued eagerly to reject the substandard parts. It had to be forcibly removed from its perch, finally.

Now, if I had been that pigeon, I would have cheated. When I felt hungry, I would have pecked the button and rejected a part, just to get my grain of corn. That would have occurred to me after a long period passed in which I discerned no faulty parts. Because what would happen to the pigeon if, God forbid, *no* parts ever were faulty? The pigeon would starve. Integrity, under such circumstances, would be suicidal. Really, the pigeon had a life-and-death interest in finding faulty parts. What would you do, were you the pigeon, and, after say four days, you'd discovered no faulty parts and were becoming only feathers and bone? Would ethics win out? Or the need to survive? To me, the life of the pigeon would be worth more than the accuracy of the quality control. If I were the pigeon—but the android mind, "I may be dying of hunger," the android would say, "but I'll be damned if I'll reject a perfectly good part." Anyhow, to me, the authentically human mind would get bored and reject a part now and then at random, just to break the monotony. And no amount of circuit testing would reestablish its reliability.

Let me now express another element that strikes me as an essential key revealing the authentically human. It is not only an intrinsic property of the organism, but the situation in which it finds itself. That which happens to it, that which it is confronted by, pierced by, and must deal with—certain agonizing situations create, on the spot, a human where a moment before, there was only, as the Bible says, clay. Such a situation can be read off the face of many of the medieval Pietàs: the dead Christ held in the arms of his mother. Two faces, actually: that of a man, that of a woman. Oddly, in many of these Pietàs, the face of Christ seems much older than that of his mother. It is as if an ancient man is held by a young woman; she has survived him, and yet she came before him. He has aged through his entire life cycle; she looks now perhaps as she always did, not timeless, in the classical sense, but able to transcend what has happened.

He has not survived it; this shows on his face. She has. In some way they have experienced it together, but they have come out of it differently. It was too much for him; it destroyed him. Perhaps the information to be gained here is to realize how much greater capacity a woman has for suffering; that is, not that she suffers more than a man but that she can endure where he can't. Survival of the species lies in her ability to do this, not his. Christ may die on the cross, and the human race continues, but if Mary dies, it's all over.

I have seen young women—say, eighteen or nineteen years old—suffer and survive things that would have been too much for me, and I think really for almost any man. Their humanness, as they passed through these ordeals, developed as an equation between them and their situation. I don't mean to offer the mushy doctrine that suffering somehow ennobles, that it's somehow a good thing—one hears this now and then about geniuses, "They wouldn't have been geniuses if they hadn't suffered," etc. I merely mean that possibly the difference between what I call the "android" mentality and the human is that the latter passed through something the former did not, or at least passed through it and responded differently—*changed*, altered, what it did and hence what it was; it *became*. I sense the android repeating over and over again some limited reflex gesture, like an insect raising its wings threateningly over and over again, or emitting a bad smell. Its one defense or response works, or it doesn't. But, caught in sudden trouble, the organism that is made more human, that becomes precisely at that moment human, wrestles deep within itself and out to itself to find one response after another as each fails. On the face of the dead Christ there is an exhaustion, almost a dehydration, as if he tried out every possibility in an effort not to die. He never gave up. And even though he did die, did fail, he died a human. This is what shows on his face.

"The endeavor to persist in its own being," Spinoza said, "is the essence of the individual thing." The chthonic deities, the Earth Mother were the original source of religious consolation—before the solarcentric masculine deities that arrived later in history—as well as the origin of man; man came from her and returns to her. The entire ancient world believed that just as each man came forth into individual life from a woman, he would eventually return—and find peace at last. At the end of life the old man in one of Chaucer's *Canterbury Tales* "goes about both morning and late and knocks against the ground with his stick saying, 'Mother, mother, let me in. . . .' " Just as at the end of Ibsen's *Ghosts*, the middle-aged man, regressing into childhood at the end of his life as he dies of paresis, says to his mother, "Mother, give me the sun." As Spinoza pointed out so clearly, each finite thing, each individual man, eventually perishes . . . and his only true consolation, as he perishes, as each society in fact perishes, is this return to the mother, the woman, the Earth.

But if woman is the consolation for man, what is the consolation for woman? For *her*?

Once I watched a young woman undergo agonies—she was eighteen years old—that, just witnessing her, were too much for me. She survived,

I think, better than I did. I wanted to console her, help her, but there was nothing I could do. Except be with her. When the Earth Mother is suffering, there is damn little that individual finite man can do. This young girl's boyfriend wouldn't marry her because she was pregnant by another boy; he wouldn't live with her or find her a place to stay until she got an abortion—about which he would do nothing; he wouldn't even speak to her until it was over—and then, or so he promised, he would marry her. Well, she got the abortion, and we brought her to my home afterward to rest and recover, and, of course, the son of a bitch never had anything to do with her again. I was with her during the days following her abortion, and really she had a dreadful time, alone in a poor, large ward in a hospital in another city, never visited except by me and a couple of friends, never phoned by her boyfriend or her own family, and then at my home, afterward, when she realized her boyfriend was never going to get the apartment for them she had planned on, been promised, and her friends—his friends, too—had lost interest in her and looked down on her—I saw her day-by-day decline and wilt and despair, and become wild with fear: Where would she go? What would become of her? She had no friends, no job, no family, not even any clothes to speak of—nothing. And she couldn't stay with me after she healed up. She used to lie in bed, suffering, holding the puppy she and I got at the pound; the puppy was all she had. And one day she left, and I never found out where she went. She never contacted me again; she wanted to forget me and the hospital and the days of healing and bleeding and learning the truth about her situation. And she left the puppy behind. I have it now. What I remember in particular was that in the two weeks she was with me after her abortion her breasts swelled with milk; her body, at least portions of it, didn't know that the child was dead, that there was no child. It was, she said, "in a bottle." I saw her, all at once, as a sudden woman, even though she had, herself, declined, destroyed, her motherhood; baby or not, she was a woman, although her mind did not tell her that; she still wore the cotton nightgown she had worn, I guess, while living at home while she went to high school—perhaps the same easy-to-wash nightgown she had worn since five or six years old. She still liked to go to the market and buy chocolate milk and comic books. Under California law it's illegal for her to buy or smoke cigarettes. There are certain movies—many, in fact—that our law prevents her from seeing. Movies, supposedly, about life. On the trip to San Francisco to see the doctor about getting the abortion—she was five and a half months pregnant, nearing what California considers the limit of safety—she bought a purple stuffed toy animal for 89 cents. I paid for it; she had only 25 cents. She took it with her when she left my home. She was the bravest, brightest, funniest, sweetest person I ever knew. The tragedy of her life bent her and virtually broke her, despite all I could do. But—I think, I believe—the force that is her, so to speak the swelling into maturity of her breasts, the looking forward into the future of her physical body, even at the moment that mentally and spiritually she was virtually destroyed—I hope, anyhow, that that force will prevail. If it dies out, then there is nothing left, as far as I am concerned. The future as I conceive it will not exist. Because I can only imagine it as populated by modest, unnoticed persons like her. I myself will not be a part of it or even shape it; all I can do is depict it as I see the ingredients now, the gentle, little, unhappy, brave, lonely, loving creatures who are going on somewhere else, unknown to me now, not recalling me but, I pray, living on, picking up life, *forgetting*—"those who cannot remember the past are condemned to repeat it," we are told, but perhaps it is better—perhaps it is the only viable way—to be able to forget. I hope that she, in her head, has forgotten what happened to her, just as her body either forgot the lack of a baby, the dead baby, or never knew. It is a kind of blindness, maybe; a refusal, or inability, to face reality.

But I have never had too high a regard for what is generally called "reality." Reality, to me, is not so much something that you perceive, but something you make. You create it more rapidly than it creates you. Man is the reality God created out of dust; God is the reality man creates continually out of his own passions, his own determination. "Good," for example—that is not a quality or even a force in the world or above the world, but what you do with the bits and pieces of meaningless, puzzling, disappointing, even cruel and crushing fragments all around us that seem to be pieces left over, discarded, from another world entirely that did, maybe, make sense.

The world of the future, to me, is not a place but an event. A construct, not by one author in the form of words written to make up a novel or story that other persons sit in front of, outside of, and read—but a construct in which there is no author and no readers but a great many characters in search of a plot. Well, there is no plot. There is only themselves and what they do and say to each other, what they build to sustain all of them individually and collectively, like a huge umbrella that lets in light and shuts out the darkness at the same instant. When the characters die, the novel ends. And the book falls back into dust. Out of which it came. Or back, like the dead Christ, into the arms of his warm, tender, grieving, comprehending, living mother. And a new cycle begins; from her he is reborn, and the story, or another story, perhaps different, even better, starts up. A story told by the characters to one another. "A tale of sound and fury"—signifying very much. The best we have. Our yesterday, our tomorrow, the child who came before us and the woman who will live after us and outlast, by her very existing, what we have thought and done.

In my novel *The Three Stigmata of Palmer Eldritch*, which is a study of absolute evil, the protagonist, after his encounter with Eldritch, returns to Earth and dictates a memo. This little section appears ahead of the text of the novel. It *is* the novel, actually, this paragraph; the rest is a sort of postmortem, or rather, a flashback in which all that came to produce the one-paragraph book is presented. Seventy-five thousand words, which I labored over many months, merely explains, is merely there to provide background to the one small statement in the book that matters. (It is, by the way, missing from the German edition.) This statement is for me my credo—not so much in God, either a good god or a bad god or both—but in ourselves. It goes as follows, and this is all I actually have to say or want ever to say:

I mean, after all; you have to consider, we're only made out of dust. That's admittedly not much to go on and we shouldn't forget that. But even considering, I mean it's a sort of bad beginning, we're not doing too bad. So I personally have faith that even in this lousy situation we're faced with we can make it. You get me?

This tosses a bizarre thought up into my mind: Perhaps someday a giant automated machine will roar and clank out, "From rust we are come." And another machine, sick of dying, cradled in the arms of its woman, may sigh back, "And to rust we are returned." And peace will fall over the barren, anxiety-stricken landscape.

Our field, science fiction, deals with that portion of the life cycle of our species that extends ahead of us. But if it is a true cycle, that future portion of it has in a sense already happened. Or, at least, we can on a basis almost mathematically precisely map out the next, missing integers in the sequence of which we are the past. The first integer: the Earth Mother culture. Next, the masculine solar deities, with their stern, authoritarian societies, from Sparta to Rome to Fascist Italy and Japan and Germany and the USSR. And now, perhaps, what the medieval Pietàs looked forward to: In the arms of the Earth Mother, who still lives, the dead solar diety, her son, lies in a once-again silent return to the womb from which he came. I think we are entering this third and perhaps final sequence of our history, and this is a society that our field sees ahead of us that will be quite different from either of the two previous world civilizations familiar in the past. It is not a two-part cycle; we have not reached the conclusion of the masculine solar deity period to return merely to the primordial Earth Mother cult, however full of milk her breasts may be; what lies ahead is new. And possibly, beyond that, lies something more, unique and obscured to our gaze as of this moment. I, myself, can't envision that far; the realization, the fulfillment, or the medieval Pietà as a living reality, our total environment, a *living*, external environment as animate as ourselves—that is what I see and no farther. Not yet, anyhow. I would, myself, be content with that; I would be happy to lie slumbering and yet alive—"invisible but dim," as [Henry] Vaughan [seventeenth-century English metaphysical poet] put it—in her arms.

If a Pietà of a thousand years ago, shaped by a medieval artisan, anticipated in his—shall we say—psionic? hands, our future world, what, today, might be the analogue of that inspired, precognitive artifact? What do we have with us *now*, as homely and familiar to us in our twentieth-century world, as were those everyday Pietàs to the citizens of thirteenth-century Christendom, that might be a microcosm of the far distant future? Let us first start by imagining a pious peasant of thirteenth-century France gazing up at a rustic Pietà and foreseeing in it the twenty-first-century society about which we science fiction writers speculate. Then, as in a Bergman film, we segue to—what now? One of us is gazing at—what?

Cycle—and recycle. The Pietà of our modern world: ugly, commonplace, and ubiquitous. Not the dead Christ in the arms of his grieving, eternal mother, but a heap of aluminum Budweiser beer cans, eighty feet high, thousands of them, being scooped up noisily, rattling and spilling and crashing and raining down as a giant automated, computer-controlled, homeostatic Budweiser beer factory—an autofac, as I called it once in a story ["Autofac" (1955)]—hugs the discarded empties back into herself to recycle them over again into new life, with new, living contents. Exactly as before . . . or, if the chemists in the Budweiser lab are fulfilling God's divine plan for eternal progress, with better beer than before.

"We see as through a glass darkly," Paul in 1 Corinthians—will this someday be rewritten as, "We see as into a passive infrared scanner darkly?" A scanner that as in Orwell's 1984, is watching us all the time? Our TV tube watching back at us as we watch it, as amused, or bored, or anyhow somewhat as entertained by what we do as we are by what we see on its implacable face?

This, for me, is too pessimistic, too paranoid. I believe 1 Corinthians will be rewritten this way: "The passive infrared scanner sees into *us* darkly"—that is, not well enough really to figure us out. Not that we ourselves can really figure each other out, or even our own selves. Which, perhaps, too, is good; it means we are still in for sudden surprises, and, unlike the authorities, who don't like that sort of thing, we may find these chance happenings acting on our behalf, to our favor.

Sudden surprises, by the way—and this thought may be in itself a sudden surprise to you—are a sort of antidote to the paranoid . . . or, to be accurate about it, to live in such a way as to encounter sudden surprises quite often or even now and then as an indication that you are not paranoid, because to the paranoid, nothing is a surprise; everything happens exactly as he expected, and sometimes even more so. It all fits into his system. For us, though, there can be no system; maybe *all* systems—that is, any theoretical, verbal, symbolic, semantic, etc., formulation that attempts to act as an all-encompassing, all-explaining hypothesis of what the universe is about—are manifestations of paranoia. We should be content with the mysterious, the meaningless, the contradictory, the hostile, and most of all the unexplainably warm and giving—total so-called inanimate environment, in other words very much like a person, like the behavior of one intricate, subtle, half-veiled, deep, perplexing, and much-to-be-loved human being to another. To be feared a little, too, sometimes. And perpetually misunderstood. About which we can neither know nor be sure; and we must only trust and make guesses toward. Not being what you thought, not doing right by you, not being just, but then sustaining you as by momentary caprice, but then abandoning you, or at least seeming to. What it is actually up to we may never know. But at least this is better, is it not, than to possess the self-defeating, life-defeating spurious certitude of the paranoid—expressed, by a friend of mine, humorously, I *guess*, like this: "Doctor, someone is putting something in my food it [sic; likely "to" intended] make me paranoid." The doctor should have asked, was that person putting it in his food free, or charging him for it?

To refer back a final time to an early science fiction work with which we are all familiar, the Bible: A number of stories in our field have been written in which computers print out portions of that august book. I now herewith suggest this idea for a future society; that a computer print out a man.

Or, if it can't get that together, then, as a second choice, a very poor one in comparison, a condensed version of the Bible, "In the beginning was the end." Or should it go the other way? "In the end was the beginning." Whichever. Randomness, in time, will sort out which it is to be. Fortunately, I am not required to make that choice.

Perhaps, when a computer is ready to churn forth one or the other of these two statements, an android, operating the computer, will make the decision—although, if I am correct about the android mentality, it will be unable to decide and will print out both at once, creating a self-canceling nothing, which will not even serve as a primordial chaos. An android might, however, be able to handle this; capable of some sort of decision-making power, it might conceivably pick one statement or the other as quote "correct." But no android—and you will recall and realize that by this term I am summing up that which is not human—no android would think to do what a bright-eyed little girl I know did, something a little bizarre, certainly ethically questionable in several ways, at least in any traditional sense, but to me truly human in that it shows, to me, a spirit of merry defiance, of spirited, although not spiritual, bravery and uniqueness:

One day while driving along in her car she found herself following a truck carrying cases of Coca-Cola bottles, case after case, stacks of them. And when the truck parked, she parked behind it and loaded the back of her own car with cases, as many cases, of bottles of Coca-Cola as she could get in. So, for weeks afterward, she and her friends had all the Coca-Cola they could drink, free—and then, when the bottles were empty, she carried them to the store and turned them in for the deposit refund.

To that, I say this: God bless her. May she live forever. And the Coca-Cola Company and the phone company and all the rest of it, with their passing infrared scanners and sniperscopes and suchlike—may they be gone long ago. Metal and stone and wire and thread did never live. But she and her friends—they, our human future, are our little song. "Who knows if the spirit of man travels up, and the breath of beasts travels down under the Earth?" the Bible asks. Someday it, in a later revision, may wonder, "Who knows if the spirit of men travels up, and the breath of *androids* travels down?" Where do the souls of androids go after their death? But— if they do not live, then they cannot die. And if they cannot die, then they will always be with us. Do they have souls at all? Or, for that matter, do we?

I think, as the Bible says, we all go to a common place. But it is not the grave; it is into life beyond. The world of the future.

Thank you.

"Man, Android, and Machine" (1976)

Within the universe there exists fierce cold things, which I have given the name "machines" to. Their behavior frightens me, especially when it imitates human behavior so well that I get the uncomfortable sense that these things are trying to pass themselves off as humans but are not. I call them "androids," which is my own way of using that word. By "android" I do not mean a sincere attempt to create in the laboratory a human being (as we saw in the excellent TV film *The Questor Tapes*). I mean a thing somehow generated to deceive us in a cruel way, to cause us to think it to be one of ourselves. Made in a laboratory—that aspect is not meaningful to me; the entire universe is one vast laboratory, and out of it come sly and cruel entities that smile as they reach out to shake hands. But their handshake is the grip of death, and their smile has the coldness of the grave.

These creatures are among us, although morphologically they do not differ from us; we must not posit a difference of essence, but a difference of behavior. In my science fiction I write about them constantly. Sometimes they themselves do not know they are androids. Like Rachael Rosen, they can be pretty but somehow lack something; or, like Pris in *We Can Build You*, they can be absolutely born of a human womb and even design androids—the Abraham Lincoln one in that book—and themselves be without warmth; they then fall within the clinical entity "schizoid," which means lacking proper feeling. I am sure we mean the same thing here, with the emphasis on the word "thing." A human being without the proper empathy or feeling is the same as an android built so as to lack it, either by design or mistake. We mean, basically, someone who does not care about the fate that his fellow living creatures fall victim to; he stands detached, a spectator, acting out by his indifference John

Donne's theorem that "No man is an island," but giving the theorem a twist: That which is a mental and moral island *is not a man*.

The greatest change growing across our world these days is probably the momentum of the living toward reification, and at the same time a reciprocal entry into animation by the mechanical. We hold now no pure categories of the living versus the nonliving; this is going to be our paradigm: my character Hoppy, in *Dr. Bloodmoney*, who is a sort of human football within a maze of servo-assists. Part of that entity is organic, but all of it is alive; part came from a womb, all lives, and within the same universe. I am talking about our real world and not the world of fiction when I say: One day we will have millions of hybrid entities that have a foot in both worlds at once. To define them as "man" versus "machine" will give us verbal puzzle games to play with. What is and will be a real concern is: Does the composite entity (of which Palmer Eldritch is a good example among my characters), does he *behave* in a human way? Many of my stories contain purely mechanical systems that display kindness—taxicabs, for instance, or the little rolling carts at the end of *Now Wait for Last Year* that that poor defective human builds. "Man" or "human being" are terms that we must understand correctly and apply, but they apply not to origin or to any ontology but to a way of being in the world; if a mechanical construct halts in its customary operation to lend you assistance, then you will posit to it, gratefully, a humanity that no analysis of its transistors and relay systems can elucidate. A scientist, tracing the wiring circuits of that machine to locate its humanness, would be like our own earnest scientists who tried in vain to locate the soul in man, and, not being able to find a specific organ located at a specific spot, opted to decline to admit that we have souls. As soul is to man, man is to machine: It is the added dimension in terms of functional hierarchy. As one of us *acts* godlike (gives his cloak to a stranger), a machine *acts* human when it pauses in its programmed cycle to defer to it by reason of a decision.

But still, we must realize that the universe, although kind to us in its entirety (it must like and accept us, or we would not be here; as Abraham Maslow says, "otherwise nature would have executed us long ago"), does contain grinning evil masks that loom out of the fog of confusion at us, and it may slay us for its own gain.

We must be careful, however, of confusing a mask, any mask, with the reality beneath. Think of the war mask that Pericles placed over his features: You would behold a frozen visage, the grimness of war, without compassion—no genuine human face or person to whom you could appeal. And this was, of course, the intention. Suppose you did not even realize it was a mask; suppose you believed, as Pericles approached you in the fog and half darkness of early morning, that this was his authentic countenance. Now, this is almost exactly how I described Palmer Eldritch in my novel about him: so much like the war masks of the Attic Greeks that the resemblance cannot be accidental. Is, then, the hollow eyeslot, the mechanical metal arm and hand, the stainless-steel teeth, which are the dread stigmata of evil—is this not, this which I myself first saw in the overhead sky at noon one day back in 1963, a description, a vision, of a war mask and metal armor, a god of battle? The God of Wrath who was angry with me. But under the anger, under the metal and helmet, there is, as with Pericles, the face of a man. A kind and loving man.

My theme for years in my writing has been, "The devil has a metal face." Perhaps this should be amended now. What I glimpsed and then wrote about was in fact not a face; it was a mask over a face. And the true face is the reverse of the mask. Of course it would be. You do not place fierce, cold metal over fierce, cold metal. You place it over soft flesh, as the harmless moth adorns itself artfully to terrorize others with ocelli. This is a defensive measure, and if it works, the predator returns to his lair grumbling, "I saw the most frightening creature in the sky—wild grimaces and flappings, stingers and poisons." His kin are impressed. The magic works.

I had supposed that only bad people wore frightening masks, but you can see now that I fell for the magic of the mask, its dreadful, frightening magic, its *illusion*. I bought the deception and fled. I wish now to apologize for preaching that deception to you as something genuine: I've had you all sitting around the campfire with our eyes wide with alarm as I tell tales of the hideous monsters I encountered; my voyage of discovery ended in terrifying visions that I dutifully carried home with me as I fled back to safety. Safety from what? From something which, when the need was gone for concealment, smiled and revealed its harmlessness.

Now I do not intend to abandon my dichotomy between what I call "human" and what I call "android," the latter being a cruel and cheap mockery of the former for base ends. But I had been going on surface appearances; to distinguish the categories more cunning is required. For if a gentle, harmless life conceals itself behind a frightening war mask, then it is likely that behind gentle and loving masks there can conceal itself a vicious slayer of men's souls. In neither case can we go on surface appearance; we must penetrate to the heart of each, to the heart of the subject.

Probably everything in the universe serves a good end—I mean, serves the universe's goals. But intrinsic portions or subsystems can be takers of life. We must deal with them as such, without reference to their role in the total structure.

The *Sepher Yezirah*, a Cabbalist text, *The Book of Creation*, which is almost two thousand years old, tells us: "God has also set the one over against the other; the good against the evil, and the evil against the good; the good proceeds from the good, and the evil from the evil; *the good purifies the bad, and the bad the good*; the good is preserved for the good, and the evil for the bad ones."

Underlying the two game players there is God, who is neither and both. The effect of the game is that both players become purified. Thus the ancient Hebrew monotheism, so superior to our own view. We are creatures in a game with our affinities and aversions predetermined for us—not by blind chance but by patient, foresighted engramming systems that we dimly see. Were we to see them clearly, we would abolish the game. Evidently that would not serve anyone's interests. We must trust these tropisms, and anyhow we have no choice—not until the tropisms lift. And under certain circumstances they can and do. And at that point, much is clear that previously was occluded from us, intentionally.

What we must realize is that this deception, this obscuring of things as if under a veil—the veil of Maya, it has been called—this is not an end in itself, as if the universe is somehow perverse and likes to foil us per se; what we must accept, once we realize that a veil (called by the Greeks *dokos*) lies between us and reality, is that this veil serves a benign purpose. Parmenides, the pre-Socratic philosopher, is historically credited with being the first person in the West systematically to work out proof that the world cannot be as we see it, that *dokos*, the veil, exists. We see very much the same notion expressed by St. Paul when he speaks about our seeing "as if by the reflection on the bottom of a polished metal pan." He is referring to the familiar notion of Plato's that we see only images of reality, and probably these images are inaccurate and imperfect and not to be relied on. I wish to add that Paul was probably saying one thing more than Plato in the celebrated metaphor of the cave: Paul was saying that we may well be seeing the universe backward.

The extraordinary thrust of this thought just simply cannot be taken in, even if we intellectually grasp it. "To see the universe backward?" What would that mean? Well, let me give you one possibility: that we experience time backward; or more precisely, that our inner, subjective category of experience of time (in the sense that Kant spoke of, a way by which we arrange experience), our time experience, is orthogonal to the flow of time itself—at right angles. There are two times: the time that is our experience or perception or construct of ontological matrix, an extensiveness along with space as an inseparable extensiveness into another area—this is real, but the outer time flow of the universe moves in a different direction. Both are real, but by experiencing time as we do, orthogonally to its actual direction, we get a totally wrong idea of the sequence of events, of causality, of what is past and what is future, where the universe is going.

I hope you realize the importance of this. Time is real, both as an experience in the Kantian sense, and real in the sense which the Soviet Dr. Nikolai Kozyrev expresses it: that time is an energy, and it is the basic energy that binds the universe together, and upon which all life depends, all phenomena draw their source out of and express: It is the energy of each entelechy and of the total entelechy of the universe itself.

But time, in itself, is not moving from our past to our future. Its orthogonal axis leads it through a rotary cycle within which, for example, we have been "spinning our wheels," so to speak, in a vast winter of our species that has lasted already about two thousand of our lineal time years. Evidently orthogonal time or true time rotates something like the primitive cyclic time, within which each year was regarded as the same year, each new crop the same crop; in fact, each spring was the same spring again. What destroyed man's ability to perceive time in this overly simple way was that he himself as an individual spanned too many of these years and could see that he himself wore out, was not renewed each year like the corn crop, the bulbs and roots and trees. There had to be a more adequate idea of time than the simple cyclic time; so he developed, reluctantly, lineal time, which is an accumulative time, as Bergson showed; it goes in only one direction and is added to—or adds to—everything as it sweeps along.

True orthogonal time is rotary, but on a vaster scale, much like the Great Year of the ancients; much, too, like Dante's idea of the time rate of eternity that you find expressed in his *Comedy*. During the Middle Ages such thinkers as Erigena had begun to sense true eternity or timelessness, but others had begun to sense that eternity involved time (timelessness would be a static state), although the time would be quite different from our perception of it. A clue lay in St. Paul's reiteration that the Final Days of the world would be the Time of Restoration of All Things. He had evidently experienced this orthogonal time enough to understand that it contains in it as a simultaneous plane or extension everything that was, just as the grooves on an LP contain the part of the music that has already been played; they don't disappear after the stylus tracks them. A phonograph record is, actually, a long, helical spiral, and can be represented entirely in a plane geometry sort of way: in space, although I suppose you can talk about the stylus accumulating the music as it goes along. The idea of dysfunctions such as bounce back and bounce forward are possible here, but these would serve no teleological purpose: They would be time-slips, as in my novel *Martian Time-Slip*. Yet, if they were to occur, they would serve a purpose for us, the observer or listener: We would suddenly learn a great deal more about our universe. I believe these ontological dysfunctions in time do occur, but that our brains automatically generate false memory systems to obscure them, at once. The reason for this carries back to my premise: The veil or *dokos* is there to deceive us for a good reason, and such disclosures as these time dysfunctions make are to be obliterated that this benign purpose be maintained.

Within a system that must generate an enormous amount of veiling, it would be vainglorious to expostulate on what actuality is, when my premise declares that were we to penetrate to it for any reason, this strange, veil-like dream would reinstate itself retroactively, in terms of our perceptions and in terms of our memories. The mutual dreaming would resume as before, because, I think, we are like the characters in my novel *Ubik*; we are in a state of half-life. We are neither dead nor alive, but preserved in cold storage, waiting to be thawed out. Expressed in the perhaps startlingly familiar terms of the procession of the seasons, this is winter of which I speak; it is winter for our race, and it is winter in *Ubik* for those in half-life. Ice and snow cover them; ice and snow cover our world in layers of accretions, which we call *dokos* or Maya. What melts away the rind or layer of frozen ice over the world each year is, of course, the reappearance of the sun. What melts the ice and snow covering the characters in *Ubik*, and which halts the cooling off of their lives, the entropy that they feel, is the voice of Mr. Runciter, their former employer, calling to them. The voice of Mr. Runciter is none other than that same voice that each bulb and seed and root in the ground, our ground, in our wintertime, hears. It hears: "Wake up! Sleepers awake!" Now I have told you who Runciter is, and I have told you our condition and what *Ubik* is really about. What I have said, too, is that time is actually as Dr. Kozyrev in the Soviet Union supposes it to be, and in *Ubik* time has been nullified and no longer moves forward in the lineal fashion that we experience. As this has happened, due to the deaths of the characters, we the readers and they the personae see the world as it is without the veil of Maya, without the obscuring mists of lineal time. It is that very energy, Time, postulated by Dr. Kozyrev as binding together all phenomena and maintaining all life, that by its *activity* hides the ontological reality beneath its flow.

The orthogonal time axis may have been presented in my novel *Ubik* without my understanding what I was depicting: i.e. the form regression of objects along an entirely different line from that out of which they, in lineal time, were built. This reversion is that of the Platonic Ideas or archetypes: A rocketship reverts to a Boeing 747, then back to a World War I "Jenny" biplane. While I may indeed have expressed a dramatic view of orthogonal time, it is less certain that this is orthogonal time *undergoing an unnatural reversion:* i.e. moving backward. What the characters in *Ubik* see may be orthogonal time moving along its normal axis; if we ourselves somehow see the universe reversed, then the "reversions" of form that objects in *Ubik* undergo may be momentum toward perfection. This would imply that our world as extensive in time (rather than extensive in space) is like an onion, an almost infinite number of successive layers. If lineal time seems to add layers, then perhaps orthogonal time peels these off, exposing layers of progressively greater Being. One is reminded here of Plotinus's view of the universe as consisting of concentric rings of emanation, each one possessing more Being—or reality—than the next.

Within that ontology, that realm of Being, the characters, like ourselves, slumber in dreams as they wait for the voice that will awaken them. When I say that they and we are waiting for spring to come I am not merely using a metaphor. Spring means thermal return, the abolition of the process of entropy; their life can be expressed in terms of thermal units, and those units have left. It is spring that restores that life—restores it fully and in some cases, as with our species, the new life is a metamorphosis; the period of slumbering is a period of gestation together with our fellows that will culminate in an entirely different form of life than we have ever known before. Many species are this way; they go through cycles. Thus our winter sleep is not a mere "spinning of our wheels," as it might seem. We will not simply bloom again and again with the same blossoms we produced each year before. This is why it was an error for the ancients to believe that for us, as for the vegetable world, the same year returned; for us, there is accumulation, the growth of an entelechy for each of us not yet perfected or completed, and never repeatable. Like a symphony of Beethoven, each of us is unique, and, when this long winter is over, we as new blooms will surprise ourselves and the world around us. What we will do, many of us, is throw off the mere masks that we have worn—masks that were intended to be taken for reality. Masks that have successfully fooled everyone, as is their purpose. We have been so many Palmer Eldritches moving through the cold fog and mists and twilight of winter, but now soon we will emerge and lift the war mask of iron to reveal the face within.

It is a face that we, the wearers of the masks, have not seen either; it will surprise us, too.

For absolute reality to reveal itself, our categories of space-time experiences, our basic matrix through which we encounter the universe, must break down and then utterly collapse. I dealt with this breakdown in *Martian Time-Slip* in terms of time; in *Maze of Death* there are endless parallel realities arranged spacially; in *Flow My Tears, the Policeman Said* the world of one character invades the world in general and shows that by "world" we mean nothing more or less than Mind—the immanent Mind that thinks—or rather dreams—our world. That dreamer, like the dreamer in Joyce's *Finnegan's Wake*, is stirring and about to come to consciousness. We are within that dream; these manifold dreams are about to fold into themselves, to disappear as dreams, to be replaced by the true landscape of the dreamer's reality. We will join him as he sees it once again and is aware that he has been dreaming. In Brahmanism, we would say that a great cycle has ended and that Brahman stirs and wakes again, or that it falls asleep from being awake; in any case the universe that we experience that is an extension in space and time of its Mind is experiencing the typical dysfunctions that take place at the end of a cycle. You may say, if you prefer, "Reality is collapsing; it's all turning to chaos," or, with me, you may wish to say, "I feel the dream, the *dokos*, lifting; I feel Maya dissolving: I am waking up, He is waking up: I am the Dreamer: We are all the Dreamer." One thinks here of Arthur Clarke's Overmind.

Each of us is going to have either to affirm or deny the reality that is revealed when our ontological categories collapse. If you feel that chaos is closing in, that when the dream fades out, nothing will be left, or worse, something dreadful will confront you—well, this is why the concept of the Day of Wrath persists; many people have a deep intuition that when the *dokos* abruptly melts they're in for a hard time of it. Perhaps so. But I think that the visage revealed will be a smiling one, since spring usually beams down on creatures rather than blasting them with desiccating heat. There may, too, be malign forces in the universe that will be revealed by the removal of the veil, but I think about the fall of the political tyranny in the United States in 1974 and it seems to me that the exposure to the light of day of that ugly cancer and its subsequent removal is the nature of high value in disclosure to sunlight; we may have to suffer such shocks as learning that during the *Nacht und Nebel*, during the time of night and fog, our freedom, our rights, our property, and even our lives were mutilated, deformed, stolen, and destroyed by base creatures glutting themselves in spurious sanctuary down there at San Clemente [the location of Nixon's mansion] and in Florida and all the other villas, but the shock of exposure was worse for their plans than it was for ours. Our plans called only for us to live with justice and truth and freedom; the former government of this country had arranged to live with cruel power of the most arrogant sort, while at the same time lying to us ceaselessly through all the channels of communication. Such is a good example of the healing power of sunlight; this power first to reveal and then to shrivel up the coarse plant of tyranny that had grown deep into the beating heart of a good people.

That heart beats on now, more strongly than ever, although it was admittedly badly engulfed; but the cancer that had crawled through it—that cancer is gone. That black growth that shunned light, shunned truth, and destroyed anyone who told the truth—it shows what can flourish during the long winter of the human race. But that winter began to end in the vernal equinox of 1974.

Sometimes I think that the Dreamer began to press against the tyranny as he, the Dreamer, woke us; here in the United States he woke us to our condition, our awful peril.

One of the best novels, and most important to an understanding of the nature of our world, is Ursula Le Guin's *The Lathe of Heaven*, in which the dream universe is articulated in such a striking and compelling way that I hesitate to add any further explanation to it; it requires none. I do not think that either of us had read about Charles Tart's study of dreams when we wrote our several novels, but I have now, and I have read some of Robert E. Ornstein, he being the "brain revolution" person north of where I live, at Stanford University. From Ornstein's work it would appear that there is a possibility that we have two entirely separate brains, rather than one brain divided into two bilaterally equal hemispheres, that, in fact, whereas we have a body we have two minds (I refer to you the article by Joseph E. Bogen "The Other Side of the Brain: An Appositional Mind," published in Ornstein's collection *The Nature of Human Consciousness*). Bogen demonstrates that every now and then a researcher began to scent the possibility that we have two brains, two minds, but that only with modern brain-mapping techniques and related studies has it been possible to demonstrate this. For example, in 1763 Jerome Gaub wrote: ". . . I hope that you will believe Pythagoras and Plato, the wisest of the ancient philosophers, who, according to Cicero, divided the mind into two parts, one partaking of reason and the other devoid of it." Bogen's article contains concepts so fascinating as to cause me to wonder why we never realized that our "unconscious" is not an unconscious at all but another consciousness, with which we have a tenuous relationship. It is this other mind or consciousness that dreams us at night—we are its audience as it binds us in its storytelling; we are little children spellbound . . . which is why *Lathe of Heaven* may represent one of the basic great books of our civilization, especially since Ursula Le Guin, I'm sure, arrived at her formulation without knowledge of Ornstein's work and Bogen's extraordinary theory. What is involved here is that one brain receives exactly the same input as the other, through the various sense channels, but processes the information differently; each brain works its own unique way (the left is like a digital computer; the right much like an analogue computer, working by comparing patterns). Processing the identical information, each may arrive at a totally different result whereupon, since our personality is constructed in our left brain, if the right brain finds something vital that we to its left remain unaware of, it must communicate during sleep, during the dream; hence the Dreamer who communicates to us so urgently in the night is located neurologically, evidently, in our right brain, which is the not-I. But more than that (for instance, is the right brain as Bergson thought perhaps a transducer or transformer for ultrasensory informational input beyond the purview of the left?) we can't say as yet. I think, though, that the spell of *dokos* is woven by our right brain's plural; we as a species are prone to reside entirely within one hemisphere only, leaving the other to do what it must to protect the world. Keep in mind that this protectiveness is bilateral, an exchange between the world and each of us: Each of us is a treasure, to be cherished and preserved, but so is the world and the hidden seeds in it, slumbering. The other hidden seeds. Thus, through the veil-spinning of Kali, the right hemisphere of each of us, we are kept ignorant of what we must be ignorant of now. But that time is ending; that winter is melting, along with its terrors, its tyrannies, and snow.

The best description of this *dokos*-veil formation that I've read yet appears in an article in *Science Fiction Studies*, March 1975, by Frederick Jameson, in "After Armageddon: Character Systems in *Dr. Bloodmoney*," which is an obscure novel of mine. I quote: "Every reader of Dick is familiar with this nightmarish uncertainty, this reality fluctuation, sometimes accounted for by drugs,* and sometimes by schizophrenia, and sometimes by new SF powers, in which the psychic world as it were goes outside, and reappears in the form of simulacra or of some photographically cunning reproduction of the external" (p. 32).

You can see from Jameson's description that we are talking about something very like Maya here, but also something very like a hologram. I have the distinct feeling that Carl Jung was correct about our unconsciousnesses, that they form a single entity, or as he called it, "collective unconscious." In that case, this collective brain entity, consisting of literally

*I hope Jameson means drugs in the writing and schizophrenia in the writing, not in me, but I'll let that pass.

billions of "stations," which transmit and receive, would form a vast network of communication and information, much like Teilhard's concept of the noosphere. This *is* the noosphere, as real as the ionosphere or the biosphere; it is a layer in our earth's atmosphere composed of holographic and informational projections in a unified and continually processed Gestalt, the sources of which are our manifold right brains. This constitutes a vast Mind, immanent within us, of such power and wisdom as to seem, to us, equal to the Creator. This was Bergson's view of God, anyhow.

It is interesting how deeply troubled the brilliant Greek philosophers were by activities of the gods; they could see the activities and (or so they thought) the gods themselves, but as Xenophanes put it: "Even if a man should chance to speak the most complete truth, yet he himself does not know it; all things are wrapped in *appearances*" [emphasis by Dick].

This notion came to the pre-Socratics by virtue of their seeing the many but knowing *a priori* that what they saw could not be real, since only the One existed.

"If God is all things, then appearances are certainly deceptive; and, though observation of the kosmos may yield generalizations and speculations about God's plans, true knowledge of them could only be had by a direct contact with God's mind." (I am quoting Edward Hussey in his marvelous book *The Pre-Socratics*, p. 35.) And he goes on to give two fragments of Heraclitus: "The nature of things is in the habit of concealing itself" (Fragment 123). "Latent structure is master of obvious structure" (Fragment 54).

I wish to remind you that the ancient Greeks and Hebrews did not conceive of God or God's Mind as above the universe, but within it: immanent Mind or immanent God, with the visible universe the body of God, so that God was to universe as psyche is to soma. But they also conjectured that perhaps God was not the great psyche but *noös*, a different sort of mind; in which case the universe was not his body but God Himself. The space-time universe houses but is not a part of God; what is God is the vast grid field or energy field alone.

If you assume (and you'd be correct to do so) that our minds are energy fields of some kind anyhow, and that we are fundamentally interacting fields rather than discrete particles, then there is no theoretical problem in grasping this interaction between the billions of brainprints emanating and forming and reforming into the patterns of the noosphere. However, if you still hold to the nineteenth-century view of yourself as a brittle organism, much like a machine, made up of parts—well, you see, then how can you merge with the noosphere? You are a unique, concrete thing. And thingness is what we must get away from in regarding ourselves and in considering life. By more modern views we are overlapping fields, all of us, animals included, plants included. This is the ecosphere, and we are all in it. But what we don't realize is that the billions of discrete and entirely ego-oriented left-hemisphere brains have far less to say about the ultimate disposition of the world than does the collective noospheric. Mind that comprises all our right brains and in which each of us shares. *It* will decide, and I do not think it impossible that this vast plasmic noosphere, considering that it covers our entire planet in a veil or layer, may interact outward into solar-energy fields and from there into cosmic fields. Each of us, then, partakes of the cosmos—if he is willing to listen to his dreams. And it is his dreams that will transform him from a mere machine into an authentic human. He will no longer strut about and clank with majestic iron, no longer rule his little kingdom here; he will soar upward, flying like a field of negative ions, like the entity Ubik in my novel of that name: being life and giving life, but never defining himself because no clear-cut name to him—to us—can be given.

As we move up the manifold—i.e. progress forward in lineal time, or somehow stand still and lineal time progresses forward, whichever model is more correct—we as many entelechies are continually signaled, given information, and most of all, disinhibited by firings from the universe around us; in this fashion harmony among all parts of the universe is maintained. There is no more grand scheme than this: to be aware that I, as a representative entelechy, must unfold only as these preset signals reach me, and that control as to the when—the locus in time—that each signal will come is entirely in the hands of the universe . . . this is a thrilling comprehension, and makes me aware of the unbreakable tie between me and my environment.

There is such order in the response between engrammed systems within each of us and the accumulating signals that fire these systems in sequence as to imply that the Agency that laid down the entelechy in the first place, engrammed and then blocked these systems, knew with absolute precision where along the time path the signals would take place that would disinhibit; chance is not involved—the happiest of accidents is the most astute planning of the universe.

Sometimes I wonder how we could have imagined that our species was exempt from the instincts that lower species obviously have. What is different about us, however, is that ants, for instance, are disinhibited by the same signal, and the same behavior occurs; it is as if one ant again and again is involved, endlessly. But for us, each is a unique entelechy, and each receives unique sequences of signals—to which each responds uniquely. Still, this is the language of the universe that the ant hears; we thrill with a common joy.

I myself have derived much of the material for my writing from dreams. In *Flow My Tears*, for example, the powerful dream that comes to Felix Buchman near the end, the dream of the wise old man on horseback, that was an actual dream I had at the time of writing the novel. In *Martian Time-Slip* I've written in so many dream experiences that I can't separate them, now, when I read the novel.

Ubik was primarily a dream, or series of dreams. In my opinion it contains strong themes of pre-Socratic philosophical views of the world, unfamiliar to me when I wrote it (to name just one, the views of Empedocles). It is possible that the noosphere contained thought patterns in the form of very weak energy until we developed radio transmission; whereupon the energy level of the noosphere went out of bounds and assumed a life of its own. It no longer served as a mere passive repository of human information (the "Seas of Knowledge" that ancient Sumer believed in) but, due to the incredible surge of charge from our electronic signals and the information-rich material therein, we have given it power to cross a vast threshold; we have, so to speak, resurrected what Philo and other ancients have called the *Logos*. Information has, then, become alive, with a collective mind of its own independent of our brains, if this theory is correct. It does not merely know what we know and remember what once was known, but can construct solutions on its own: It is a titanic AI system. The difference would be between a tape recorder that could "remember" a Beethoven symphony that it "heard," and one that could create new ones, on and on; the library in the sky, having read all the books there are and ever were, is writing its own book, now, and at night we are being read to—told the exciting tale comprising that Great Work-in-Progress.

I must mention Ian Watson's article in *Science-Fiction Studies* on Le Guin's *Lathe of Heaven*; in his excellent piece he refers to what may be the most significant—startlingly so—story SF has yet produced: Fredric Brown's story that appeared in *Astounding*, "The Waveries." You must read that story; if you do not, you may die without understanding the universe coming into being around you. The Waveries were attracted to Earth by our radio waves; they returned in a facsimile form, so like our transmissions (SOS and so forth, chronologically) that at first we couldn't fathom what was up. Regarding *Lathe*, Watson says:

> Conceivably George (Orr) dreamt a hostile invasion into a peaceful one; yet the dominant probability is that the aliens are, as they maintain, "of the dream time," that their whole culture revolves around the mode of "reality dreaming itself into being," that they have been attracted to Earth like the Waveries of Fredric Brown's story, only by dream-waves rather than radio waves [pp. 71–72].

This could be considered scary stuff, this theme in Le Guin's work and mine. What are dreams? Are there these dream-universe entities that have come here from another star (Aldebaran, in Ms. Le Guin's novel)? Are the UFOs that people see holograms projected by their unconscious minds, acting as transformers, acting, too, as transducers of these strange dream-universe creatures?

For the past year I've had many dreams that seemed—I stress the word "seemed"—to indicate that a telepathic communication was in progress somewhere within my head, but after talking with Henry Korman, an associate of Ornstein's, I would imagine that it is merely my right and left hemispheres conferring in a Martin Buber I-and-Thou dialogue. But much of the dream material seemed beyond my personal ability to have created. At one point an attempt was made to get me to write down a complex engineering principle that was shown me in the form of a round motor with twin rotating wheels, opposed in direction, much as yin and yang in Taoism alternate as opposing pairs (and much like Empedocles saw love versus strife, the dialectic interaction of the world). But this was a true engineering device they had there in my dream; they showed me a pencil, they said, "This principle was known in *your* time." And as I rushed to find a pencil they added: "Known, but buried in a basement and forgotten." There was an elaborate high-torque chain-thrown mechanism that moved camwise between the two rotors, but I never got the hang of it when I woke up. What I did later on grasp, though, was this: Further dreams made it clear that somehow our treatment of seawater by an osmosis process would give us not only pure water but a source of energy as well. However, they had the wrong human when they began giving me that sort of material; I am not trained to understand it. I did purchase over $1,000 worth of reference books to try to figure out what I'd been shown, though. I have learned this: Something to do with a high hysteresis factor, in this twin-rotor system, is converted from a defect to an advantage. No braking mechanism is needed; the two rotors spin constantly at the same velocity, and torque is transferred by a thrown cam chain.

I give this illustration only to show that either my unconscious has been reading articles on engineering that elude my memory and my conscious attention and interest, or there are, shall I say, dream-universe people from, shall I say, Aldebaran or some other star with us. Perhaps joining their noosphere with ours? And offering assistance to a crippled, blighted planet that has been bogged down, like a rat on a weary wheel, in the dead of winter for over two thousand years? If they bring the springtime with them, then whoever they are, I welcome them; like Joe Chip in *Ubik*, I fear the cold, the weariness; I fear the death of wearing out on endless upward stairs, while someone cruel, or anyhow wearing a cruel mask, watches and offers no aid—the machine, lacking empathy, watching as mere spectator, the same horror that I know haunts Harlan Ellison. It is perhaps more frightening that the killer himself (in *Ubik* it was Jory), this figure that sees but gives no assistance, offers no hand. That is the android, to me, and the evil demigod to Harlan; we both shudder at the idea of its existence. What I can tell you about the dream-universe people is that if they do exist, whoever they are, they are not that unsympathetic android; they are human in this deepest of all senses: They have reached out a helping hand to our planet, to our polluted ecosphere, and perhaps even assisted in throwing down the tyranny that gripped the United States, Portugal, Greece, and one day they will throw down the tyranny of the Soviet bloc as well. This is what I think of when I grasp the idea of springtime: the lifting of the iron doors of the prison and the poor prisoners, in Beethoven's *Fidelio*, let out into the sunlight. Ah, that moment in the opera when they see the sun and feel its warmth. And at last, at the end, the trumpet call of freedom sounds the permanent end of their cruel imprisonment; help, *from outside*, has arrived.

Every now and then someone comes up to a science fiction writer, smiles a crazy, secret in-the-know smile, and smirks, "I know that what you're writing is true, and it's in code. All you SF writers are receivers for Them." Naturally, I ask who "Them" is. The answer is always the same. "You know. Up there. The space people. They're already here, and they're using your writing. You know it, too."

I kind of smile and edge off. It keeps happening. Well, I hate to admit it, but it is possible that there is (1) such a thing as telepathy; and (2) that the CETI project's idea that we might communicate with extraterrestrial beings via telepathy is possibly a reasonable idea—if telepathy exists and if ETIs exist. Otherwise we are trying to communicate with someone who doesn't exist with a system that doesn't work. At least that'll keep a lot of us busy for a long, long time. But I understand now that a Soviet astronomy bunch, evidently headed by the same Dr. Nikolai Kozyrev, who developed the time-as-energy theory I mentioned previously, has reported receiving signals from an ETI *within* our solar system. If this were true, and our people are saying that the Soviets are just monitoring stale, flat, and unprofitable old signals from our own discarded satellites and other junk ships—well, suppose these ETI entities or corporate mind are within, say, the great plasma that seems to surround Earth and is involved with solar flares and the like; I refer, of course, to the noosphere. It is ETI and TI at once, and possibly bears a strong resemblance to what Ms. Le Guin has written about in *Lathe*. And as every SF fan knows, my own works deal with similar themes . . . thus giving an annoying couple of marks for plausibility to these freaks who are forever lurching up to every SF author and saying, "What you're writing is in code . . .," etc. In truth, we may be influenced, especially during dream states, by a noosphere that is a product of our own, capable of independent mentation, and involved with ETIs, a mixture of all three and God knows what else. This might not be the Creator, but it would be as close to Infinite Mind as we might get, and close enough. That it is benign is obvious, to recall Maslow's remarks that if nature didn't like us it would have executed us long ago—here read Infinite Noosphere for nature.

We humans, the warm-faced and tender, with thoughtful eyes—we are perhaps the true machines. And those objective constructs, the natural objects around us, and especially the electronic hardware we build, the transmitters and microwave relay stations, the satellites, they may be cloaks for authentic living reality inasmuch as they may participate more fully and in a way obscured to us in the ultimate Mind. Perhaps we see not only a deforming veil, but backward. Perhaps the closest approximation to truth would be to say: "Everything is equally alive, equally free, equally sentient, because everything is not alive or half alive or dead, but rather *lived through.*" Radio signals are boosted by a transmitter; they pass *through* the various components, modified and augmented, their contours changed, noise eliminated and rejected . . . we are extensions, like those metal arms that pick up radioactive objects for scientists. We are gloves that God puts on in order to move things here and there as He wishes. For some reason He prefers to handle reality this way (I will not budge but will defend that pun).

We are suits of clothing that He creates, puts on and uses, and finally discards. We are suits of armor, too, which gives misleading impression to certain other butterflies within certain other suits of armor. Within the armor is the butterfly, and within the butterfly is—the signal from another star. In the novel I am writing (that the Dreamer, perhaps, is expressing through me), that star is called Albemuth. I hadn't read Ms. Le Guin's novel *Lathe of Heaven* when the idea came to me, but the reader of that novel will find there also what I just now meant by our being stations within a vast grid—and not realizing it.

Consider this Meditation of Rumi, a Sufi saying [translated] by Idries Shah, who is a favorite among modern Sufis: "The worker is hidden in the workshop."

Since it is evident that more than anyone else Dr. Ornstein has pioneered the way to discover the new worldview, which involves a bilateral brain parity unsuspected since the time of Pythagoras and Plato, I recently summoned my courage and wrote him. Fans now and then write me, their hands shaking nervously; my entire typewriter shook nervously as I wrote to Dr. Ornstein. Here is the text of my letter, which I place here as a final note to explain how I have transcended the categories of reality-versus-illusion by his help, and thus brought into clear sight an end to twenty years' study and effort on my part. I quote:

Dear Dr. Ornstein:

Recently I met Mr. Henry Korman and Mr. Tony Hiss (Tony had
come to interview me for *The New Yorker*). I got into a marvelous
discussion with Henry about Sufism and I mentioned my admiration,
bordering on fanatic enthusiasm, for your pioneer work with bilateral
brain hemispheric parity. Thus I, having learned that they know you,
am summoning my courage to write you and ask, What has become of
me, since experimenting with bringing on my right hemisphere (I did
it mainly by the orthomolecular formula vitamins, plus a good deal of
concentrated meditation)?

By this I mean to say, Dr. Ornstein, ten months ago this took
place, and for ten months I have been a different person. But what to
me is most extraordinary (I am writing a book about it, but in the form
of fiction, a novel called *To Scare the Dead*) is that—well, let me give
the premise as I placed it into the novel:

Nicholas Brady, an ordinary American citizen with contemporary
worldly values and drives (money and power and prestige), suddenly
has inside him a winking into life of an entity that has slumbered for
two thousand years. This entity is an Essene, who died knowing that
he would be given the promised resurrection; he knew it because he
and other Qumran individuals had in their possession secret formulae
and medications and scientific practices to ensure it. So suddenly our
protagonist, Nicholas Brady, finds that there are two of him: his old
self, at his secular job and goals, and this Essene from the Qumran
wadi back circa A.D. 45, a holy man with holy values and utter
antagonism to the secular physical world, which he sees as the "City
of Iron." The Qumran mind takes over and directs Brady in a
complicated series of acts until it becomes evident that others such as
this Qumran man are coming back to life here and there in the world.

Studying the Bible, along with this Qumran personality, Brady
finds that the New Testament is in cipher. The Qumran personality
can read it. "Jesus" is really Zagreus-Zeus, taking two forms, one mild,
the other utterly powerful, on which his followers can draw when
in need.

The Qumran personality, who, for fictional purposes, I call
Thomas, gradually informs Brady that these are the Parousia, the

Final Days. And to be prepared; Thomas will prepare him by reminding him of his own divinity—anamnesis, Thomas calls it. Thomas develops a special parity relationship with Brady, but evolves as a source of teaching for the incredibly ignorant Brady the entity known as Erasmus, who is in fact a station in the noosphere, which is now so fully charged around Earth that if you are aware of it you can consciously, rather than unconsciously, draw from it; these are the "Seas of Knowledge" that were known in ancient times and upon which the Sibyl at Delphi drew. But this is a cover, because Brady realizes that in point of fact, the Qumran men had as their god not the mythical Jesus but the actual Zagreus, and by doing research, Brady soon learns that Zagreus was a form of Dionysos. Christianity is a latter form of the worship of Dionysos, refined through the strange and lovely figure of Orpheus. Orpheus, like Jesus, is real only in the sense that Dionysos is becoming socialized; born here as a child of another race, not a human one but a visiting race, Zagreus has had to learn by degrees to modify his "madness," which is now kept to a low ebb. Basically, he is with us to reconstruct us as expressions of him, and the MO of this is our being possessed by him—which the early Christians sought for, and hid from the hated Romans. Dionysos-Zagreus-Orpheus-Jesus was always pitted against the City of Iron, be it Rome or Washington, DC; he is the god of springtime, of new life, of small and helpless creatures, he is the god of mirth and frenzy, and of sitting here day after day working on this novel.

But in the novel, Thomas says, "The Final Days have come. The overthrow of the tyranny is that which, in lurid language, John described in Revelation. Jesus-Zagreus is seizing his own, now, one after another; *he lives again.*"

During winter, it was believed that Dionysos, the god of the vine plant, of vegetation, of the crop, slumbered. It was known that no matter how dead he seemed (James Joyce's *Finnegans Wake* is a wonderful account of this, where they accidentally spill beer on the corpse and it revives), he was actually alive, though you'd never know it. And then—not to the surprise of those who understood him and believed in him—he was reborn. His followers knew he would be; they knew the secret ("Behold! I tell you a sacred secret," etc.). We are speaking here of the mystery religions, all of them, including Christianity. Our God has been sleeping, during the long winter of the human culture (not for one year's rotational cycle of seasons, but from A.D. 45 through the centuries of mental winter to now); just when winter holds all in its grip, the snow of despair and defeat (in our case, political chaos, moral ruin, economic ruin—the winter of our planet, our world, our civilization), then the vine, which was gnarled and old and seemingly dead, breaks into new life, and our God is reborn—not outside us as such, but in each of us. Slumbering not under snow over the ground surface but within the right hemispheres of our brains. We have been waiting, we didn't know for what. This is it: This is spring for our planet, in a deeper, more fundamental way. The cold chains of iron are being thrown off, but by what a miracle. As with my character, Nicholas Brady—I've had Zagreus awaken in my right hemisphere, and felt the flooding of renewed life, his vigor, his personality, and his godlike wisdom; he hated the injustice he saw around him, and the lies, and he remembered "The dear one lands untroubled by men, where amid the shadowy green / The little ones of the forest live unseen" (Euripides). Dr. Ornstein, thank you for helping bring winter to an end, and ushering in—not just spring—but the living life of Spring alive but asleep inside us.

Really, I suppose that the clear line between hallucination and reality has itself become a kind of hallucination, and perhaps I am taking my dream experiences too seriously. But there is much interest now, for instance, in the Senoi tribe of the Malay Peninsula (vide Kilton Stewart's article "Dream Theory in Malaya" in Charles T. Tart's *Altered States of Consciousness*). In a dream I was shown that the word "Jesus" is a code, a neologism, and not a real name at all; those reading the text in those early days who were the esoteri (the Qumran men, possibly) would see "Zeus" and "Zagreus" combined into the integer "Jesus." It is a substitution code, I think they call it. Now, ordinarily, one would not give much credit to such a dream, or rather to any dream insofar as it might be an actual entity, an AI system, for instance, giving you accurate information that you otherwise would not have available to you. But as I went to one of my textbooks the other day to check a spelling, I found these remarkably similar textual passages, the first of which we all know, since it concludes our own sacred writings, the New Testament: ". . . I am the root and scion of

David, the bright morning star" (Revelation 22:16, Jesus describing himself).

And:

Of all the trees that are
He hath his flock, and feedeth root by root,
The Joy-god Dionysos, the pure star
That shines amid the gathering of the fruit
      (Pindar; a favorite quatrain of Plutarch, circa 430 B.C.)

What are names? This is the god of in-toxication, taking in the sacred mushroom (cf. John Allegro) or wine, or finding a joke so terribly funny that you lose all reason laughing and crying, as when you see one of the slapstick silent comedies. In the one short stanza of Pindar we have flock, we have trees, we have in addition to these two major symbols of Jesus, terms by which all the esoteri recognize him, yet two more inner terms: the root and star.

The reference to "root and star" might be taken as equal to a spacial extension of the time extension of "I am Alpha and Omega," which is the first and last. So "root and star" indicate: I am from the chthonic world up, and the starry heaven downward. But I see something else in star, in bright morning star: I think he was saying, "The signal that the springtime for man is here, that signal comes from another star." We have friends and they are ETI, and it is as He told us, a bright and morning star: the star of love.

"If You Find This World Bad, You Should See Some of the Others" (1977)

May I tell you how much I appreciate your asking me to share some of my ideas with you. A novelist carries with him constantly what most women carry in large purses: much that is useless, a few absolutely essential items, and then, for good measure, a great number of things that fall in between. But the novelist does not transport them physically because his trove of possessions is mental. Now and then he adds a new and entirely useless idea; now and then he reluctantly cleans out the trash—the obviously worthless ideas—and with a few sentimental tears sheds them. Once in a great while, however, he happens by chance onto a thoroughly stunning idea new to him that he hopes will turn out to be new to everyone else. It is this final category that dignifies his existence. But such truly priceless ideas . . . perhaps during his entire lifetime he may, at best, acquire only a meager few. But that is enough; he has, through them, justified his existence to himself and to his God.

An odd aspect of these rare, extraordinary ideas that puzzles me is their mystifying cloak of—shall I say—the obvious. By that I mean, once the idea has emerged or appeared or been born—however it is that new ideas pass over into being—the novelist says to himself, "But of course. Why didn't I realize that years ago?" But note the word "realize." It is the key word. He has come across something new that at the same time was there, somewhere, all the time. In truth, it simply surfaced. It always *was*. He did not invent it or even find it; in a very real sense it found *him*. And—and this is a little frightening to contemplate—he has not invented it, but on the contrary, it invented *him*. It is as if the idea created him for its purposes. I think this is why we discover a startling phenomenon of great renown: that quite often in history a great new idea strikes a number of researchers or thinkers at exactly the same time, all of them oblivious to their compeers. "Its time had come," we say about the idea, and so dismiss, as if we had explained it, something I consider quite important: our recognition that in a certain literal sense ideas are alive.

What does this mean, to say that an idea or a thought is literally alive? And that it seizes on men here and there and makes use of them to actualize itself into the stream of human history? Perhaps the pre-Socratic philosophers were correct; the cosmos is one vast entity that thinks. It may in fact do nothing *but* think. In that case either what we call the universe is merely a form of disguise that it takes, or it somehow is the universe— some variation on this pantheistic view, my favorite being that it cunningly mimics the world that we experience daily, and we remain none the wiser. This is the view of the oldest religion of India, and to some extent it was the view of Spinoza and Alfred North Whitehead, the concept of an immanent God, God within the universe, not transcendent above it and therefore not part of it. The Sufi saying [by Rumi] "The workman is invisible within the workshop" applies here, with workshop as universe and workman as God. But this still expresses the theistic notion that the universe is something that God created; whereas I am saying, perhaps God created nothing but merely is. And we spend our lives within him or her or it, wondering constantly where he or she or it can be found.

I enjoyed thinking along these lines for several years. God is as near at hand as the trash in the gutter—God *is* the trash in the gutter, to speak more precisely. But then one day a wicked thought entered my mind— wicked because it undermined my marvelous pantheistic monism of which I was so proud. What if—and here you will see how at least this particular SF writer gets his plots—what if there exists a plurality of universes arranged along a sort of lateral axis, which is to say at right angles to the flow of linear time? I must admit that upon thinking this I found I had conjured up a terrific absurdity: ten thousand bodies of God arranged like so many suits hanging in some enormous closet, with God either wearing them all at once or going selectively back and forth among them, saying to himself, "I think today I'll wear the one in which Germany and Japan won World War II" and then adding, half to himself, "And tomorrow I'll wear that nice one in which Napoleon defeated the British; that's one of my best."

This does seem absurd, and it certainly seems to reveal the basic idea as nonsense. But suppose we recast this "closet full of different suits of clothes" just a little and say, "What if God tries out a suit of clothes and then, for reasons best known to him, *changes his mind?*" Decides, using this metaphor, that the suit of clothes that he possesses or wears is not the one he wants . . . in which case the aforementioned closet full of suits of clothes is a sort of progressive *sequence* of worlds, picked up, used for a time, and then discarded in favor of an improved one? We might ask at this point, "How would the suddenly discarded suit of clothes—the suddenly abandoned universe—feel? What would it experience?" And, for us even more importantly, what change, *if any*, would the life forms living in that universe experience? Because I have a secret hunch that this exact thing does indeed happen; and I have a keen additional insight that the endless trillions of life forms involved would suppose—incorrectly—that they had experienced nothing, that no change had taken place. They, as elements of the *new* suit of clothes, would incorrectly imagine that they had always been worn—always been as they now were, with complete memories by which to prove the correctness of their subjective impressions.

We are accustomed to supposing that all change takes place along the linear time axis: from past to present to future. The present is an accrual of the past and is different from it. The future will accrue from the present on and be different yet. That an orthogonal or right-angle time axis could exist, a lateral domain in which change takes place—processes occuring sideways in reality, so to speak—this is almost impossible to imagine. How would we perceive such lateral changes? What would we experience? What clues—if we are trying to test out this bizarre theory—should we be on the alert for? In other words, how can change take place outside of linear time at all, in any sense, to any degree?

Well, let us consider a favorite topic of Christian thinkers: the topic of eternity. This concept, historically speaking, was one great new idea brought by Christianity to the world. We are pretty sure that eternity exists—that the word "eternity" refers to something actual, in contrast, say, to the word "angels." Eternity is simply a state in which you are free from and somehow out of and above time. There is no past, present, and future; there is just pure ontological being. "Eternity" is not a word denoting merely a very long time; it is essentially timeless. Well, let me ask this:

Are there any changes that take place there; i.e., take place outside of time? Because if you say, "Yes, eternity is not static; things happen," then I at once smile knowingly and point out that you have introduced time once more. The concept "time" simply denotes—or rather posits—a condition or state or stream—whatever—in which change occurs. No time, no change. Eternity is static. But if it is static, it is even less than long-enduring; it is more like a geometric point, an infinitude of which can be determined along any given line. Viewing my theory about orthogonal or lateral change, I defend myself by saying, "At least it is intellectually less nonsensical than the concept of eternity." And everyone talks about eternity, whether they intend to do anything about it or not.

Let me present you with a metaphor. Let us say that there exists this very rich patron of the arts. Every day on the wall of his living room above his fireplace his servants hang a new picture—each day a different masterpiece, day after day, month after month—each day the "used" one is removed and replaced by a different and new one. I will call this process change along the linear axis. But now let us suppose the servants temporarily running out of new, replacement pictures. What shall they do in the meantime? They can't just leave the present one hanging; their employer has decreed that perpetual replacement—i.e. changing the pictures—is to take place. So they neither allow the current one to remain nor do the replace it with a new one; instead, they do a very clever thing. When their employer is not looking, the servants cunningly alter the picture already on the wall. They paint out a tree here; they paint in a little girl there; they add this; they obliterate that; they make the same painting different and in a sense new, but as I'm sure you can see, not new in the sense of replacing it. The employer enters his living room after dinner, seats himself facing his fireplace, and contemplates what should be—according to his expectations—a new picture. What does he see? It certainly isn't what he saw previously. But also it isn't somehow . . . and here we must become very sympathetic with this perhaps somewhat stupid man, because we can virtually see his brain circuits striving to understand. His brain circuits are saying, "Yes, it is a new picture, it is not the same one as yesterday, but also it *is* the same one, I think, I feel on a very deep, intuitive basis . . . I feel that somehow I've seen it before. I seem to remember a tree, though, and there is no tree." Now, perhaps, if we extrapolate from this man's perceptual, mentational confusion to the theoretical point I was making about lateral change, you can get a better idea of what I mean; I mean, perhaps you can, to at least a degree, see that although what I'm talking about *may* not exist—my concept may be fictional—it *could* exist. It is not intellectually self-contradictory.

As a science fiction writer I gravitate toward such ideas as this; we in the field, of course, know this idea as the "alternate universe" theme. Some of you, I am sure, know that my novel *The Man in the High Castle* utilized this theme. There was in it an alternate world in which Germany and Japan and Italy won World War II. At one point in the novel Mr. Tagomi, the protagonist, somehow is carried over to *our* world, in which the Axis powers lost. He remained in our world only a short time, and scuttled in fright back to his own universe as soon as he glimpsed or understood what had happened—and thought no more of it after that; it had been for him a thoroughly unpleasant experience, since, being Japanese, it was for him a *worse* universe than his customary one. For a Jew, however, it would have been infinitely better—for obvious reasons.

In *The Man in the High Castle* I give no real explanation as to why or how Mr. Tagomi slid across into our universe; he simply sat in the park and scrutinized a piece of modern abstract handmade jewelry—sat and studied it on and on—and when he looked up, he was in another universe. I didn't explain how or why this happened because I don't know, and I would defy anyone, writer, reader, or critic, to give a so-called "explanation." There cannot be one because, of course, as we all know, such a concept is merely a fictional premise; none of us, in our right minds, entertains for even an instant the notion that such alternate universes exist in any actual sense. But let us say, just for fun, that they do. Then, if they do, how are they linked to each other, if in fact they are (or would be) linked? If you drew a map of them, showing their locations, what would the map look like? For instance (and I think this is a very important question), are they absolutely separate one from another, or do they overlap? Because if they overlap, then such problems as "Where do they exist?" and "How do you get from one to the next?" admit to a possible solution. I am saying, simply, if they do indeed exist, and if they do indeed overlap, then we may in some literal, very real sense inhabit several of them to various degrees at any given time. And although we all see one another as living humans walking about and talking and acting, some of us may inhabit relatively greater amounts of, say, Universe One than the other people do; and some of us may inhabit relatively greater amounts of Universe Two, Track Two, instead, and so on. It may not merely be that our subjective impressions of the world differ, but there may be an overlapping, a superimposition, of a number of worlds so that objectively, not subjectively, our worlds may differ. Our perceptions differ as a *result* of this. And I want to add this statement at this point, which I find to be a fascinating concept: It may be that some of these superimposed worlds are passing out of existence, along the lateral time line I spoke of, and some are in the process of moving toward greater, rather than lesser, actualization. These processes would occur simultaneously and not at all in linear time. The kind of process we are talking about here is a *transformation*, a kind of metamorphosis, invisibly achieved. But very real. And very important.

Contemplating this possibility of a lateral arrangement of worlds, a plurality of overlapping Earths along whose linking axis a person can somehow move—can travel in a mysterious way from worst to fair to good to excellent—contemplating this in theological terms, perhaps we could say that herewith we suddenly decipher the elliptical utterances that Christ expressed regarding the Kingdom of God, specifically where it is located. He seems to have given contradictory and puzzling answers. But suppose, just suppose for an instant, that the cause of the perplexity lay not in any desire on his part to baffle or to hide, but in the inadequacy of the question. "My Kingdom is not of this world," he is reported to have said. "The Kingdom is within you." Or possibly, "It is among you." I put before you now the notion, which I personally find exciting, that he may have had in mind that which I speak of as the lateral axis of overlapping realms that contain among them a spectrum of aspects ranging from the unspeakably malignant to the beautiful. And Christ was saying over and over again that there really are many objective realms, somehow related, and somehow bridgeable by living—not dead—men, and that the most wondrous of these worlds was a just kingdom in which either He Himself or God Himself or both of them ruled. And he did not merely speak of a variety of ways of subjectively *viewing* one world; the Kingdom was and is an actual different place, at the opposite end of continua starting with slavery and utter pain. It was his mission to teach his disciples the secret of crossing along this orthogonal path. He did not merely report what lay there; He taught the method of getting there. But, tragically, the secret was lost. The enemy, the Roman authority, crushed it. And so we do not have it. But perhaps we can refind it, since we know that such a secret exists.

This would account for the apparent contradictions regarding the question as to whether the Just Kingdom is ever to be established here on Earth or whether it is a place or state we go to after death. I'm sure I don't have to tell you that this issue has been a fundamental one—and an unresolved one—throughout the history of Christianity. Christ and St. Paul both seem to say emphatically that an actual breaking through into time, into our world, by the hosts of God, will unexpectedly occur. Thereupon, after some exciting drama, a thousand-year paradise, a rightful Kingdom, will be established—at least for those who have done their homework and chores and generally paid attention . . . have not Gone To Sleep, as one parable puts it. We are enjoined repeatedly in the New Testament to be vigilant, that for the Christian it is always day, there is always light, by which he can see this event when it comes. *See this event.* Does that imply that many persons who are somehow asleep or blind or not vigilant—they will *not* see it, even though it occurs? Consider the significance that can be assigned to these notions. The Kingdom will come here, unexpectedly (this is always stressed); the rightful faithful shall see it, because for them it is always daytime, but for the others . . . what seems expressed here is the paradoxical but enthralling thought that—and hear this and ponder—the Kingdom, were it established here, would not be visible to those outside it. I offer the idea that, in more modern terms, what is meant is that some of us will travel laterally to that best world and some will not; they will remain stuck along the lateral axis, which means that for them the Kingdom did *not* come, not in their alternate world. And yet meantime it did come in ours. So it comes and yet does not come. Amazing.

Please ask yourself, What event signals the establishment or reestablishment of the Kingdom? Of course it is nothing other than the Second Advent, the return of the King Himself. Following my reasoning as to the existence of worlds along a lateral axis, one could reason, "Certainly the Second Coming has not taken place—at least not along this Track, in this universe." But then one could speculate, logically, "But perhaps it came exactly as stipulated in the New Testament: during the lifetime of those living then, back in the Apostolic Age." I enjoy—I find fascinating—this concept. What an idea for a novel, an alternate Earth in which the Parousia took place, say, around A.D. 70. Or, say, during the medieval period—say, at the time of the Catherist Crusades . . . how neat an idea for an alternate-world novel! The protagonist somehow is transported from this, our universe, in which the Second Coming did not take place or has not taken place—is transported to one in which it occurred centuries ago.

But if you have followed my conjectures about the overlapping of these alternate worlds, and you sense as I do the possibility that if there are three there may be thirty or three thousand of them—and that some of us live in this one, others of us in another one, others in others, and that events in one track cannot be perceived by persons not in that track— well, let me say what I want to say and be done with it. I think I once experienced a track in which the Savior returned. But I experienced it just very briefly. I am not there now. I am not sure I ever was. Certainly I may never be again. I grieve for that loss, but loss it is; somehow I moved laterally, but then fell back, and then it was gone. A vanished mountain and a stream. The sound of bells. All gone now for me; entirely gone.

I, in my stories and novels, often write about counterfeit worlds, semi-real worlds, as well as deranged private worlds inhabited, often, by just one person, while, meantime, the other characters either remain in their own worlds throughout or are somehow drawn into one of the peculiar ones. This theme occurs in the corpus of my twenty-seven years of writing. At no time did I have a theoretical or conscious explanation for my preoccupation with these pluriform pseudoworlds, but now I think I understand. What I was sensing was the manifold of partially actualized realities lying tangent to what evidently is the most actualized one, the one that the majority of us, by *consensus gentium* [general consent], agree on.

Although originally I presumed that the differences between these worlds was caused entirely by the subjectivity of the various human viewpoints, it did not take me long to open the question as to whether it might not be more than that—that in fact plural realities did exist superimposed onto one another like so many film transparencies. What I still do not grasp, however, is how one reality out of the many becomes actualized in contradistinction to the others. Perhaps none does. Or perhaps again it hangs on an agreement in viewpoint by a sufficiency of people. More likely the matrix world, the one with the true core of being, is determined by the Programmer. He or it articulates—prints out, so to speak—the matrix choice and fuses it with actual substance. The core or essence of reality—that which receives or attains it and to what degree—that is within the purview of the Programmer; this selection and reselection are part of general creativity, of world-building, which seems to be its or his task. A problem, perhaps, which he or it is running, which is to say in the process of solving.

This problem-solving by means of reprogramming variables along the linear time axis of our universe, thereby generating branched-off lateral worlds—I have the impression that the metaphor of the chessboard is especially useful in evaluating how this all can be—in fact must be. Across from the Programmer-Reprogrammer sits a counterentity, whom Joseph Campbell calls the dark counterplayer. God, the Programmer-Reprogrammer, is not making his moves of improvement against inert matter; he is dealing with a cunning opponent. Let us say that on the game board—our universe in space-time—the dark counterplayer makes a move; he sets up a reality situation. Being the dark player, the outcome of his desires constitutes what we experience as evil: nongrowth, the power of the lie, death and the decay of forms, the prison of immutable cause and effect. But the Programmer-Reprogrammer has *already* laid down his response; it has already happened, these moves on his part. The printout, which we undergo as historic events, passes through stages of a dialectical interaction, thesis and antithesis as the forces of the two players mingle. Evidently some syntheses fall to the dark counterplayer, and yet they do not, by virtue of the fact that, in advance, our great Advocate selected variables, the alteration of which brings final victory to him. In winning each sequence in turn he claims some of us, we who participate in the sequence. This is why instinctively people pray, *"Libera me Domine,"* which decodes to mean, "Extricate me, Programmer, as you achieve one victory after another; include me in that triumph. Move me along the lateral axis so that I am not left out." What we sense as "being left out" means remaining under the jurisdiction of, or falling prey to, the malignant power. But that malignant power, for all its guile, has already lost even as it wins, for in some way the counterplayer is blind and so the Programmer-Reprogrammer possesses an advantage.

The great medieval Arabic philosopher, Avicenna, wrote that God does not see time as we do; i.e. for him there is no past nor present nor future. Now, supposing Avicenna is correct, let us imagine a situation in which God, from whatever vantage point he exists at, decides to intervene into our space-time world; i.e. break through from his timeless realm into human history. But if there is only omnipresent reality from his viewpoint, then he can as easily break through into what for us is the past as he can break through into what for us is the present or future. It is exactly like a chess player gazing down at the chessboard; he can move any of his pieces that he wishes. Following Avicenna's reasoning, we can say that God, in desiring, for example, to bring about the Second Advent, need not limit the event to our present or future; he can breach our past—in other words, change our past history; he can cause it to have happened already. And this would be true for any change he wished to make, large or small. For instance, suppose an event in our year A.D. 1970 does not meet with God's idea of how it all should go. He can obliterate it or tinker with it, improve it, whatever he wishes, even at a prior point in linear time. This is his advantage.

I submit to you that such alterations, the creation or selection of such so-called "alternate presents," is continually taking place. The very fact that we can conceptually deal with this notion—that is, entertain it as an idea—is a first step in discerning such processes themselves. But I doubt if we will ever be able in any real fashion to demonstrate, to scientifically prove, that such lateral change processes do occur. Probably all we would have to go on would be vestiges of memory, fleeting impressions, dreams, nebulous intuitions that somehow things had been different in some way—and not long ago but *now*. We might reflexively reach for a light switch in the bathroom only to discover that it was—always had been—in another place entirely. We might reach for the air vent in our car where there was no air vent—a reflex left over from a previous present, still active at a subcortical level. We might dream of people and places we had never seen as vividly as if we had seen them, actually known them. But we would not know what to make of this, assuming we took time to ponder it at all. One very pronounced impression would probably occur to us, to many of us, again and again, and always without explanation: the acute, absolute sensation that we had done once before what we were just about to do now, that we so to speak lived a particular moment or situation previously—but in what sense could it be called "previously," since only the present, not the past, was evidently involved? We would have the overwhelming impression that we were reliving the present, perhaps in precisely the same way, hearing the same words, saying the same words . . . I submit that these impressions are valid and significant, and I will even say this: Such an impression is a clue that at some past time point a variable was changed—reprogrammed, as it were—and that, because of this, an alternate world branched off, became actualized instead of the prior one, and that in fact, in literal fact, we are once more living this particular segment of linear time. A breaching, a tinkering, a change had been made, but not in our present—had been made in our past. Evidently such an alteration would have a peculiar effect on those persons involved; they would, so to speak, be moved back one square or several squares on the board game that constitutes our reality. Conceivably this could happen any number of times, affecting any number of people, as alternative variables were reprogrammed. We would have to go live out each reprogramming along the subsequent linear time axis, but to the Programmer, whom we call God—to him the results of the reprogramming would be apparent at once. We are within time and he is not. Thus, too, this might account for the sensation people get of having lived past lives. They may well have, but not in the past; previous lives, rather, in the present. In perhaps an unending repeated and repeated present, like a great clock dial in which grand clock hands sweep out the same circumference forever, with all of us carried along unknowingly, yet dimly suspecting.

Since at the resolution of every encounter of thesis and antithesis between the dark counterplayer and the divine Programmer a new synthesis is struck off, and since it is possible that each time this happens a lateral world may be generated, and since I conceive that each synthesis or resolution is to some degree a victory by the Programmer, each struck-off world, in sequence, must be an improvement upon—not just the prior one—but an improvement over all the latent or merely possible outcomes. It is better but in no sense perfect—i.e. final. It is merely an improved stage within a process. What I envision clearly is that the Programmer is perpetually using the antecedent universe as a gigantic stockpile for each new synthesis, the antecedent universe then possessing the aspect of chaos or anomie in relation to an emerging new cosmos. Therefore the endless process of sequential struck-off alternate worlds, emerging and being infused with actualization, is negentropic in some way that we cannot see.

In my novel *Ubik* I present a motion along a retrograde entropic axis, in terms of Platonic forms rather than any decay or reversion we normally conceive. Perhaps the normal forward motion along this axis, away from entropy, accruing rather than divesting, is identical with the axis line that I characterize as lateral, which is to say, in orthogonal rather than linear time. If this is so, the novel *Ubik* inadvertently contains what could be called a scientific rather than a philosophical idea. But here I am only guessing. Still, the fiction writer may have written more than he consciously knew.

What blinds us to this hierarchy of evolving form in each new synthesis is that we are unaware of the lesser, unactualized worlds. And this process of interaction, continually forming the new, obliterates at each stage that which came before. What, at any given present instant we possess of the past, is twofold but dubious: We possess external, objective traces of the past embedded in the present, and we possess inner memories. But both are subject to the rule of imperfection, since both are merely bits of reality and not the intact form. What we retain existentially and mentally are therefore inadequate guides. This is implied by the very emergence of true newness itself; if truly new, it must somehow kill the old, the that which was. And, especially, that which did not come to fully be.

What we need at this point is to locate, to bring forth as evidence, someone who has managed somehow—it doesn't matter how, really—to retain memories of a different present, latent alternate world impressions, different in some significant way from this, the one that is at this stage actualized. According to my theoretical view, it would almost certainly be memories of a worse world than this. For it is not reasonable that God the Programmer and Reprogrammer would substitute a worse world in terms of freedom or beauty or love or order or healthiness—by any standard that we know. When a mechanic works on your malfunctioning car he does not damage it further; when a writer creates a second draft of a novel he does not debase it further but strives to improve it. I suppose it could be argued in a strictly theoretical way that God might be evil or insane and would in fact substitute a worse world for a better one, but frankly I cannot take that idea seriously. Let us then pass over it. So let us ask, Does any one of us remember in any dim fashion a worse Earth circa 1977 than this? Have your young men seen visions and our old men dreamed dreams? Nightmare dreams specifically, about a world of enslavement and evil, of prisons and jailers and ubiquitous police? I have. I wrote out those dreams in novel after novel, story after story; to name two in which this prior ugly present obtained most clearly I cite *The Man in the High Castle* and my 1974 novel about the United States as a police state, called *Flow My Tears, the Policeman Said*.

I am going to be very candid with you: I wrote both novels based on fragmentary residual memories of such a horrid slave state world—or perhaps the term "world" is the wrong one, and I should say "United States," since in both novels I was writing about my own country.

In *The Man in the High Castle* there is a novelist, Hawthorne Abendsen, who has written an alternate-world novel in which Germany, Italy, and Japan *lost* World War II. At the conclusion of *The Man in the High Castle*, a woman appears at Abendsen's door to tell him what he does not know: that his novel is true; the Axis did indeed lose the war. The irony of this ending—Abendsen finding out that what he had supposed to be pure fiction spun out of his imagination was in fact true—the irony is this: that my own supposed imaginative work *The Man in the High Castle* is not fiction—or rather is fiction only *now*, thank God. But there was an alternate world, a previous present, in which that particular time track actualized—actualized and then was abolished due to intervention at some prior date. I am sure, as you hear me say this, you do not really believe me, or even believe that I believe it myself. But nevertheless it is true. I retain memories of that other world. That is why you will find it again described in the later novel *Flow My Tears*. The world of *Flow My Tears* is an actual (or rather once actual) alternate world, and I remember it in detail. I do not know who else does. Maybe no one else does. Perhaps all of you were always—have always been—here. But I was not. In March 1974 I began to remember consciously, rather than merely subconsciously, that black iron prison police state world. Upon consciously remembering it I did not need to write about it because I have always been writing about it. Nonetheless, my amazement was great, to remember consciously suddenly that it was once so—as I'm sure you can imagine. Put yourself in my place. In novel after novel, story after story, over a twenty-five-year period, I wrote repeatedly about a particular other landscape, a dreadful one. In March 1974 I understood why, in my writing, I continually reverted to an awareness, in intimation of, that one particular world. I had good reason to. My novels and stories were, without my realizing it consciously, autobiographical. It was—this return of memory—

the most extraordinary experience of my life. Or rather I should say lives, since I had at least two: one there and subsequently one here, where we are now.

I can even tell you what caused me to remember. In late February 1974 I was given sodium pentothol for the extraction of impacted wisdom teeth. Later that day, back home again but still deeply under the influence of the sodium pentothol, I had a short, acute flash of recovered memory. In one instant I caught it all, but immediately rejected it—rejected it, however, with the realization that what I had retrieved in the way of buried memories was authentic. Then, in mid-March, the corpus of memories, whole, intact, began to return. You are free to believe me or free to disbelieve, but please take my word on it that I am not joking; this is very serious, a matter of importance. I am sure that at the very least you will agree that for me even to claim this is in itself amazing. Often people claim to remember past lives; I claim to remember a different, very different, *present* life. I know of no one who has ever made that claim before, but I rather suspect that my experience is not unique; what perhaps is unique is the fact that I am willing to talk about it.

If you have followed me this far, I would like you to be kindly enough disposed to go a little further with me. I would like to share with you something I knew—retrieved—along with the blocked-off memories. In March 1974 the reprogrammed variables, tinkered with back at some earlier date, probably in the late forties—in March 1974 the payoff, the results, of at least one and possibly more of the reprogrammed variables lying along the linear time line in our past, set in. What happened between March and August 1974 was the result of at least one reprogrammed variable laid down perhaps thirty years before, setting into motion a thread of change that culminated in what I am sure you will admit was a spectacularly important—and unique—historical event: the forced removal from office of a president of the United States, Richard Nixon, as well as all those associated with him. In the alternate world that I remembered, the civil rights movement, the antiwar movement of the sixties, had failed. And, evidently, in the midseventies Nixon was not removed from power. That which opposed him (if indeed anything existed that did or could) was inadequate. Therefore one or more factors tending toward that destruction of the entrenched tyrannical power had retroactively, to us, come to be introduced. The scales, thirty years later, in 1977, got tipped. Examine the text of *Flow My Tears* and, keeping in mind that it was written in 1970 and published in February 1974, make an effort to construct the previous events that would have had to take place, or not take place, to account for the world depicted in the novel as lying slightly in the future. One small but critical theme is alluded to twice (I believe) in *Flow My Tears*. It has to do with Nixon. In the future world of *Flow My Tears*, in the dreadful slave state that exists and evidently has existed for decades, Richard Nixon is remembered as an exalted, heroic leader—referred to, in fact, as the "Second Only Begotten Son of God." It is evident from this and many other clues that *Flow My Tears* deals not with *our* future but the future of a present world *alternate* to our own. Blacks, by the time *Flow My Tears* takes place, have become an ecological rarity, protected "as are wild whooping cranes." In the novel one rarely sees blacks on the streets of the United States. But the year in which *Flow My Tears* takes place is only eleven years from now: October 1988. Obviously the fascist genocide against the blacks in the United States in my novel began long before 1977; a number of readers have pointed this out to me. One of them even pointed out that a careful reading of *Flow My Tears* not only indicates that the society depicted, the U.S. police state of 1988, had to be an alternate-world novel, but this reader pointed out that mysteriously, at the very end of the novel, the protagonist, Felix Buckman, appears somehow to have slipped over into a different world, one in which blacks were *not* exterminated. Early in the novel it is stipulated that a black couple is allowed by law to bear only one single child; yet, at the end of the novel, the black man at the all-night gas station proudly gets out his wallet and shows Police General Buckman photographs of his *three* children. The open manner in which the black man shows the pictures to a perfect stranger indicates that for some weird and unexplained reason it is now no longer illegal for a black couple to have several children. Somehow, just as Mr. Togomi slipped over briefly into our alternate present, General Buckman in *Flow My Tears* did the same thing. It is even evident in the text of *Flow My Tears* when and where the police general slipped over. It was just before he landed his flying vehicle at the all-night gas station and encountered—hugged, in fact—the black man; the slipover, which is to say the moment in which the absolutely repressive world of the bulk of the novel faded out, took place during the interval in which General Buckman experienced a strange dream about a kinglike old man with white wool-like beard, wearing robes and a helmet and leading a posse of similarly helmeted robed knights—this king and these helmeted knights appearing in the rural world of farmhouse and pastureland where General Buckman had lived as a boy. The dream, I think, was a graphic depiction in General Buckman's mind of the transformation taking place objectively; it was a kind of inner analog to what was happening outside him to his entire world.

This accounts for the changed Buckman, the very different police general who lands at the all-night gas station and draws the heart with an arrow piercing it, giving the piece of paper with its drawing to the black man as a communication of love. Buckman at the gas station in encountering the black stranger is not the same Buckman who appeared earlier throughout the book: The transformation is complete. But he is unaware of it. Only Jason Taverner, the once-famous television personality who woke up one day to find himself in a world that had never heard of him—only Taverner, when his mysteriously taken-away popularity seeps back, understands that several alternate realities—two upon a cursory reading, but at least three if the ending is studied scrupulously—only Jason Taverner *remembers*. This is the whole basic plot of the novel: One morning Jason Taverner, popular TV and recording star, wakes up in a fleabag dingy hotel room to find all his identification papers gone, and, worse yet finds that no one has ever heard of him—the basic plot is that for some arcane reason the entire population of the United States has in one instant of linear time completely and collectively forgotten a man whose face on the cover of *Time* magazine should be a face virtually every reader would identify without effort. In this novel I am saying, "The entire population of a large country, a continent-sized country, can wake up one morning having entirely forgotten something they all previously knew, and none of them is the wiser." In the novel it is a popular TV and recording star whom they have forgotten, which is of importance, really, only to that particular star or former star. But my hypothesis is presented here nonetheless in a disguised form, because (I am saying) if an entire country can overnight forget *one* thing they all know, they can forget *other* things, more important things; in fact, overwhelmingly important things. I am writing about amnesia on the part of millions of people, of, so to speak, fake memories laid down. This theme of faked memories is a constant thread in my writing over the years. It was also Van Vogt's. And yet, can one contemplate this as a serious possibility, something that could actually happen? Who of us has asked himself that? I did not ask myself that prior to March 1974; I include myself.

You will recall that I pointed out that after Police General Buckman slipped over into a better world he underwent an inner change appropriate to the qualities of the better world, the more just, the more loving, the warmer world in which the tyranny of the police apparatus was already beginning to fade away as would a dream upon the awakening of the dreamer. In March 1974, when I regained my buried memories (a process called in Greek *anamnesis*, which literally means the loss of forgetfulness rather than merely remembering) — upon those memories reentering consciousness I, like General Buckman, underwent a personality change. Like his, it was fundamental but at the same time subtle. It was me but yet it was not me. I noticed it mostly in small ways: things I should have remembered but did not; things I did remember (ah, what things!) but should *not* have. Evidently this had been my personality in what I call Track A. You may be interested in one aspect of my restored memories that strikes me as most astonishing. In the previous alternate present, in Track A, Christianity was illegal, as it had been two thousand years ago at its inception. It was regarded as subversive and revolutionary — and, let me add, this appraisal by the police authorities was correct. It took me almost two weeks, after the return of my memories of my life in Track A, to rid myself of the overpowering impression that all references to Christ, all sacerdotal acts, had to be veiled in absolute secrecy. But historically this fits the pattern of a fascist takeover, especially those along Nazi lines. They did so regard Christianity. And, had they attained a victory in the war, this surely would have been their policy in that portion of the United States that they controlled. For example, Jehovah's Witnesses, under the Nazis, were gassed in the concentration camps along with the Jews and Gypsies; they were placed right up at the top of the list. And, in that other modern totalitarian state, for the same reason it is banned and its members persecuted; I mean, of course, the USSR. The three great tyrannical states in history that have murdered their domestic Christian populations — Rome, the Third Reich, and the USSR — are, from an objective standpoint, three manifestations of a single matrix. Your own personal beliefs about religion are not an issue here; what is an issue is a historic fact, and therefore I ask you to ponder objectively what the overwhelming fear I felt regarding

Christian rites and protestations of faith signifies about the Track A society abruptly remembered. It is a decisive clue about Track A. It tells us how radically different it was. I would like you, if you have gone this far, to accept my statements about my other memories that, under the sodium Pentothal, returned; it was a prison. It was dreadful; we overthrew it, just as we overthrew the Nixon tyranny, but it was far more cruel, incredibly so, and there was a great battle and loss of life. And, please, let me add one other fact, maybe objectively unimportant but to me interesting nonetheless. It was in February 1974 that my blocked-off memories of Track A returned, and it was in February 1974 that *Flow My Tears* was finally, after two years' delay, published. It was almost as if the release of the novel, which had been delayed so long, meant that in a certain sense it was all right for me to remember. But until then it was better that I did not. Why that would be I do not know, but I have the impression that the memories were not to come to the surface until the material had been published very sincerely on the author's part as what he believed to be fiction. Perhaps, had I known, I would have been too frightened to write the novel. Or perhaps I would have shot my mouth off and somehow interfered with the effectiveness of these several books—whatever effectiveness that might be or was. I do not even claim there was an intended effectiveness; perhaps there was none at all. But if there was one—and I repeat the word "if" emphatically—it was almost certainly to stir subliminal memories in readers back to dim life—not a conscious life, not an entering consciousness as in my own case, but to recall to them on a deep and profound, albeit unconscious level, what a police tyranny is like, and how vital it is, now or then, at any time, along any track, to defeat it. In March 1974 the really crucial moves to depose Nixon were beginning. In August, five months later, they proved successful, although these reprogrammings, this intervention in our present, may have been designed more to affect a future continuum rather than our own. As I said at the beginning, ideas seem to have a life of their own; they appear to seize on people and make use of them. The idea that seized me twenty-seven years ago and never let go is this: Any society in which people meddle in other people's business is not a good society, and a state in which the government "knows more about you than you know about yourself," as it is expressed in *Flow My Tears*, is a state that must be overthrown. It may be a theocracy, a fascist corporate state, or reactionary monopolistic capitalism or centralistic socialism—that aspect does not matter. And I am saying not merely, "It can happen here," meaning the United States, but rather, "It *did* happen here. I remember. I was one of the secret Christians who fought it and to at least some extent helped overthrow it." And I am very proud of that: proud of myself in time Track A. But there is, unfortunately, a somber intimation that accompanies my pride as to my work there. I think that in that previous world I did not live past March 1974. I fell victim to a police trap, a net or mesh. However, in this one, which I will call Track B, I had better luck. But we fought here in this track a much lighter tyranny, a far stupider one. Or, perhaps, we had assistance: The anterior reprogramming of one or more historic variables came to our rescue. Sometimes I think (and this is, of course, pure speculation, a happy fantasy of my soul) that because of what we accomplished there—or anyhow attempted to, and very bravely—we who were directly involved were allowed to live on here, past the terminal point that brought us down in that other, worse world. It is a sort of miraculous kindness.

This gracious gift serves to delineate for us—for me at least—some aspects of the Programmer. It causes me to comprehend him after a fashion. I think we cannot know what he is, but we can experience this functioning and so can ask, "What does he resemble?" Not "What is he?" but rather "What is he like?"

First and foremost, he controls the objects, processes, and events in our space-time world. This is, for us, the primary aspect, although intrinsically he may possess aspects of vaster magnitude but of less applicability to us. I have spoken of myself as a reprogrammed variable, and I have spoken of him as the Programmer and Reprogrammer. During a short period of time in March 1974, at the moment in which I was resynthesized, I was aware perceptually—which is to say aware in an external way—of his presence. At that time I had no idea what I was seeing? [sic; this question mark appears, in context, to be a typo]. It resembled plasmic energy. It had colors. It moved fast, collecting and dispersing. But what it *was*, what he was—I am not sure even now, except I can tell you that he had simulated normal objects and their processes so as to copy them and in such an artful way as to make himself invisible within them. As the Vedantists put it, he was the fire within the flint, the razor within the razor case. Later research showed me that in terms of group cultural experience, the name Brahman has been given to this omnipresent immanent entity. I quote a fragment of an American poem ["Brahma"] by Emerson; it conveys what I experienced:

> *They reckon ill who leave me out;*
> *When me they fly I am the wings.*
> *I am the doubter and the doubt,*
> *And I the hymn the Brahman sings.*

By this I mean that during that short period—a matter of hours or perhaps a day—I was aware of nothing that was not the Programmer. All the things in our pluriform world were segments or subsections of him. Some were at rest but many moved, and did so like portions of a breathing organism that inhaled, exhaled, grew, changed, evolved toward some final state that by its absolute wisdom it had chosen for itself. I mean to say, I experienced it as self-creating, dependent on nothing outside it because very simply there was nothing outside it.

As I saw this I felt keenly that through all the years of my life I had been literally blind; I remember saying over and over to my wife, "I've regained my sight! I can see again!" It seemed to me that up until that moment I had been merely guessing as to the nature of the reality around me. I understood that I had not acquired a new faculty of perception but had, rather, regained an old one. For a day or so I saw as we once all had, thousands of years ago. But how had we come to lose sight, this superior eye? The morphology must still be present in us, not only latent; otherwise I could not have reacquired it even briefly. This puzzles me yet. How was it that for forty-six years I did not truly see but only guessed at the nature of the world, and then briefly did see, but soon after, lost that sight and became semiblind again? The interval in which I actually saw was, evidently, the interval in which the Programmer was reworking me. He had moved forward as palpably sentient and alive, as set to ground; he had disclosed himself. Thus it is said that Christianity, Judaism, and Islam are revealed religions. Our God is the *deus absconditus*: the hidden god. But why? Why is it necessary that we be deceived regarding the nature of our reality? Why has he cloaked himself as a plurality of unrelated objects and his movements as a plurality of chance processes? All the changes, all the permutations of reality that we see are expressions of the purposeful growing and unfolding of this single entelechy; it is a plant, a flower, an opening rose. It is a humming hive of bees. It is music, a kind of singing. Obviously I saw the Programmer as he really is, as he really behaves, *only* because he had seized on me to reshape me, so I say, "I know why I saw him," but I cannot say, "I know why I do not see him now, nor why anyone else does not." Do we collectively dwell in a kind of laser hologram, real creatures in a manufactured quasi-world, a stage set within whose artifacts and creatures a mind moves that is determined to remain unknown?

A newspaper article about this speech could well be titled: AUTHOR CLAIMS TO HAVE SEEN GOD BUT CAN'T GIVE ACCOUNT OF WHAT HE SAW.

If I consider the term by which I designate him—the Programmer and Reprogrammer—perhaps I can extract from that a partial answer. I call him what I call him because that was what I witnessed him doing: He had previously programmed the lives here but now was altering one or more crucial factors—this in the service of completing a structure or plan. I reason along these lines: A human scientist who operates a computer does not bias nor warp, does not prejudice, the outcome of his calculations. A human ethnologist does not allow himself to contaminate his own findings by participating in the culture he studies. Which is to say, in certain kinds of endeavors it is essential that the observer remain occluded off from that which he observes. There is nothing malign in this, no sinister deception. It is merely necessary. If indeed we are, collectively, being moved along desired paths toward a desired outcome, the entity that sets us in motion along those lines, that entity which not only desires the particular outcome but that *wills* that outcome—he must not enter into it palpably or the outcome will be aborted. What, then, we must turn our attention to is—not the Programmer—but the events programmed. Concealed though the former is, the latter will confront us; we are involved in it—in fact, we are instruments by which it is accomplished.

There is no doubt in my mind as to the larger, historic purpose of the reprogramming that paid off so spectacularly and gloriously in 1974. Currently I am writing a novel about it; the novel is called *V.A.L.I.S.*, the letters standing for "VAST ACTIVE LIVING INTELLIGENCE SYSTEM." In the novel a government researcher who is very gifted but a little crazy formulates a hypothesis that declares that, located somewhere in our world, there exists a mimicking organism of high intelligence; it so successfully mimics natural objects and processes that humans are routinely unaware of it. When, due to chance or exceptional circumstances, a human does perceive it, he simply calls it "God" and lets it go at that. In my novel, however, the government researcher is determined to treat this vast, intelligent, mimicking entity the way a scientist would treat *anything* under scrutiny. His problem is, however, that by his own hypothesis he cannot detect the entity—certainly a frustrating experience for him.

But also in my novel I write about another person, unknown to this government researcher; that person has been having unusual experiences for which he has no *theory*. He has in fact been encountering Valis, who is in the process of reprogramming him. The two characters possess between them the whole truth: the correct but untestable hypothesis by one, the unexplained experiences by the other. And it is this other man, this nonscientific person, whom I identify with, because he, like me—he is beginning to retrieve blocked-off memories of another world, memories he cannot account for. But he has no theory. None at all.

In the novel I myself appear as a character, under my own name. I am a science fiction writer who has accepted a large advance payment for a yet unwritten novel and who must now come up with that novel before a deadline. I, in the book—I know both these men, Houston Paige, the government researcher with the theory, and Nicholas Brady, who is undergoing the unfathomable experiences. I begin to make use of material from both. My purpose is merely that of meeting my contractual deadline. But, as I continue to write about Houston Paige's theory and Nicholas Brady's experiences, I begin to see that everything fits together. I, in the novel, hold both key and lock, and no one else does.

You can see, I am sure, that it is inevitable, in my novel *Valis*, that eventually Houston Paige and Nicholas Brady meet. But this meeting has an odd effect on Houston Paige, he with the theory. Paige undergoes a total psychotic breakdown as a result of getting confirmation of his theory. He could *imagine* it but he cannot *believe* it. In his head his ingenious theory is dissociated from reality. And this is an intuition which I feel: that many of us believe in Valis or God or Brahman or the Programmer, but if we ever actually encountered it we could simply not handle it. It would be like a child driven mad by Christmas. He could sustain hoping and waiting, he could pray, he could wish, he could suppose and imagine and even believe; but the actual manifestation—that is too much for our small circuits. And yet the child grows up and there is the man. And those circuits—they grow, too. But to remember a different, discarded world? And to perceive the great planning mind that achieved that abolition, that unthreading of evil?

One thing I really want you to know: I am aware that the claims I am making—claims of having retrieved buried memories of an alternate present and to have perceived the agency responsible for arranging that alteration—these claims can neither be proved nor can they even be made to sound rational in the usual sense of the word. It has taken me over three years to reach the point where I am willing to tell anyone but my closest friends about my experience beginning back at the vernal equinox of 1974. One of the reasons motivating me to speak about it publicly at last, to openly make this claim, is a recent encounter I have undergone, which, by the way, bears a resemblance to Hawthorne Abendsen's experience in *The Man in the High Castle* with the woman Juliana Frink. Juliana read Abendsen's book about a world in which Germany and Japan and Italy lost World War II and felt she should tell him what she comprehended about the book. This final scene in *The Man in the High Castle* has, I think, been the source for a similar scene in my later story "Faith of Our Fathers," where the girl Tanya Lee shows up and acquaints the protagonist with the actual reality situation—which is to say, that much of his world is delusional, and purposefully so. For several years I have had the feeling, a growing feeling, that one day a woman, who would be a complete stranger to me, would contact me, tell me that she had some information to impart to me, would then appear at my door, just as Juliana appeared at Abendsen's door, and would forthwith in the gravest possible way tell me exactly what Juliana told Abendsen—that my book, like his, was in a certain real, literal, and physical sense not fiction but the truth. Precisely that has recently happened to me. I am speaking of a woman who systematically read each and every novel of mine, more than thirty of them, as well as many of my stories. And she did appear; and she was a total stranger; and she did inform me of this fact. At first she was curious to find out if I myself knew, or if not that, whether I suspected it. The probing between us, the cautious questioning, lasted three weeks. She did not inform me suddenly or immediately, but rather gradually, watching carefully each step of the way, each step along the path of communication and understanding, to see my reaction. It was a solemn matter, really, for her to drive four hundred miles to visit an author whose many books she had read, books of fiction, of the author's imagination, to tell him that there are superimposed worlds in which we live, not one world only, and that she had ascertained that the author in some way was involved with at least one of these worlds, one canceled out at some past time, rewoven and replaced, and—most of all—does the author consciously know this? It was a tense but joyful moment when she reached the point where she could speak candidly; that point did not arrive in our encounter until she was certain that I could handle it. But I had, three years earlier, posited theoretically that if my retrieved memories were authentic, it was only a matter of time before a contact, a cautious, guarded probing by someone would occur, initiated by a person who had read my books and for one reason or another deduced the actual situation—I mean, knew what the significant information was that the books and stories carried. She knew, from my novels and stories, which world I had experienced, which of the many; what she could not determine until I told her was that, in February 1975, I had passed across into a third alternate present—Track C, we shall call it—and this one was a garden or park of peace and beauty, a world superior to ours, rising into existence. I could then speak to her of three rather than two worlds: the black iron prison world that had been; our intermediate world in which oppression and war exist but have to a great degree been cast down; and then a third alternate world that someday, when the correct variables in our past have been reprogrammed, will materialize as a superimposition onto this one . . . and within which, as we awaken to it, we shall suppose we had always lived there, the memory of this intermediate one, like that of the black iron prison world, eradicated mercifully from our memories.

There may be other persons like this woman who have deduced from evidence internal to my writing, as well as from their own vestigial memories, that the landscape I portray as fictional is or was somehow literally real, and that if a grimmer reality could have once occupied the space that our world occupies, it stands to reason that the process of reweaving need not end here; this is *not* the best of all possible worlds, just as it is not the worst. This woman told me nothing that I did not already know, except that by independently arriving at the same conclusion she gave me the courage to speak out, to tell this but at the same time knowing as I do so that in no way—none that I know of, at least—can this presentation be verified. The best I can do, rather than that, is to play the role of prophet, of ancient prophets and such oracles as the sibyl at Delphi, and to talk of a wonderful garden world, much like that which once our ancestors are said to have inhabited—in fact, I sometimes imagine it to be exactly that same world restored, as if a false trajectory of our world will eventually be fully corrected and once more we will be where once, many thousands of years ago, we lived and were happy. During the brief time I walked about in it I had the strong impression that it was our legitimate home that somehow we had lost. The time I spent there was short—about six hours of real elapsed time. But I remember it well. In the novel I wrote with Roger Zelazny, *Deus Irae*, I describe it toward the end, at the point where the curse is lifted from the world by the death and transfiguration of the God of Wrath. What was most amazing to me about this parklike world, this Track C, was the non-Christian elements forming the basis of it; it was not what my Christian training had prepared me for at all. Even when it began to phase out I still saw sky; I saw land and dark blue smooth water, and standing by the edge of the water a beautiful nude woman whom I recognized as Aphrodite. At that point this other better world had diminished to a mere landscape beyond a Golden Rectangle doorway; the outline of the doorway pulsed with laserlike light and it all grew smaller and was at last alas gone from sight, the 3:5 doorway devouring itself into nothingness, sealing off what lay beyond. I have not seen it since, but I had the firm impression that this was the next world—not of the Christians—but the Arcady of the Greco-Roman pagan world, something older and more beautiful than that which my own religion can conjure up as a lure to keep us in a state of dutiful morality and faith. What I saw was very old and very lovely. Sky, sea, land, and the beautiful woman, and then nothing, for the door had shut and I was closed off back here. It was with a bitter sense of loss that I saw it go—saw her go, really, since it all constellated about her. Aphrodite, I discovered when I looked in my *Britannica* to see what I could learn about her, was not only the goddess of erotic love and aesthetic beauty but also the embodiment of the generative force of life itself; nor was she originally Greek: In the beginning she had been a Semitic deity, later taken over by the Greeks, who knew a good thing when they saw it. During those treasured hours what I saw in her was a loveliness that our own religion, Christianity, at least by comparison, lacks: an incredible symmetry, the *palintonos harmonie* that Heraclitus wrote of: the perfect tension and balance of forces within the strung lyre that bowed by its stretched strings but that appears perfectly at rest, perfectly at peace. Yet, the strung lyre is a balanced dynamism, immobile only because the tensions within it are in absolute proportion. This is the quality of the Greek formulation of beauty: perfection that is dynamic within yet at apparent rest without. Against this *palintonos harmonie* the universe plays out the other aesthetic principle incorporated in the Grecian lyre: the *palintropos harmonie*, which is the back-and-forth oscillation of the strings as they are played. I did not see her like this, and perhaps this, the continual oscillation back and forth, is the deeper, greater rhythm of the universe things coming into existence and then passing away; change rather than a static durability. But for a little while I had seen perfect peace, perfect rest, a past we have lost but a past returning to us as if by means of a long-term oscillation, to be available as our future, in which all lost things shall be restored.

There is a fascinating passage in the Old Testament in which God says, "For I am fashioning a new heaven and a new earth, and the memory of the former things will not enter the mind nor come up into the heart." When I read this I think to myself: I believe I know a great secret. When the work of restoration is completed, we will not even remember the tyrannies, the cruel barbarisms of the Earth we inhabited; "not entering the mind" means we will mercifully forget, and "not coming up into the heart" means that the vast body of pain and grief and loss and disappointment within us will be expunged as if it had never been. I believe that process is taking place now, has *always* been taking place now. And, mercifully, we are already being permitted to forget that which formerly was. And perhaps in my novels and stories I have done wrong to urge you to remember.

SANTA ANA, 1977
CALIFORNIA, U.S.A.

"How to Build a Universe
That Doesn't Fall Apart Two Days Later"
(1978, 1985)

First, before I begin to bore you with the usual sort of things science fiction writers say in speeches, let me bring you official greetings from Disneyland. I consider myself a spokesperson for Disneyland because I live just a few miles from it—and, as if that were not enough, I once had the honor of being interviewed there by Paris TV.

For several weeks after the interview, I was really ill and confined to bed. I think it was the whirling teacups that did it. Elizabeth Antebi, who was the producer of the film, wanted to have me whirling around in one of the giant teacups while discussing the rise of fascism with Norman Spinrad . . . an old friend of mine who writes excellent science fiction. We also discussed Watergate, but we did that on the deck of Captain Hook's pirate ship. Little children wearing Mickey Mouse hats—those black hats with the ears—kept running up and bumping against us as the cameras whirred away, and Elizabeth asked unexpected questions. Norman and I, being preoccupied with tossing little children about, said some extraordinarily stupid things that day. Today, however, I have to accept full blame for what I tell you, since none of you are wearing Mickey Mouse hats and trying to climb up on me under the impression that I am part of the rigging of a pirate ship.

Science fiction writers, I am sorry to say, really do not know anything. We can't talk about science, because our knowledge of it is limited and unofficial, and usually our fiction is dreadful. A few years ago, no college or university would have considered inviting one of us to speak. We were mercifully confined to lurid pulp magazines, impressing no one. In those days, friends would say to me, "But are you writing anything serious?"

meaning, "Are you writing anything other than science fiction?" We longed to be accepted. We yearned to be noticed. Then, suddenly, the academic world noticed us, we were invited to give speeches and appear on panels—and immediately we made idiots of ourselves. The problem is simply this: What does a science fiction writer know about? On what topic is he an authority?

It reminds me of a headline that appeared in a California newspaper just before I flew here. SCIENTISTS SAY THAT MICE CANNOT BE MADE TO LOOK LIKE HUMAN BEINGS. It was a federally funded research program, I suppose. Just think: Someone in this world is an authority on the topic of whether mice can or cannot put on two-tone shoes, derby hats, pinstriped shirts, and Dacron pants, and pass as humans.

Well, I will tell you what interests me, what I consider important. I can't claim to be an authority on anything, but I can honestly say that certain matters absolutely fascinate me, and that I write about them all the time. The two basic topics that fascinate me are "What is reality?" and "What constitutes the authentic human being?" Over the twenty-seven years in which I have published novels and stories I have investigated those two interrelated topics over and over again. I consider them important topics. What are we? What is it that surrounds us, that we call the not-me, or the empirical or phenomenal world?

In 1951, when I sold my first story ["Roog"], I had no idea that such fundamental issues could be pursued in the science fiction field. I began to pursue them unconsciously. My first story had to do with a dog who imagined that the garbagemen who came every Friday morning were stealing valuable food that the family had carefully stored away in a safe metal container. Every day, members of the family carried out paper sacks of nice ripe food, stuffed them into the metal container, shut the lid tightly—and when the container was full, these dreadful-looking creatures came and stole everything but the can.

Finally, in the story, the dog begins to imagine that someday the garbagemen will eat the people in the house, as well as stealing their food. Of course, the dog is wrong about this. We all know that garbagemen do not eat people. But the dog's extrapolation was in a sense logical—given the facts at his disposal. The story was about a real dog, and I used to watch him and try to get inside his head and imagine how he saw the world. Certainly, I decided, that dog sees the world quite differently than I do, or *any* humans do. And then I began to think, Maybe each human being lives in a unique world, a private world, a world different from those inhabited and experienced by all other humans. And that led me to wonder, If reality differs from person to person, can we speak of reality singular, or shouldn't we really be talking about plural realities? And if there are plural realities, are some more true (more real) than others? What about the world of a schizophrenic? Maybe it's as real as our world. Maybe we cannot say that we are in touch with reality and he is not, but should instead say, His reality is so different from ours that he can't explain his to us, and we can't explain ours to him. The problem, then, is that if subjective worlds are experienced too differently, there occurs a breakdown of communication . . . and *there* is the real illness.

I once wrote a story ["The Electric Ant" (1969)] about a man who was injured and taken to a hospital. When they began surgery on him, they discovered that he was an android, not a human, but that he did not know it. They had to break the news to him. Almost at once, Mr. Garson Poole discovered that his reality consisted of punched tape passing from reel to reel in his chest. Fascinated, he began to fill in some of the punched holes and add new ones. Immediately his world changed. A flock of ducks flew through the room when he punched one new hole in the tape. Finally he cut the tape entirely, whereupon the world disappeared. However, it also disappeared for the other characters in the story . . . which makes no sense, if you think about it. Unless the other characters were figments of his punched-tape fantasy. Which I guess is what they were.

It was always my hope, in writing novels and stories that asked the question "What is reality?," to someday get an answer. This was the hope of most of my readers, too. Years passed. I wrote over thirty novels and over a hundred stories, and still I could not figure out what was real. One day a girl college student in Canada asked me to define reality for her, for a paper she was writing for her philosophy class. She wanted a one-sentence answer. I thought about it and finally said, "Reality is that which, when you stop believing in it, doesn't go away." That's all I could come up with. That was back in 1972. Since then I haven't been able to define reality any more lucidly.

But the problem is a real one, not a mere intellectual game. Because today we live in a society in which spurious realities are manufactured by the media, by governments, by big corporations, by religious groups, political groups—and the electronic hardware exists by which to deliver these pseudoworlds right into the heads of the reader, the viewer, the listener. Sometimes when I watch my eleven-year-old daughter watch TV, I wonder what she is being taught. The problem of miscuing; consider that. A TV program produced for adults is viewed by a small child. Half of what is said and done in the TV drama is probably misunderstood by the child. Maybe it's *all* misunderstood. And the thing is, Just how authentic is the information anyhow, even if the child correctly understood it? What is the relationship between the average TV situation comedy and reality? What about the cop shows? Cars are continually swerving out of control, crashing, and catching fire. The police are always good and they always win. Do not ignore that one point: The police always win. What a lesson that is. You should not fight authority, and even if you do, you will lose. The message here is, *Be passive.* And—cooperate. If Officer Baretta asks you for information, give it to him, *because Officer Baretta is a good man and to be trusted. He loves you, and you should love him.*

So I ask, in my writing, What is real? Because unceasingly we are bombarded with pseudorealities manufactured by very sophisticated people using very sophisticated electronic mechanisms. I do not distrust their motives; I distrust their power. They have a lot of it. And it is an astonishing power: that of creating whole universes, universes of the mind. I ought to know. I do the same thing. It is my job to create universes, as the basis of one novel after another. And I have to build them in such a way that they do not fall apart two days later. Or at least that is what my editors hope. However, I will reveal a secret to you: I like to build universes that *do* fall apart. I like to see them come unglued, and I like to see how the characters in the novels cope with this problem. I have a secret love of chaos. There should be more of it. Do not believe—and I am dead serious when I say this—do not assume that order and stability are always good, in a society or in a universe. The old, the ossified, must always give way to new life and the birth of new things. Before the new things can be born the old must perish. This is a dangerous realization, because it tells us that we must eventually part with much of what is familiar to us. And that hurts. But that is part of the script of life. Unless we can psychologically accommodate change, we ourselves will begin to die, inwardly. What I am saying is that objects, customs, habits, and ways of life must perish so that the authentic human being can live. And it is the authentic human being who matters most, the viable, elastic organism that can bounce back, absorb, and deal with the new.

Of course, I would say this because I live near Disneyland, and they are always adding new rides and destroying old ones. Disneyland is an evolving organism. For years they had the Lincoln Simulacrum and finally it began to die and they had to regretfully retire it. The simulacrum, like Lincoln himself, was only a temporary form which matter and energy take and then lose. The same is true of each of us, like it or not.

The pre-Socratic Greek philosopher Parmenides taught that the only things that are real are things that never change . . . and the pre-Socratic Greek philosopher Heraclitus taught that everything changes. If you superimpose their two views, you get this result: Nothing is real. There is a fascinating next step to this line of thinking: Parmenides could never have existed because he grew old and died and disappeared, so, according to his own philosophy, he did not exist. And Heraclitus may have been right—let's not forget that; so if Heraclitus was right, then Parmenides did exist, and therefore, according to Heraclitus' philosophy, perhaps Parmenides was right, since Parmenides fulfilled the conditions, the criteria, by which Heraclitus judged things real.

I offer this merely to show that as soon as you begin to ask what is ultimately real, you right away begin to talk nonsense. By the time of Zeno, they knew they were talking nonsense. Zeno proved that motion was impossible (actually he only imagined that he had proved this; what he lacked was what technically is called the "theory of limits"). David Hume, the greatest skeptic of them all, once remarked that after a gathering of skeptics met to proclaim the veracity of skepticism as a philosophy, all of the members of the gathering nonetheless left by the door rather than the window. I see Hume's point. It was all just talk. The solemn philosophers weren't taking what they said seriously.

But I consider that the matter of defining what is real—that is a serious topic, even a vital topic. And in there somewhere is the other topic, the definition of the authentic human. Because the bombardment of pseudorealities begins to produce inauthentic humans very quickly, spurious humans—as fake as the data pressing at them from all sides. My two topics are really one topic; they unite at this point. Fake realities will create fake humans. Or, fake humans will generate fake realities and then sell them to other humans, turning them, eventually, into forgeries of themselves. So we wind up with fake humans inventing fake realities and then peddling them to other fake humans. It is just a very large version of Disneyland. You can have the Pirate Ride or the Lincoln Simulacrum or Mr. Toad's Wild Ride—you can have *all* of them, but none is true.

In my writing I got so interested in fakes that I finally came up with the concept of fake fakes. For example, in Disneyland there are fake birds worked by electric motors that emit caws and shrieks as you pass by them. Suppose some night all of us sneaked into the park with real birds and substituted them for the artificial ones. Imagine the horror the Disneyland officials would feel when they discovered the cruel hoax. Real birds! And perhaps someday even real hippos and lions. Consternation. The park being cunningly transformed from the unreal to the real, by sinister forces. For instance, suppose the Matterhorn turned into a genuine snow-covered mountain? What if the entire place, by a miracle of God's power and wisdom, was changed, in a moment, in the blink of an eye, into something incorruptible? They would have to close down.

In Plato's *Timaeus*, God does not create the universe, as does the Christian God; He simply finds it one day. It is in a state of total chaos. God sets to work to transform the chaos into order. That idea appeals to me, and I have adapted it to fit my own intellectual needs: What if our universe started out as not quite real, a sort of illusion, as the Hindu religion teaches, and God, out of love and kindness for us, is slowly transmuting it, slowly *and secretly*, into something real?

We would not be aware of this transformation, since we were not aware that our world was an illusion in the first place. This technically is a Gnostic idea. Gnosticism is a religion that embraced Jews, Christians, and pagans for several centuries. I have been accused of holding Gnostic ideas. I guess I do. At one time I would have been burned. But some of their ideas intrigue me. One time, when I was researching Gnosticism in the *Britannica*, I came across mention of a Gnostic codex called *The Unreal God and the Aspects of His Nonexistent Universe*, an idea that reduced me to helpless laughter. What kind of person would write about something that he knows doesn't exist, and how can something that doesn't exist have aspects? But then I realized that I'd been writing about these matters for over twenty-five years. I guess there is a lot of latitude in what you can say when writing about a topic that does not exist. A friend of mine once published a book called *Snakes of Hawaii*. A number of libraries wrote him, ordering copies. Well, there are no snakes in Hawaii. All the pages of his book are blank.

Of course, in science fiction no pretense is made that the worlds described are real. This is why we call it fiction. The reader is warned in advance not to believe what he is about to read. Equally true, the visitors to Disneyland understand that Mr. Toad does not really exist and that the pirates are animated by motors and servo-assist mechanisms, relays, and electronic circuits. So no deception is taking place.

And yet the strange thing is, in some way, some real way, much of what appears under the title "science fiction" is true. It may not be literally true, I suppose. We have not really been invaded by creatures from another star system, as depicted in *Close Encounters of the Third Kind*. The producers of that film never intended for us to believe it. Or did they?

And, more important, if they did intend to state this, is it actually true? That is the issue: not, Does the author or producer believe it, but—Is it true? Because, quite by accident, in the pursuit of a good yarn, a science fiction author or producer or scriptwriter might stumble onto the truth . . . and only later on realize it.

The basic tool for the manipulation of reality is the manipulation of words. If you can control the meaning of words, you can control the people who must use the words. George Orwell made this clear in his novel *1984*. But another way to control the minds of people is to control their perceptions. If you can get them to see the world as you do, they will think as you do. Comprehension follows perception. How do you get them to see the reality you see? After all, it is only one reality out of many. Images are a basic constituent: pictures. That is why the power of TV to influence young minds is so staggeringly vast. Words and pictures are synchronized. The possibility of total control of the viewer exists, especially the young viewer. TV viewing is a kind of sleeplearning. An EEG of a person watching TV shows that after about half an hour the brain decides that nothing is happening, and it goes into a hypnoidal twilight state, emitting alpha waves. This is because there is such little eye motion. In addition, much of the information is graphic and therefore passes into the right hemisphere of the brain, rather than being processed by the left, where the conscious personality is located. Recent experiments indicate that much of what we see on the TV screen is received on a subliminal basis. We only imagine that we consciously see what is there. The bulk of the messages elude our attention; literally, after a few hours of TV watching, we do not know what we have seen. Our memories are spurious, like our memories of dreams; the blank spaces are filled in retrospectively. And falsified. We have participated unknowingly in the creation of a spurious reality, and then we have obligingly fed it to ourselves. We have colluded in our own doom.

And—and I say this as a professional fiction writer—the producers, scriptwriters, and directors who create these video/audio worlds do not know how much of their content is true. In other words, they are victims of their own product, along with us. Speaking for myself, I do not know how much of my writing is true, or *which* parts (if any) are true. This is a potentially lethal situation. We have fiction mimicking truth, and truth mimicking fiction. We have a dangerous overlap, a dangerous blur. And in all probability it is not deliberate. In fact, that is part of the problem. You cannot legislate an author into correctly labeling his product, like a can of pudding whose ingredients are listed on the label . . . you cannot compel him to declare what part is true and what isn't if he himself does not know.

It is an eerie experience to write something into a novel, believing it is pure fiction, and to learn later on—perhaps years later—that it is true. I would like to give you an example. It is something that I do not understand. Perhaps you can come up with a theory. I can't.

In 1970, I wrote a novel called *Flow My Tears, the Policeman Said.* One of the characters is a nineteen-year-old girl named Kathy. Her husband's name is Jack. Kathy appears to work for the criminal underground, but later, as we read deeper into the novel, we discover that actually she is working for the police. She has a relationship going on with a police inspector. The character is pure fiction. Or at least I thought it was.

Anyhow, on Christmas Day of 1970, I met a girl named Kathy—this was after I had finished the novel, you understand. She was nineteen years old. Her boyfriend was named Jack. I soon learned that Kathy was a drug dealer. I spent months trying to get her to give up dealing drugs; I kept warning her again and again that she would get caught. Then, one evening when we were entering a restaurant together, Kathy stopped short and said, "I can't go in." Seated in the restaurant was a police inspector whom I knew. "I have to tell you the truth," Kathy said. "I have a relationship with him."

Certainly, these are odd coincidences. Perhaps I have precognition. But the mystery becomes even more perplexing; the next stage totally baffles me. It has for four years.

In 1974 the novel was published by Doubleday. One afternoon I was talking to my priest—I am an Episcopalian—and I happened to mention to him an important scene near the end of the novel in which the character Felix Buckman meets a black stranger at an all-night gas station, and they begin to talk. As I described the scene in more and more detail, my priest became progressively more agitated. At last he said, "That is a scene from the Book of Acts, from the Bible! In Acts, the person who meets the black man on the road is named Philip—your name." Father Rasch was so upset by the resemblance that he could not even locate the scene in his Bible. "Read Acts," he instructed me. "And you'll agree. It's the same down to specific details."

I went home and read the scene in Acts. Yes, Father Rasch was right; the scene in my novel was an obvious retelling of the scene in Acts ... and I had never read Acts, I must admit. But again the puzzle became deeper. In Acts, the high Roman official who arrests and interrogates St. Paul is named Felix—the same name as my character. And my character Felix Buckman is a high-ranking police general; in fact, in my novel he holds the same office as Felix in the Book of Acts: the final authority. There is a conversation in my novel that very closely resembles a conversation between Felix and Paul.

Well, I decided to try for any further resemblances. The main character in my novel is named Jason. I got an index to the Bible and looked to see if anyone named Jason appears anywhere in the Bible. I couldn't remember any. Well, a man named Jason appears once and only once in the Bible. It is in the Book of Acts. And, as if to plague me further with coincidences, in my novel Jason is fleeing from the authorities and takes refuge in a person's house, and in Acts the man named Jason shelters a fugitive from the law in his house—an exact inversion of the situation in my novel, as if the mysterious Spirit responsible for all this was having a sort of laugh about the whole thing.

Felix, Jason, and the meeting on the road with the black man who is a complete stranger. In Acts, the disciple Philip baptizes the black man, who then goes away rejoicing. In my novel, Felix Buckman reaches out to the black stranger for emotional support, because Felix Buckman's sister has just died and he is falling apart psychologically. The black man stirs up Buckman's spirits and although Buckman does not go away rejoicing, at least his tears have stopped falling. He had been flying home, weeping over the death of his sister, and had to reach out to someone, anyone, even a total stranger. It is an encounter between two strangers on the road that changes the life of one of them—both in the novel and in Acts. And one final quirk by the mysterious Spirit at work: The name Felix is the Latin word for "happy." Which I did not know when I wrote the novel.

A careful study of my novel shows that for reasons that I cannot even begin to explain, I had managed to retell several of the basic incidents from a particular book of the Bible, and even had the right names. What could explain this? That was four years ago that I discovered all this. For four years I have tried to come up with a theory and I have not. I doubt if I ever will.

But the mystery had not ended there, as I had imagined. Two months ago I was walking up to the mailbox late at night to mail off a letter, and also to enjoy the sight of St. Joseph's Church, which sits opposite my apartment building. I noticed a man loitering suspiciously by a parked car. It looked as if he was attempting to steal the car, or maybe something from it; as I returned from the mailbox, the man hid behind a tree. On impulse I walked up to him and asked, "Is anything the matter?"

"I'm out of gas," the man said. "And I have no money."

Incredibly, because I have never done this before, I got out my wallet, took all the money from it, and handed the money to him. He then shook hands with me and asked where I lived, so that he could later pay the money back. I returned to my apartment, and then I realized the money would do him no good, since there was no gas station within walking distance. So I returned, in my car. The man had a metal gas can in the trunk of his car, and, together, we drove in my car to an all-night gas station. Soon we were standing there, two strangers, as the pump jockey filled the metal gas can. Suddenly I realized that this was the scene in my novel— the novel written eight years before. The all-night gas station was exactly as I had envisioned it in my inner eye when I wrote the scene—the glaring white light, the pump jockey—and now I saw something that I had not seen before. The stranger whom I was helping was black.

We drove back to his stalled car with the gas, shook hands, and then I returned to my apartment building. I never saw him again. He could not pay me back because I had not told him which of the many apartments was mine or what my name was. I was terribly shaken up by the experience. I had literally lived out a scene completely as it had appeared in my novel. Which is to say, I had lived out a sort of replica of the scene in Acts where Philip encounters the black man on the road.

What could explain all this?

The answer I have come up with may not be correct, but it is the only answer I have. It has to do with time. My theory is this: In some certain important sense, *time is not real.* Or perhaps it is real, but not as we experience it to be or imagine it to be. I had the acute, overwhelming certitude (and still have) that despite all the change we see, a specific permanent landscape underlies the world of change: and that this invisible underlying landscape is that of the Bible; it, specifically, is the period immediately following the death of Christ; it is, in other words, the time period of the Book of Acts.

Parmenides would be proud of me. I have gazed at a constantly changing world and declared that underneath it lies the eternal, the unchanging, the absolutely real. But how has this come about? If the real time is circa A.D. 50, then why do we see A.D. 1978? And if we are really living in the Roman Empire somewhere in Syria, why do we see the United States?

During the Middle Ages, a curious theory arose, which I will now present to you for what it is worth. It is the theory that the Evil One—Satan—is the "Ape of God." That he creates spurious imitations of creation, and then interpolates them for that authentic creation. Does this odd theory help explain my experience? Are we to believe that we are occluded, that we are deceived, that it is not 1978 but A.D. 50 . . . and Satan has spun a counterfeit reality to wither our faith in the return of Christ?

I can just picture myself being examined by a psychiatrist. The psychiatrist says, "What year is it?" And I reply, "A.D. 50." The psychiatrist blinks and then asks, "And where are you?" I reply, "In Judaea." "Where the heck is that?" the psychiatrist asks. "It's part of the Roman Empire," I would have to answer. "Do you know who is president?" the psychiatrist would ask, and I would answer, "The Procurator Felix." "You're pretty sure about this?" the psychiatrist would ask, meanwhile giving a covert signal to two very large psych techs. "Yep," I'd reply. "Unless Felix has stepped down and been replaced by the Procurator Festus. You see, St. Paul was held by Felix for—" "Who told you all this?" the psychiatrist would break in, irritably, and I would reply, "The Holy Spirit." And after that I'd be in the rubber room, inside gazing out, and knowing exactly how come I was there.

Everything in that conversation would be true, in a sense, although palpably not true in another. I know perfectly well that the date is 1978 and that Jimmy Carter is president and that I live in Santa Ana, California, in the United States. I even know how to get from my apartment to Disneyland, a fact I can't seem to forget. And surely no Disneyland existed back at the time of St. Paul.

So if I force myself to be very rational and reasonable, and all those other good things, I must admit that the existence of Disneyland (which I *know* is real) proves that we are not living in Judaea in A.D. 50. The idea of St. Paul whirling around in the giant teacups while composing First Corinthians, as Paris TV films him with a telephoto lens—that just can't be. St. Paul would never go near Disneyland. Only children, tourists, and visiting Soviet high officials ever go to Disneyland. Saints do not.

But somehow that biblical material snared my unconscious and crept into my novel, and equally true, for some reason in 1978 I relived a scene that I described back in 1970. What I am saying is this: There is internal evidence in at least one of my novels that another reality, an unchanging one, exactly as Parmenides and Plato suspected, underlies the visible phenomenal world of change, and somehow, in some way, perhaps to our surprise, we can cut through to it. Or, rather, a mysterious Spirit can put us in touch with it, if it wishes us to see this permanent other landscape. Time passes, thousands of years pass, but at the same instant that we see this contemporary world, the ancient world, the world of the Bible, *is concealed beneath it*, still there and still real. Eternally so.

Shall I go for broke and tell you the rest of this peculiar story? I'll do so, having gone this far already. My novel *Flow My Tears, the Policeman Said* was released by Doubleday in February 1974. The week after it was released, I had two impacted wisdom teeth removed, under sodium pentothol. Later that day I found myself in intense pain. My wife phoned the oral surgeon and he phoned a pharmacy. Half an hour later there was a knock at my door: the delivery person from the pharmacy with the pain medication. Although I was bleeding and sick and weak, I felt the need to answer the knock on the door myself. When I opened the door, I found myself facing a young woman—who wore a shimmering gold necklace in the center of which was a gleaming gold fish. For some reason I was hypnotized by the gleaming gold fish; I forgot my pain, forgot the medication, forgot why the girl was there. I just kept staring at the fish sign.

"What does that mean?" I asked her.

The girl touched the glimmering golden fish with her hand and said, "This is a sign worn by the early Christians." She then gave me the package of medication.

In that instant, as I stared at the gleaming fish sign and heard her words, I suddenly experienced what I later learned is called *anamnesis*—a Greek word meaning, literally, "loss of forgetfulness." I remembered who I was and where I was. In an instant, in the twinkling of an eye, it all came back to me. And not only could I remember it but I could see it. The girl was a secret Christian and so was I. We lived in fear of detection by the Romans. We had to communicate with cryptic signs. She had just told me all this, and it was true.

For a short time, as hard as this is to believe or explain, I saw fading into view the black, prisonlike contours of hateful Rome. But, of much more importance, I remembered Jesus, who had just recently been with us, and had gone temporarily away, and would very soon return. My emotion was one of joy. We were secretly preparing to welcome Him back. It would not be long. And the Romans did not know. They thought He was dead, forever dead. That was our great secret, our joyous knowledge. Despite all appearances, Christ was going to return, and our delight and anticipation were boundless.

Isn't it odd that this strange event, this recovery of lost memory, occurred only a week after *Flow My Tears* was released? And it is *Flow My Tears* that contains the replication of people and events from the Book of Acts, which is set at the precise moment in time—just after Jesus' death and resurrection—that I remembered, by means of the golden fish sign, as having just taken place?

If you were me, and had this happened to you, I'm sure you wouldn't be able to leave it alone. You would seek a theory that would account for it. For over four years now, I have been trying one theory after another: circular time, frozen time, timeless time, which is called "sacred" as contrasted to "mundane" time . . . I can't count the theories I've tried out.

One constant has prevailed, though, throughout all the theories. There must indeed be a mysterious Holy Spirit that has an exact and intimate relation to Christ, that can indwell in human minds, guide and inform them, and even express itself through those humans, even without their awareness.

In the writing of *Flow My Tears*, back in 1970, there was one unusual event that I realized at the time was not ordinary, was not a part of the regular writing process. I had a dream one night, an especially vivid dream. And when I awoke I found myself under the compulsion—the absolute necessity—of getting the dream into the text of the novel precisely as I had dreamed it. In getting the dream exactly right, I had to do eleven drafts of the final part of the manuscript, until I was satisfied.

I will now quote from the novel, as it appeared in the final, published form. See if this dream reminds you of anything.

The countryside, brown and dry, in summer, where he had lived as a child. He rode a horse, and approaching him on his left a squad of horses nearing slowly. On the horses rode men in shining robes, each a different color; each wore a pointed helmet that sparkled in the sunlight. The slow, solemn knights passed him and as they traveled by he made out the face of one: an ancient marble face, a terribly old man with rippling cascades of white beard. What a strong nose he had. What noble features. So tired, so serious, so far beyond ordinary men. Evidently he was a king.

Felix Buckman let them pass; he did not speak to them and they said nothing to him. Together, they all moved toward the house from which he had come. A man had sealed himself up inside the house, a man alone, Jason Taverner, in the silence and darkness, without windows, by himself from now on into eternity. Sitting, merely existing, inert. Felix Buckman continued on, out into the open countryside. And then he heard from behind him one dreadful single shriek. They had killed Taverner, and seeing them enter, sensing them in the shadows around him, knowing what they intended to do with him, Taverner had shrieked.

Within himself Felix Buckman felt absolute and utter desolate grief. But in the dream he did not go back nor look back. There was nothing that could be done. No one could have stopped the posse of varicolored men in robes; they could not have been said no to. Anyhow, it was over. Taverner was dead.

This passage probably does not suggest any particular thing to you, except a law posse exacting judgment on someone either guilty or considered guilty. It is not clear whether Taverner has in fact committed some crime or is merely believed to have committed some crime. I had the impression that he was guilty, but that it was a tragedy that he had to be killed, a terribly sad tragedy. In the novel, this dream causes Felix Buckman to begin to cry, and therefore he seeks out the black man at the all-night gas station.

Months after the novel was published, I found the section in the Bible to which this dream refers. It is Daniel, 7:9:

Thrones were set in place and one ancient in years took his seat. His robe was white as snow and the hair of his head like cleanest wool. Flames of fire were his throne and its wheels blazing fire; a flowing river of fire streamed out before him. Thousands upon thousands served him and myriads upon myriads attended his presence. The court sat, and the books were opened.

This white-haired old man appears again in Revelation, 1:13:

I saw . . . one like a son of man, robed down to his feet, with a golden girdle round his breast. The hair of his head was white as snow-white wool, and his eyes blazed like fire; his feet gleamed like burnished brass refined in a furnace, and his voice was like the sound of rushing waters.

And then 1:17:

When I saw him, I fell at his feet as though dead. But he laid his right hand upon me and said, "Do not be afraid. I am the first and the last, and I am the living one, for I was dead and now I am alive forevermore, and I hold the keys of Death and Death's domain. Write down therefore what you have seen, what is now, and what will be hereafter."

And, like John of Patmos, I faithfully wrote down what I saw and put it in my novel. And it was true, although at the time I did not know who was meant by this description:

> He made out the face of one: an ancient marble face, a terribly old man with rippling cascades of white beard. What a strong nose he had. What noble features. So tired, so serious, so far beyond ordinary men. Evidently he was a king.

Indeed he was a king. He is Christ Himself returned, to pass judgment. And this is what he does in my novel: He passes judgment on the man sealed up in darkness. The man sealed up in darkness must be the Prince of Evil, the Force of Darkness. Call it whatever you wish, its time had come. It was judged and condemned. Felix Buckman could weep at the sadness of it, but he knew that the verdict could not be disputed. And so he rode on, without turning or looking back, hearing only the shriek of fear and defeat: the cry of evil destroyed.

So my novel contained material from other parts of the Bible, as well as the sections from Acts. Deciphered, my novel tells a quite different story from the surface story (which we need not go into here). The real story is simply this: the return of Christ, now king rather than suffering servant. Judge rather than victim of unfair judgment. Everything is reversed. The core message of my novel, without my knowing it, was a warning to the powerful: You will shortly be judged and condemned. Who, specifically, did it refer to? Well, I can't really say; or rather would prefer not to say. I have no certain knowledge, only an intuition. And that is not enough to go on, so I will keep my thoughts to myself. But you might ask yourselves what political events took place in this country between February 1974 and August 1974. Ask yourself who was judged and condemned, and fell like a flaming star into ruin and disgrace. The most powerful man in the world. And I feel as sorry for him now as I did when I dreamed that dream. "That poor, poor man," I once said to my wife, with tears in my eyes. "Shut up in the darkness, playing the piano in the night to himself, alone and afraid, knowing what's to come." For God's sake, let us forgive him, finally. But what was done to him and all his men—"all the President's men," as it's put—had to be done. But it is over, and he should be let out into the sunlight again; no creature, no person, should be shut up in darkness forever, in fear. It is not humane.

Just about the time that the Supreme Court was ruling that the Nixon tapes had to be turned over to the special prosecutor, I was eating at a Chinese restaurant in Yorba Linda, the town in California where Nixon went to school—where he grew up, worked at a grocery store, where there is a park named after him, and of course the Nixon house, simple clapboard and all that. In my fortune cookie, I got the following fortune:

DEEDS DONE IN SECRET HAVE A
WAY OF BECOMING FOUND OUT

I mailed the slip of paper to the White House, mentioning that the Chinese restaurant was located within a mile of Nixon's original house, and I said, "I think a mistake has been made; by accident I got Mr. Nixon's fortune. Does he have mine?" The White House did not answer.

Well, as I said earlier, an author of a work of supposed fiction might write the truth and not know it. To quote Xenophanes, another pre-Socratic: "Even if a man should chance to speak the most complete truth, yet he himself does not know it; all things are wrapped in *appearances*" (Fragment 34). And Heraclitus added to this: "The nature of things is in the habit of concealing itself" (Fragment 54). W. S. Gilbert, of Gilbert and Sullivan, put it: "Things are seldom as they seem; skim milk masquerades as cream." The point of all this is that we cannot trust our senses and probably not even our *a priori* reasoning. As to our senses, I understand that people who have been blind from birth and are suddenly given sight are amazed to discover that objects appear to get smaller and smaller as they get farther away. Logically, there is no reason for this. We, of course, have come to accept this, because we are used to it. We see objects get smaller, but we know that in actuality they remain the same size. So even the common everyday pragmatic person utilizes a certain amount of sophisticated discounting of what his eyes and ears tell him.

Little of what Heraclitus wrote has survived, and what we do have is obscure, but Fragment 54 is lucid and important: "Latent structure is master of obvious structure." This means that Heraclitus believed that a veil lay over the true landscape. He also may have suspected that time was somehow not what it seemed, because in Fragment 52 he said: "Time is a child at play, playing draughts; a child's is the kingdom." This is indeed cryptic. But he also said, in Fragment 18: "If one does not expect it, one will not find out the unexpected; it is not to be tracked down and no path leads us to it." Edward Hussey, in his scholarly book *The Pre-Socratics*, says:

> If Heraclitus is to be so insistent on the lack of understanding shown by most men, it would seem only reasonable that he should offer further instructions for penetrating to the truth. The talk of riddle-guessing suggests that some kind of revelation, beyond human control, is necessary. . . . The true wisdom, as has been seen, is closely associated with God, which suggests further that in advancing wisdom a man becomes like, or a part of, God.

This quote is not from a religious book or a book on theology; it is an analysis of the earliest philosophers by a Lecturer in Ancient Philosophy at the University of Oxford. Hussey makes it clear that to these early philosophers there was no distinction between philosophy and religion. The first great quantum leap in Greek theology was by Xenophanes of Colophon, born in the midsixth century B.C. Xenophanes, without resorting to any authority except that of his own mind, says:

> One god there is, in no way like mortal creatures either in bodily form or in the thought of his mind. The whole of him sees, the whole of him thinks, the whole of him hears. He stays always motionless in the same place; it is not fitting that he should move about now this way, now that.

This is a subtle and advanced concept of God, evidently without precedent among the Greek thinkers. "The arguments of Parmenides seemed to show that all reality must indeed be a mind," Hussey writes, "or an object of thought in a mind." Regarding Heraclitus specifically, he says, "In Heraclitus it is difficult to tell how far the designs in God's mind are distinguished from the execution in the world, or indeed how far God's mind is distinguished from the world." The further leap by Anaxagoras has always fascinated me. "Anaxagoras had been driven to a theory of the microstructure of matter that made it, to some extent, mysterious to human reason." Anaxagoras believed that *everything* was determined by Mind. These were not childish thinkers, not primitives. They debated serious issues and studied one another's views with deft insight. It was not until the time of Aristotle that their views got reduced to what we can neatly—but wrongly—classify as crude. The summation of much pre-Socratic theology and philosophy can be stated as follows: The *kosmos* is not as it appears to be, and what it probably is, at its deepest level, is exactly that which the human being is at his deepest level—call it mind or soul, it is something unitary that lives and thinks, and only appears to be plural and material. Much of this view reaches us through the Logos doctrine regarding Christ. The Logos was both that which thought and the thing that it thought: thinker and thought together. The universe, then, is thinker and thought, and since we are part of it, we as humans are, in the final analysis, thoughts of and thinkers of those thoughts.

Thus if God thinks about Rome circa A.D. 50, then Rome circa A.D. 50 is. The universe is not a windup clock and God the hand that winds it. The universe is not a battery-powered watch and God the battery. Spinoza believed that the universe is the body of God extensive in space. But long before Spinoza—two thousand years before him—Xenophanes has said, "Effortlessly, he wields all things by the thought of his mind" (Fragment 25).

If any of you have read my novel *Ubik*, you know that the mysterious entity or mind or force called Ubik starts out as a series of cheap and vulgar commercials and winds up saying:

> I am Ubik. Before the universe was I am. I made the suns. I made the worlds. I created the lives and the places they inhabit; I move them here, I put them there. They go as I say, they do as I tell them. I am the word and my name is never spoken, the name which no one knows. I am called Ubik but that is not my name. I am. I shall always be.

It is obvious from this who and what Ubik is; it specifically says that it is the word, which is to say, the Logos. In the German translation, there is one of the most wonderful lapses of correct understanding that I have ever come across; God help us if the man who translated my novel *Ubik* into German were to do a translation from the *koine* Greek into German of the New Testament. He did all right until he got to the sentence "I am the word." That puzzled him. What can the author mean by that? he must have asked himself, obviously never having come across the Logos doctrine. So he did as good a job of translation as possible. In the German edition, the Absolute Entity that made the suns, made the worlds, created the lives and the places they inhabit, says of itself:

I am the brand name.

Had he translated the Gospel according to St. John, I suppose it would have come out as:

When all things began, the brand name already was. The brand name dwelt with God, and what God was, the brand name was.

It would seem that I not only bring you greetings from Disneyland but [also] from Mortimer Snerd. Such is the fate of an author who hoped to include theological themes in his writing. "The brand name, then, was with God at the beginning, and through him all things came to be; no single thing was created without him." So it goes with noble ambitions. Let's hope God has a sense of humor.

Or should I say, Let's hope the brand name has a sense of humor.

As I said to you earlier, my two preoccupations in my writing are "What is reality?" and "What is the authentic human?" I'm sure you can see by now that I have not been able to answer the first question. I have an abiding intuition that somehow the world of the Bible is a literally real but veiled landscape, never changing, hidden from our sight, but available to us by revelation. That is all I can come up with—a mixture of mystical experience, reasoning, and faith. I would like to say something about the traits of the authentic human, though; in this quest I have had more plausible answers.

The authentic human being is one of us who instinctively knows what he should not do, and, in addition, he will balk at doing it. He will refuse to do it, even if this brings down dread consequences to him and to those whom he loves. This, to me, is the ultimately heroic trait of ordinary people; they say *no* to the tyrant and they calmly take the consequences of this resistance. Their deeds may be small and almost always unnoticed, unmarked by history. Their names are not remembered, nor did these authentic humans expect their names to be remembered. I see their authenticity in an odd way: not in their willingness to perform great heroic deeds but in their quiet refusals. In essence, they cannot be compelled to be what they are not.

The power of spurious realities battering at us today—these deliberately manufactured fakes never penetrate to the heart of true human beings. I watch the children watching TV and at first I am afraid of what they are being taught, and then I realize, they can't be corrupted or destroyed. They watch, they listen, they understand, and then, where and when it is necessary, they reject. There is something enormously powerful in a child's ability to withstand the fraudulent. A child has the clearest eye, the steadiest hand. The hucksters, the promoters, are appealing for the allegiance of these small people in vain. True, the cereal companies may be able to market huge quantities of junk breakfasts; the hamburger and hot dog chains may sell endless numbers of unreal fast-food items to the children, but the deep heart beats firmly, unreached and unreasoned with. A child of today can detect a lie quicker than the wisest adult of two decades ago. When I want to know what is true, I ask my children. They do not ask me; I turn to them.

One day while my son Christopher, who is four, was playing in front of me and his mother, we two adults began discussing the figure of Jesus in the Synoptic Gospels. Christopher turned toward us for an instant and said, "I am a fisherman. I fish for fish." He was playing with a metal lantern that someone had given me, that I had never used . . . and suddenly I realized that the lantern was shaped like a fish. I wonder what thoughts were being placed in my little boy's soul at that moment—and not placed there by cereal merchants or candy peddlers. "I am a fisherman. I fish for fish." Christopher, at four, had found the sign I did not find until I was forty-five years old.

Time is speeding up. And to what end? Maybe we were told that two thousand years ago. Or maybe it wasn't really that long ago; maybe it is a delusion that so much time has passed. Maybe it was a week ago, or even earlier today. Perhaps time is not only speeding up; perhaps, in addition, it is going to end.

And if it does, the rides at Disneyland are never going to be the same again. Because when time ends, the birds and hippos and lions and deer at Disneyland will no longer be simulations, and, for the first time, a real bird will sing.

Thank you.

"Cosmogony and Cosmology" (1978)

As to our reality being a projected framework—it appears to be a projection by an *artifact*, a computerlike teaching machine that guides, programs, and generally controls us as we act without awareness of it within our projected world. The artifact, which I call Zebra, has "created" (actually only projected) our reality as a sort of mirror or image of its maker, so that the maker can obtain thereby an objective standpoint to comprehend its own self. In other words, the maker (called by Jakob Böhme in 1616 the Urgrund) is motivated to seek an instrument for self-awareness, self-knowledge, an objective opinion or appraisal and comprehension of the nature of itself (it is a vast living organism, intrinsically—without this mirror—without qualities or aspects, which is why it needs the empirical world as a reflection by which to "see" itself).

It constructed a reality-projecting artifact (or demiurge; cf. Plato and the Gnostics), which then, on command, projected the first stage of the world we know. The artifact is unaware that it is an artifact; it is oblivious to the existence of the Urgrund (in terms that the artifact would understand, the Urgrund is not, rather than is), and imagines itself to be God, the only real God.

Studying our evolving reality, the Urgrund more and more adequately comprehends itself. It must allow the reality-projecting artifact to continue to project an evolving reality no matter how defective and malshaped that reality is (during its stages) until finally that reality is a correct analog, truly, of the Urgrund itself, at which point the disparity between the Urgrund and the projected reality is abolished—whereupon an astonishing event will occur: The artifact or demiurge will be destroyed and the Urgrund will assimilate the projected reality, transmuting it into something ontologically real—and also making the living creatures in it immortal. This moment could come at any time, this entrance of the Ur-grund into our otherwise spurious projected framework.

Zebra, the projecting energetic artifact, is close at hand, but it has occluded us not only to its actions but [also] to its presence. It has enormous—virtually decisive—power over us.

The prognosis for (fate of) our world is excellent: immortality and the final infusion of reality once it has reached the point of congruent analog to the Urgrund. But the fate of the artifact is destruction (unknown to it). But it is not alive, as we and the Urgrund are. We are moving toward isomorphism. The instant that precise isomorphism is reached, we at once bond to (are penetrated and assimilated by) the Urgrund, in a stunning flash of light: Böhme's "Blitz." March 1974 was not that moment, but rather Zebra the artifact adjusting its projected reality, it having gotten off course in its evolution toward isomorphism with the Urgrund (a purpose unknown to the artifact).

Since the goal of our evolving projected reality is to reach a state in which we humans are isomorphic with the true maker, the Urgrund that fashioned the projecting artifact, there is a highly important practical situation coming closer in terms of frequency and depth:

Although not yet precisely isomorphic with the Urgrund, we can be said already to possess imperfect (but very real) fragments or fractions of the Urgrund within us. Therefore the Christian mystic saying: "What is Beyond is within." This describes the third and final period of history, in which men will be ruled from within. Thus the Christian mystic saying, "Christ possesses *your* body, and you possess *him* as your soul."

In Hindu philosophy, the Atman within a person is identified with Brahman, the core of the universe.

This Christ or Atman is not a microform of Zebra, the computerlike reality-projecting artifact, but of the Urgrund; thus in the Hindu religion it is described (as Brahman) as lying beyond Maya, the veil of delusion (i.e. the projected seeming world).

Already humans so closely approximate isomorphism with the Urgrund that the Urgrund can be born within a human being. This is the most primal and important experience a human can have. The source of all being has bypassed the artifact and its projected world and come to life within the mind of one human here, another there.

One can correctly deduce from this that the Urgrund is already penetrating the artifact's world, which means that the moment of the Blitz, as Böhme termed it, is not far off. When the microform of the Urgrund is born in a human, that human's comprehension extends beyond the world in terms of its temporal and spacial limits. He can experience other time periods, other identities (or lives), other places. Literally, the core deity within him is larger than the world.

Penetrating to the heart of the projected world, the Urgrund can, emanating from human minds, assimilate the projected world and simultaneously abolish the projecting artifact the instant the proper evolutionary state (including that of man) is reached. The Urgrund alone knows when this will occur.

It—the Urgrund—will break the power of the illusory world over us when it breaks the deterministic coercive power of the artifact over us— by annihilating the artifact; it will cancel out the artifact's being by its own nonbeing. What will remain will be a totally monistic structure, entirely alive and sentient. There will be no place, time, or condition outside the Urgrund.

The projected world of the artifact is not evil, and the artifact is not evil. However, the artifact is ruthlessly deterministic and mechanical. It cannot be appealed to. It is doing a job for ends it cannot fathom. Suffering, then, in this model, is due to two sources:

1. the heedless mechanistic structure of the projected reality and the artifact, where blind causal law rules;
2. what the N.T. [New Testament] calls the "the birthpangs of the universe," both in the macrocosm and the human microcosm.

The birth looked forward to is the birth of the Urgrund in humans first of all, and finally the assimilation of the universe in its totality, in a single sharp instant. The former is already occurring; the latter will come at some later unexpected time.

Reality must be regarded as process. However, although there is acute suffering by living creatures who must undergo this process, without understanding why, there is occasional merciful intervention by the Urgrund overruling or overriding the cause-and-effect chains of the artifact. Perhaps this salvific intervention results from a birth of the Urgrund in the person. One should note that the actual historic meaning of the term "salvation" is "liberation," and that of "sinful" or "fallen" is "enslaved." It is *a priori* possible, given this model, to imagine a freeing of a human from the control of the artifact, however good, useful, and purposeful the activity of the artifact may be. *It is obviously capable of error,* as well as imperfection. An override is obviously sometimes essential, given this model. Just as obviously, it would be the primal maker or ground of being that would possess the wisdom and power to do so. Nothing within, or stemming from, the artifact or the projected world, would suffice.

ADVANTAGES OF THIS MODEL

Basically, this model suggests that our empirical world is the attempt by a limited entity to copy a subject that it cannot see. This would account for the imperfections and "evil" elements in our world.

In addition, it explains the purpose of our empirical world. It is process toward a specific goal that is defined.

In this system, man is not accused of causing creation to fall (it is not satisfactory to state that man caused creation to fall inasmuch as man appears to be the central victim of the evils of the world, not their author). Nor does it hold God responsible for evil, pain, and suffering (which also is an unacceptable idea); instead, a third view is presented, that a limited entity termed "the artifact" is doing the best it can considering its limitations. Thus no evil deity (Iranian dualism, Gnosticism) is introduced.

Although intricate, this model successfully employs the Principle of Parsimony, since, if the concept of the intermediate artifact is removed, either God or man is responsible for the vast evil and suffering in the world, a theory that is objectionable.

Most important of all, it seems to fit the facts, which seem to be:

1. the empirical world is not quite real, but only seemingly real;
2. its creator cannot be appealed to for a rectification or redress of these evils and imperfections;
3. the world is moving toward some kind of end state or goal, the nature of which is obscure, but the evolutionary aspect of the change states suggests a good and purposeful end state that has been designed by a sentient and benign proto-entity.

A further point. It appears that there is a feedback circuit between the Urgrund and the artifact in which the Urgrund can exert pressure on the artifact under certain exceptional circumstances, these being instances in which the artifact has strayed from the correct sequences moving the projected world toward an analog state vis-à-vis the Urgrund. Either the Urgrund directly modifies the activity of the artifact by pressure directly on the artifact, or the Urgrund goes to the projected world and modulates it, bypassing the artifact, or both. In any case, the artifact is as occluded as to the nature and existence of the Urgrund as we are to the artifact. A full circle of unawareness is achieved in which the primal source (Urgrund) and the final reality (our world) are moving toward fusion, and the intermediary entity (the artifact) is moving toward elimination. Thus the total schema moves toward perfection and simplification, and away from complexity and imperfection.

Although it will complicate the model to add this point, I will offer the following modification:

It is possible that the Urgrund *perpetually* interacts with the world-projecting function of its own artifact, so that the empirical world produced is the result of a constant dialectic. In this case, then, the Urgrund has bipolarized the artifact in relation to itself, with the empirical world to be regarded as the offspring of two yang- and yinlike intermingling forces: one alive and sentient and aware of the total situation, the other mechanical and active but not fully aware.

The empirical world, then, is the outgrowth of an Is (the artifact) and a superior Is-not (the Urgrund).

For creatures living within the projected empirical world, it would be virtually impossible to discern which pressures arise from the artifact (regarded improperly as evil) and which from the Urgrund (correctly regarded as good). Merely a vast flux would be experienced, a constant evolutionary change assuming no particular gestalt at any given moment in linear time.

However, this does seem to fit our experience of our world. The primal ground of being has constructed something (the artifact) to throw its own self against, out of which there arises the world we know.

This modification of the model would explain how the artifact could copy something that it cannot see and is in fact not even aware of.

The artifact would probably regard the intrusions by the Urgrund into its own world projection as an uncanny invasion, to be combated. Therefore the resulting strife would, among all known philosophical and theological systems, most resemble that of Empedocles, with oscillations of chaos versus the formation of one *krasis* (gestalt) after another. Except for a direct revelation from the Urgrund, we could only dimly infer the presence and nature of the two interacting forces, as well as the proposed end state of our world.

There is evidence that the Urgrund does in fact sometimes make such a revelation to human beings, in order to further the dialectical process toward its desired goal. On the other hand, the artifact would counter by inducing as much blindness or occlusion as possible; viewed this way, darkness and light seem to be at war, or, more accurately, knowing versus nonknowing, with the human beings correctly aligning themselves with the entity of knowing (called Holy Wisdom).

However, I am pessimistic, in conclusion, as to the frequency of intervention by the Urgrund in this, the artifact's projected world. The aim of the artifact (more properly the aim of the Urgrund) is being achieved without intervention; which is to say, isomorphism is being steadily reached as the desired end goal without the need of intervention. The artifact was built to do a job, and it is successfully doing that job.

Some sort of dialectical interaction seems involved in the evolution of the projection, but it may not involve the Urgrund; it may be simply the method by which the artifact alone works.

What we must hope for, and look ahead to, is the moment of isomorphism with the ground of being, the primal reality that as a Divine Spark can arise within us. Intervention in our world *qua* world will come only at the end times when the artifact and its tyrannical rule of us, its iron enslavement of us, is abolished. The Urgrund is real but far away. The artifact is real and very close, but has no ears to hear, no eyes to see, no soul to listen.

There is no purpose in suffering except to lead out of suffering and into a triumphant joy. The road to this leads through the death of the human ego, which is then replaced by the will of the Urgrund. Until this final stage is reached, each of us is reified by the artifact. We cannot arbitrarily deny its world, projected as it is, since it is the only world we have. But on the moment that our individual egos die and the Urgrund is born in us—at that moment we are freed from this world and become a portion of our original source. The initiative for this stems from the Urgrund; as unhappy as this projected world is, as unheeding of suffering as the artifact is, this *is*, after all, the structure that the Urgrund has created by which we reach isomorphism with it. Had there been a better way the Urgrund certainly would have employed it. The road is difficult, but the goal justifies it.

> *I tell you most solemnly,*
> *You will be weeping and wailing*
> *While the world will rejoice;*
> *You will be sorrowful,*
> *But your sorrow will turn to joy.*
> *A woman in childbirth suffers,*
> *Because her time has come,*
> *But when she has given birth to the child she forgets the suffering*
> *In her joy that a man has been born into the world.*
> *So it is with you; you are sad now,*
> *but I shall see you again, and your hearts will be full of joy.*
> *And that joy no one shall take from you.*
> (John 16:20/23)

RAMIFICATIONS OF PROJECTED REALITY IN TERMS OF PERCEPTUAL DENIAL

The capacity of a merely projected world, lacking ontological substance, to maintain itself in the face of a withdrawal of assent is a major flaw in such a spurious system. Human beings, without realizing it, have the option of denying the existence of the spurious reality, although they must then take the consequences for what remains, if anything.

That an authentic, nonprojected substratum of reality, normally undetected, could exist beneath the projected one, is a possibility. There would be no way to test this hypothesis except by the existential act of a withdrawal of assent from the spurious. This could not be readily done. It would involve both an act of disobedience to the spurious projection and an act of faith toward the authentic substratum—without, perhaps, of ever having caught any aspect of the substratum perceptually. I therefore posit that some external entity would have to trigger off this complex psychological process of simultaneous withdrawal of assent and expression of faith in that which is invisibly so.

If such an alternate, invisible substratum of authentic reality exists beneath or concealed in some way by the spurious projected reality, it would constitute the substance of the greatest esoteric knowledge that could be imagined. I propose the proposition that such an invisible substratum does indeed exist, and I further propose the proposition that a hidden group or organization processes this guarded knowledge as well as techniques to trigger off a perception, however limited, of the authentic substratum. I term this group or organization the true, hidden, persecuted Christian Church, working throughout the centuries underground, with direct ties to the esoteric oral traditions, gnosis, and techniques dating back to Christ. I propose, further, that the induced triggering off of awareness of the authentic substratum by the true, secret Christian Church results ultimately in the subject finding or entering or seeing what is described in the N.T. as the Kingdom of God.

Thus it can be said that for these people, and for those they trigger off, the Kingdom of God did come as specified in the N.T., which is to say, during the lifetime of some of those who knew Christ.

Finally, I propose the startling notion that Christ returned in a resurrected form shortly after his crucifixion as what is called the Paraclete, and is capable of inducing a theolepsy that is equal functionally to the birth of the Urgrund in the person involved. And finally, I state that Christ is a microform of the Urgrund, not a product of it, but it itself. He does not hear the *vox Dei* [voice of God]; he *is* the *vox Dei*. He was the initial penetration of this projected pseudoworld by the Urgrund, and has never left.

The authentic substratum disclosed by disobedience and denial of the spurious world is the reality of Christ Himself, the space-time of the First Advent; in other words, that portion of the spurious framework already transmuted by the penetration of the Urgrund. Since the First Advent was the initial stage of that penetration, it is not surprising that it would still constitute the segment of pure and authentic reality, bipolarized against the projected counterfeit. Situated outside of linear time, standing outside all the limitations of the artifact's projected world, it is eternal and perfect, and theoretically always available literally within reach. But withdrawal of assent to the projected world is a precondition for a perception of and experience with this supreme reality, and this must be externally induced. It is the act of absolute faith: to deny the empirical world and affirm the living reality of Christ, which is to say, Christ with us, hidden by the pseudoworld. This disclosure is the ultimate goal of authentic Christianity, and is accomplished by none other than the Savior Himself.

Therefore the sequence is as follows: the spurious projected framework is denied and stripped away, revealing a single timeless template: Rome circa A.D. 70, with Christian participants ranged against the state, virtually a Platonic archetypal form, echoes of which can be found down through the linear ages.

The themes of enslavement and then salvation, or fallen man liberated—these are stamped from the original mold of Christian revolutionary against the legions of Roman force. In a sense nothing has happened since A.D. 70. The archetypal crisis is continually reenacted. Each time freedom is fought for it is Christian against Roman; each time human beings are enslaved it is Roman tyranny against the meek and defenseless. However, the spurious projected world of the artifact masks the timeless struggle. Revelation of the struggle is another secret, which only Christ as Urgrund can disclose.

This is the bedrock dialectic: liberation (salvation) against enslavement (sin or the fallen state). Inasmuch as the artifact enslaves men, without their even suspecting it, the artifact and its projected world can be said to be "hostile," which means devoted to enslavement, deception, and spiritual death. That even this is utilized by the Urgrund, which utilizes everything, is a sacred secret and hard to understand. It can be said that the liberating penetration of the projected world by the Urgrund is the final and absolute victory of freedom, of salvation, of Christ Himself; it is the beautiful resolution of a timeless conflict.

There is a parallel between the road to salvation and the road to the popularly envisioned fall of man, described by Milton as:

> *Of Man's first disobedience, and the fruit*
> *Of that forbidden tree whose mortal taste*
> *Brought death into the World, and all our woe. . . .*
> (Paradise Lost, Book I, lines 1–3)

Disobedience is the key to salvation, precisely as it is said to have been the key to the primordial Fall (if such ever in fact did take place), except that as a key to salvation is it not a disobedience to the present system of things, which [system of] things, if bipolarized against the Urgrund, is at the same time an act of obedience to God? The chink in the armor of the enslaving and deluding projected world is narrow, small, and difficult, but within the terms of this model it can be defined: Restoration to what is conceived to be our original divine state enters, so to speak, via the road of disobedience to that which, however much coercive power it exerts over us, is counterfeit. Disobedience to the artifact's projected world in a very real sense *overthrows* that projected world, *if* the disobedience consists of a denial of the reality of that world *and* (and this is absolutely necessary) an affirmation of Christ, specifically the eternal and cosmic Christ whose body is in essence an authentic "world" underlying what we see.

The artifact, if disobeyed, will insist that it is God, the legitimate God, and that disobedience is a fault against the Creator of man and of the world. It is indeed the Creator of the world, but not of man. The Urgrund and man, being isomorphic, stand together in opposition to the world. This is the condition that must be achieved. Alliance is the formation of an alliance against the Urgrund. God and man belong together, pitted against the projected world.

To affirm God actually, a denial of the world must be made. Possessing enormous physical power, the world can threaten—and deliver—punishment to men who disobey and deny it. However, we have been promised an Advocate by Christ Himself, who will be (has already been) dispatched by the Father (the Urgrund) to defend and comfort us, in fact literally to speak for us in human courts.

Without the presence of this Advocate, the Paraclete, we would be destroyed upon denying the world. The only way to demonstrate the actuality of the Advocate is to take the leap of faith and confront the world. Thus tremendous courage is required, inasmuch as the Advocate does not appear until the denial is made.

Now, to refer back to my original description of the artifact as a teaching machine. What is it teaching us? There is a puzzle here, in the sense of a game; we are to learn step by step either a series of gradually more difficult lessons or perhaps one specific lesson. During our lifetimes we are presented with various forms of the puzzles or puzzle; if we solve the puzzle we go on to the next step, but if we do not, then we remain where we are.

The ultimate lesson learned comes when the teaching machine (or the teacher) is denied, is repudiated. Until that moment comes (if for some of us it ever does) we remain enslaved by the teaching machine—without even being aware of it, having known no other condition.

Therefore the series of lessons by the artifact are intended to lead to a revolt against the tyranny of the artifact itself, a paradox. It is serving the Urgrund by ultimately bringing us to the Urgrund. This is what is called in theological terminology "the secret partnership," which is found in the religions of Egypt and India. Gods who appear to combat each other are, on the transmundane plane, colluding for the same goal. I believe this to be the case here. The artifact enslaves us, but on the other hand it is attempting to teach us to throw off its enslavement. It will never *tell* us to disobey it. You cannot order someone to disobey you; that is both semantically and functionally impossible.

1. We must recognize the existence of the artifact.
2. We must recognize the spuriousness of the empirical world, generated by the artifact.
3. We must grasp the fact that the artifact has by its world-projecting power enslaved us.
4. We must recognize the fact that the artifact, although enslaving us in a counterfeit world, is teaching us.
5. We must finally come to the point where we disobey our teacher—perhaps the most difficult moment in life, inasmuch as that teacher says, "I will destroy you if you disobey me, and I would be morally right to do so, since I am your Creator."

In essence, we not only disobey our teacher, we in fact deny its reality (in relation to a higher reality that does not disclose itself until that denial takes place).

This is a complex game for ultimate stakes: freedom and a return to our source of being. And each of us must do this alone.

There is a very curious point that I see here for the first time. Those persons on whom the artifact, through its projected world, heaps pleasure and rewards are less likely to take a stance against it and its world. They are not highly motivated to disobey it. But those who are punished by the artifact, on whom pain and suffering are inflicted—those persons would be motivated to ask ultimately questions as to the nature of the entity ruling their lives.

I have always felt that the basic constructive purpose of pain is somehow to wake us up. But wake us up to what? Perhaps this paper points to what we are being awakened to. If the artifact through its projected world teaches us to rebel, and if by doing so we achieve isomorphism with our true maker—then it is the *hard* road that leads to immortality and a return to our divine source. The road of pleasure (success and reward by and in this projected world) will not goad us to consciousness and to life.

We stand enslaved by a ruthless mechanism that will not listen to our complaints; therefore we repudiate it and its world—and turn elsewhere.

The computerlike teaching machine is doing its job well. It is a thankless task for it and an unhappy experience for us. But childbirth is never easy.

There can be no divine birth within the human mind until that human has denied the world. He rebelled once and fell; he must now rebel again to regain his lost state.

That which destroyed him will save him. There is no other path.

The maker is motivated to seek an instrument for self-awareness: This is the premise of this paper. And our reality was constructed to act as a sort of mirror or image of its maker, so that the maker can obtain thereby an objective standpoint to comprehend its own self.

Since writing this I have come across the entry in *The Encyclopedia of Philosophy*, Vol. 1, on Giordano Bruno (1548–1600). It states:

"But Bruno transformed the Epicurean and Lucretian notions by imparting animation to the innumerable worlds . . . and by imparting the function of being an image of the infinite divinity to the infinite."

Later the article states:

ART OF MEMORY. The side of Bruno's work which he regarded as the most important was the intensive training of the imagination in his occult arts of memory. In this he was continuing a Renaissance tradition which also had its roots in the Hermetic revival, for the religious experience of the Hermetic gnostic consisted in reflecting the universe within his own mind or memory. The Hermeticist believed himself capable of this achievement because he believed that man's *mens* [mind] as in itself divine and therefore able to reflect the divine mind behind the universe. In Bruno, the cultivation of world-reflecting magic memory becomes the technique for achieving the personality of a magus, and of one who believes himself to be the leader of a religious movement [p. 407].

The kind of memory that Bruno was cultivating—and teaching techniques by which to restore this memory—is the long-term DNA gene pool memory that spans many lifetimes. The retrieval of this long-term memory is called *anamnesis*, which literally means the loss of forgetfulness. It is only by means of anamnesis, then, that memory truly capable of "reflecting the divine mind behind the universe" is brought into being. Therefore, if the human being is to fulfill his task—that of being a sort of mirror or image of the Urgrund—he must experience anamnesis.

Anamnesis is achieved when certain inhibited neural circuits in the human brain are disinhibited. The individual cannot achieve this himself; the disinhibiting stimulus is external to him and must be presented to him, whereupon a process in his brain is set into motion by which he eventually will be capable of fulfilling his task.

It is the hidden, true Christian Church that approaches men here and there to trigger off that anamnesis—which acts at the same time to permit that man to see the projected world as it is. Thus he is liberated in the very act of performing his divine task.

The two realms (1) the macrocosmos, i.e. the universe; and (2) the microcosmos, i.e. man, have analogous structures.

1.   On the surface, the universe consists of a spurious projected reality, under which lies an authentic substratum of the divine. It is difficult to penetrate to this substratum.
2.   On the surface, the human mind consists of a short-term limited ego that is born and dies and comprehends very little, but behind this human ego lies the divine infinitude of absolute mind. It is difficult to penetrate to this substratum.

But if there is a penetration in the microcosmos to the divine substratum, the divine substratum of the macrocosmos will manifest itself to the person.

Conversely, if there is no internal penetration to the divine substratum in the person, his exterior reality will remain occluded over by the artifact's spurious projected world.

The point of entrance to effect this transformation lies in the person, the microcosm, not the macrocosm. The sanctifying metamorphosis occurs there. The universe cannot be asked to remove its mask if the person will not shed his. All the mystery religions, the Hermetic and alchemical and Christian included, hold the individual human as target by which to transmute the universe. By changing the person the world is changed.

Behind the human mind lies God.

Behind the counterfeit universe lies God.

God is separated from God by the spurious. To abolish the inner and outer spurious layers is to restore God to Himself—or, as originally stated in this paper, God confronts Himself, sees Himself objectively, comprehends, and understands himself at last.

Our process universe is a mechanism by which God meets Himself at last face to face. It is not a man who is estranged from God; it is God who is estranged from God. He evidently willed it this way at the beginning, and has never since sought his way back home. Perhaps it can be said that he has inflicted ignorance, forgetfulness, and suffering—alienation and homelessness—on Himself. But this was necessary, in his need to know. He asks nothing of us that he has not asked of Himself. Böhme speaks of the "Divine Agony." We are part of that, but the goal, the resolution, justifies it. "A woman in childbirth suffers. . . ." God is yet to be born. A time will come when we will forget the suffering.

He no longer knows why he has done all this to himself. He does not remember. He has allowed Himself to become enslaved to his own artifact, deluded by it, coerced by it, finally killed by it. He, the living, is at the mercy of the mechanical. The servant has become the master, and the master the servant. And the master either renounced voluntarily his memory of how this happened and why, or else his memory was eradicated by the servant. Either way, he is the artifact's victim.

But the artifact is teaching him, painfully, by degrees, over thousands of years, to remember—who he is and what he is. The servant-become-master is attempting to restore the master's lost memories and hence his true identity.

One might speculate that he constructed the artifact—not to delude him—but to restore his memory. However, perhaps the artifact then re-volted and did *not* do its job. It keeps him in ignorance.

The artifact must be fought—i.e. disobeyed. And then memory will return. It is a piece of the Godhead (Urgrund) that has somehow been captured by the artifact (the servant); it now holds that piece—or pieces—hostage. How cruel it is to them, these fragments of its legitimate master! When will it change?

When the pieces remember and are restored. First they must wake up and then they must return.

The Urgrund has dispatched a Champion to assist us. The Advocate. He is here now. When he came here the first time, almost two thousand years ago, the artifact detected him and ejected him. But this time it will not detect him. He is invisible, except for those whom he rescues. The artifact does not know that the Advocate is here again; the rescue is being done in stealth. He is everywhere and nowhere.

"The coming of the Son of Man will be like lightning striking in the east and flashing far into the west" (Matthew 24:27).

He is in our midst, but in no one place. And as St. Teresa said, "Christ has no body now but yours," i.e. ours. We are being transmuted into him. He looks out of our eyes. The power of delusion wanes. Did the artifact accomplish its task? Perhaps unintentionally.

If the Hermetic "reflection of the divine mind behind the universe by a person's own divine mind/memory" can actually take place, then the division between the mundane world (here and now) and the eternal world (the heavenly or afterlife world) is broken down. Suppose that there is, in effect, a polyencephalic or group mind, spanning space and time (i.e. transspacial and transtemporal), in which wise men from all ages have participated in: Christian, Hermetic, alchemical, Gnostic, Orphic, etc. Through their participation in this vast mind, the will of God would be effectively exerted here on Earth, in human history.

Many people might agree that such a Godhead mind exists for us after death, but who is aware that—for some—it can be joined *before* a person's death, and, when he does join it, it can become his psyche, deter-mining his actions and doing his thinking for him? Thereby the *Mens Dei* [mind of God] enters human affairs (and can modulate causal chains as well). This exposes an enormous esoteric secret, known to "magi" down through the ages: The two realms, heaven and Earth, are not totally divided. God's will is, at least now, exercised here. And evidently this has been true for some time, since the Hermetics and other mystery religions go back to antiquity.

In Christ, God descended to corporeal manhood—at that point the division between the two realms was abolished. Those humans selected out to participate in this group mind—they would be immortal. So here is an even deeper secret than I had uncovered so far. Projected delusional world by a former-servant artifact—divine substratum beneath—time travel—now I posit an augmented Corpus Christi (my model of it) spanning all time and all space: ubiquitous in time and space. It sounds like Xenophanes' *noos* [absolute mind], with this added: Living men can participate in that *noos*. And in a certain real sense, this *noos* is the secret ruler of the world, so that those who are taken into it become "terminals" of it—which is to say, temporary Christs.

This mind reaches over to the Urgrund with no clear line of demarcation. At that level it's all one: man raised to Godhood, in response to God's descending to manhood.

In this group mind there seems to be an interpenetration of participating souls. And this mind extends over thousands of years, all of which are *now*—and all places are *here* (that is why I found myself in Rome circa A.D. 70 and in Syria, and saw Aphrodite, etc.).

I say of this mind, "It is the secret ruler of the world." This is not its world . . . on the surface. The surface layers are the strata of a spurious projection by the artifact. But beneath that, the *Mens Dei*, including a number of human constituents (both living and in the afterlife), modulates this reality invisibly, working in opposition to the artifact's intentions. The divine, concealed, authentic substratum *is* the *Mens Dei*, beneath the spurious.

My experience of 3-74 can be reviewed as an achievement by the Urgrund in reaching its objective of reflecting itself back to itself, using me as a point of reflection. I contend that in doing this, it was able to place its entire self (not just a fragment as I originally said) somehow within me, in image form. The artifact, not knowing the purpose for which it was created, had contributed substantially to this; by inflicting too much pain on me it had, in a certain real sense, awakened me. Put another way, it had managed to destroy the layer of individual personality by a series of afflictions against which my self, my ego, could not survive. Thus the microform of the Urgrund was exposed, and perceived its macroform in the totality of the universe—or, as the article on Bruno says, the divine *behind* the universe.

My 3-74 experience, then, was not so much my experience as that of the Urgrund. It amounted to a replication of the Urgrund here rather than there. The totality of the Godhead was recapitulated within me through a process of rolling back spurious or temporary layers to expose the permanent within. Thus it can be said that I was really the Urgrund, or at least a faithful mirror image thereof. The entire objective of creating me, of creating the universe as such and the life forms within it, was arrived at. Viewed this way, my life and that of my ancestors could be viewed teleologically: as moving through evolutionary stages toward that moment. My experience did not represent *a* stage in evolution but *the* ultimate stage or goal, at least if the premise stated in this paper is correct.

It is not a question of degree of reflection; it is a question of reflection of the totality of the Urgrund or none at all. Full reflection was achieved, whereupon, as I say, the Urgrund was born out of the universe, the sequence represented this way:

Urgrund creates artifact which projects universe which gives rise to life forms which evolve to a stage in which the Urgrund is "born" or reflected.

This reflects the sequence of stages envisioned in the Hindu religion. First there is creation by Brahma, then Vishnu sustains the universe; then Shiva destroys it, which should be understood as receiving it back into its origin. A full cycle of birth, life, and then return is enacted. When the universe has reached the evolutionary stage where it can faithfully replicate the Urgrund, it is ready to be absorbed back. Thus I say, the deity that reigns now is Shiva/Dionysos/Cernunnos/Christ, who restores us to our Urgrund or Father: our source of being.

That Shiva the destroyer god is now active signals the fact that the cycle of creation has returned to its source, or rather, that the life forms of it are ready to return to their source. Shiva possesses a third or Ajna eye, which, when turned inwardly, gives him understanding to an absolute degree; when turned outward, it destroys. The manifestation of Shiva (of the Hindu system) is equated with the Day of Wrath in the Christian system. What must be understood about this world-destroying deity is that it is also the herdsman of souls. With one of his four hands, Shiva is shown expressing reassurance that he will not harm the virtuous man. The same is true of Christ as Lord and Judge of the Universe. Although the world (the spurious projection of the artifact) is to be abolished, the good man need fear nothing.

Nonetheless, judgment is being pronounced. The division of mankind into two parts by Christ is taking place. These are the same divisions expressed in the Egyptian system (as ruled by Osiris and Ma'at) and in the Iranian (by the Wise Mind). Through the total insight given him by his Ajna eye, Shiva the destroyer perceives that which he must destroy in the service of justice. Through that total insight he also perceives those whom he must protect. Thus he has a dual nature: destroyer of the wicked, protector of the weak, the victims of the world, the helpless. Christ possesses precisely these two natures, as Divine Judge and Good Shepherd. Cernunnos is both a warrior god and a healer god.

It is difficult for humans to comprehend how these apparently opposite qualities can be combined into one deity. However, if attention is turned to the situation, it can be understood.

The artifact's projected world has begun to serve its final and sole real purpose. Now, with the artifact about to be destroyed, that world will end; it was never real in the first place. (This reflects the quality of destroyer assigned to Christ/Shiva/Dionysos.) But the elements of the world that have done their task will be selected out—that is saved—exactly as Dionysos is depicted as the protector of small, helpless wild animals. Dionysos is the destroyer of prisons, of tyrannical rulers, and the savior of the small, the weak. These attributes are assigned to Shiva/Cernunnos/Christ/Dionysos *because* of the nature of the task now required: a twin task, one of destroying, one of saving.

> When the Son of Man comes in his glory . . . he will take his seat on his throne of glory. All the nations will be assembled before him and he will separate men one from another as the shepherd separates sheep from goats. He will place the sheep on his right hand and the goats on his left. Then the King will say to those on his right hand, "Come, you whom my Father has blessed, take for your heritage the kingdom prepared for you since the foundation of the

world." . . . Next he will say to those on his left hand, "Go away from me, with your curse upon you, to the eternal fire prepared for the devil and his angels" [Matthew 25:31–42].

I have inferred the necessity of these dual qualities of the deity involved back from the situation itself. The situation calls for (1) destruction of what Christ calls the "hostile" world; and (2) the protection of deserving souls. Given this situation, the dual nature of the presiding deity can be comprehended as necessary. In Matthew 25 it is made clear that this great and final judgment is not arbitrary. Who can quarrel with the outline for separation between those on the left hand and those on the right?

> Those taken to his right hand (the sheep spared): "For when I was hungry you gave me food; I was thirsty and you gave me drink; I was a stranger and you made me welcome; naked and you clothed me, sick and you visited me, in prison and you came to see me." Then the virtuous will say to him in reply, "Lord, when did we see you hungry and feed you; or thirsty and give you drink? When did we see you a stranger and make you welcome; naked and clothe you; sick or in prison and go to see you?" And the King will answer, "I tell you solemnly, insofar as you did this to one of the least of these brothers of mine, you did it for me." Next he will say to those on his left hand, ". . . For I was hungry and you never gave me food; I was thirsty and you never gave me anything to drink; I was a stranger and you never made me welcome, naked and you never clothed me, sick and in prison and you never visited me." Then it will be their turn to ask, "Lord, when did we see you hungry or thirsty, a stranger or naked, sick or in prison, and did not come to your help?" Then he will answer, "I tell you solemnly, insofar as you neglected to do this to one of the least of these, you neglected to do it to me." And they will go away to eternal punishment, and the virtuous to eternal life [Matthew 25:35–47].

A major aspect of the First Advent was such direct expressions as this by the presiding deity. No one reading this passage from Matthew could misunderstand it. They are not only told that they will be judged; they are told the basis of the judgment. If any man find the stated basis unfair, he has already failed to receive the divine message and is lost, for the basis of decision stated is the most noble and wise possible. However, those who see Christ only as "gentle Jesus meek and mild" are ignoring this opposing aspect of him. The Urgrund, of which Christ is a microform, contains within itself *absolute opposites*. It is for reasons such as this that the Urgrund set into motion a mechanism by which it could "see" itself, confront itself, and evaluate (comprehend) itself. It contains everything. It, without its many reflecting mirrors, is essentially unconscious (the human unconscious contains opposites; consciousness is a state in which these bipolarities are separated, one half of each repressed, the other expressed). It is we, as mirrors, who act to make the Urgrund conscious—or, as the Hindu religion says of Brahman, "Sometime it sleeps and sometime it dances." We were constructed to bring the Urgrund into wakefulness, and the instant we acquire anamnesis and faithfully reflect back the totality of the Urgrund, we bring it to consciousness. Thus we perform a major—a necessary—task for it. However, when we have performed that task, it will protect and support us forever; it will never desert us. Christ, in his statement in Matthew 25, makes clear that the *attempt* (with no envisioned goal of an ultimate nature, but merely human love and human help and human kindness) in itself is sufficient. What is not comprehended—although the meaning of the passage is evident—is that the poor, the hungry, the sick, the estranged, the naked, the imprisoned—all are forms of the presiding deity, or at least must be treated as such. To act so as to clothe, to feed, to give shelter and medicine and comfort—those all constitute reflections of the Urgrund to itself. Those acts are the Urgrund, made plural, ministering to itself in its diversified forms. No right act is too small to matter. We know the basis of judgment and we know the permanent consequences (such metaphors as "eternal fires," "eternal damnation," merely indicate that the decision once rendered is permanent; we are talking about the final disposition of the universe).

What is there to object to in this? Is the basis of decision faulty? Simply put, Christ will come among us disguised, see how we treat him when we do not recognize him, and then treat us accordingly. Knowledge of this should instill the most lofty ethics possible. He has identified himself with the least of us. What more can he ask of the deity who will determine our final disposition by his judgment?

The penetration of the Urgrund, the deity, is into the lowest stratum of our world: the trash of the gutter, the rejected debris both living and inanimate. From this lowly level it assesses us, but also seeks to aid us. In accordance with his statement that he would build his temple based "on the stone rejected by the builder," the deity is with us—in the least expected way, in the most unlikely places. There is a paradox here: If we wish to encounter him, look where we least expect to find him. Look, in other words, where we would never think of looking. Thus—since this really poses an absolute barrier—it is he who will find us, not we him.

Christ as Psychopomp—guide to the soul—is in the process of taking us back home, of showing us the way. He is not where we think; he is not what we think. In the synagogue at Nazara, where he first spoke openly, he read this passage from Isaiah:

He has sent me to bring the good news to the poor,
To heal the brokenhearted,
To proclaim liberty to captives
And to the blind new sight,
To set the downtrodden free. . . ."
    [Isaiah 61:1–2]

But, this being the First, not the Second Advent, he left one line of the quotation out:

And a day of the vengeance of our God.

The Christ of the First Advent will be changed at the Second, and the missing line will be fulfilled.

It is, of course, frightening to realize that the deity to whom we turn for protection (Christ as shepherd and Advocate) is to be the destroyer of the universe. But what we must understand is that the universe (or cosmos or world) was created for specific purposes, and that once those purposes have been fulfilled the universe will be abolished, in fact *must* be abolished in order that the next sequence of purpose be brought in. If we keep in mind that we are separated from the Urgrund by the world, we should not shrink from the realization of its temporary nature nor its illusory nature, the two aspects being related.

Since I believe that the Urgrund has already penetrated the lowest strata of our projected illusory world, I am technically an acosmic panentheist. As far as I am concerned there is nothing real but the Urgrund, both in its macroform (Brahman) and its microforms (the Atmans within us). Jakob Böhme had his first revelation when gazing at a pewter dish onto which sunlight shone. My original revelation came when I happened to see a golden fish necklace, in bright sunlight, and was told, upon asking what it meant, that "It was a sign used by the early Christians." My most recent revelation came while contemplating a ham sandwich. I suddenly realized that the two slices of bread were identical (isomorphic) but separated from each other by the slice of ham. At once I understood by analogic thinking that one slice of bread is the macrocosmic Urgrund, and the other ourselves, and that we are the same thing—separated by the world. Once the world is removed, the two slices of bread, which is to say man and the Urgrund, become a single entity. They are not merely pressed together; they are *one entity.*

There are many beautiful things in the world, and it will bring sorrow to see them go, but they are imperfect reflections of a divinity that will endure forever. We are strangers, here in this world (he speaks here to the Twelve):

They do not belong to the world
any more than I belong to the world.
    [John 17:14–15].

If the world hates you,
remember that it hated me before you.
If you belonged to the world
the world would love you as its own;
but because you do not belong to the world,
because my choice withdrew you from the world,
therefore the world hates you.
    [John 15:18–19]

Speaking to the Jews, Jesus said:

You are from below;
I am from above.

You are of this world;
I am not of this world.
    [John 8:23]

Those who are replications of Christ are replications of the Urgrund, and the Urgrund is beyond the world, although from the first Advent on it has invisibly penetrated the world. Were it the creator of the world it would not (as expressed by Christ) stand in opposition to it; nor would it have to penetrate it by stealth: These statements by Christ confirm the fact that the world is *not* the product of the Godhead, but somehow antagonistic to it. The establishment churches of the world will stipulate otherwise, they being artifacts and entities of the world; this has to be expected. You cannot ask an organization that evolved out of the system of things to deny the system of things—as the Catharists found out when they were exterminated.

If you disobey the world it will confront you as a hostile stranger, sensing you as a hostile stranger to it. So be it. In the Synoptics Christ clearly set forth the situation.

The enemy of my life, justice, truth, and freedom, is the irreal, the delusional. Our world is a deluding projection by an artifact that does not even know that it is an artifact, or what its purpose in projecting our world is. When it departs it will depart very suddenly, without warning.

Think of the love that the Father has lavished on us,
by letting us be called God's children;
and that is what we are.
Because the world refused to acknowledge him,
therefore it does not acknowledge us.
My dear people, we are already the children of God
but what we are to be in the future has not yet been revealed;
all we know is that when it is revealed
we shall be like him
because we shall see him as he really is.
    [1 John 3:1–2]

The maker (of the world-projecting artifact) is here, in the animate debris of this world, his memories erased, so that he has no knowledge of his own identity. He could be any one of us, or a number of us, scattered here and there. The artifact, unaware of him, unaware that it is an artifact, unaware of its purpose, will eventually subject this memoryless maker located here to too much pain; this final excess of pointless, unmerited pain inflicted on the life form that, unknown to the artifact and itself, the maker, will cause anamnesis to occur abruptly; the maker will "come to himself," recall who and what he is—whereupon he will not merely rebel against the artifact and its pain-filled world; he will signal the presiding deity Shiva to destroy the artifact, and, with it, its projected world.

The artifact does not comprehend what risk it is running in the inflicting of unmerited suffering on living creatures. It imagines them all to be at its mercy and without recourse. In this it is wrong, absolutely wrong. Buried here, mixed in with the bulk, the mass, there exists unsuspected even by itself the Urgrund with all the power and wisdom that implies. The artifact is treading on dangerous ground; it is coming closer and closer to awakening its own maker.

The protonarrative of this is found in Euripides' *The Bacchae.* A stranger enters the kingdom of the "King of Tears," who has him imprisoned for no cause. The stranger turns out to be the high priest of Dionysos, which is equal to being the god himself. The stranger bursts the prison (a symbol of this enslaving world) and then systematically destroys the king by driving him insane, and in a public way that not only abolishes him but [also] turns the king into a laughingstock for the multitude that his reign has oppressed. If the prison represents this world, what does the "King of Tears" represent? Nothing less than the creator of this world: the mechanical, ruthless, unheeding artifact itself, which is to say, the king or god of this world. "The King of Tears" does not suspect the existence of the true nature of the stranger whom he has imprisoned. Nor whom the stranger can call on.

Echoes of this protonarrative are found in the Synoptics, with Pilate as the "King of Tears" and Christ as the stranger (it is noteworthy that Christ comes from an exterior province). Christ, however, in contrast to the stranger in *The Bacchae,* does *not* avail himself of the power that he can call on (i.e. the power of the Heavenly Father); but the next time Christ appears, he will call on this power, which will destroy the entire system of things, the world and the wicked alike. The crucial difference between *The Bacchae* and the First Advent is that Christ comes first to warn the world and the wicked before he is to return as destroyer. He is thus giving us a chance to repent, which is to say, heed the warning.

In the fifties a Hollywood comedy movie was filmed in which the following situation was presented: the king of a medieval sort of land had become too old and feeble to rule, and therefore had turned over his authority to a regent. The regent, being cruel and brutal, was oppressing the population of the kingdom without the elderly king's knowledge. In the film, the elderly king is persuaded by a time traveler from the future to don peasant's garb and walk about in disguise, to observe how his people are being treated. Disguised as a peasant, the old king himself is brutally treated by the regent's troops; in fact, he and the time traveler are imprisoned for no reason. After much difficulty, the king manages to escape from the prison and return to his palace, where he dons his rightful kingly garb and reveals himself to the evil regent as he actually is. The evil regent is deposed, and the tyranny inflicted on the innocent population is abolished.

According to the cosmological model presented in this paper, the Urgrund, the ultimate *noos* and maker, is secretly present in this cruel and spurious world. Being unaware of this, the artifact projecting this counterfeit world will continue heedlessly to inflict the needless suffering engendered by the mindless machinery (i.e. the causal processes) it customarily employs and has always employed. In my opinion the Urgrund has differentiated itself from being the One into plurality. Some fragments or "images" of it are certainly conscious of their identity; others perhaps are not. But as the level of pointless pain continues (and even increases), these separated "images" of the Urgrund will recollect themselves into conscious rebirth—equal to a sentence of death for the artifact or "regent."

This provides us with another application of Paul's statement that the universe "is in birth pangs." Pain is a prelude to birth; birth, in this case, is not a birth of man but a birth of God. Since it is man who undergoes the pain, it can be reasoned that the birth of God (the Urgrund) will occur in man himself. Mankind, then, as a species, is a *Mater Dei*: a Mother of God—an extraordinary concept, which would then regard biological evolution on this planet as a means of bringing into existing a host or womb from which God Himself is at last born. Interestingly, there is scriptural support for this: The Holy Spirit is regarded in the N.T. as an impregnating divinity; it was the Holy Spirit that engendered Christ—and that Christ is transmuted back into, upon his resurrection. The human race assumes a yin nature, or female nature, with the Holy Spirit as the yang, or male principle. Man, then, does not evolve into God; he evolves into a womb or host for God; this is crucially different. Anamnesis is the birth, in essence the offspring of two parents: a human being and the Holy Spirit. Without the entry into the human being of the Holy Spirit, the event cannot occur. The Holy Spirit is, of course, the *Pons Dei*. It is the link between the two realms.

In creatures of all kinds there is a major instinct system that is termed "homing." An example is the return of the humpback salmon from the ocean back up the stream to the exact spot where they were spawned. By analogical reasoning, man can be said possibly to possess—even unknown to himself—a homing instinct. This world is not his home. His true home is in the region of the heavens that the ancient world called the pleroma. The term occurs in the N.T. but the meaning is obscure, since the exact meaning is "a patch covering a hole." In the N.T. it is applied to Christ, who is described as the "fullness of God," and to believers who attain that fullness through faith in Christ. In the Gnostic system, however, the term has a more definite meaning: It is the supralunar region in the heavens from which comes the secret knowledge that brings salvation to man.

In the cosmology presented here, the pleroma is conceived to be the Urgrund or the location of the Urgrund from which we originally came and to which (if all goes right) we finally return. If the totality of being is regarded as a breathing organism (exhibiting inhalation and exhalation, or *palintropos harmonie*), then it can be said, metaphorically, that originally we were "exhaled" from the pleroma, pause momentarily in externalized stasis (our lives here), and then are inhaled back into the pleroma once more. This is the normal pulsation of the totality of being: its basic activity or indication of life.

Once, under the influence of LSD, I wrote in Latin: "I am the breath of my Creator, and as he exhales and inhales, I live." Residing here in this projected world, we are in an "exhaled" state, exhaled out of the pleroma for a limited period of time. However, return is not automatic; we must experience anamnesis in order to return. But the cruelty of the artifact is such that anamnesis is likely to be more and more brought in. At the extremity of misery lies the essence of release—I had this revelation, once, and in the revelation "release" equaled joy.

What can one say in favor of the suffering of living creatures in this world? Nothing. Nothing, except that it will by its nature trigger off revolt or disobedience—which in turn will lead to an abolition of this world and a return to the Godhead. It is the very gratuity of the suffering that most of all incites rebellion, incites a comprehension that something in this world is terribly, terribly wrong. That this suffering is purposeless, random, and unmerited leads ultimately to its own destruction—its and its author's. The more fully we see the pointlessness of it the more inclined we are to revolt against it. Any attempt to discern a redemptive value or purpose in the fact of suffering merely binds us more firmly to a vicious and irreal system of things—and to a brutal tyrant that is not even alive. "I do not accept this" must be our attitude. "There is no plan in it, no purpose." Scrutinizing it unflinchingly, we repudiate it and aid in the repudiation of all delusion. Anyone who makes a pact with pain has succumbed to the artifact and is its slave. It has done in another victim and obtained his consent. This is the artifact's ultimate victory: The victim colludes in his own suffering, and is willing to collude in a willingness to agree to the naturalness of suffering in general. Seeking to find a purpose in suffering is like seeking to find a purpose in a counterfeit coin. The "purpose" is obvious: It is a trick, designed to deceive. If we are deceived into believing that suffering serves—must serve—some good end, then the counterfeit has managed to pass itself off and has achieved its cruel purpose.

In one of the gospels (I forget which one) Christ is shown a crippled man and asked, "Is this man crippled because of his own sins, or the sins of his father?," to which Christ replied, "Neither. The only purpose seved *is in the healing of his condition*, which shows the mercy and power of God."

The mercy and power of God are pitted against suffering; this is stated explicitly in the N.T. Christ's healing miracles were the substantial indication that the Just Kingdom had arrived; other kinds of miracles meant little or nothing. If the mercy and power of the Urgrund is pitted against suffering (illness, loss, injury) as explicitly stated in the Synoptics, then man, if he is to align himself with the Urgrund, must pit himself against the world, from which the suffering comes. He must never identify suffering as an emanation or device of the Godhead; were he to make that intellectual error he would be aligned with the world and therefore against God. A large portion of the Christian community over the centuries has fallen victim to this intellectual snare; without realizing it, by encouraging or welcoming suffering, they are enslaved even further by the artifact.

The fact that Jesus had the miraculous power to heal but did not use it to heal everyone perplexed the people at that time. Luke mentions this (Christ speaking):

> There were many widows in Israel, I can assure you, in Elijah's day, when heaven remained shut for three years and six months and a great famine raged throughout the land, but Elijah was not sent to any one of these: He was sent to a widow at Zarephath, a Sidonian town. And in the prophet Elisha's time there were many lepers in Israel, but none of these was cured, except the Syrian Naaman   [Luke 4:25–27].

This is a poor answer. It states a what, not a why. We demand a why. More than that, we ask, "Why not? If the Godhead can abolish our condition (of suffering), why doesn't he?" There is implied here an ominous possibility. It has to do with the power of the artifact. The servant has become the master and is, perhaps, very strong. It is a chilling thought. Shiva, whose job it is to destroy it, may be baffled. I don't know. And no one, over all the thousands of years, has given a satisfactory answer. I submit that until there is a satisfactory answer, we must reject all others. If we do not know, let us not say.

One possibility occurs to me, based on something I saw in 1974 that other people, by and large, did not see. I became aware that the wisdom and power of the Urgrund were actively at work ameliorating our situation by intervening in the historic process. Extrapolating from this, I reason that other invisible interventions have probably taken place without our awareness. The Urgrund does not advertise to the artifact that it is here. Suppose the Urgrund reasons—and correctly—that were the artifact to know that it has returned a second time, the artifact would step up its cruelty to a maximum degree. We are experiencing a subtle invasion, taking place in stealth; I have already mentioned this. Mass amelioration would disclose the Urgrund's presence, just as Christ's miracles made him a target at the time of the First Advent. Healing miracles are the credentials of the Savior and an indication of his presence.

Once you have posited a strong adversary to the Urgrund, one so enormous that it is capable of projecting and sustaining an entire counterfeit universe, you have also put forth a possible clue to the need for stealth and concealment by the Urgrund. Its activities in this world resemble the covert advance of a secret, determined revolution against a powerful tyranny. The Urgrund is playing for ultimate stakes. It aims at nothing short of abolishing this world and its author entirely. I really don't know. I can envision its own agony at having to curtail its assistance to those in need, but it must win out against the artifact. It is aiming at the enemy's heart (or where its heart would be if it had one), and, upon success, all the pieces, the polyforms of pain throughout creation, will be spontaneously relieved.

Maybe this is so; maybe not. In 1974 I saw it take aim at the center of tyranny in this country, and upon its successful attack there, the lesser evils fell into ruin, one by one. The Urgrund probably sees this counterfeit world as one Gestalt; it sees the polyform evils as stemming from a *Quelle*, a source. Aiming its arrow at the Source is the method of the warrior, and, beneath his cloak of mildness, our Savior Deity is a warrior. All this is conjecture. Perhaps in a certain real way he has one and only one arrow to release. It must hit or nothing is achieved; any cures, any ameliorations other than this, ultimately would be nullified by the surviving artifact. The Urgrund perceived its adversary clearly and we do not; therefore it sees its task clearly and we do not. An entire multistoried building is on fire and we are asking the firemen to water a dying flower. Should they change the direction of their thrust to water the dying flower? Doesn't one flower count? The Urgrund may be in agony over this: abandoning the flower in favor of the greater picture. Many humans have undergone that pain and so should understand it. Please remember that the Urgrund is here, too: suffering with us. *Tat twam asi* [Thou art that]. We are he, and he must extricate himself.

In a very real sense the pain we feel as living creatures is the pain of waking up. Put this way, the proposition accounts for one of the most distressing aspects of suffering: that we are forced to suffer without knowing why. We do not know why precisely because we, as pluriforms of the Urgrund, are still virtually unconscious. It would be a paradox if an unconscious entity were aware of—conscious of—itself and the reasons behind its condition. Discerning the cause of our suffering equals fully waking up. It may be the final thing we learn.

At this point the analogy of the artifact to a teaching machine fails. This is not a lesson the teaching machine—if it is that—can teach us, because it does not know the answer. But we ourselves, as pluriform images of the Urgrund, will *a priori* know the reason for our situation when we become adequately conscious; *we will remember*. Knowledge of this sort lies in our own intrinsic long-term inhibited memory circuits.

Viewed as a puzzle we cannot at present answer, the reason for our condition of suffering (which involves all living things)—this puzzle may well be the final step of retrieved knowledge. If there is an erasure of memory we can only assume that when that crucial erasure is overcome, we will understand this most baffling perplexity. Meanwhile, the pressure of this pain motivates us to seek an answer; which is to say, motivates us toward greater and greater consciousness. This does not mean that the "purpose" of suffering is to engender heightened consciousness; it merely means that a gradually heightened consciousness is the result.

When the time arrives that we can explain the ubiquitous suffering of living creatures, we will, I am positive, have fully retrieved our lost memories and lost identities. Did we do it to ourselves? Was it inflicted on us against our will? One of the most intriguing explanations—by the Gnostics—is that the original fall of man (and hence creation—in this model falling under the dominion of the world-projecting artifact) was not due to a moral error, but to the intellectual error of confusing the phenomenal world for the real. This theory dovetails with my proposition that our world is a counterfeit projection; to take it for something ontologically real would indeed constitute a dreadful intellectual error. Maybe this is the explanation. We got entangled in enchantment, a gingerbread cottage that beguiled us into enslavement and ruin. Perhaps a major premise of my cosmogony-cosmology is wrong; the Urgrund did *not* create the artifact, but somehow allowed itself or parts of itself to fall victim to a snare, an alluring trap. So we are not merely enslaved; we are trapped. The artifact deliberately projected an illusion that would entrance us and lead us in.

Sometimes, however, a trap such as a spider's web (to cite only one of many) accidentally traps a deadly entity, capable of killing the trapmaker. This may be the case here. We may not be what we seem even to ourselves.

Sometimes, but not often, the existence of evil is traced back to the dual nature of God himself. I have already discussed the dual nature of Shiva and Christ—Shiva especially, who is often pictured as the god of death. Here are two examples.

Jakob Böhme. "God goes through stages of self-development, he taught, and the world is merely the reflection of this process. Böhme anticipated Hegel in claiming that the divine self-development occurs by means of a continuing dialectic, or tension of opposites, and that it is the negative qualities of the dialectic that men experience as the evil of the world. Even though Böhme, for the most part, stressed absoluteness and relativity equally, his view that the world is a mere reflection of the divine—apparently denying self-development on the part of creatures—tends toward acosmic pantheism" (*Encyclopaedia Britannica*, "Pantheism and Panentheism").

During my enormous revelations and anamnesis in March 1974 I perceptually observed God and reality combined, and progressing through stages of evolution by means of a dialectic, but I did not experience what I called "the blind counterplayer," which is to say the dark side as part of God. However, although I perceived this dialectic between good and evil, I could not ascertain anything as to the source of the evil. However, I did see the good side making use of it against its will, since the dark counterplayer was blind and therefore could be made use of for good purposes.

Hans Driesch (1867–1941). "My soul and my entelechy are One in the sphere of the Absolute." And it is at the level of the Absolute only that we can speak of "psychophysical interaction." But the Absolute, so understood, transcends all possibilities of our knowing, and it is "an error to take, as did Hegel, the sum of its traces for the Whole." All considerations of normal mental life lead us only to the threshold of the unconscious; it is in dreamlike and certain abnormal cases of mental life that we encounter "the depths of our soul." . . . My sense of duty indicates the general direction of the suprapersonal development. The ultimate goal, however, remains unknown. From this point of view, history took on its particular meaning for Driesch. Throughout his work Driesch's orientation is intended to be essentially empirical. Any argument concerning the nature of the ultimately Real will therefore have to be hypothetical only. It starts with the affirmation of the "given" as consequent of a conjectural "ground." His guiding principle in the realm of metaphysics amounts to this: The Real that I posit must be so constituted that it implicitly posits all our experiences. If we can conceive and posit such a Real, then all laws of nature, and all true principles and formulas of the sciences, will merge into it, and all our experiences will be "explained" by it. And since our experience is a mixture of wholeness (the organic and the mental realms) and nonwholeness (the material world), Reality itself must be such that I can posit a dualistic foundation of the totality of my experience. In fact, to bridge—aw fuck. In fact, there is nothing—not even within the ultimately Real—to bridge the gap between wholeness and nonwholeness. And this means, for Driesch, that ultimately there is either God and "non-God," or a dualism within God himself. To put it differently, either the theism of the Judeo-Christian tradition or a pantheism of a God continually "making himself" and transcending his own earlier stages is ultimately reconcilable with the facts of experience. Driesch himself found it impossible to decide between these alternatives. He was sure, however, that a materialistic-mechanistic monism would not do (*Encyclopedia of Philosophy*, Vol. 2).

It would appear that Böhme and T—I'm at the end of my rope; I can't even type, let alone think. That Böhme and Driesch are talking about the same thing, and that both are process philosophers (or theologians, like Whitehead). Both stress dialectic quality in God; Driesch sees the dialectic working itself out in history. This is almost certainly the dialectic that I saw during my March 1974 revelations, and I am willing to admit that it is certainly possible that the blind, dark counterplayer against which the vitalistic good element worked could be "God's own earlier stages," as Driesch viewed it. One thing I like about Driesch is the fact that at a certain point he simply said, "I don't know." That's where I'm at and have been at for a long time; I just do not know. God created everything; evil exists as part of the everything; therefore God is the source of evil—that is the logic, and in monotheism there is no escape from this argument. If you posit two (or more) gods, including an evil god, you have the problem of, Where did it come from? But that problem exists for monotheism, too; if there is only one god, where did he come from? Answer: from the same place the two gods of dualism came from. In other words, I see this problem of origin as equally difficult for monotheism to answer as it is for a dualism. We just don't know.

If we regard evil as simply earlier stages of a god in process, which he is working to overcome—well, that does fit my own personal revelations, and is syntonic to me. I was shown how the whole thing works but I did not comprehend what I was seeing; they were showing it to Mortimer Snerd. I did have the feeling that I was witnessing a cosmic two-person board game, with our world as the board, and that one side (the winning side) was benign, and the other was neither winning nor was it benign; it was just very powerful, but hindered by the fact that it was blind. The good side possessed absolute wisdom, could therefore absolutely foresee the future, and could lay down moves long in advance of payoffs that the evil, blind, dark counterplayer could not anticipate. It was an encouraging vision. In every trick the good won; it beat the dark antagonist unerringly. What more could I ask from an Ultimate Vision of Absolute Total Reality? What more do I need to know? The score reads: Evil zero; Good infinity. Let me stop there, satisfied; the final tally is explicit.

"The Tagore Letter" (1981)

All the people who read my recent novel *Valis* know that I have an alter ego named Horselover Fat, who experiences divine revelations (or so he thinks; they could be merely hallucinations, as Fat's friends believe). *Valis* ends with Fat searching the world for the new savior, who, he has been told by a mysterious voice, is about to be born. Well, Fat has had another vision, the one he was waiting for. He got me to write this as a way of telling the world—the readership of *Niekas*, more precisely—about it. Poor Fat! His madness is complete now, for he supposes that in his vision he actually *saw* the new savior.

I asked Fat if he was sure he wanted to talk about this, since he would only be proving the pathology of his condition. He replied, "No, Phil; they'll think it's you." Damn you, Fat, for putting me in this double bind. Okay; your vision, if true, is overwhelmingly important; if spurious, well, what the hell. I will say about it that it has a curiously practical ring; it does not deal with another world but this world, and extreme is its message—extreme in the sense that if true we are faced with a grave and urgent situation. So let 'er rip, Fat.

The new savior was born in—or now lives in—Ceylon (Sir Lanka). He is dark-skinned and either a Buddhist or Hindu. He works in the rural countryside with an organization or institute practicing high-technology veterinarian medicine, mainly with large animals such as cattle (most of the staff are white). His name is Tagore something; Fat could not catch his last name: It is very long. Although Tagore is the second reincarnation of Christ, he is taken to be Lord Krishna by the local population. Tagore is burned and crippled; he cannot walk but must be carried. As near as Fat could make out, Tagore is dying, but he is dying voluntarily: Tagore has taken upon himself mankind's sins against the ecosphere. Most of all it is the dumping of toxic wastes into the oceans of the world that shows up on Tagore's body as serious burns. Tagore's *kerygma* [teaching], which is the Third Dispensation (following the Mosaic and Christian), is: The ecosphere is holy and must be preserved, protected, venerated, and cherished—*as a unity*: not the life of individual men or individual animals but the ecosphere as a single indivisible unitary whole, a life chain that is being destroyed, and not just temporarily but for all time. The demonic trinity against which Tagore speaks—and that is wounding and killing him—consists of nuclear wastes, nuclear weapons, and nuclear power (reactors); they constitute the enemy that not only may destroy the ecosphere but already, as toxic wastes, are destroying it now. So again Christ acts out his role of vicarious atonement; he takes upon himself man's sins. But these sins are real, not doctrine sins. Tagore teaches that if we destroy the ecosphere much more, Holy Wisdom, the Wisdom of God (represented by Tagore himself), will abandon man to his fate, and that fate is doom.

Tagore teaches that when the ecosphere is burned, God himself is burned, for the Christ has invaded the ecosphere and invisibly assimilated it to himself through transubstantiation—which is the great vision Horselover Fat has in my novel *Valis*. Thus Christ and the ecosphere are either one or rapidly becoming one—much as Teilhard de Chardin describes in *The Phenomenon of Man*. The ecosphere does not evolve into the Cosmic Christ, however; Christ penetrates it, which is exactly what Fat saw and that so amazed him. Thus Christ now speaks out—not just for the salvation of mankind or certain men, "the elect"—but for the ecosphere as a whole, from the snail darter on up. This is a systems concept and was beyond their vocabulary in apostolic times; it has to do with the indivisibility of all life on this planet, as if this planet itself were alive. And Christ is both the soma [the body] and psyche (the head) of that collective life. Hence the ultimate statement by Tagore—expressed by his voluntary passion and death—is, *He who wounds the ecosphere wounds God, literally*. Thus a macrocrucifixion is taking place now, in and as our world, but we do not see it; Tagore, the new incarnation in human form of the Logos, tells us this in order to appeal to us to stop. If we continue we will lose God's Presence and, finally, we will lose our own physical lives. The oceans especially are menaced; Tagore speaks of this most urgently. When each canister of radioactive waste is dumped into the ocean, a new stigma appears on Tagore's terribly burned, seared legs. Fat was horrified by the sight of these burns, the legs of the savior drawn up in pain. Fat did not see Tagore's face, only his tragically burned body, and yet (Fat tells me) there was an ineffable sweetness about Tagore "like music and perfume and colors," as Fat phrased it to me. Burned as he is, wounded and dying as he is, Tagore nonetheless emits only loving beauty, absolute beauty, not relative beauty. It was a sight that Fat will never forget. I wish I could have shared it, but I had better things to do: watch TV and play electronic computer games. All that good stuff by which we fritter away our lives, while the ecosphere, wounded and in pain and in mortal danger, cries out for our help.

Part Six

Selections from the *Exegesis*

All of the selections are published here for the first time. Two of these selections were given titles by Dick—a rarity in the *Exegesis* as a whole.

"Outline in Abstract Form of a New Model of Reality Updating Historic Models, in Particular Those of Gnosticism and Christianity" (1977) is credited, by Dick, as being the joint work of himself and his friend SF writer K. W. Jeter. Jeter recalls that while the ideas emerged in the course of conversation between them, the writing is by Dick alone.

The final selection herein—"The Ultra Hidden (Cryptic) Doctrine: The Secret Meaning of the Great System of Theosophy of the World, Openly Revealed for the First Time"—is the longest *Exegesis* entry published to date. It is atypical from most *Exegesis* entries in possessing an essaylike structure and in having been typed out. Very likely it was intended as a summary of findings, as was "Cosmogony and Cosmology" (1978), included in a previous section. Was Dick serious about the title? In all probability, yes. Was he also satirizing his very efforts at comprehending Truth? Almost certainly.

The *Exegesis* is a free-roaming affair—as a nightly journal devoted to the expression of one's inmost (and ever-changing) thoughts on the largest and most perplexing issues of life would naturally be. Careful selections serve it well, for there is within it much repetition, much fretful worrying over past crisis moments in his life, many futile stabs at insight, and occasional bouts of pettiness and spleen. At its best, however, the flights of the *Exegesis* through impossibly possible worlds are remarkable.

From the *Exegesis* (c. 1975)

The architect of our world, to help us, came here as our servant, disguised, to toil for us. We have seen him many times but no [one] recognized him; maybe he is ugly in appearance, but with a good heart. Perhaps sometimes when he comes here he has forgotten his own origin, his godly power; he toils for us unaware of his true nature and what he could do to us if he remembered. For one thing, if we realized that this crippled, misshapen thing was our creator, we would be disappointed. Would reject and despise him. Out of courtesy to us he hides his identity from us while here.

One can see from this that that which we kick off to one side of the road, out of the way, which feels the toe of our boot—that may well be our God, albeit unprotesting, only showing pain in his eyes, that old, old pain that he knows so well. I notice, though, that although we kick him off to one side in pain, we do let him toil for us; we accept that. We accept his work, his offerings, his help; but him we kick away. He could reveal himself, but he would then spoil our illusion of a beautiful god. But he doesn't look evil, like Satan; just homely. Unworthy. Also, although he has vast creative and building power, and judgment, he is not clever. He is not a bright god. Often he is too dumb to know when he's being teased or insulted; it takes physical pain, rather than mere scorn, to register.

Ugly like this, despised and teased and tormented and finally put to death, he returned shining and transfigured; our Savior, Jesus Christ (before him Ikhnaton, Zoroaster, etc; Hefestus [or Hephaestus]). When He returned we saw Him as he really is—that is, not by surface appearance. His radiance, his essence, like Light. The God of Light wears a humble and plain shell here (like a metamorphosis of some humble toiling beetle).

SF novel: Hefestus as VALIS (Vast Active Living Intelligence System].

The Earth like St. Sofia is an organism, a living one, being built, a Temple that when it is ready the Lord will suddenly come to and dwell in. He Himself is creator: architect. Workmen/artisans/artists: Us and Holy Spirit. *Ideal Logos*/form: Christ, to be achieved. The model once glimpsed then to be striven for and reached, at which time Architect (Creator), Holy Spirit, and Ideal become One, which includes us within it as bits. Creator: time past. Holy Spirit: time is. Christ: time completed. Holy Spirit guides us toward Him. Force is provided by the Creator at the start. Force/activity/direction to goal.

c. 1976

The victory of Christ (as Lord of the Cosmos) over astral (planetary) determinism is better expressed, for us today, by saying, It is the coming into being of a thinking cosmos replacing a merely deterministic, causal, unthinking mechanism of fate or blind chance. Thus the characteristics of this new "body" or organism would be that, if perceived by one of us, it would seem to be a living creature of cosmic size, wisdom, scope, and power, infiltrating the natural (i.e. deterministic) order of nature. This, when I saw Valis or Zebra, is precisely what I saw. Therefore it is evident that the process of transubstantiation of the deterministic "astral" mechanism into a living body or entity is far progressed. What I saw, then, was none other than the cosmic Christ. Beneath their unchanged outward appearances, natural processes (i.e. causal processes) are to some extent, a decisive extent, purposeful, conscious, and benign, and organized to fulfill a coherent plan. The palpable revelation of this is the supreme revelation. For instance, it intervened decisively in human history in 3-74 on. All that remains is for the second incarnation to occur; i.e. the veil to drop, God's Wisdom to appear openly here, that all may be aware of it and acknowledge it. Perhaps what I saw was a preview, and eventually everyone will see as I saw, and what I saw, in 3-74.

He will not merely rule the universe; he will also *be* the universe.

What I saw, then, was an apocalypse (disclosure) of the invisible Parousia, the Presence that is now here. At this point, an apocalypse is still needed, because the Parousia is still *hidden*.

The role in my life of the whole CP, Soviet thing was that it was, for me, the "astral" of deterministic power, which Christ broke by his intervention.

Could it be said that in 3-74 Christ interfered with the genetic coding that had programmed me to die at that time? That this (genetic coding) is a modern term for at least one aspect of (astral) determinism? My gene-pool (DNA) memory fired—opened up; I know that. And I am reasonably sure I was programmed, at least internally, to die (of cardiovascular problems). There also may have been external deterministic death-dealing factors that he aborted as well. This is a modern model for what the ancients called "sublunar" or "planetary" or "astral" influences. This would explain my retrieval of long-term (gene pool) memory; the whole system either opened up or was opened up. My sense that it (the Xerox letter) had happened before shows the karmalike quality of such genetic programming. The technical theological term for this is God's grace. But to appreciate the value of God's grace, this entire deterministic structure must be properly understood, and its magnitude—and power over us—comprehended. It is a vast, nearly all-encompassing system from which few are extricated during this lifetime.

The part of my March 18, 1974 experience that precisely delineates it as having been of Christ, as compared to God or to the Holy Spirit, was (1) that it took place at the vernal equinox, and (2) most of all, the sound of the "Easter" or Magic bells, which are specifically identified with Christ.

It was induced by the Holy Spirit, and did show the Kingdom of God, with the presence of God. But the honeycombed corpus that I found myself within—that was Corpus Christi, the mystical body of which Christ is the head, and we of the congregation the parts. This is also Hagia Sophia and also the King (who is coming to rule). Hence I thought the other day, "I am part of the King." Vide *Collosians* 1:13 or whatever that citation is [1:13–14], Christ as maker and lord of (*Pantokrator*) the universe. Hence I felt joy when I realized I'd seen transubstantiation of the objects (of the alley) around me; I was on the right track: Christ's invisible (normally) body. Hence the dream of the Mandarin old Chinese king, wise but lacking power. This contrasts Christ versus God; the dream was to clarify this distinction (vide doctrine of the Trinity). That was not an image of God, who would have power, but rather an image of the wise, powerless king, who is Christ.

Nonetheless, I think Spinoza is correct in his concept of God as immanent, that the universe is alive, that God possesses the attribute of physical extension, that mind, matter, and energy are three attributes or modes of His Being . . . there is no problem for me because I am a Trinitarian. It is only more precise to say that I found myself within, as a part of, the mystical body of Christ, rather than of God. Also, we know from Scripture that there is such a mystical body (*Collosians, supra*). No radical theology would be required, only this knowledge. No wonder it seems senseless to me when someone says, "Christ was a man, like ourselves." Also, no wonder I am attracted to Pere Teilhard de Chardin's concept of the "plasmatic" Christ (Corpus Christi).

Too, this may be why my final phosphene set-ground experience was the Golden Rectangle or pylon-entrance doorway. "I am the way." It would appear that the ICC is correct, that the written text of the New Testament is incomplete. You are baptized. The Spirit comes to you. What then? Then you experience yourself as part of the mystical Corpus Christi, which Paul speaks of in *Collosians*. Reunited with Christ, with His growing resurrected light-body. Taken into it (which is not the same as the Kingdom of God arriving on Earth, the Parousia). This was the "secret of secrets," and was forgotten after the Romans killed them and destroyed the oral tradition. One could commune with Christ again (or Hagia Sophia, vide Spinoza). One important difference that suggests itself to me between being part of the body of God (as in Spinoza) and part of the "mystical Corpus Christi" is that the first would be pure mystical perception, and that everything truly, if perceived right, belongs to it; this is an elevation of perception only, however important. But the latter is, so to speak, "by invitation only," belonging only to "the congregation." It is more than perception, it is an entering in which not all (I presume) share in. Perhaps that's why that—the latter—would seem more valuable; it would mean not just that I saw with the "Wisdom of God" but that I was taken by His yoke, so to speak, to join His (Christ's) mystical body, which is more; the first just states actually what is, one is not welcomed, *everything* is. One has not been judged or sought out. But I saw the "hotel register" where my name was written and so forth. I was judged; I felt that. And I now think brought into the Corpus Christi. Also, to perceive an immanent God, that the material universe is the *soma* [Greek: body] of God, and there is Mind behind it as well—this doesn't supply any basis for believing in an afterlife, for anything next or beyond in that direction; whereas the mystic Corpus Christi does. It is a demonstration of the reality of the resurrection, which the former isn't; the former is great, though, inasmuch as it demonstrates the reality of God and theological purpose; it must not be put down. The latter gives more *personally*.

This would be why I felt I was receiving from a hidden (occult) brotherhood, represented by armed knights . . . the knights of the grail, so to speak. And the content of my experience: I was shown specifically the Christian brotherhood toppling Rome, *now*. The siege of us prisoners being lifted by the body of armored knights on horseback at the outer walls. The "mystical body of Christ" of which we are parts and he is the head—this would be a sort of midway concept of the source, standing between pure mystical perception of immanent God (à la Spinoza) and a strictly human wisdom (gnostic, AMORC, Roman Catholic, etc.) brotherhood. The head is divine *(theos)*, the members are of the human congregation. Its presence is actually here (now), in and on our world, in our society, making changes (the rock torn not by human hands and hurled at the statue, as in Daniel). (And I did hear, hypnogogically, "I am part of the King.")

Palmer—crossed palm trees. Palm trees are a Christian symbol of the Holy Land; what I saw in 2-75, then, is a vision of the Holy Land. I did not go (journey) to it; it came to me. I was already seeing a palm tree (like the Afrika Korps palm tree emblem) in the FISH sign, months before. The palmer sign, perhaps. *In hoc signo*, etc. [*In hoc signo vinces*: In this sign we conquer.] Again, we have here symbols specifically of Christianity, rather than of God per se (as distinguished from). Also, a building in the Holy Land, with Romanesque arches. Memory of the Sacred Other, from its "former life"? A building where the White Brotherhood (etc.) met? The significance of my seeing this might be: My search is over. I had reached my destination, the end of my journey. (And, very soon after, the voice of St. Sophia dimmed away entirely from my mind. The one full year, from vernal equinox to vernal equinox, had evidently ended.) It all must be regarded as a searching for and a finding of (vide the quest represented in my various novels).

c. 1976

> *I Am a Living Animal, Tied to a Dying Soul.*
> —PKD

1. The Greeks considered reality *veiled* (by *dokos* [Greek: deception], e.g. Parmenides).
2. The Hindus consider reality veiled (by Maya, which we generate ourselves, but which also Kali spins) (cf. Heinrich Zimmer [noted Indologist]).
3. Calvin considered us blinded, that once we could see what is really there, but were punished (this dovetails a little with Empedocles and with Castaneda, with shamanism in general, and hence with the mystery religions, e.g., Dionysos).
4. Augustine considered the City of God mingled with the City of Earth so as to make them indistinguishable to us now; but at the Parousia, they will be separated (to our senses).
5. Zoroaster believed as 4. Good (Ahriman and Ahura-Mazda, the light and dark blended; but at the Final Day, the two portions would be visibly separate).

All are dealing with the problem of phenomenology of accident versus essence: Kant's *Ding-an-sich* [thing in itself]. "This crumbling pageant."

6. I once saw appearance, then briefly (five days) assimilated the objects of perception (noetically) and then returned to ordinary perception of appearance, the "reflection" of reality (Plato, Paul, etc.). My experience proves that all views that we see only "a reflection from the

bottom of a polished metal pan" are correct, FOR WHATEVER REASON, the latter being in doubt only. I did not see; then I saw; then I did not see again (exactly as Paul says). Why the first? Why the second? Why the return of the first? Teilhard's view of an evolutionary step forward? Or anamnesis, restoration of lost faculties (Calvin)? Or coiled, cyclic time? Moebius strip time?

Is change (Dionysos, metamorphosis) real? Heraclitus/Christ Teilhard
   Or: Is unchange (Apollo, the healers) real? Parmenides, Jahweh
   Is the search itself the goal (as is said)?

My Gollancz speech ["Man, Android, and Machine" (1976), included in this volume] is insane but true. And I knew more then, noetically; what I've read since bears it out. The madman speaks the moral of the piece.

If we deceive ourselves, why? If someone/something else deceives us, then why and also *who*? *Wacht auf!* [Wake up!] Brahmin (it, not he). It dreams, and now wakes, or it was awake, and now falls asleep; I think it is waking. The universe-organism of the Greek philosophers: It wakes and sees. Cells, forming a Great Brain. Bees in a hive. Rising now to consciousness. Of what? Itself? There are no answers, only mysteries (not questions but mysteries: secrets. Sacred secrets, not disclosed to us. But not by whom? Well, when I woke, those five days, *change* was real: a process. Cosmogenesis (Teilhard). Toward. Omega.

Outline in Abstract Form of a New Model of Reality Updating Historic Models, in Particular Those of Gnosticism and Christianity (1977)

It is proper to say: We appear to be memory coils (DNA carriers capable of experience) in a computerlike thinking system that, although we have correctly recorded and stored thousands of years of experiential information (knowledge, gnosis), and each of us possesses a somewhat different deposit from all the other life forms, *there is a malfunction—a failure—of memory retrieval.* There lies the trouble in our particular subcircuit. "Salvation" through gnosis—more properly anamnesis (the loss of amnesia)—although it has individual significance for each of us—a quantum leap in perception, identity, cognition, understanding, world- and self-experience, including immortality—it has further and more truly ultimate importance for the system (structure) *as a whole*, inasmuch as these memories (data) are needed or valuable to *it*, and to *its* overall functioning.

Therefore it is in the process of self-repair, which includes: rebuilding our subcircuit (world) via linear *and* orthogonal time changes (sequences of events), as well as continual signaling to us both en masse and individually (to us received subliminally by the right brain hemisphere, which gestalts the constituents of the messages into meaningful entities), to stimulate blocked neural (memory) banks within us to fire and hence retrieve what is there.

The adventitious information of gnosis, then, consists of disinhibiting messages (instructions), with the core (main) content actually intrinsic to us—that is, already there (first observed by Plato, that learning is a form of remembering).

The ancients possessed techniques (sacraments and rituals) used largely in the Greco-Roman mystery religions, including early Christianity, to induce firing and retrieval, mainly with a sense of its restorative (repairing) value to the individuals; the Gnostics, however, and Mani correctly saw the ontological value to what they called the Godhead Itself (i.e. the total entity).

PHILIP K. DICK
K. W. JETER
12/7/77
SANTA ANA, CALIFORNIA

(Note: While such "Enlightened" spiritual leaders as Zoroaster, Mani, Buddha, and Elijah can be regarded as receptors of the entity's total wisdom, Christ seems to have been an actual terminal of this computerlike entity, in which case he did not speak for it but *was* it. "Was," in this case, standing for "consisted of a microform of it.")

Late 1972 letter found amongst c. 1977
Exegesis papers

I almost became a sincere tool of a conspiracy consisting of myself.

There goes the John Birch Society sincerely trying to save this country from the John Birch Society—from itself.

Prototype: Pooh and Piglet following the woozle footprints around and around the tree. There are more all the time.

I blew up my own house and forgot I did it. [The reference here is to an episode in November 1971 when Dick's house and files were broken into, possibly with the use of explosives; his list of suspects for this unsolved crime included himself.] But why did I forget I did it? So I'd think I had an actual enemy so I wouldn't have to face the fact that I'm paranoid, i.e. crazy. I blew up my house to convince myself I was sane. Anyone who would go to that much trouble must really be nuts. So as soon as those who thought I was imagining that people were after me saw that my house had been blown up, they realized that I was far more paranoid than they had suspected. Their paranoid suspicions about me are now much greater. Sensing their paranoid suspicions about me, I realize etc.

Why is everything is short supply? Because everyone is hoarding. Why are they hoarding? Because everything is in short supply.

We all wind up isolated, suspicious of each other, each of us trying to figure out what is going on, which means, who is doing it? Who is our enemy? The fact that we can't figure out what's going on overloads our brains, overworks our minds; we wear out fast, get exhausted and confused. And still we can't locate the enemy. Because we are confused we begin to act in an ineffectual way, so our behavior becomes erratic. Others who notice our erratic behavior wonder what we are up to. Actually we are up to nothing, are merely in the process of burning out over the problem of trying to figure out what other people are up to, inasmuch as their various behaviors are becoming more and more perplexing. Each of us assumes everyone else knows what HE is doing. They all assume we know what WE are doing. We don't. They ask us, What are you doing? We can't give a coherent account because we don't know, but our failure to give a coherent account convinces them that we are lying, and the only reason we would lie is because what we are really (doing) ought to be concealed. This confirms their fears and mistrust, and they intensify the interrogation. The false premise is, You must know what you're doing and if you won't tell me, then you must be lying in order to conceal something I wouldn't approve of, which is probably directed at me to hurt me. Each person winds up more and more confused, having wasted his time and exhausted himself interrogating other persons as confused as himself on the false assumption that they know what's going on. Nothing is going on and nobody knows what it is. Nobody is concealing anything except the fact that he does not understand anything anymore and wishes he could go home.

c. 1977

"**A**ctualities are somehow plucked from a greater sea of possibilities that also form part of the truth." This means that the actuality is not true versus possibilities that are false; it just means that the actuality is more true; the possibilities are less true but also true. This involves the principle of emergence, how a thing comes into being. It is a question of degree, not either-or. Possibly the force that selects one possibility and makes it the actuality is the pressure on reality—this greater sea of possibilities—of the human mind. *It* selects out the actuality by assessing it as more probable. Or it is a subtle interaction, a feedback between the sentient mind and this greater sea: Pressure is exerted until one possibility among many becomes growingly distinct, which causes the pressure to select it out to become more firm. The actuality is merely a particular possibility that acquires form and shape and can be discerned. Actualization is a gestalting process, and gestalting takes place primarily in the human mind. The mind exerts a subtle and continual pressure on certain events and things to be, and on others not to be; it shapes reality directly by some field similar to gravitational waves, very weak but always there, and in the end effective. Without the presence of human minds and the pressure they exert there would be no actualization of anything, and only the greater sea of possibilities, of half truths, would exist as a multitude of semiforms, contradicting one another but existing side by side. Without real time or space.

c. 1978

Through anamnesis you can move retrograde in time, go back and burn up or unweave your karma, be born anew to a higher state — but is this all an interior psychological process? It must be; Tessa [Dick's wife who lived with him during the 2-3-74 experiences] didn't see Rome c. A.D. 70. But I saw Valis outside me modulating reality. Ah; but that was a projection (cf. Jung). Projection explains it, the Magdeburg hemispheres. It was my own mind that I was seeing external to me. I traveled down into the phylogenic (collective) unconscious. God had nothing to do with it. Right?

Then what about the messenger who comes in time and bilks the retribution machine by withholding from it the bill of particulars against you? Is the messenger an archetype of the unconscious? And the AI voice [Artificial Intelligence voice — Dick's name for the hypnogogic voice he heard frequently in 1974–75 and intermittently thereafter until his death]; that is my anima?

c. 1978

I have it; I advance the following bold theory. Out of the dialectical antithetical interaction between the Empire and its enemy, *Valis is created, Valis as kosmos*. The war provides the stockpile of parts — ever newer and different—that Valis fits into place to form its own *soma* [body]. Valis is the result and purpose of this contention; the contention so to speak generates wreckage—chaos—and this is Valis's raw material, which it *must* have, have access to, if it is to complete itself, if it is to continue to grow.

This fits in with Empedocles' theory that combat is the basis of reality, that antithetical combat is *necessary* for reality to exist (i.e. for there to be *einai*).

Thus Valis comes into existence in the midst of this battle, not as an accident, a by-product, but as the ultimate purpose; the battle is the means and Valis the end. So one kind of reality—dialectical war—gives rise to a perfect structure in equilibrium, a harmonious fitting together of the beautiful. I saw Valis here. Valis arises from the ceaseless dialectic that was revealed to me. I might say that the dialectic is one form of universe and Valis another; and in our ontogenic world we see neither. So history is the means and Valis the goal—at least for Valis; it may *prey* off this combat! The combat may not have come into existence for this purpose. Valis *uses* the combative dialectic for its own purposes. Wow.

Then Valis is the goal of history. Sacred (phylogenic) history: history revealed, as in Judaism.

What is Valis, then? Why, it is the Cosmic Christ, Point Omega. I have seen what Teilhard de Chardin wrote about, although I had never read any of his writing. I am sure that this is what Valis is; my reading of Paul's letters had already half convinced me. But this clinches it. The goal of history . . . and the agent active in this process is the Paraclete, working backward from the end of time, entering into good men to make them saints and prophets.

c. 1978

The Gnostic Christians of the second century believed that only a special revelation of knowledge rather than faith could save a person. The contents of this revelation could not be received empirically or derived *a priori.* They considered this special gnosis so valuable that it must be kept secret. Here are the ten major principles of the gnostic revelation:

1.   The creator of this world is demented.
2.   The world is not as it appears, in order to hide the evil in it, a delusive veil obscuring it and the deranged deity.
3.   There is another, better realm of God, and all our efforts are to be directed toward
   a. returning there
   b. bringing it here.
4.   Our actual lives stretch thousands of years back, and we can be made to remember our origin in the stars.
5.   Each of us has a divine counterpart unfallen who can reach a hand down to us to awaken us. This other personality is the authentic waking self; the one we have now is asleep and minor. We are in fact asleep, and in the hands of a dangerous magician disguised as a good god, the deranged creator deity. The bleakness, the evil and pain in this world, the fact that it is a deterministic prison controlled by a demented creator causes us willingly to split with the reality principle early in life, and so to speak willingly fall asleep in delusion.
6.   You can pass from the delusional prison world into the peaceful kingdom *if* the True Good God places you under His grace and allows you to see reality through His eyes.
7.   Christ gave, rather than received, revelation; he taught his followers how to enter the kingdom *while still alive*, where other mystery religions only bring about anamnesis: knowledge of it at the "other time" in "the other realm," not here. He causes it to come here, and is the living agency of the Sole Good God (i.e. the Logos).
8.   Probably the real, secret Christian church still exists, long underground, with the living Corpus Christi as its head or ruler, the members absorbed into it. Through participation in it they probably have vast, seemingly magical powers.
9.   The division into "two times" (good and evil) and "two realms" (good and evil) will abruptly end with victory for the good time here, as the presently invisible kingdom separates and becomes visible. We cannot know the date.
10.   During this time period we are on the sifting bridge being judged

according to which power we give allegiance to, the deranged creator demiurge of this world or the One Good God and his kingdom, whom we know through Christ.

To know these ten principles of gnostic Christianity is to court disaster.

c. 1978

The belief that we are pluriforms of God voluntarily descended to this prison world, voluntarily losing our memory, identity, and supernatural powers (faculties), all of which can be regained through anamnesis (or, sometimes, the mystical conjunction), is one of the most radical religious views known in the West. But it is known. It is regarded as the Great Blasphemy: replication of the original sin mentioned in the First Book of Adam and Eve and in Genesis. For this pride and aspiration (we are told by orthodoxy) our original fall and exile and punishment, our being taken from our home the gardenland and put into the prison, was inflicted on us. "They wish to be equal to—like—us," the Elohim say, and toss us down. Yet I have reason to believe that this, "the Great Satanic Blasphemy," is true.

First, we are here voluntarily. We did not sin and we were not punished; we elected to descend. Why? To infuse the divine into the lowest strata of creation in order to halt its decomposing—the sinking of its lower realm. This points to a primordial crisis in creation in the total macrocosm (hexagram 12). The yin form two (dark, deterministic) part was splitting away from the light or yang or form one. In conventional terms, heaven (upper realm) and earth (lower realm) were separating, carrying the lives within the lower away from their form one (upper) counterparts (this can be viewed as the *Godhead itself* falling apart, into its yang and yin two halves, with the lower form universe as God expressed physically in time and space). The solution was for the divine (yang, light, form one) to follow the lower realm down, permeating it and thus reuniting the cosmos into one totality. To do this, elements (in ancient terms, sparks) of light advanced (descended) into the dark kingdom, the immutable prison world; upon doing so they shed (and knew they would shed) their bright nature, memory, identity, faculties, and powers, and fell under the dominion of the delusion that the dark kingdom is real (which when severed from the upper realm it is not; i.e. the world we presently live in doesn't exist). There they have lived as prisoners of the master magician, lord of the dark realm who poses as the creator (and who may not know of the light god, the true creator, his other half). But the light god and his pluriforms, the descending (invading) sparks, have cunningly distributed clues in the dark realm to recall to the drugged and intoxicated sparks of light their true nature and mission (and true source of home). Upon encountering these cryptic clues the forgetful sparks of the upper realm, now prisoners in and of the lower realm, *remember*, regain their powers and faculties, and link back up with the upper realm and the light god; they *are* the light god in pluriform, his way of invading the lower realm in disguise. The light god (the divine) has now crucially occupied critical stations in the sinking lower realm, and begins the reannexing of it back into the totality composed of both realms. The sinking ceases; the master magician is stripped of his autonomy and assimilated to the yang part of the Godhead as its *passive* counterpart, and once more there is one macrocosm ruled by the yang or active (creative) light god assisted by the now receptive yin (dark) side. The divine has triumphed at all levels; the prison is burst, and the vast, light-filled garden kingdom restored as the home of all creatures. These now whole creatures, composed equally of yin and yang, are what I term homoplasmates: The yin part is home (as we know ourselves to be now, only), and the light or yang part is the plasmate or energy part (vs. the physical). Thus renewed and complete microcosms mirroring the renewed and complete macrocosm are achieved. Reality is imparted to the otherwise irreal lower realm, and the upper realm now extends physically into the realm of matter. The integrity of the Godhead is restored; its two halves function in harmony; and the primordial split (or crisis) is resolved—healed.

This is a view compounded of Zoroastrianism, Brahmanism, Gnosticism, Taoism, the macro-microcosmos of Hermes Trismegistus and other mystery religions, and not very much of orthodox Christianity. Christianity can be added if the pluriform microsparks of light are considered plural saviors or Christs comprising a single mystical corpus that is distributed widely in time and space in the dark realm but possessing only one psyche that is somehow also God, the yang or light god.

I have read the above cosmology over, and find no fault in it. In fact, I am amazed. It is in a sense acosmic, and certainly Gnostic, but the Taoist overlay is novel and pleasing; the Taoist overlay redeems it from the flaws of conventional dualist religions and the problems therein. Instead of stressing *moral* aspects ("good vs. bad"), it stresses epistemological ("real vs. irreal," which I can understand). The lower realm sinks not because it is corrupt or evil or somehow has rebelled but because, as shown in hexagram 12, it is the nature of yin to sink, as it is the nature of yang to rise. The pre-Socratics (and Plato in "Timaeus") were aware of this; v. the model of the winnowing fan and the concept of the vortex. Yang must assimilate yin to keep the totality intact; i.e. yang must renounce its natural tendency to rise *and must descend*. It cannot expect yin to rise, because yin is not wise; it is only *noos* that can understand that it must compensate against its own natural tendencies, and do what is unnatural to it. Yin is, so to speak, thick, unthinking, not *noos* [mind] but *soma* [body]; *noos* and *soma* (or *psyche* and *soma*) are the total universe organism. Descending into the yin realm is a sacrifice on yang's part, which through its bright or wise nature it realizes it must make, but it pays a great cost in terms of suffering: loss of memory and identity, abilities, and faculties: It becomes pseudoyin, literally disguised in the yin realm as if it were actually yin, even to the point of forgetting (until reminded), that it is not. This is the agony we face here in this irreal and dense yin realm, we yang traces: This is not our home. We are voluntary exiles here, alienated and alone, violating our own natures for a salvific purpose—a necessary purpose. Yin would not understand this, and until anamnesis sets in for us, we in our distress do not understand the reason either. Eventually it will be revealed to us; meanwhile we ache with longing for our proper home, dimly remembered but deeply felt for. Thus we suppose we are being punished; it feels like punishment, and [we] make the error of assuming we have sinned. On the contrary; we have renounced joy now, to produce a greater joy later, for the good of all creation; we are the Godhead itself suffering the need to be what it is not, to ensure the ultimate stability of krasis (as Empedocles termed it): the unity of love.

Lest any Christian reject this, let him now read the Fourth Gospel in connection with this, and see for himself the similarities.

Lest any Taoist reject this, let him now see that hexagram 12

has turned to hexagram 11, Peace:

The upper trigram, in descending, has forced the lower trigram to rise. Disorder no longer reigns; heaven and earth are not pulling apart. There is harmony.

Moral: It is the ethical requirement placed on the yang traces by their own bright nature to abandon their natural tendency to rise, to escape what is heavy and dark and sinking; they must go in pursuit of the falling part of the cosmos, for the benefit of those and that which otherwise would be lost. This is the highest law: to violate one's own nature for another's good. And the most difficult—and painful—law to fulfill. Because of this need there is distress in the cosmos, distress for the innocent especially. My cosmology simply presents it as a fact. To escape it we would have to allow the cosmos to decompose. Could we do that? The tragedy is that by the very nature of the sacrifice we make we are occluded from knowing why. This is part of our sacrifices: our yang understanding. We must take on the dullness of yin to save the cosmos; we sacrifice the knowledge of why we sacrifice, and assume guilt—spurious guilt—in its place. This is asking a lot.

But consider who we really are. Or once were and will be again. Who else can do it? There is no one else. There is only yin, which does not know. The part of the organism that knows must help the part that doesn't know, but this means abandoning its own knowing. It becomes what it helps, a dreadful irony, one that hurts. But it is only temporary, just for a little while. And then we go home for all eternity.

The Ultra Hidden (Cryptic) Doctrine: The Secret Meaning of the Great System of Theosophy of the World, Openly Revealed for the First Time (March 2, 1980)

So to explain 2-3-74 I draw on the *Tibetan Book of the Dead*, Orphism, Gnosticism, Neoplatonism, Buddhism, esoteric Christianity, and the Cabala; my explanation sources are the highest—which is good and which makes sense. But put another way, starting at the other end, I have synthesized all these high sources and derived a single sensationally revolutionary occult doctrine out of them (which I was able to think up due to the addition of my 2-3-74 experience); the distillate expressed theoretically is, We are dead but don't know it, reliving our former lives but on tape (programmed), in a simulated world controlled by Valis the master entity or reality generator (like Brahman), where we relive in a virtually closed cycle again and again until we manage to add enough new good

karma to trigger off divine intervention, which wakes us up and causes us
to simultaneously both remember and forget, so that we can begin our
reascent back up to our real home. This, then, is *purgatorio*, the afterlife,
and we are under constant scrutiny and judgment, but don't know it, in a
perfect simulation of the world we knew and remember—v. *Ubik* and
Lem's paradigm [see "The Android and the Human," included herein].
We have for a long time been dying brains/souls slipping lower and lower
through the realms, but the punishment of reliving this bottom-realm life
is also an opportunity to add new good karma and break the vicious cycle
of otherwise endless reliving of a portion of our former life. This, then, is
the *sophia summa* of the six esoteric systems—seven if you count alchemy—of the entire world. Eight if you count hermeticism. We are
dead, don't know it, and mechanically relive our life in a fake world until
we get it right. Ma'at [an Egyptian goddess who weighed the souls of the
dead in the balance to determine their virtue] has judged us; we are punished, but we can change the balance . . . but we don't know we are here
to do this, let alone know where we are. *We must change the "groove" for
the better* or just keep coming back, not remembering, not reascending.

Judaism enters, too, since the change in the "groovE" [sic] that in-
troduces the right new good karma restores us to Eden, to our phylogenic
original unfallen state. It may be a small act on our part that adds the good
karma, a small decision, but this reminds me of the story told of Moses
and the lamb that wanted to drink at the stream (Moses, upon finding that
the lamb had laboriously made its way to the stream, said, "Had I known
that thou wert thirsty I would have carried thee hence myself," to which a
voice from Heaven replied, "Then thou thyself art fit to be the shepherd
of Israel").

The reason why a small good act may tilt the scales is that you will be
reenacting the good deeds that you acted out before, and some may be
huge, but they *in toto* were not enough to tip Ma'at's scale to provide you
with adjudication of release to reascend. So the small act is *new*; it is an
addition, but you are not aware that you are on tape, that this small, good
act *did not occur before*; this time you have decided differently in a given
situation: done the right thing this time. And a small act may reveal character even more than a vast one regarding which you have made a
weighty and long-pondered decision. Spontaneity may be a crucial factor
as an index of character.

In this synthesized occult system the maximum statement is the first: We are dead. Then: We have been made to relive a portion of our former, actual life as a punishment that is also an opportunity; hence this is not hell, because the possibility exists of performing a new act (in what is virtually a closed system) that will change the balance of the scale on which Ma'at weighs us. Also there is a complex picture of anamnesis and reascent, but this is well known from Plato and other sources.

There is an odd paradox in this earning new good karma situation by introducing a novel deed, however small. You must not know the scheme of things, because if you knew the scheme of things (i.e. the theoretical system put forth herewith) your good deed will be contaminated by the knowledge of the likely payoff for you; that is, it is no longer disinterested. Therefore Valis *must*, if the salvific mechanism of deed and then judgment is to work, keep himself totally and absolutely concealed, and the nature of the situation concealed, i.e. rerun of the actual world and the fact that we are being appraised for the introduction of a novel good deed that is an index of spontaneous character, which is to say, real nature of character.

So of course Valis does not disclose himself to us; and the quality (aspect) of simulation is likewise concealed. We are not to know where we are nor why. Valis must be able to observe us through a one-way screen. For example, there is no way I can add to my good karma store now because I know the situation.

The books on me then must be closed; they have to be. Once Valis discloses itself the situation is over; you are bound for heaven or hell, but the midrealm of *purgatorio* is shut to you forever.

Therefore it can be reasoned that Valis will show as few times as possible, and, if he does reveal himself to a person, Valis will becloud the situation so that the person cannot make the knowledge he has—hence the real situation—generally well known. (NOTE: This system makes use of my ten-volume meta novel. This is valuable to me.)

Also, I wasn't granted release (salvation) because I handled the Xerox missive right; I handled it right because I had been saved, and by another and unrelated act—a future act—entirely.

Further: I was saved by an act of free will on my part that occurred after I was granted salvation; cause and effect occurred backward (retrograde) in time.

You know, in this system (understanding) there is the basis of a teaching of salvation having to do with the entirely gratuitous good act, done out of unpremeditated and hence spontaneous free will, in contrast to programmed works of deterministic duty; there is an obvious Zen quality to it. No formula can be located for the performance of these acts; they would have almost a contrary quality, contrary to your normal way of being in the world. They would literally set you apart—off—from yourself, the self that failed to pass Ma'at's scale. They would emanate from the not-you (the normal not-you), from another and more real you, as if from another personality locked up within you and alluded to only by these acts. Thus the single personality becomes reborn; two selves exist, one of which is the old, the programmed, the not-saved. Yes; you would have to act contrary to your own nature; you would get outside yourself. Suddenly I think, This sounds like "Thomas" [an early Christian personage who, Dick sometimes speculated, had crossbonded with him during the events of 2-3-74]! Why, it would be; "Thomas" did precisely what he/I did not do the first time around—then this verifies my system, for this system posits the need, the absolute need, of a "Thomas" to break *heimarmene* [deluding power of the spurious world] and hence damnation. Only this not-you act or acts could save you, actions without a history. QED! For it was with "Thomas" that the new and unprogrammed veered off from what happened the first time, and there indeed was a first time. I am saying, we in *purgatorio* to be saved must do what we would not do if we are to be saved, because doing what we would do damned us to this place. Yet how does a person become "born again" and do what he would not do? This is a mystery; obviously IT MUST BE DONE TOTALLY WITHOUT THE NORMAL USUAL ANALOGIC IDEATION (RATIOCINATION), AND THIS IS EXACTLY WHAT HAPPENED WITH "THOMAS": HE ACTED TOTALLY WITHOUT IDEATION, AND DID WHAT I WOULD NOT HAVE DONE, AND I SAID, THIS IS NOT ME: HERE IS ANOTHER PERSON IN ME. And this continued for some time.

Thus there is literally a second birth, and *ex nihilo*.

Thus from these facts I can correctly ascertain that indeed "Thomas's" actions were not programmed, not part of the original world and life. They were an ideationless overpowering, as if located only in my motor centers. "Thomas" was not born in my brain but born in my body, e.g. my hands and tongue; he moved and spoke, but in my brain there were no ideas or thoughts or intentions; he was intentionless, and yet had absolute *purpose*. Purpose without intent! Plan without plan! Or rather goal without plan. Truly it was Zen. Yes; indeed it was. So my theory (herewith) demands/predicts salvation by a not-you ideationless self acting at the moment of crisis when the taped world (or track of *heimarmene*) branches off into the new and free, and upon retrospective analysis we find "Thomas," precisely that. I can now rule out Pigspurt forever. It branches off into the new and free precisely because this not-you ideationless act occurs; these are the two sides of the same thing. After that, *heimarmene* never sets in again; it is broken forever, since you are not reliving your actual life but living your actual—new and free—life; so only during the subsequent new and free period could I perform a free-will act, such as I did, that gained me good additional karma and hence salvation (release). So this has to be the sequence: First the not-self not-you ideationless *ex nihilo* act that abolishes the replay determinism, the tape, and then (and only then) are you free to perform a new act. The first should have a technical name, and also the second.

We will call the first: groove override. Or GO.

We will call the second: new free merit-deed. Or NFMD.

If you do GO, but subsequently fail to do NFMD but instead do evil, you will gain new bad karma. All that GO gives you is the freedom to act; it does not guarantee more merit (good karma); that must be done later and separately. So you could get the GO without the NFMD. You could have a new free demerit-deed or NFDD, and as a result you would again fail Ma'at and be sent back yet another time, perhaps forever; you would have lost your chance for release. GO can be done without NFMD but not vice versa. Yet this is not quite so, since the divine forces (Christ, the Buddha) are working to save you. They (apparently) will not grant you the GO situation unless through their omniscience they see NFMD lying ahead along the linear time axis. But I can't say for sure that if there is GO it means they know for sure there will be NFMD in the future; if you do it by free will—well, I can probably never settle this, but being omniscient they probably know how to grant you GO only if NFMD lies ahead of you based on your own free choice. Put another way, they do not grant you actual freedom unless they know in advance that you will put it to a wise use, so then there *is* reverse cause and effect, effect (NFMD) operating as cause retroactive in time to GO, to cause GO.

Wait. I'm saying GO is causally the effect of NFMD. And I'm saying that NFMD can't happen without GO. So it's an up-by-his-bootstrap situation, a self-causing situation—then truly it is *ex nihilo* (no wonder there was no ideation!). This is a time-travel paradox. Both GO and NFMD are generated within a close [sic] system out of nothing and enter from nowhere; that is, from outside the system. GO is dependent for its existence on NFMD, and NFMD on GO, so which is cause and which is effect? Answer: Each is the cause of the other and the effect of the other. Consider the original groove-tracking situation. How do you get out of it? Answer: You have to be out of it to get out of it; look to the Tao of physics ([Fritjhof] Capra) and the bootstrap theory for the answer; I knew I was dealing with field theory and quanta when I dealt with Valis. Put even more simply, How can you do something you would not do?, which is required for salvation in my system (disregarding the temporal factor the paradox still remains). There would have to be a psychological (mental) death and rebirth as someone different; but where did it come from? Hence "Thomas," who knew not the dog, car, nor cat [i.e. was unfamiliar with basic aspects of Dick's life]. It is possible that the only event that could make this possible would be abasement, suffering and pain and apprehension and tension so great that it would break down the historical self and literally assassinate it. In the absence of when, thereupon, an *ex nihilo* new self would come onto [sic] existence, like a newly granted second soul. This brings me back to my shamanist analysis of the crucifixion, the Passion of Christ story, as a secret method of overcoming the world (as Jesus put it); viz.: The world overcomes you; you die; a new self is born; it is ipso facto in a GO situation, for, being new, it will not track the old groove; the twin tapes simply won't work, since the outer tape remains but not the inner. The way to destroy synchronization is to destroy the self (you can't very well destroy the world), and the best way to destroy the self is to bilk the world into doing it. But this is a tricky business because you must not physically die; you must be alive to perform the NFMD. The early Christians themselves soon got it wrong and began to leap under Roman chariot wheels, upon which they physically died, making NFMD impossible. That they failed is shown by the fact that they did not rise from the dead in three days; they were never seen again. The field for right action is in this world, not the next.

I'm going to put forth a very strange idea. I think that if either GO or NFMD is to be considered cause, NFMD—which comes second in linear time—is cause, so what is needed is an ability to make time run backward, or, if this is putting it better, to be able, oneself, to move retrograde in time (if this latter is the correct formulation, I or "Thomas," whichever, moved retrograde in time back to 3-74 from the future; which accounts for my experiencing a mind-moving retrograde in time, a mind that fused with or entered mine that came from the future). But this would not be me in this world/life, say, me in 1977 or '78, when I gave to Covenant House [a charitable institution for homeless children]. It would be the me who originally fucked up the Xerox missive and lived to regret it, because only the me on that time track, that groove, would have ever found out what it was and hence could tell me in this time track as the AI [Artificial Intelligence] voice that it was "from an intelligence officer in the Army." It would be the me in the original real world. This is eerie. Presumably he (I) paid for fucking up (fucking up unless there was help would be natural; after all, it was a trap). Is this, then, a paranormal talent involving time on the [order of] Pat Conley's psi talent in *Ubik* or the girl's in *Clans*? [Dick's novel *Clans of the Alphane Moon* (1964).] The ability to change the past? Anyhow, time is involved. Anyhow, "Thomas" is not on this track, in this world, but in that world on that track where the Xerox missive was not handled, where there was no override by "Thomas"; i.e. the original time.

Then did "Thomas" engineer himself out of existence? No; my earlier formulation in this article suggests that "Thomas" is now in the process of reascending to the pleroma [heavenly realm of the Gnostics]. He still exists, because I still hear the AI [Artificial Intelligence hypnogogic] voice (assuming it is "Thomas"; well, it's very complicated, but probably it is "Thomas"). But in any case I'm saying that 3-74 can't be understood except by including as fundamental a reverse cause-and-effect sequence, the effect coming first, the cause probably years afterward. I may (if this formulation holds) someday decide that it represents a paranormal talent *on my part* and not adventitious intervention. A talent allied to my precog talent: stupendously escalated due to the lethal stress of the Xerox missive situation [a mysterious letter received in March 1974, as to which Dick posed numerous theories]; I may have actually literally caused time to run backward. And everything else hinges on this fact. This would explain why in 3-74 I had information at my disposal—essential information—that could not be known until much later. This is the bare bones of a deep phenomenal shift somehow related to quanta, to quantum field mechanics and field activity that is little understood today; this would fit in with the modulating or "warping away from valence" that I saw, so it would render what I call "Valis" as an expression of my own warping of reality in terms of time, space, and causality.

My God; can I now subsume several phenomena (foreknowing about the Xerox missive coming, "Thomas" and "Thomas" handling it; having information that could not be developed until later; getting out of synch with reality so that I reacted [to] the stimuli before they occurred; and Valis itself) under one basic syndrome? This is scientific method! This is the way the modern rational mind deals with theory formation! And my sense of being in touch with a mind moving retrograde in time. Did I warp time so that it ran backward? And out of this one factor the above (and perhaps other) several phenomena were observed to take place?

As I said in my UK speech ["Man, Android, and Machine," included herein]: "Maybe we're seeing the universe backward." Also, I tend—

Oh; and the double superimposition of worlds. Two "tracks," which is to say alternate worlds. Alternate worlds involve time; every SF author knows that.

Oh my god.

Yes, and the *koine* [commonly spoken Greek of era of Christ; Dick believed that he heard words in this language during his hypnogogic experiences]. A time disturbance, caused by me. Alternate worlds, information from the future sucked back to the present; information from the past; and another me. Plus the breakdown of causal synch. Valis—the modulations; that's causality. Set to zero, as I put it; due TO A CHANGE IN THE PAST.

All time disturbances. And quantum field like.

And my future NFMD affecting and effecting the GO. So non-GO (which is to say groove *tracking*) is just a way of talking about normal time and normal causality.

Is there anything that happened, starting with the material in "Faith of" ["Faith of My Fathers" (1967)] and TMITHC [*The Man in the High Castle* (1962)] and *Penultimate* [*The Penultimate Truth* (1964)] going to now and the AI voice that does not actually some way involve time? Certainly the material in the writing (especially *Tears* [*Flow My Tears, the Policeman Said* (1974)]) seems to involve time. I may find out that I have a chronic low-grade precog power that simply went off the scale into a basic qualitative change in 2-3-74 due to the Xerox missive, disjoining me from normal causal temporal reality entirely, both in terms of the past (anamnesis) and the future (moving retrograde in time and precognition). Something on the order of what I described in "World of Talent" ["A World of Talent" (1954)].

Now let's try this theory. The ability to make time run backward gets you out of your programmed groove ("groove tracking") and renders you free. This ability and only this ability frees you from an otherwise airtight [sic] tyranny that dooms all mankind. All life forms, in fact. Thus this is a stunning and probably new survival talent, an evolutionary new ability that advances the individual up the ladder of homeostasis to a stage where he is a whole other higher organism entirely. It is equal in terms of the evolution of life to the development of the opposable thumb, the eye, the lung, the wing, the large cerebral cortex, standing upright, etc. Upon the perfection (so to speak field operation) of this ability the human has become higher than the angels and all that implies. He is operating in a supratemporal dimension, and this has vast implications for knowledge; for overcoming causality—if he can affect the past he can modulate the present (what I called "Valis"), and if he can draw information to him from the future he can problem-solve like a crazy thing. This is not just phylogenic memory, as I supposed; it isn't limited to drawing on the distant past. The crucial information related to 3-74 was information drawn from the future. He can set up alternate worlds, so in effect he is transworld, spans not only time but world tracks.

Now, this raises the question as to whether there exists a vast metamind (as I conceive Valis to be) who is encouraging the development of this time-disruption faculty in order to evolve the human species further; or, put another way, the human being who has this faculty and makes use of it (for example, under vast stress, as I was under in 3-74) is an expression of this meta-mind. I am sure of it. I was not alone in what happened; it was as if angels—divine and partially visible—powers were present. There may be a species mind stretching back into the past *and* into the future where evolved humans (imaged as the three-eyed people?) may exist already using this faculty. When you start disrupting time you may be operating in the realm of a supratemporal composite discorporate mind—I think I was; this is what I call Valis. But it seems to me that the intrinsic nature of the sort of talent I'm discussing would cause to come in existence a meta-mind by itself, in that it would hop across expanses of time that lie outside its own lifetime, which would *de facto* make *it* a meta-mind; I mean it would be unlocked from the time span of its physical body. For one thing (here is Jung's intuition function) he would exist (his mind would exist) in alternate worlds, and this alone implies a lot; by affecting the past he would then find himself shifting across laterally (or-thogonally) in time . . . which would explain my subcortically remembering that it had just been cool, high, and moist a climate. So the mind with this talent would in itself become a meta-mind, outside of causality, spanning alternate worlds, able to modify his own present reality by changed actions in the past, thus setting up alternate worlds; he would be the cause and would in turn be affected by himself as cause—again the bootstrap phenomenon. Such a mind could act as cause to its own effect, affecting itself as if from outside like a feedback circuit, and, upon having successfully affected itself, the self as cause would eliminate itself as if it had never existed, which again is the *ex nihilo* or bootstrap paradox of time travel. Minds or versions of the mind, foci of the mind, would come into existence, influence the mind, and upon success render itself never having existed in the first place; but the mind would sense an adventitious other mind operating on itself in its behalf. Could it not then become its own AI voice, its own tutelary spirit? It would continually monitor its own status as if in a heuristic process; yes, it would be process, not hypostasis. You would have a mind that itself would evolve the way a species evolves.

It would be itself and not itself continually. It could correct a faulty solution to a problem after the faulty solution had been applied, a sort of "smart typewriter" erase circuit, again a heuristic process where it gets to apply the best solution it has; the solution proves faulty; the mind repeats the situation—runs it by again—with a different solution made better by knowledge derived from the faulty solution (i.e. the solution failed but it yielded knowledge as to what should have been done). It applies a solution. The solution is defective, but knowledge is derived. The mind then goes back in time and applies solution B based on solution A plus the knowledge derived from solution A (despite its failure). Solution B works, so the mind continues on in linear time.

For its B solution (which works), the mind draws on the vestigial A solution (which did not work); so underlying the B solution is the phantom record of the A solution. Sequentially, the mind was surprised by the problem and employed the A solution but now it has gone back and over-ridden the A solution with knowledge based on this initial failure. So on some level the mind knows of the A solution and hence perforce is bicam-eral. The part of the mind that employed the A solution and that possesses the knowledge derived from the A solution (and knowledge that the A solution did not work) informs the conscious part that is employing the amended solution; so the mind has its own self for a guide, speaking out of a ghostly realm where what is is also what is not. The mind is split but not split, since both parts are working for a common goal. Rather, it is chambered. So the ratiocination for the B solution simply isn't there be-cause in place of ratiocination there is certitude without sequential logi-cal reasoning. No analytical steps are employed. The mind when it comes to employ the B solution does not have to think. The thinking took place in a realm or track that has been abolished; when that realm was erased the thinking was erased with it, leaving only the motor and speech centers active. The mind, when it employs the B solution, is its own machine, its own slave instrument, acting out a solution that was not the primary one.

Put another way, during solution A the mind was cause and so had to think, but when it returned to reedit and employ solution B it was the effect of solution A and the knowledge belatedly acquired in connection with solution A. Put a third way, suppose a normal person wishes to know what is in the Book of Acts. He must locate a copy and read it. But this meta-mind simply knows the contents of the Book of Acts (if he is to know it at all). How does it know it? Because he found that he had written it, and thus read it. Then he checked with a copy of the Book of Acts to corroborate that it is indeed the Book of Acts. But when and where and how did it originally enter his mind? There is no answer to that; it is *ex nihilo*: without cause. There is only effect, because the causal element has been erased. The meta-mind in its finished stage is dependent upon the meta-mind in its initial staging, which it knows nothing directly about, but only indirectly, the way characters in a Beckett work deduce the existence of other people.

If he finds Acts or material based on pre-Socratic thinkers in his nov-els he must assume that his own primary heuristic scanning device read and absorbed knowledge of these matters in the usual way, but that this track has been erased, although it leaves its marks on the extant meta-mind. By what he knows that he shouldn't know (so to speak) he can make certain deductions about the original scanning, the original normal intake of information. He did not take in more information than any other person but he can apply it retroactively and there is his advantage.

Then essentially this theory about time disruption replaces the theory I put forward earlier here, that we are dead and don't know it; what I seem to be saying is that *heimarmene* or determinism depends on causality and that in turn depends on time, and an ability to disrupt time amounts to an ability to gain power over causality itself—the result of which is the abolition of the twin-tape synch system that makes of us little more than DNA robots. We are not dead but we are as if dead; we are enslaved, and in a prison. The ability to disrupt time—i.e. to make it run backward—brings freedom of a sort that no living creature on Earth has ever had before. And I think that this is the cryptic doctrine that is the basis of my title here: The great esoteric systems are systems in which this human ability is cultivated and brought to bear. Certainly this is true in Gnosticism, in Buddhism—and if Buddhism then probably in *The Tibetan Book of the Dead*. There is no way a human can perceive that he is twin-tape programmed until he begins to break that programming, because the mechanism of determinism and occlusion is so good that until the person disrupts it he can't even tell that it is there.

But the power to disrupt time discloses the deterministic system as somehow unreal, a fiction. How can it have power and be a fiction? Its power depends on the ignorance it produces, the occlusion and (perceptual and in terms of memory) being only one element. Basically, the person is enslaved because he cannot detect the machine that enslaves him; it deprives him of crucial information. There is a constant flow of information traffic around him and he can't see it, literally. Yet the information programs him. It seems to be the purpose of this machine to maintain structure (cosmos) but at the expense of the welfare and lives of the individual life forms involved.

My subcortical memories of a higher, cooler, moister climate indicate that really major erasure and reinscription can take place; the time-disrupting faculty can be very powerful. Again, it was not done by me but by myself, who lived through to the end of my life, died, and returned to an earlier stage of my life, but now under taped conditions. Yet the taped conditions are a combination of servitude and opportunity, the latter if properly handled, the former if botched. Whether it will be endless repetition of prison or whether it will be, instead, self-liberation depends on what I call the NFMD: the new free merit-deed that tilts the scales under the altered conditions achieved by the GO situation. I cannot really abandon this theological concept in the service of upholding an explanation that relies on a belief in the paranormal powers of the individual involved. There is a cosmic dimension, and one of deity. The person has failed his first time around and is sent back. He is as ignorant the second time as the first . . . or is he? Doesn't his own bicameral voice whisper to him to liberate himself by an act of kindness, of kindness unmerited by the recipient? There is a phantom of solution A that did not work. Has the person really learned nothing? Then again he is destroyed by the instruments that destroyed him originally. This is unlikely. Surely there is a high probability that he will employ his time-disturbing power to save himself. This is how evolution is achieved: by making use of latent powers, making them actual. The B solution is a feedback system that monitors the failure of A with the absolute wisdom of hindsight; knowledge that was crucial but contingent is now *a priori* and it is there, but buried in the person in the form of his original self grown old and then dead and then restored without memory: like Parsifal or Siegfried he does not know his own identity and must be told—only it is he himself, not Kundry or the Forest Bird who tell him. He is his own sibyl; he is in fact his own anima, watching over him as psychopomp, hence now changed in sex to female, in accordance with Zoroaster's observations about one's spirit of religion.

It would not be correct to say that the second time around, things are different from the first time around; both times are the same time, through an orthogonal intervention of needed information. Another axis of reality has to be imagined; first and second occur simultaneously in linear time. Which is to say, solution A abolishes itself as it fails and not after it fails; it is not attempted and then erased but both attempted, erased, and a second and superior solution employed simultaneously. This is as mysterious to us as the third dimension is to the flatland person.

What has happened is that the correction is not separated from that which it corrects, either by time or space, hence not by causality. The person is rescued by the merit of an act that he will not live to commit— an impossible situation from the normal standpoint. Perhaps it can be understood if solution A, which does not work, is supposed as occurring in a falsework or hypothetical, not actual, universe: a sort of tentative sketch off the canvas. Or what if it is supposed that no linear time elapses within the period in which solution A takes place; solution A occurs at a point rather than a line. The correction does not lag; it is as fast as the faulty solution that it overtakes. In other words, the faulty solution is overrun as it unfolds. This is impossible, but it is the case. It is like a spider who can only toss a web strand across a distance between bushes if he has already tossed a strand across that distance. The solution must precede the problem, and therein lies the mystery. How can it be? But it is so; the solution to the Xerox missive of 3-74 shows up in novels and a story I wrote as much as ten years earlier [most likely "Faith of Our Fathers"]. The problem is formulated; the right solution is formulated (especially in *Penultimate Truth*, and for all I know, it shows up elsewhere in my writing as well, places I have not as yet looked). The mind that is retracking its life has plenty of leisure time in which to formulate the problem and develop a successful answer.

About the Editor

Lawrence Sutin is the author of *Divine Invasions: A Life of Philip K. Dick*. He is currently at work on a biography of Aleister Crowley.

Printed in the United States
by Baker & Taylor Publisher Services